THEOLOGY FOR TEACHERS

THEOLOGY
FOR
TEACHERS

IAN KNOX, C.S.SP.

NOVALIS

Cover: Blair Turner

Layout: Suzanne Latourelle

3rd Edition © 1999, Novalis, Saint Paul University, 223 Main Street, Ottawa, Ontario, K1S 1C4 Canada

Business Offices:

Novalis Publishing Inc.
10 Lower Spadina Avenue, Suite 400
Toronto, Ontario, Canada
M5V 2Z2

Novalis Publishing Inc.
4475 Frontenac Street
Montréal, Québec, Canada
H2H 2S2

Phone: 1-800-387-7164
Fax: 1-800-204-4140
E-mail: books@novalis.ca
www.novalis.ca

Nihil obstat: Rev. John Boissonneau, D.Th., Censor deputatus

Imprimatur: +Aloysius Ambrozic, Archbishop of Toronto, February, 1999

We wish to thank sincerely the publishers who gave permission to print substantial material for which they hold the copyright. All sources are acknowledged in the notes that accompany each quotation.

Every effort has been made to trace sources of material quoted in this edition. Sources will be attributed in future editions on receipt of publication information.

We acknowledge the financial support of the Government of Canada through the Book Publishing Industry Development Program (BPIDP) for our publishing activities.

Canadian Cataloguing in Publication Data: C99-901052-2

ISBN: 978-2-89507-020-7

Reprint 2005, 2007

Printed in Canada

CONTENTS

FOREWORD

The Master Teacher gathered his disciples, took them aside to train and form them, opened their eyes and their understanding, made connections between their everyday life, their contemporary culture and the kingdom of God. Gradually they "picked up his moves" as they saw him in action, in conversation, in relationship with people. Eventually they were ready to go into action themselves.

Over the years their initial enthusiasm was tempered by reality, their faith tested by Calvary, their hope renewed by Easter, their hesitation to go public swept away by Pentecost, their insights honed by new situations, their teaching enlarged by new questions, their family and temple rituals replaced by basilica and church sacraments, their practices codified, their message adapted (sometimes too slowly) to many diverse peoples. But in and through all these changes and developments the deep down core of their proclamation remained the Master Teacher.

Ian Knox quotes the Canadian Conference of Catholic Bishops: "The heart of the Christian message is Jesus Christ. The centre of the Christian life is Jesus Christ. Even more, the Christian message itself is Jesus Christ. For Christians, 'To live is Christ.'" His book spells out the many-layered consequences of this core proclamation. Its intended audience is teachers who hope to teach in Catholic schools, heirs to a long educational tradition carried in the hearts and mouths and deeds of many generations.

The message – ever ancient, ever new – now reaches the second millennium on its marathon torch-bearing run. For the last fifteen hundred years it has been handed on through monastic schools and wandering friars, through universities and religious communities of women and men with their network of schools, through family practice and church attendance, through sacramental preparation and adult faith formation. It has informed and formed millions who call themselves Catholic Christians. Today's Catholic schools in Canada are staffed by lay persons open to the movement of contemporary history. How will they pass the torch to a generation spanning both a century and a millennium?

Ian Knox gives us valuable insights into what to hand on and how best to do it. He discards the sometimes all too familiar framework of disparate watertight compartments. He establishes connections and relationships and encourages teachers to understand the Christian message as an organic whole. He fosters a disciplined approach to religious education, but reminds us that it all follows from our relationship with Jesus: "The formulation of beliefs comes after a dedication to a way of life that Jesus taught. Religion is never simply a system of beliefs." He quotes more than once the incisive words of Pope John Paul II: "The definitive aim of catechesis is to put people not merely in touch, but in communion, in intimacy with Jesus Christ."

His is a theology for teachers – the subject matters and so does the approach. His conviction is that "we do not study theology for its own sake; we study it that it may affect our daily life and bring us closer to the living God." Thus his theology combines with a spirituality based on the biblical conviction that "God calls us from the depth of our experience." His approach to theology is truly catholic – scripture, the *Catechism of the Catholic Church*, personal anecdote, story, human reason, sacrament, and prayer combine to probe and provoke, to provide food for the soul, explanations for the mind, a stirring of the imagination and a transformation of the heart. In his book reason and revelation are on speaking terms, faith and understanding walk hand in hand. He encourages teachers to prepare the ground. He warns against separating the material, the worldly and the moral from the spiritual. He gives teachers in training an organic sense of Catholic theology as distinct from a disconnected list of doctrines, practices and rituals. He presents the subject matter whole, makes it palatable and as an engaging host invites his guests to taste and see. They in turn sit down to good rich food and fine strained wine and are encouraged to let the well-prepared meal nourish them as bite by bite they probe what they really believe deep down and would wish to pass on to a younger generation.

Each chapter concludes with Reflection Questions (e.g., What does it mean to say that the biblical story of the Israelites is a story told through the eyes of faith? Articulate carefully why you want to teach in a Catholic school; Why was the older brother in the parable of the Prodigal Son probably more at fault than the one who left home?) and some recommended Further Reading. A Glossary of Terms (e.g., Analogy, Mystery, Myth, Synoptic, Hierarchy, Testament, Heresy) is found at the end of the book. Method and message go hand in hand – a trait much appreciated by Ian's own students at the Faculty of Education, University of Toronto.

Much of the text will surely be underlined or hi-lited by its readers. Some personal highlights include:

• God is never so hidden that faith is impossible, but at the same time God is never so clearly revealed that faith is inevitable.

• God is the supreme paradox. We don't solve paradoxes, we learn to live with them.

- To say what God is like is not to say what God is.
- The Spirit suffers from an "image problem".
- All experience of God is *mediated* – God calls us from the depth of our experience.
- There is only one Tradition, but there are many traditions.
- The Bible contains error, but teaches no error.
- Christianity cannot escape its Jewish roots.
- No one followed Jesus around with a notebook and a tape recorder.
- The parables invite us to make adult decisions about our own lives.
- The word miracle itself appears nowhere in the scriptures.
- History tries to get at accurate detail and fact; theology tries to understand the working of God in human experience.
- Jesus attracted bands of followers during his lifetime; they would not have known the word "church" or the word "Christian".
- Taking account of the fact that we are body-persons is a basic and extremely important principle in all of Roman Catholic theology.
- We must not allow only the law to sensitise us and do our thinking for us.
- We help people to gather the tools for making their own good moral decisions; we do not make moral decisions for them.
- Our God is a God of life and human history.
- Gospel values are human values, they are not merely religious values.

This book will leave teachers in training with a renewed sense of the privilege and responsibility that is theirs. If Canadian Catholic teachers need additional encouragement they might ponder what Pope John Paul II said to them in Newfoundland: "No one else will ever be where you are. No one else will ever have the opportunity you have – to accompany students in the search for truth, to foster in them a thirst for justice and an appreciation of the goodness of God, to lead them patiently and lovingly in their journey of faith." Ian Knox encourages them to teach in such a manner that their students may come to grasp the Christian way as something worthwhile, as something speaking to their life. In his final chapter he encourages teachers to present to the students the challenge of Jesus, the challenge of faith, the challenge of vocation and commitment. "Are you with me or against me?"

Those who digest this book will move beyond information to formation and transformation. Beginning teachers could choose no better guidebook along the path of Catholic Christian discipleship. All real teaching is continuing education and so even those who have borne the heat of the day will be refreshed by the book's clarity and renewed by its spirituality.

Patrick Fitzpatrick, C.S.Sp.

Part I

PRINCIPLES OF FAITH
AND
FAITH GROWTH

1

Knowing God

There is no doubt that the effort to proclaim the Gospel to the people of today, who are buoyed up by hope but at the same time often oppressed by fear and distress, is a service rendered to the Christian community but also to the whole of humanity.[1]

Thus begins Pope Paul VI's landmark encyclical *On Evangelization in the Modern World.* "Gospel" derives from an Old English word meaning "good news," the good news of Our Lord Jesus Christ, the "good news of great joy for all the people" (Lk 2:10). "Jesus Christ is good news today because he still comes into our lives . . . . We want to repeat this message again and again. We want to live it more deeply. The heart of the Christian message is Jesus Christ. The centre of the Christian life is Jesus Christ. Even more, the Christian message itself is Jesus Christ. For Christians, 'living is Christ' (Phil 1:21)."[2]

"The Christian message itself is Jesus Christ." The message is a person. To come to know and understand the message we must come to know and understand the person. Unfortunately, the English word "know" is not a very rich word. It does not distinguish between knowing *something* and knowing *someone.* Further, the word does not distinguish between knowing *about* a person and knowing *the person* through the experience of a close personal relationship. It is perfectly possible for us to come to know a lot *about* Jesus. We can come to know the circumstances of his life and ministry (such as are available to us); we can come to know his message of salvation. But we can learn all this in an objective, non-involved, dry, academic fashion through textbooks of theology and history without ever coming to meet the person of Jesus deep in our hearts and without responding to him in a relationship of love. In other words, we can know a lot about Jesus without meeting and responding to him as a person.

Responding to the person of Jesus is an essential aspect of knowing him. It is not enough to know in the sense of possessing knowledge in our mind. Both the Old and the New Testament, the Hebrew and Christian Scriptures, insist that to know God is to love, to obey and to believe. Thus, for example, "Whoever

---

[1]   Pope Paul VI, *Evangelii nuntiandi*, No. 1 (Washington, D.C.: Publications Office, United States Catholic Conference, 1975).
[2]   Canadian Conference of Catholic Bishops, *Jesus Christ, Centre of the Christian Life* (Ottawa: CCCB Publications Service, 1981), p. 3.

does not love does not know God, for God is love" (1 Jn 4:8). Paul prays for the Colossians that they "may lead lives worthy of the Lord, fully pleasing to him, as you bear fruit in every good work and as you grow in the knowledge of God" (Col 1:10). Thomas Groome comments:

> In the Biblical sense, then, to know God is a dynamic, experiential, relational activity involving the whole person and finding expression in a *lived response of loving obedience to God's will.* Without loving action God is not known.[3]

And again:

> God is not "known" unless God's will is done, and it is only in the doing that God is truly known. . . . It is because Jesus did the will of God perfectly that he could claim to know the Father best. It is because of his obedience that he can be our model of faith.[4]

To know God involves a whole life-orientation, an active and enduring commitment. To know God is an *active* knowing of believing, trusting and doing, not merely a passive possession of knowledge.

But there is another side to the coin. It is possible to develop an intimate personal relationship with Jesus without really knowing too much about him. The beginnings of faith, the beginnings of a personal relationship with God, may have come for many of us through the example of loving and dedicated parents, or through the example of someone we much admire, or through groups of friends with whom we share and experience love. Perhaps we have met the Lord Jesus in the quiet experience of personal prayer, or in the experience of the beauty of creation—the silence of the forest, the pounding of waves on a rocky shore, the kaleidoscopic colours of the aurora borealis. The point is that there are many faith-filled holy people who have done little or no formal study of theology or religion, who perhaps know little about God. Such people have a strong, emotional, gut-level attachment to God in Jesus, a love relationship that gives meaning to their lives: they *know* the Lord Jesus. This deep, personal, intimate, experiential knowledge is a foretaste of the happiness that God has prepared for those who love him.[5] "Now I know only in part; then I will know fully, even as I have been fully known" (1 Cor 13:12).

---

[3]   Thomas Groome, *Christian Religious Education* (San Francisco: Harper San Francisco, 1980), p. 144; emphasis added.

[4]   *Ibid.*, p. 64.

[5]   There is no gender in God. Since we believe that God is personal, our language does not allow us to treat God as neuter. We have no choice: when referring to God, we are forced to use either the masculine or the feminine pronoun, unless we adopt some inelegant and awkward circumlocutions, such as Him/Her, He/She, or even S/He. Some languages other than English allow for fine distinctions that obviate, to some extent, this problem. For example, in Arabic the supreme

But if we are truly in love with someone, it goes without saying that we will want to know more about the person we love. A true love relationship cannot be sustained without a growth in intimacy, a progressive revelation of person to person, a deeper and deeper knowledge. To love Jesus is to want to understand him more, to search out and make our own the values that motivated him, to grasp more and more fully the heart of his message, to know more about him. F.J. Sheed, in *Theology for Beginners,* makes this point with humour and insight:

> I cannot say how often I have been told that some old Irishman saying his rosary is holier than I am, with all my study. I dare say he is. For his own sake, I hope he is. But if the only evidence is that he knows less theology than I, then it is evidence that would convince neither him nor me. It would not convince him because all the rosary-loving, tabernacle-loving old Irishmen I have ever known (and my own ancestry is rich with them) were avid for more knowledge of the Faith. It does not convince me for while it is obvious that an ignorant man can be virtuous, it is equally obvious that ignorance is not a virtue; men have been martyred who could not have stated a doctrine of the church correctly, and martyrdom is the supreme proof of love: yet with more knowledge of God they would have loved Him more still.[6]

The justification for studying theology is that it sustains and expands our love-relationship with God in the person of Jesus. The duty of "proclaiming the gospel" belongs, in the first place, to those to whom it has been specially entrusted: namely, the Pope and bishops as successors of the apostles. But all true believers share in this responsibility. Perhaps the principal work of those entrusted with the education of the young (i.e., teachers and parents) is to help those young people develop and sustain a love-relationship with God as an expression of their faith. This important task should take precedence over all other educational work.

The *Catechism of the Catholic Church* (hereinafter referred to as CCC, or as the Catechism) defines catechesis as "an *education in the faith* of children, young people, and adults" (CCC 5). Without doubt this is a privileged sharing in the work of proclaiming the gospel. For all those who teach, therefore, Pope John Paul in his encyclical *Catechesi tradendae* makes a point of capital importance. "The definitive aim of catechesis," he says, "is to put people not

---

name for God is *al-Lah* (masculine) but the word for God's essence is *al-Dhat* (feminine). The Catechism points out that "God transcends the human distinction between the sexes. He is neither man nor woman: he is God" (CCC 239). As can be seen, in spite of this statement the Catechism opts for the use of the masculine pronoun. Since this terminology has been more conventional and traditional, in this book we shall also use the masculine pronoun.

[6]   F.J. Sheed, *Theology for Beginners* (New York: Sheed & Ward, 1964), p. 5.

merely in touch, but in communion, intimacy, with Jesus Christ," for "only he can lead us to the love of the Father in the Spirit and make us share in the life of the Holy Trinity."[7]

In this book we shall consider many of the truths, doctrines, traditions and practices that are expressions of our Catholic faith. We do not study these things for their own sake; we study them so that we may be led to a closer and closer relationship with God in Jesus Christ, so that we may come to *know* the Lord Jesus in the fullest sense of the word.

---

[7]   Pope John Paul II, *Catechesi tradendae,* No. 5 (Ottawa: Canadian Conference of Catholic Bishops, 1979).

2

FAITH: ITS MEANING AND PRACTICE

Faith: A Human Phenomenon

Let us begin by saying that one need not be a religious person to have faith. In truth and in fact, faith is a significant factor in every human life because we all need to believe in something to make life meaningful and manageable. Thus, for example, we frequently talk of the need to "believe in ourselves" if we are to meet life's challenges creatively and purposefully. We believe our doctors, our teachers, our scientific experts and countless others who are significant in our lives. We need to believe, too, because we simply do not and cannot have absolute certainty about everything when we have to make an important decision. We cannot foresee the future, and therefore cannot know in advance whether our decision will be the right one. Since finding absolute certitude in every aspect of life is impossible, we must have some form of faith to keep our psychological balance or we might become neurotic. Faith, therefore, is our constant human companion.

It should be clear from the above statements that the object of our faith is always beyond the immediate scope of our senses; we cannot "claim" it or "own" it in the sense that we have absolute certitude. Faith gives us the assurance and conviction that make life manageable. Importantly, therefore, faith relates to something or someone that we do not completely control. Nevertheless, we trust in that something or someone not to let us down. What we are trying to say is neatly captured in the words of the Letter to the Hebrews: "Now faith is the assurance of things hoped for, the conviction of things not seen" (Heb 11:1).

Religious Faith

How, we may ask, does religious faith differ from ordinary human faith? For Christians, Jews and Muslims the answer is that the object of their religious faith is not something but *someone*, someone who relates to us and to whom we can relate in a personal way. We call this reality God. Some people claim that there is no God; they are called atheists*.[8] (from the Greek *athe[os]*, "godless") (CCC 2123-2126). There are others who claim that God may or may not exist, but that we really cannot know for sure. Since we cannot know whether God exists, they claim, we cannot commit ourselves to any form of religious observance. Such people are called agnostics*   (from the Greek *agnost[os]*, "not known") (CCC 2127-2128).

Christians, Jews and Muslims not only believe in a personal God but, very importantly, they believe that this God is not an arbitrary or capricious God. On the contrary, they believe that he is a good and gracious God who has the well-being of the world, of the whole of creation, at heart. Furthermore, this gracious God has made himself known to us, has revealed himself so that we can come to know him. God has spoken to us, made himself available to us. Christians believe that God has spoken to us most especially in Jesus of Nazareth: a man like us in all things but sin, but also the Son of God. Thus we read in the Letter to the Hebrews: "Long ago God spoke to our ancestors in many and various ways by the prophets, but in these last days he has spoken to us by a Son, whom he appointed heir of all things, through whom he also created the worlds" (Heb 1:1-2).

In what way, we might ask, does Christian faith differ from all other forms of religious faith? What makes Christian faith distinctive, or unique, is that it focuses on the person of Jesus of Nazareth, the Son of God. Christians believe that Jesus' whole life and teaching are God's message to us. Christians believe that God calls us to a close personal relationship with him. "By his Revelation, 'the invisible God, from the fullness of his love, addresses men as his friends, and moves among them, in order to invite and receive them into his own company'" (CCC 142; *Dei verbum* 2). Because Jesus is human and speaks to us in human language, it is through him that we are able to enter into a personal relationship with God, a relationship that will lead to eternal life. "And this is eternal life, that they may know you, the only true God, and Jesus Christ whom you have sent" (Jn 17:3).

More about Faith

1. Faith Is a Gift of God

Tommy turned out to be the "atheist in residence" in my Theology of Faith course. He constantly objected to, smirked at, or whined about the possibility of an unconditionally loving Father-God. We lived with each other in relative peace for one semester, although I admit that he was for me at times a serious pain in the back pew. When he came up at the end of the course to turn in his final

---

[8]   Items with an asterisk appear in the glossary at the end of the book.

exam, he asked in a slightly cynical tone: "Do you think I'll ever find God?" I decided on a little shock therapy. "No," I said emphatically. "Oh," he responded, "I thought that was the product you were pushing." "Tommy!" I said, "I don't think you'll ever find him, but I'm absolutely certain he will find you."

Later I heard that Tommy was graduated and I was duly grateful. Then a sad report. I heard that Tommy had terminal cancer. Before I could search him out, he came to see me. When he walked into my office, his body was badly wasted, and the long hair had fallen out as a result of chemotherapy. "Tommy," I said, "I've thought about you so often. I hear you are sick."

"Oh yes, very sick. I have cancer in both lungs. It's a matter of weeks."

"Can you talk about it, Tom?"

"Sure, what would you like to know?"

"What it's like to be only 24 and dying?"

"Well, it could be worse."

"Like what?"

"Well, like being 50 and having no values and ideals, like being 50 and thinking that booze, seducing women and making money are the real biggies in life.

"But what I came to you about," Tom said, "is something you said to me on the last day of class.

"I asked you if you thought I would ever find God and you said 'No!', which surprised me. Then you said 'But he will find you.' I thought about that a lot, even though my search for God was hardly intense at the time.

"But when the doctors removed a lump from my groin and told me that it was malignant, then I got serious about locating God. And when the malignancy spread to my vital organs, I really began banging bloody fists against the bronze doors of heaven. But God did not come out. In fact, nothing happened. Did you ever try anything for a long time with great effort and with no success? You get psychologically glutted, fed up with trying. And then you quit. Well, one day I woke up and instead of throwing a few more futile appeals over the high brick wall to a God who may or may not be there, I just quit. I decided that I really didn't care . . . about God, about an afterlife, or anything like that.

"I decided to spend what time I had left doing something more profitable. I thought about you and I remembered something else you had said: 'The essential sadness is to go through life without loving. But it would be almost equally sad to go through life and leave this world without ever telling those you loved that you had loved them.'

"So I began with the hardest one: my Dad. He was reading the newspaper when I approached him.

'Dad. . .'

'Yes, what?' he asked without lowering the newspaper.

'Dad, I would like to talk with you.'

'Well, talk.'

'I mean . . . it's really important.'

"The newspaper came down three slow inches. 'What is it?'

'Dad, I love you. I just wanted you to know that.'

Tom smiled at me and said with obvious satisfaction, as though he felt a warm and secret joy flowing inside him: "The newspaper fluttered to the floor. Then my father did two things I could never remember him ever doing before. He cried and he hugged me. And we talked all night, even though he had to go to work in the morning.

"It was easier with my mother and little brother. They cried with me, too, and we hugged each other, and started saying real nice things to each other. We shared the things we had kept secret for so many years. I was only sorry about one thing: that I had waited so long. Here I was in the shadow of death, and I was just beginning to open up to all the people I had actually been close to.

"Then one day I turned around and God was there. He didn't come to me when I pleaded with him. I guess I was like an animal trainer holding out a hoop, 'C'mon, jump through. C'mon I'll give you three days . . . three weeks.' Apparently God does things in his own way and at his own hour.

"But the important thing is that he was there. He found me. You were right. He found me even after I stopped looking for him."[9]

This beautiful story is related by John Powell, S.J., in his book *Unconditional Love*. The story poignantly illustrates the gift dimension of faith and the intrinsic link between faith and love.

Religious faith is God's gift, a supernatural virtue infused into us by the power of the Holy Spirit: we cannot demand it as a right. It is faith that enables us to believe in God and in all that he has revealed (CCC 1814). It is through faith that we come into contact with the ever-present God and enter into a personal relationship with him. We cannot achieve this by natural reason alone but only by the grace of God. It is faith that gives us the certainty of God's presence in our life (CCC 157). Further, since faith is God's gift we cannot give one another

---

[9]   John Powell, S.J., *Unconditional Love* (Allen, Texas: Tabor Publishing, 1978), pp. 110 ff. Used with permission.

faith. Our parents and teachers do not give us faith. The best they can do is to prepare the ground: they dispose us to receive God so that when the gift of faith is offered we shall respond positively. As we see from Tommy's story, one of the best ways that we can become disposed to receive the gift of faith is to learn the true meaning of love for one another, for love is the heart of Jesus' gospel message. Faith is a gift. We are free to accept it or reject it; God respects our freedom at all times (CCC 160).

Since it is evident, from our own experience, that some people come to faith while others do not, one may object that God is quite arbitrary in giving the gift of faith. God, it seems, really puts some people at a grave disadvantage by not granting them the gift of faith. Is God "unfair"? Not so. First, we must state unequivocally, in the words of Vatican II, that ". . . we must hold that theHoly Spirit offers to all the possibility of being made partners, in a way known to God, in the paschal mystery."[10] Second, those who receive and respond to the gift of faith do so freely; they are not forced by God in any way (CCC 160). But this free choice brings with it the responsibility of expressing that gift in everyday life, as Jesus says in the gospel: "From everyone to whom much has been given, much will be required; and from the one to whom much has been entrusted, even more will be demanded" (Lk 12:48). The gift of faith does place obligations on us. Third, we believe in a good and gracious God. Hence, we believe that, in the words of Vatican II, "Divine providence [does not] deny the assistance necessary for salvation to those who, without any fault of theirs, have not yet arrived at an explicit knowledge of God, and who, not without grace, strive to lead a good life"[11] (see also CCC 847).

2. Faith Is a Verb

Generally, when we speak of faith we make it sound as though it is something that we have or possess. Thus, we speak of someone "having" faith, or having "the faith." The very notion that faith is a gift makes us think of it as some "thing" that is given to us in much the same way as material gifts are given. We also speak, for example, of someone "losing" their faith, as if they have lost some possession such as their handkerchief, or their hair. We also speak of someone "growing" in faith, as if it were something that could increase in size. Therefore, the language we use often makes us speak of faith as though it were a noun, a "thing"; we reify (thing-ify) faith. Unfortunately, as is often the case when we are dealing with intangibles, our language traps us into a mode of

---

[10]   *Vatican Council II: The Basic Sixteen Documents,* Austin Flannery, O.P. ed. (New York: Costello Publishing, 1996) *Pastoral Constitution on the Church in the Modern World (Gaudium et spes),* No. 22.
[11]   *Vatican Council II: The Basic Sixteen Documents, Dogmatic Constitution on the Church (Lumen gentium),* No. 16.

expression that leaves us with an incorrect idea of the reality. Since language is one of the major factors in shaping our consciousness, we must be careful to correct such misconceptions.

In reality, faith is a verb because faith is manifested only in action. The word "faith" describes "faithing" acts, just as grace describes gracious acts. We act in a certain way because of our faith. Rather than saying, for example, that someone "has" faith, we should more correctly speak of a "faithing" person. Rather than saying that someone has "lost" the faith, we should more correctly say that they have "stopped faithing." "Losing the faith" always involves a free choice; what actually happens is that we make a conscious decision to no longer "faith" actively. For us to use faith as a verb in this manner is linguistically ugly, but it would certainly be more accurate and would focus our attention on the fact that faith is active and dynamic, not merely a static possession.

3. Active Expression of Faith

Faith, then, is an essential component of the active expression in our daily life of our relationship with God. The other active components are hope and love. As we shall see, these three virtues – faith, hope and love – are inextricably bound together. A faith-relationship is also a hope-relationship and a love-relationship. When referring to our relationship to God, some people prefer to speak of this relationship as the spiritual life. They envision it, therefore, as a relationship between God, who is Spirit, and the very inner principle of our own being, our "soul," which is also spirit. Pursuing this line of thought has led to the tendency to separate a "spiritual" life from ordinary human or moral life: that is, the way one normally acts in the world. Thus, if we want to be close to God, we must become more and more "spiritual," less "worldly." We must become less concerned with mere human things and more oriented towards the "spiritual," the "otherworldly." Put another way, what we do at Eucharist on a Sunday has little or no relationship with what we do during the rest of the week.

An extreme form of this type of thinking is well illustrated by the following story, as related by Thomas Day. Day was told by a retired F.B.I. agent about the interrogation of Joseph Valachi, a vicious Mafia criminal who turned government informer in the 1960s. Valachi told the interrogators about a particular Mafia chieftain who was old, gentlemanly, self-educated and, according to rumour, an ex-seminarian. This don gave Valachi and an associate the job of rubbing out one of his competitors (whom we shall call Mario), but they failed. They returned to the don's house to ask for an extension on the contract. The old don was very understanding when he heard their story, and he gave them another week to accomplish their task. "By the way," he added, "did you boys go to Mass today?" (It was Sunday.) Why, no, said Valachi (who had no use for religion), they had been too busy trying to rub out Mario. The old man shook his head.

"Rubbing out Mario is important for business," he said, "but going to Mass is important for your soul."[12]

The tendency to separate the "material," the "worldly," the "moral" from the "spiritual" has plagued the religious life of many Christians down through the centuries. We express our faith and develop our relationship with God in and through the way we go about the everyday business of living. A well-lived human life of faith involving the whole person – intellect, will, emotions, desires – is also a spiritual life. As one commentator on Celtic spirituality puts it, the spiritual person is the person who feels at home in both worlds.

Faith in Daily Life

Let us now take a look at how we express our faith in our daily life and so develop our relationship with God. Here we shall take as our guide the schema proposed by Thomas Groome.[13]

1. Believing

"Faith" and "belief" are frequently confused in popular understanding and usage. They are not necessarily the same thing. Faith enlightens us so that we can see God revealed in the midst of human life, at the heart of our human experience. We interpret our faith (that is, our way of perceiving God) and we articulate it more clearly by a series of beliefs. A belief, therefore, is a clear and precise articulation, in a specific instance, of our much broader commitment of faith in God who is present to our life. Examples of such beliefs are the belief that Jesus is both God and man, the belief in the real presence of Christ in the eucharist, the belief in the Assumption of Mary, the belief in the church as the Mystical Body of Christ. Thomas Groome expresses it well:

> That Christianity makes certain historical, moral and cognitive claims and proposes them to people as a way of making meaning in their lives is beyond doubt. The activity of Christian faith, therefore, requires, in part, a firm conviction about the truths proposed as essential beliefs of the Christian faith.[14]

Believing, therefore, is an aspect of faith, a way of expressing faith. As mentioned earlier, in English we use faith almost exclusively as a noun. When we need a verb to express faith, we use "believe." In its early and original meaning, to believe signified "to hold dear," "to prize," "to give allegiance," "to be loyal to"; therefore it is not merely an act of the mind but of the whole person.

---

[12] Adapted from Thomas Day, *Why Catholics Can't Sing* (New York: Crossroad, 1991), p. 115.

[13] See Groome, *Christian Religious Education,* pp. 57-66.

[14] *Ibid.*, p. 57.

In present English usage, however, to believe usually refers to something cognitive, engaging principally the mind, the intellect, the rational part of us. As we noted above, on a purely natural, non-religious level all human believing involves accepting certain situations and outcomes for which there is no adequate "proof." Believing means that we accept things that we do not fully grasp or control, even though we do not have scientific certainty. Believing requires a certain submission of the mind.

The same applies to religious believing. We believe, for example, that Jesus is really present in the Eucharist despite the fact that the evidence of our senses indicates that there is nothing there but bread and wine. Why do we believe these religious truths? We believe them, in the first place, because God has revealed them to us and we believe that God is gracious, loving and cannot deceive us (CCC 156). Second, we believe these truths because believing them makes a difference to our lives, makes life more meaningful and helps us to cope with life better. As the great theologian Karl Barth has said: "If a man believes and knows God, he can no longer ask, 'What is the meaning of my life?' But by believing he actually lives the meaning of his life." That bit of advice is worth repeating and emphasizing. Religious believing is an active element in living our religious life. And that brings us to the next dimension of active faith: faith as trusting.

2. Trusting

As we have seen, believing faith is always a "leap in the dark." We believe, even though we do not have all the evidence that would produce certainty. In fact, if we do have absolute certainty about some particular thing, then we cannot have faith in that thing. For example, if I know with certainty that it is two o'clock in the afternoon I cannot have faith in that. If, on the other hand, someone tells me that it is two o'clock in the afternoon and I believe it to be so, then, ultimately, I believe it because I trust that the other person is not deceiving me. Trust is the basis of all faith, as the following story illustrates.

A man came out from a supermarket and saw that the side of his car had been badly dented. He was only somewhat relieved when he saw a note under his windshield wiper. The note read: "Dear Sir, I have just bumped into the side of your car. The people who saw me do this are still watching, and they believe that I am now leaving my name and address on this piece of paper. But they are wrong."

What does it mean to trust? At its simplest and most fundamental psychological level, to trust someone means that we must relinquish control, we must let go, we must stop managing things and let someone else do it. If you have ever been in a car with a back seat driver, you will understand what this means. There are some people who simply cannot trust another driver to drive well.

Why are we afraid to trust? Precisely because we are afraid. We are afraid of an accident, afraid of being hurt, afraid of being blamed for someone else's mistakes, afraid of losing the esteem of our peers or of the boss, afraid of losing our property, afraid of being conned in business, afraid of death. Yes, we are afraid of death: that is the bottom line. All the other fears are just small ways of dying. They are ways of being deprived of things we hold dear – health, wealth, reputation, a loved one. When we lose the things we are attached to, a little bit of us dies. If we read any of the numerous books and articles on death and dying, we shall find the author making the point that to attain some form of peace and serenity, the dying person must agree to let the world go on without them. We have to agree to give up managing our own affairs, we have to agree to let someone else take control, we have to trust someone to look after our future. For us Christian believers, that someone to whom we surrender is God. As death approaches, we shall have to make the ultimate act of trust. As Jesus said on the cross, "Father, into your hands I commend my spirit" (Lk 23:46).

Trusting is an intrinsic part of believing. Many of us can remember the time when, as a child unable to swim, we were encouraged to jump into a swimming pool because there was some adult there to catch us. We believe God, for we trust that God will not deceive us; he loves us, is faithful to us, and will look after us. Because we trust, we have the confidence to throw ourselves into the arms of God, who will not let us drown. When Jesus called upon Peter to walk on the water (Mt 14:29), it was Peter's trust that failed him, until he called out, "Lord, save me!"

It is interesting to note that the English word "faith" is derived from the Latin *fidere,* meaning "to trust." Trusting belongs to the heart, to the emotions. To say to someone "I believe you" is to say that we accept what the other person has told us as being correct, or true, even though we ourselves have not checked it out. But to say to someone "I believe in you" is to convey a deep, personal trust, an expression of confidence born of a loving relationship. It is because we believe in God that we accept God as our Lord, our creator, the giver of life, the one whom we reverence, wonder at, are grateful to and seek a close union with. It is our trusting faith that leads us to pray from the heart, seeking to cement our relationship with the God who has been called by the poet Francis Thompson "This Tremendous Lover."

Odd as it may sound, the truth is that we shall learn to trust God more, the more we learn to trust one another. What does that mean? We must begin to look at any experience of human trust as an experience of trusting God. We have to learn to see God as an integral part of every facet of our life. To trust is an essential aspect of love; loving and trusting must go together, just as "faithing" and trusting must go together. As we are told in the gospel, we can only learn to love God by learning to love one another. Similarly, we can only learn to trust God if we learn to trust one another.

3. Doing

It is possible, though not probable, that someone may overemphasize the trusting dimension of faith. Overemphasis on trust would tend to make us believe that all we need to do in life is to trust God. Ultimately, such an attitude implies, God will accomplish everything. We really don't have to worry about anything, or even do anything, just leave it all to God.

Admirable as such sentiments may be, we instinctively know that there is more to faith than that. We have to work with God, we have to cooperate with God in an active manner in and through the very fabric of our everyday life. St. Augustine makes the point in one of his oft-cited aphorisms: God, who made us without ourselves, will not save us without ourselves.

There is a well-known story of a man who always had complete trust in God. After many days of rain, the river was about to flood its banks and all the residents in the area were warned to seek higher ground. The man ignored the warning because he was certain that God would not let this happen to him. As the flood waters rose, the man climbed to the upstairs part of his house. A boat came by taking off people who, like himself, had left it too late to leave. He refused a ride in the boat because he was certain that God would help him. As the water rose further, he climbed on to the roof of his house, at which point a helicopter, rescuing the few remaining survivors, came by and lowered a rope for him. No, he said, God would look after him. And, in time, he drowned.

The man arrived in heaven and, being very angry at the way he had been treated, complained to St. Peter that God had let him down despite his great faith and trust. St. Peter replied: "Did we not give you ample warning to seek higher ground? And did we not send a boat to collect you when you did not heed the first warning? And then did we not even send a helicopter for you? It seems to me that we really did answer your prayers!" According to the old Danish proverb, "In the storm pray to God, but keep rowing!"

To cooperate with God in an active manner is to act on our faith in the midst of our Christian life. But the crucial question is this: How can we know what God asks of us – what must we do? To answer this question we must look to the life of Jesus, his teaching about how we should live, and his active promotion of the kingdom of God. His message to us is that we can only love God by loving one another. This active love of one another manifests itself in active work to help establish the kingdom of God on earth.

The kingdom of God is a kingdom of justice – we must help to promote justice in all its forms and we must try to eradicate injustice, discrimination, dishonesty, deceit, insincerity, and cheating. The paramount importance of promoting justice was emphasized by the Synod of Bishops gathered in Rome on November 30, 1971. "Action on behalf of justice," they say, "and participation in the transformation of the world fully appear to us as a constitutive dimension of preaching the gospel, or, in other words, of the Church's mission for the redemption of the human race and its liberation from every oppressive situation."

The kingdom of God is a kingdom of peace – we must become peacemakers, seeking to reconcile those who are enemies, those who are fighting or feuding, those who are alienated and angry.

The kingdom of God is a kingdom in which there is no hurt or suffering – we must seek to alleviate suffering in whatever way we can. We must minister to the sick, the injured, the disabled, the aged, the bereaved, the hungry, the homeless.

The kingdom of God is a kingdom of love. Its headline is the love of Jesus, who says to us, "Love one another as I have loved you" (Jn 15:12).

The principle of an active faith is a constant theme in the New Testament, but perhaps nowhere more clearly than in the Letter of James. It is worth quoting the passage:

> What good is it, my brothers and sisters, if you say you have faith but do not have works? Can faith save you? If a brother or sister is naked and lacks daily food, and one of you says to them, "Go in peace; keep warm and eat your fill," and yet you do not supply their bodily needs, what is the good of that? So faith by itself, if it has no works, is dead. . . . You see that a person is justified by works and not by faith alone. . . . For just as the body without the spirit is dead, so faith without works is also dead. (Jas 2:14-17, 24, 26)

From all this it should be evident that we cannot call ourselves "faithing" people if we *do nothing* about our faith. In fact, we can say without hesitation that there is no such thing as a non-practising believer. A non-practising believer is a contradiction. True faith is a blending of all the dimensions we have mentioned; it is active believing, trusting and doing. No one dimension is more important than any other; all three must be present. Faith, when all is said and done, is a way of living. Christian faith finds its expression in a truly Christian lifestyle. The faith-filled life is a thoroughly moral life, a spiritual life.

As teachers and religious educators, we must be careful to promote all three dimensions of faith in our teaching.

Reflection Questions

1. As I look back over my journey with God, who are the significant people in my life that I would name as "faithing" persons? What influence did they have on me? Is there anyone who negatively influenced my faith journey? Why?

2. Can I write my own creed? From my own experience, whom and what do I believe? Try to state three or four deeply held beliefs.

3. As a "faithing" person, where do I feel called to grow in trust these days?

4. What actions in my life would testify to my "faithing"?

5. Helen, a devout and well-educated Catholic, was married to Eric, a Christian but of no particular persuasion. They had been married for over 30 years and had raised seven children. Eric used to accompany his wife and family to Eucharist every Sunday but had not given any indication that he wanted to become a Catholic. After Mass one Sunday that seemed to be no different from any other Sunday, he suddenly announced that he wanted to be received into the church. "But Eric," his wife expostulated, "why, after all these years?" "I don't know," he said, "I can't explain it. I just believe."

    Comment on this true story.

    Distinguish between faith and belief.

6. Explain the following quotations:

    "Faith is the sight of an inward eye." (Alexander Maclaren)

    "We must learn that to expect God to do everything while we do nothing is not faith, but superstition." (Martin Luther King)

    "I have never discarded beliefs deliberately. I have left them in the drawer, and, after a while when I opened it, there was nothing there at all." (William Graham Sumner)

Further Reading

Cunningham, Lawrence. *Faith Rediscovered* (New York: Paulist Press, 1987). See particularly Chapter 2, "Faith and the Faith."

Groome, Thomas. *Christian Religious Education* (San Francisco: Harper San Francisco, 1980). Though published some years back, this remains a most significant work in religious education. It is used as a basic text in many university-level courses. It is not always an easy book to read, but many sections (such as the one on faith and on the suggested process of religious education) are clear and helpful. It will repay study and is an excellent reference.

Link, Mark, S.J. *Path Through Catholicism* (Allen, TX: Tabor Publishing, 1991). A highly recommended text for high school religious education. Chapter 1 deals with faith.

Shea, John. *Stories of Faith* (Chicago: Thomas More Press, 1980). A wide-ranging treatment of various aspects of faith in narrative (story-telling) form. Has received high acclaim from the critics.

3

GOD – MYSTERY PRESENT

God Is Mystery

> We firmly believe and confess without reservation that there is only one true God, eternal, infinite (*immensus*) and unchangeable, incomprehensible, almighty and ineffable, the Father and the Son and the Holy Spirit; three persons indeed, but one essence, substance or nature entirely simple. (CCC 202, Source: Lateran Council IV: DS 800)

This is a clear and comprehensive statement of what Christians believe about God. God is infinite and therefore infinitely surpasses our human efforts to understand him. God is mystery,* but there is no need to be frightened of mystery. For most of us, the worlds of nuclear physics and computer chip technology are a mystery, but that doesn't prevent us from getting on with life. God and God's dealings with us – the whole panoply of what we call religion – is shot through with mystery. It cannot be otherwise because of who God is and who we are. But God has revealed himself to us, has opened himself to us so that we can relate to him; God has made himself present to us (CCC 203-207). Therefore, Christians believe that this mystery of God is present to their lives, and is something that can be experienced and with which they are in touch. The God who is transcendent* is also the God who is immanent,* or present in the midst of creation. God is mystery present. Furthermore, this is the God who calls us to enter into a personal relationship with him (CCC 2567). In the course of this relationship we should not be surprised that there will always be things that remain mysterious and beyond our grasp.

But mystery is not something we *cannot* know; it is something we cannot *fully* or *wholly* know. The fact that God is mystery means that while God remains hidden, at the same time God discloses himself to us. In other words, "The presence of God is never so clear that belief is inevitable, nor ever so obscure that belief is impossible."[15] Mystery always presents an invitation to us to penetrate it ever more deeply. Mystery is what F.J. Sheed calls "an inexhaustible well of Truth from which the mind may drink and drink again in the certainty that the

---

[15] Richard P. McBrien, *Catholicism*, New ed., (San Francisco: Harper San Francisco, 1994), p. 272.

well will never run dry."[16] It is as though we live in a circle of light surrounded
by darkness. We cannot see beyond the edge of the light; our vision and
experience are limited. We must aim to push outward the boundary of darkness
so that we may see and experience more and more of the mystery. Pushing
outward the boundary of darkness is one of the things we are aiming to do in this
book so that God becomes more intimate to us, more accessible, more present.

Our Search for God

The Bible puts it very succinctly: "No one has ever seen God. It is God the
only Son, who is close to the Father's heart, who has made him known" (Jn
1:18). It is in Jesus, therefore, that we "see" and know God most clearly and
fully. Jesus is the full and complete revelation of God to us. We Christians
believe that God, who is mystery, has nevertheless entered our lives in a
definitive way, and we know this especially through the revelation of Jesus as
God. God calls to us, God searches for us, God reaches out to us in the ordinary
processes of our lives. No one has ever seen God, and we have never seen Jesus
Christ, but we can become convinced of God's existence and his presence in our
lives in a variety of ways. Often enough we are not able to explain clearly why
we are convinced; we just know it "in our bones."

Let us now take a look at some of the ways we may find God.

One way is to look around us, to study the evidence from our own life
experiences, to reflect on the order and beauty in the world. In his fine book *Path
Through Catholicism*, Mark Link, S.J., begins the section on God by telling the
story of the movie *Laura*. Laura is murdered in her apartment, and over the next
few days the detective assigned to the case, Mark MacPherson, searches assiduously for clues among Laura's personal belongings – he even reads her diary.
Learning more and more about Laura from examining her life and effects, Mark
is strongly attracted to her. One night, as he sits in Laura's apartment thinking
about her, he falls asleep. Something awakens him, and as he opens his eyes,
there is Laura standing in the doorway. It turns out that Laura had only gone
away for a few days but had not read a newspaper or heard the radio reports of
her own death. One of Laura's friends had used the apartment in her absence and
she was the one who had been murdered. The happy ending to the movie is, of
course, that Mark and Laura fall in love and marry. Mark Link sees in this story
a parable of God's presence in the world and of our relationship to God. The
world is God's "apartment." By searching assiduously in the apartment we can
discover God's personal effects, as it were, and thus get to know him.

---

[16]   F.J. Sheed. *Theology and Sanity* (New York: Sheed & Ward, 1962), p. 18.

Sacred Scripture points to the same phenomenon. In his letter to the Romans, St. Paul indicates that the pagans really have no excuse for not coming to know God. "For what can be known about God is plain to them, because God has shown it to them. Ever since the creation of the world his eternal power and divine nature, invisible though they are, have been understood and seen through the things he has made" (Rom 1:19-20). By contemplating the created universe and reflecting upon it we can come to know the unseen God (CCC 54).

A second way we can come to know that God exists is by some direct and ineffable personal experience. Religious experience takes many and varied forms and exhibits many different characteristics. One characteristic that has been reported is the experience of a "Presence" which is not human or finite, a presence of "the Other," the transcendent. Religious experience may also give one a feeling of great peace, of joy, of the sense of being "saved," or of a sense of the "holy" which moves us to respect and worship. Consider the following story.

It happened in my room at Peterhouse on the evening of 1 February 1913, when I was an undergraduate at Cambridge. If I say that Christ came to me I should be using conventional words which would carry no precise meaning; for Christ comes to men and women in different ways. When I tried to record the experience at the time I used the imagery of the vision of the Holy Grail; it seemed to me to be like that. There was, however, no sensible vision. There was just the room with its shoddy furniture and the fire burning in the grate and the red-shaded lamp on the table. But the room was filled by a Presence, which in a strange way was both about me and within me, like light or warmth. I was overwhelmingly possessed by Someone who was not myself, and yet I felt I was more myself than I had ever been before. I was filled with an intense happiness, and almost unbearable joy, such as I had never known before and have never known since. And over all was a deep sense of peace and security and certainty.[17]

While this experience seems to be very out of the ordinary, it is safe to say that similar experiences are not uncommon. What may be even more surprising is that they occur in the lives of very ordinary people who would not in any way consider themselves to be religious mystics. It is interesting to compare the mystical experience related above with those recorded in the New Testament, such as those of St. Paul (Acts 9; 22:6-16; 26:12-18). God is never far away from any of us.

---

[17]   F.C. Happold, quoted by Andrew M. Greeley and William C. McCready, "Are We a Nation of Mystics?" in *New York Times* Sunday Supplement Magazine, January 26, 1975.

A third way we may find God is through the example of others who have touched us in some special way, who are close to us and influence us: our parents, a teacher, a pastor, friends and others who are people of faith and who express that faith through worship. Here, for example, is the story of Paul Stookey (of the musical trio Peter, Paul and Mary).

> I started reading the New Testament. [Bob] Dylan was right, because I began discovering that all the truths I sought were contained in the life of this man. . . . It was fantastic. . . . He set a good example, but it never occurred to me that he could really be the Son of God. . . .
>
> Then I was backstage during a concert in Austin, Texas, once, walking along, click clack, click clack, across the hall . . . and there was a cat standing there in a Navajo jacket with curly blond hair . . . . And he said, "Could I talk to you?" . . . I sorta walked close to him and said, "What is it you'd like to talk to me about?" I wanted to be sort of a father to him. And he said, "I want to talk to you about the Lord!"
>
> Whack! . . .
>
> Somehow, this guy made all the reading in the Scriptures make sense because he explained to me that while Jesus himself did in fact live this life, Jesus is real. . . . I said: "Well, I know he is real. I mean, he was real." He said: "No. He's a spirit and he says in the Scriptures: Behold I knock; if any man asks me to enter I will come and dwell with him."
>
> So, wow! I started to pray with him, and I asked Jesus to come in and take over my life. And I started to cry and he started to cry. . . .
>
> When you say, "All right, Lord. . . . You point out where you want me to go". . . . even then you are continually being called back into the world . . . But once you have seen the light . . . you just keep coming back to it."[18]

God comes to us and touches our lives in a variety of ways, ways that will be unique to each one of us, ways that will depend on our own personal faith story. Paul Stookey's faith story had begun much earlier than the incident related above. It had begun with his desire to find some meaning in life – it had begun with the curiosity he felt about his "spiritual nature." It is important for each of us to reflect often on our own faith story, the experiences and the people that put us in touch with God. Our early faith experiences, the influence of parents, teachers, clergy – the whole nurturing process and how we reacted to it – has a lot to do with how we now "see" and relate to God, how we understand what God may be saying to us. As Bernard Cooke says, "Religiously, the manner in which each

---

[18] From Bob Combs and Scott Ross, "Peter, Me, and Mary," *Campus Life*, May, 1972.

of us interprets her or his personal experience is the springboard for thinking about the divine."[19] We must do our best to become aware of our experiences, particularly the early ones which have shaped and formed us, if we are to grow in understanding and intimacy with God. We may well need ultimately to rid ourselves of many of the false images of God that we have grown up with.

How, then, do we "see" God? How do we try to capture the transcendent mystery so that it becomes real to us? We do it largely by attempting to form images of God that speak to us.

Images of God

Let us now take a look at some of the more common images that people have of God. Can we, perhaps, find our own preferred image in any of the following?

Artistic impressions and images of God affect many people. Thus, for example, God is often portrayed in stained glass windows and in paintings as a kindly old man with a beard, perhaps sitting on a throne in heaven attended by angels. A well-educated grown man once told the author that whenever the sun broke through the clouds in the form of rays he always thought of God. As a child, most of the pictures of God he had seen portrayed God with a luminous halo and rays of light coming out from behind him! That was one of the earliest images that he could remember. Another way artists have portrayed God is as a God of power. The famous creation scene in Michaelangelo's painting on the ceiling of the Sistine Chapel in the Vatican portrays God in this way.

In all these cases God is portrayed as a man. God is anthropomorphized,* that is, made into the form of a human person (from the Greek *anthropos*, human person, and *morphe*, form). Because we are human, it is difficult, if not impossible, to think about God unless we form some image of God. It is terribly important for us to clarify our images of God because first, we need to replace the wrong and misleading images, and second, we need to understand better how we relate to God and how this relationship affects the expression of our faith.

The Bible provides us with several very homely, down-to-earth and appealing images of God. Thus, God is a *shepherd* who leads his flock along the right paths to green pastures (Ps 23), the shepherd who will "seek the lost," "bring back the strayed" and "strengthen the weak" (Ezek 34:16). God is a *mother* who never forgets the child of her womb (see Isa 49:15), or the mother eagle who cares for her offspring and teaches them to fly (see Deut 32:11). God is a loving *parent*: "I was to them like those who lift infants to their cheeks. I bent down to them and fed them" (Hos 11:1-4). God is a *gracious host*: "You prepare a table

---

[19]   Bernard Cooke, *Sacraments and Sacramentality* (Mystic, CT: Twenty-Third Publications, 1983), p. 34.

before me in the presence of my enemies; you anoint my head with oil; my cup overflows" (Ps 23:5). God is the *creator* (Ps 24:1-2), a king of glory strong and mighty (Ps 24:8), the Holy One before whom the angels bow and cry out, "Holy, holy, holy is the Lord of hosts; the whole earth is full of his glory" (Isa 6:3).

Some other images of God, also basically biblical, may also strike a chord with us. Here are some examples.

God is the one we *fear*. God can send us to hell (Mt 25:41). God doesn't like it when we have too much fun. Having too much pleasure causes us to "look over our shoulder," causes feelings of guilt. As one high school student put it, "God is an old fogey who is always on the lookout for people who are having fun so that he can put a stop to it"!

God is the great *manipulator*. God arranges things in the world, somewhat like a puppeteer (Ps 35). Thus, when things go wrong we call on God to fix them. God goes around working minor miracles: arranging this, fixing that, averting accidents, healing sickness, giving special wisdom at exam time, and so on. We blame God when things go wrong. "Why didn't God do something?" we exclaim (Ps 10:1); "Why did God let it happen to me?"

God is someone with whom we can *bargain*. And so, for example, if we promise to say a lot of prayers God will give us what we want. We make pacts with God: "If you will do this for me, I will do that for you" (Jer 10:10 ff). We "use" God when we want something.

God is the one who *provides comfort* and security amid the awful vicissitudes of life. We look to God for solace in our troubles. It is easy to persuade ourselves that God wants us to have a comfortable and secure life.

God is the *Transcendent One*. God is a sort of Olympian figure, somewhat distant. God is "out there." God is *light*, the light associated with the near-death experience.[20]

The Bible uses these, and several other images, to help us form some sort of idea about God, the God who surpasses all human ideas and images.

It is useful to try to determine what is our dominant image of God, the one that most easily comes to mind, the one that most frequently takes precedence over all others. Discovering our dominant image often will give us a clue to understanding why we order our life in a certain way, how our belief in God affects the way we live. Particularly, those who teach religion should encourage

---

[20] Some of these images are adapted from Chapter 5 of Philip Sheldrake, S.J., *Images of Holiness* (Notre Dame, IN: Ave Maria Press, 1987). Useful material on various images of God and how they affect our prayer may be found in Pat McCloskey, O.F.M., *Naming Your God* (Notre Dame, IN: Ave Maria Press, 1991), and in Gerard Hughes, S.J., *God of Surprises* (New York: Paulist Press, 1985).

and help their students to look into their lives and try to identify the kind of person they perceive God to be, and to search out why this image may be dominant. One way of doing this is to examine how we pray. When we try to reach out to God in prayer, what are we thinking of? How do we approach God? The very way we go about trying to reach God reveals our own particular vision and understanding of God.

Trying to form an imaginative picture of God, whether as a human being or as any other form of being, can be very misleading. The only way we can truly imagine God is to imagine our Lord Jesus Christ while remembering Jesus' words to the apostle Philip. Jesus said to him, "Have I been with you all this time, Philip, and you still do not know me? Whoever has seen me has seen the Father. How can you say, 'Show us the Father'?" (Jn 14:9). Our real problem is that we are always trying to make God into our own image. It is reported that one Protestant pastor, angry that one of his congregation had become a Catholic, told his people, "And I want you all to remember one thing: God is who *I* say God is." Subconsciously, we want to control and domesticate God – we want to drag God down to our own level. As Gerard Hughes says, "We are constantly tempted to make God into our own image, to divinise our narrowness and self-importance and then call it the will of God."[21]

But, wonder of wonders, this God who is mystery comes to us in the flesh as our Lord Jesus Christ. This God calls to us in love and asks for our love in return. It is this most important quality of God, the God who is love (as exhibited in the life and teaching of Jesus) that we should focus on most of all. Any image, therefore, that will help us to focus on the God who is love is one that we should cultivate and make our own. [22] The great danger we must guard against is getting caught up in the many false and misleading ideas about love that are so prevalent in today's culture, which tends to over-sentimentalize love and often is unable to distinguish between the true love of another and a destructive self-love. There is a strong tendency in modern culture to turn God into some sort of divine Mary Poppins who dispenses "warm fuzzies": the "do-gooder" God.[23]

Finally, we need to be warned again and again that any image that is overemphasized does a disservice to our understanding of and relationship to God. We should never allow ourselves to be totally captivated by any image of God. God is all of them, and none of them. That may sound like a paradox, and

---

[21]   Gerard Hughes S.J., *God of Surprises,* p. 33.

[22]   The Catechism (CCC 218-221) deals eloquently with this great truth that God is love.

[23]   Thomas Day has brilliantly and insightfully traced the metamorphosis of the "hard," the "awesome," the "terrible" God more familiar to previous generations into the "soft," "cuddly" God of the modern era. See *Why Catholics Can't Sing,* (New York: Crossroad, 1990), p. 69.

indeed it is, for God is the supreme paradox. We don't solve paradoxes; we learn to live with them.

The Language Gap and God

While we cannot wholly know God, all the same there is much that we can know. Our problem is that in coming to know God and in speaking about God we have to use human language – it's all we have. The problem is compounded because, in this age of science and technology, our language is becoming more and more "earthbound": strictly related to what can be scientifically determined and proved, the "nuts and bolts" kind of stuff. Our consciousness is so largely shaped by our earthbound language that anything that cannot be described in scientific terms tends to lose its meaning for us. This point is well illustrated by Mark Twain. Twain had mastered the technicalities of piloting a steamboat on the Mississippi, noting familiar landmarks, gauging the currents, avoiding the sandbars, taking advantage of deep water. But he found that with the accumulation of all this scientific knowledge of the great river he had lost something too, something that "could never be restored to me while I live. All the grace and beauty, the poetry had gone out of the majestic river!"

Mystery cannot be trapped in scientific categories; we cannot easily bring it down to earth, so to speak, domesticate it, control it, which is what we are always trying to do. We need a language of symbol and metaphor, a language that leaves room for the poetic and the aesthetic, a language that lifts us beyond the drab and the mundane and points us in the direction of the transcendent. Language about mystery is always more evocative and engaging when it is right-brain language* rather than left-brain language.* Consider, for example, the following descriptions of God.

Francis Thompson, in his magnificent poem *The Hound of Heaven,* describes his own flight from God and how God, the hound of heaven, the tremendous lover, pursued him with the deliberate speed and majestic instancy of a pursuing hound:

I fled Him down the nights and down the days;
I fled Him down the arches of the years;
I fled Him down the labyrinthine ways
Of my own mind. . . .
But with unhurrying chase
And unperturbed pace
Deliberate speed, majestic instancy,
They beat – and a Voice beat
More instant than the Feet -
All things betray thee, who betrayest Me.

Or consider this one by St. Augustine of Hippo, full of brilliant images of a soul that yearns for God. It is taken from his *Confessions,* in which he laments the many years he spent estranged from God.

Late have I loved you, O beauty so ancient and so new; late have I loved you! . . . . You called and cried to me and broke upon my deafness; and you sent forth your beam and shone upon me, and chased away my blindness; you breathed fragrance upon me, and I drew in my breath and do not pant for you; I tasted you and I now hunger and thirst for you; you touched me and I now burned for your peace.

Compare these statements about God with the dry-bones philosophical description of God as "the unmoved first mover" or the "uncaused first cause." Descriptions like these may enlighten the mind, but they fail to reach the depths of the whole person, mind and heart. The same may be said of many of the theological formulae that are used about God.

God and Analogy

Human language is the product of human experience; it is, therefore, inadequate to fully express the mystery that is God because God transcends all human experience. When we use human language to speak about God, we use analogies. We speak of God after the analogy* of what is human. Thus, we look at the human, we look at what we know and experience, and say "God is like this." For example, when we say "God is good," or "God is just," or "God is loving," we are using the words "good," "just," "loving" as we understand them from human experience. And so we say that God is "loving" because God is like our human understanding of what it is to be loving.

Take another specific example, an example we shall elaborate in the next chapter. We understand God as personal, as having personal characteristics; that is, we understand God to be someone we can know and love. We can only call God a person because of our understanding of human persons. We apply personal characteristics to God derived from our experience of human persons. It is the essence of persons to have intellect and will: they can know and they can love. We know, also from our experience, that it is essential for human persons to communicate, to relate to one another; in fact, human personality is only formed through a process of communication and interrelationship. Deprived of human relationship we cannot develop into full human persons. If we say that God is personal, after the analogy of human persons, then we must mean that God can communicate with us, relate to us, and we can do the same with God. Our spiritual personality, what we Christians believe to be our true self, will develop in and through communication and relationship with God.

To repeat this most important principle, *all language about God is analogical and symbolic*. However, to say what God is like is not to say what God *is*. The depth of God's being and essence is always beyond our full comprehension. Before the glory and infinity of God we can but take the advice of the prophet Habakkuk: "let all the earth keep silence before him!" (Hab 2:20, see also Ps 46:10). One of the great things we have to look forward to in the next life is precisely a more vivid, a more intimate and captivating revelation of the depth of God's being.

> *For we know only in part, and we prophesy only in part; but when the complete comes, the partial will come to an end. When I was a child, I spoke like a child, I thought like a child, I reasoned like a child; when I became an adult, I put an end to childish ways. For now we see in a mirror, dimly, but then we will see face to face. Now I know only in part; then I will know fully, even as I have been fully known. (1 Cor 13:9-12)*

Importance for Religious Education

The field of religious education has been greatly affected by our contemporary bias in favour of left-brain language. Many religious education programs see the main task of religious education as providing what might be termed "religious information," or knowledge about religion – Scripture, doctrine, church history, liturgy and morality – albeit with some application to practical living. The designers of such programs refer to the information as "content"; they tend to be suspicious of courses that lack "content." Clearly, it is important for us to be theologically correct in our statements about God. We must have the necessary information about religion, knowledge about religion and faith. But religious education can never lose sight of the vital necessity of fostering the dimension of the aesthetic, the symbolic. Good religious educators will make use of all avenues that open up the aesthetic experience, such as music, poetry, art, story, dance and drama. They must also try to foster a sense of awe, of wonder and of reverence as befits the transcendent and mysterious God. It is the aesthetic, the experience of symbol, that is often the best way of putting us in touch with the God who is mystery, of making God "real" to us. Religious educators who neglect this dimension will miss out on an important – in fact, an essential – way of helping students to appreciate and relate to the God who is present and whom we can reach only through the realm of the symbolic.

The whole question of religious symbolism will be dealt with more fully when we come to consider sacramentality. But next we must say something about an important aspect of the Christian belief in God: that the one God is also a community of persons, Father, Son and Holy Spirit – the Blessed Trinity.

Reflection Questions

1. Can you identify and name three or four images of God that have been important or strong in your life at any time?

2. Can you link them with certain stages in your life? With what stages do you associate them?

3. Are there particular events or people who were influential in shaping these images of God for you?

4. Have these images changed over time? Why? How? What reaction and response has it provoked in you when these images had to change?

5. Add to the list given in this chapter any images of God that are meaningful to you.

6. What do we mean when we say that God is love?

7. Can you think of some teaching strategies that would help in fostering an appreciation for the aesthetic and symbolic experience?

Further Reading

Flynn, Eileen, and Gloria Thomas. *Living Faith: An Introduction to Theology* (Kansas City, MO: Sheed & Ward, 1989). Particularly Chapter 1. A good, readable and fairly simple survey of fundamental theological themes. Presumes no previous knowledge of theology. Very useful reference book.

Hughes, Gerard W., S.J. *God of Surprises* (New York: Paulist Press, 1985). A book that helps us grow in intimacy with God as we clarify our images of the One who loves us.

Martin, James (ed.) *How Can I Find God?* (Liguori, MO: Triumph Books, 1997). Several prominent and not so prominent people speak sincerely of their quest for God in their lives and how they visualize, recognize, experience and understand God. Excellent and deeply spiritual reading.

Shea, John. *Stories of God* (Chicago: Thomas More Press, 1978). An outstanding book of narrative theology, which attempts to explain our experience of God in story form. Has received wide critical acclaim and will repay reading and study.

4

GOD – A COMMUNITY

OF PERSONS

Christianity cannot escape its Jewish roots. The major tenets of Jewish faith are in fact the building blocks for Christian faith. Jewish faith has as its foundation a single belief: there is but ONE God (monotheism*). This monotheistic faith is clearly expressed in what is now known as the First Commandment. This commandment was given by God to Moses as part of the covenant between God and the Jewish people: "I am the Lord your God, who brought you out of the land of Egypt, out of the house of slavery; you shall have no other gods before me" (Ex 20:2-3).

Jesus was born into and raised in this tradition of strict monotheism. However, in the course of his life and teaching he came to reveal that, while there is but one God, in this one God there are three persons: the Father, the Son and the Holy Spirit. "We do not confess three Gods, but one God in three persons, the 'consubstantial Trinity.' The divine persons do not share the one divinity among themselves but each of them is God whole and entire" (CCC 253). And so, after his resurrection, Jesus gives the following commission to his apostles:

All authority in heaven and on earth has been given to me. Go therefore and make disciples of all nations, baptizing them in the name of the Father, and of the Son and of the Holy Spirit, and teaching them to obey everything that I have commanded you. (Mt 28:18-20a)

One God in three divine persons – Father, Son and Holy Spirit, the Blessed Trinity – is the "central mystery of Christian faith and life" (CCC 234), a mystery that could never have been known unless revealed by God (CCC 237). We profess this faith every time we make the sign of the cross, every time we recite the Creed. We begin and end our prayers with it to remind ourselves of its importance.

Persons in God

As we saw in the previous chapter, when we use the word "person" we use it after the analogy of our understanding of human persons. But a word of caution. To the modern mind, when we hear the word "person" we tend to think of a unique and distinct individual, someone who has a unique and distinctive centre of consciousness, *a* person. Clearly, we cannot think of God as having three distinct centres of consciousness, for then we would have three Gods, not one. No, we must think of the persons of the Trinity as distinct from one another but in relationship with one another after the analogy of how we understand human persons to enter into relationships, by knowledge and love. Thus, the Blessed Trinity – God – is in fact a community of persons.

"The Fathers of the Church distinguish between theology *(theologia)* and economy *(oikonomia)*. 'Theology' refers to the mystery of God's inmost life within the Blessed Trinity and 'economy' to all the works by which God reveals himself and communicates his life" (CCC 236). The theology of God's inmost life is extremely difficult and is beyond the scope of this book. We shall concentrate, rather, on the economy (the root of which is the Greek *oicos,* meaning *home,* or *house*): how God relates to us and we to God "at home," in the midst of our life.

As we struggle to find ways of expressing our experience of God, all human language fails us. Down through the centuries Christian theologians, preachers and writers have tried to find images that might help to put people in touch with the mystery of Blessed Trinity. Stories are told of St. Patrick who, when preaching to his Irish neophytes, used the shamrock, one leaf yet three-pronged. Another image proposed is that of water. Water is a single chemical substance, but yet it exists in three different states: solid, liquid and vapour. John Wesley, the founder of Methodism, sometimes used the symbol of light. "Tell me how it is that in this room there are three candles but one light, and I will explain to you the mode of divine existence." The candles are distinct candles but together give off a single light.

In the economic sense, as affecting our lives, what the Blessed Trinity really means for us is that the one God is revealed to us as three distinct persons. We can experience God as entering our lives and relate to the God who loves us in a special way through each distinct person. And so, the Blessed Trinity is not a mere theological formula or a theological curiosity that has no real effect on our lives. As Andrew Greeley puts it, "The doctrine of the Holy Trinity was not revealed to us to test our faith or to provide an abstruse puzzle for metaphysically inclined theologians. It was revealed to tell us something about God, and hence something about the purpose and meaning of human life."[24]

---

[24]   Andrew Greeley, *The Great Mysteries: An Essential Catechism* (New York: Seabury Press, 1976), p. 36.

God the Father

Consider this beautiful passage from St. Paul's Letter to the Romans:

For you did not receive a spirit of slavery to fall back into fear, but you have received a spirit of adoption. When we cry, "Abba! Father!" it is that very Spirit bearing witness with our spirit that we are children of God . . . . (Rom 8:15-16)

It is Jesus who taught us to call God *Abba.* Abba is an Aramaic word (the language that Jesus spoke); it is the familiar and familial word for father, a term of intimacy and endearment. The word is still used by Palestinian children of our day. For a Palestinian Jew of that time, even to utter the name of God was blasphemy, yet Jesus speaks to God in this radically intimate way. It seems clear that as a human being Jesus really experienced God as Abba and even understood himself in terms of this close relationship. Jesus called upon his disciples to pray to God as Abba (see Rom 8:15; Gal 4:6), and so should we. Again, Abba speaks of intimacy; we are God's children, we are on intimate terms with God just as Jesus was on intimate terms with his Father. God is our Abba, Father.

After the example and teaching of Jesus, we experience God as exhibiting all the qualities we might expect from a loving, caring father with whom we are on intimate terms. God is the giver of life, who sustains us, who supports us, to whom we turn in difficulty, to whom we owe everything. We pray to God as Jesus taught us: Our Father. We experience God as Father after the analogy of a human father, but why not after the analogy of a human mother? Does not a mother do for her child everything a father does, and more? Does not everything we have said of human fathers also apply to human mothers? Of course it does. Furthermore, the Bible does have several references to the maternal aspect of God. For example, "As a mother comforts her child, so I will comfort you; you shall be comforted in Jerusalem" (Isa 66:13). And again: "Can a woman forget her nursing child, or show no compassion for the child of her womb? Even these may forget, yet I will not forget you. See, I have inscribed you on the palms of my hands; your walls are continually before me" (Isa 49:15-16).

There is no gender in God. The limitations of our human experience and language force us to use gender when we are speaking of human persons and, consequently, by analogy when we speak of God. The analogical or metaphorical use of the term "father" when speaking of God in no way implies that God is of the masculine sex. George Montague, S.M., quotes St. John Damascene (645–750) as follows: "We have to regard it as indispensable to apply our earthly words to the divinity in a metaphorical sense, especially those that for us concern parenting. Do you imagine that

God is the masculine sex because we call him Theos and Father?"[25] In speaking of God as Father, or Mother, we are applying the qualities of a good human parent, as we understand them, to God. It is important for us to keep in mind that in calling God "Father" we do not use that term primarily as one denoting authority and power, as opposed to the more maternal qualities of caring and tenderness. Our strong tendency is to associate authority and power with maleness and thus with human fathers. On the other hand, we tend to think of caring and tenderness as more maternal qualities, more befitting a female. But, as Montague reminds us, "In prophetic thought [in the Old Testament]. . . the image of father was not primarily one of authority and power, but one of adoptive love, covenant bonding, tenderness and compassion. It combined what we understand today as roles of both father and mother."[26] Thus the power of God is not the power of force associated with physically strong people or with armies. No, the power of God means the power of one faithful to us in love, the power of a friend.

In all of sacred Scripture God is never specifically called "Mother." Jesus never calls God his mother; he calls only Mary his mother. It is true that Jesus, being fully human, grew up in a patriarchal society. He was influenced by the social mores of his time, as he was by the cultural and linguistic patterns of his own people. Nevertheless, even granted that Jesus' manner of speaking was historically conditioned, we still have to take into account the underlying meaning of what he said. And so, even if Jesus had specifically referred to God as our mother, the essential message that God is our loving parent would be the same. We know and relate to God as a person whose personhood is expressed as father after the analogy of human father (parent).

God the Father, the First Person of the Blessed Trinity.

God the Son

We Christians believe that Jesus of Nazareth, who belongs in history at a specific time and place, is both God and man; Jesus is "the human face of God." In the New Testament, Jesus is also called the Word of God. Jesus is the Son of God speaking to us in human language, that is, in a word that we can understand. "And the Word became flesh and lived among us, and we have seen his glory, the glory as of a father's only son, full of grace and truth" (Jn 1:14). This Jesus, who speaks God's word to us, constantly refers to God as his Father. Further-

---

[25] George Montague, S.M., "Freezing the Fire: The Death of Relational Language," *America*, March 13, 1993, p. 5.

[26] George Montague, S.M., *Our Father, Our Mother* (Steubenville, OH: Franciscan University Press, 1990), p. 18. That the word *Abba* need not essentially and necessarily be associated with maleness and patriarchy, see Brian Wren, *What Language Shall I Borrow?* (New York: Crossroad, 1991), pp 183-188. See also Thomas Groome, *Language for a "Catholic" Church* (Kansas City, MO: Sheed & Ward, 1991), pp. 25-26, 37.

more, close to one hundred times the Christian Scriptures use the title "Son of God" for Jesus. Jesus says, "The Father and I are one" (Jn 10:30). And again, "Whoever has seen me has seen the Father.... Do you not believe that I am in the Father and the Father is in me?" (Jn 14:9-10). Jesus is very conscious of his own unique relationship with God. It is a relationship of unity and equality, but at the same time a relationship of son to father. Jesus understands and expresses his whole mission on earth as that of a dutiful son. His duty is to "do the will of my Father in heaven." "I do nothing on my own," he says, "but I speak these things as the Father instructed me. And the one who sent me is with me; he has not left me alone, for I always do what is pleasing to him" (Jn 8:28-29).

The historical fact is that Jesus was male; it is quite natural for him to refer to himself as son. He was the son of his Father. But as we did for God the Father, we must look beyond the maleness of Jesus; we must look to the trans-historical significance of this revelation of God as son. Reading the gospels, it is not difficult for us to see how Jesus exhibits all the qualities we like to associate with good children, both sons and daughters: he is obedient, faithful, loyal, reliable, helpful, loving. In Jesus we can relate to God in a special way as sons and daughters. Jesus is our brother; we are part of God's family.

In Jesus we experience and relate to God after the analogy of human sons and daughters. We experience God as Son.

God the Son, the Second Person of the Blessed Trinity.

God the Spirit

At the baptism of Jesus in the Jordan, the Spirit of God was seen to descend on him in the form of a dove (Mk 1:10; Lk 3:21-22). It is because of this incident that God's Spirit is frequently represented in art as a bird (a dove). The pervasiveness of this image has led to stories such as the one related by Anthony Bloom, in which he quotes a Japanese person: "In the Christian religion I think I understand about the Father and the Son, but I can never discover the signifi-cance of the honourable bird"![27] The Spirit of God also appears in other forms in the New Testament, such as the tongues of fire that rested on the apostles on the day of Pentecost (Acts 2:3). We may recall, from the incident of Moses and the burning bush (Ex 3), that fire is used as a symbol of the presence of God.

Down through the centuries many theologians, spiritual writers and preach-ers have complained that the Spirit of God has been "neglected" or "forgotten" in the teaching and spiritual life of the church. In our present time, as a result of the discussions at Vatican Council II, the church has witnessed a growth in aware-ness of the importance of the Spirit. The birth of the Charismatic Renewal

---

[27]   Quoted by Mark Link, S.J., *Path Through Catholicism* (Allen, TX; Tabor Publishing, 1991) p. 62.

movement in 1967 and its subsequent spread have focused a lot of attention on what the Spirit does. But the question of what the Spirit is like as a person and how we can relate to the Spirit as a person has not received much attention. To put it in a nutshell, the Spirit suffers from an "image problem." Because of the very nature and meaning of spirit as we usually understand it (i.e., something that is not material, not having a body), it is not easy to completely eliminate the image problem for the Spirit of God. It will be helpful, however, for us to take a look at how we experience spirit in our everyday life.

1. We speak of "the human spirit" or, more pointedly, of "my spirit'" (for example, "my spirits are low," or, someone is "high-spirited"). Thus, spirit refers to something deep down in me which cannot be easily defined or grasped, something which makes me unique, the source of my vitality, the power within me, something which directs and energizes me as a human person. Can we come to appreciate that this power of energy and life in me is the Spirit of God, God's personal gift of love?

2. In Hebrew the word for spirit is *ruah*; in Latin it is *spiritus* (from which the English word "spirit" is derived). Both these words mean breath, wind (CCC 691). The Spirit of God is the breath of God. In the first book of the Bible the creation of the first human is described as follows: "then the Lord God formed man from the dust of the ground, and breathed into his nostrils the breath of life; and the man became a living being" (Gen 2:7). God's breath (spirit) is in me. God dwells in me. God gives me life, God sustains me, God gives me my spirit. If God were to cease breathing in me I would cease to exist. The Spirit of God is the love of God in me calling to me to respond to that love.

3. The Bible usually associates God's works of power with the Holy Spirit. Thus, the creation of the world, bringing order out of chaos, is attributed to the spirit, "a wind from God" (Gen 1:2) (CCC 703, 704). The Bible refers to the miracle at the Sea of Reeds, when the Israelites were saved from the pursuing Egyptians, as follows: "At the blast of your nostrils the waters piled up, the floods stood up in a heap; the deeps congealed in the heart of the sea" (Ex 15:8). The power of God's Spirit came upon the apostles on the day of Pentecost "like the rush of a violent wind" (Acts 2:2), giving them the strength and courage to witness to the word of God, to work miracles and to bring healing in his name. Peter announced that the same outpouring of the Spirit would be given to everyone to proclaim God's message (Acts 2:17), and not only to proclaim God's message but also to accomplish God's work in the world. Thus the Christian Scriptures speak of how the Holy Spirit gives different gifts to different people, gifts that work together for "building up the body of Christ" (Eph 4:12) which is the church (CCC 768, 798-801).

It is the power of the Spirit that unites the many different peoples into one body, the church (CCC 813). "To each is given the manifestation of the Spirit for the common good. To one is given through the Spirit the utterance of wisdom . . . to another gifts of healing by the one Spirit, to another the working of miracles, to another prophecy, to another the discernment of spirits . . . ." (1 Cor 12:7-10) (CCC 1830). We all have received the power of God's Spirit to do God's work in the world.

4.   Jesus refers to the Spirit of God as the Paraclete (CCC 692). The Greek word *parakletos* means advocate. That alone tells us something about the personality of the Spirit. The Spirit argues our case before God, as it were – puts us in God's presence, teaches, leads and defends us. The Spirit bridges the gap between us and God, overcomes the sense of our own unworthiness. The Spirit is love-giving and life-giving, for God is love. The Spirit of God is the love of God given to us; wherever we experience God's love we experience the Spirit of God.

Therefore,

1.   I experience and relate to God's Spirit as life-giving, as life, as the breath of life in me, God's gift of love.

2.   I experience and relate to God's Spirit as the inmost part of me, the very depth of my personality, that which makes me unique, able to respond to God's call to personal intimacy.

3.   I experience and relate to God's Spirit as the power in my life, the power to work for the spread of God's message, the power to "do what is pleasing to him," the power of God's love in me and my power to respond to that love.

4.   I experience God's Spirit as paraclete, advocate, and the one who brings me into the centre of God's own life, God's all-encompassing love.

We experience and relate to the person of God the Spirit expressed as Spirit and Life.

We may well conclude this section with the words of the Catechism: "To believe in the Holy Spirit is to profess that the Holy Spirit is one of the persons of the Holy Trinity, consubstantial with the Father and the Son: 'with the Father and the Son he is worshipped and glorified'"(CCC 685).

God the Holy Spirit, the Third Person of the Blessed Trinity.

The Fruit of the Spirit

The greatest gift of God's Spirit to us is the gift of love. This is beautifully expressed in the First Letter of John:

No one has ever seen God; if we love one another, God lives in us, and his love is perfected in us. By this we know that we abide in him and he in us,

because he has given us of his Spirit. . . . God is love, and those who abide
in love abide in God, and God abides in them. (1 Jn 4:12-13, 16b)

The power, the qualities and the effects of that love in us are also beautifully expressed in other passages in the Christian Scriptures, particularly in the letters of St. Paul. Perhaps its most powerful and most quoted statement is in the first letter to the Corinthians, Chapter 13. But in the letter to the Galatians (Gal 5:22), Paul also indicates what he calls the fruit of the Spirit, the practical effects of God's love in a human life: love, joy, peace, patience, kindness, generosity, faithfulness, gentleness and self-control. If we are conscious of these qualities in our life, then we have a very practical indication of the presence of God's Spirit. This list of the fruit of the Spirit also provides us with a good instrument of discernment, an excellent litmus test, as it were. A constant problem for us is how we can know what God asks of us in a particular circumstance: how can we know whether what we have done, or contemplate doing, is what God really wants? There are no easy answers to this problem. However, if we are conscious of peace and joy and self-control, if we are convinced that we have done the loving thing with patience, kindness and generosity, then we can be quite sure that we have done what God wants because the Holy Spirit is present.

Conclusion

And so, God's personhood is expressed as Father, as Son and as Holy Spirit. For us in our everyday life, this means three distinct persons in God and so three ways of entering into a personal relationship with God, but only one God. We call this the Blessed Trinity. Therefore, God is one, but God is not solitary. Just as we relate to God through each distinct person, so does each divine person relate to the other persons in the very inner life of the Trinity. God is a community of persons calling us to live together as a community and to love one another. In the words of Jesus' own prayer, "I ask not only on behalf of these, but also on behalf of those who will believe in me through their word, that they may all be one. As you, Father, are in me and I am in you, may they also be in us, so that the world may believe that you have sent me" (Jn 17:20-21). The Blessed Trinity, three persons in one God, is not simply a theological formula: it is at the root of our life-relationship to God, how God reaches out to us and touches our lives. The revelation of the Trinity, as detailed in the Christian Scriptures, belongs to the earliest and most essential expression of Christian faith.

Glory be to the Father, and to the Son, and to the Holy Spirit.

Reflection Questions

1. Out of which life experience at this time do you name God as parent/Father, brother/friend, Spirit?

2. In honest reflection, name the gifts of the Spirit of which you are aware in your life.

3. Using the fruit of the Spirit (Gal 5:22), how would you discern your call to the ministry of teaching as being "from God"?

4. How would you attempt to bring your students to appreciate the presence of the Trinity in their lives?

5. Write a short paragraph on what the Spirit of God means for you.

6. Why is water a useful analogy for explaining the Trinity?

7. What does it mean to address God as Abba?

Further Reading

Fatula, Mary Ann, O.P. *The Triune God of Christian Faith* (Collegeville, MN: Michael Glazier, The Liturgical Press, 1990). Short, basic treatment of the theology of the Trinity together with some excellent applications of faith in the Trinity to everyday Christian life.

Foley, Leonard. "The Trinity: The Mystery at the Heart of Life," in *Catholic Update* (Cincinnati, OH: St. Anthony Messenger Press, 1988). A short, readable, and useful treatment which combines some basic theology with the spiritual aspect of our relationship to God in Three Persons.

5

THE DEVELOPMENT OF FAITH

Earlier we noted that two important factors affect the way we practise our faith: our concept of God and our concept of ourselves. The first of these we dealt with in Chapter 3. Now we must take a look at the second of these: our concept of ourselves in the context of faith development.

As we have already indicated, faith is a gift of God. Of ourselves we cannot come to faith; "No one can say 'Jesus is Lord' except by the Holy Spirit" (1 Cor 12:3). To acknowledge Jesus as Lord, to make an act of faith in Jesus as God and Saviour, is a gift of the Holy Spirit. But faith is not an abstract thing; faith is only expressed in and through our human personality. Who and what we are affects the way we express our faith in the course of human life.

Because the expression of our faith is intimately related to our human personality, it undergoes changes; it waxes, wanes, develops, matures and changes perspective. Our faith-expression is affected by the changes that take place in our continuing development as human persons. The process of faith development will be a gradual process of coming to know and to accept God as a God of love. This God is present in our life in a most intimate way and calls us to respond to that love.

Crises of Faith

Most of us will go through crises of faith. Most of us will experience times when doubt creeps in, and we wonder how we can respond to God in the circumstances that we now face. Rare is the person whose faith is not tried and tested in the cauldron of life. In fact, it is probably true to say that without some crises our faith will not reach the mature expression it should. As our personality changes and develops, as we move into new experiences and circumstances, we shall have to reassess our former faith-expression, our images of God, our prayer, our way of understanding how God works in the world. Often this can be a bewildering, painful process that produces a crisis of faith.

Here is the true story of one such crisis. Elie Wiesel, a Hungarian Jew, was only a boy in his early teens when he was forced, with his family, into a Nazi concentration camp during World War II. He survived, but his parents did not. They were among the six million Jews and others who were exterminated or who died in the camps. Together with the many other atrocities, as a warning and an example to all prisoners, the guards would conduct public executions for minor crimes, such as stealing. On this particular occasion, the guards had selected for hanging two adults and one young boy.

> The SS [guards] seemed more preoccupied, more disturbed than usual. To hang a young boy in front of thousands of spectators was no light matter. . . . The three victims mounted together on to the chairs. The three necks were placed at the same moment within the nooses. . . . "Where is God? Where is He?" someone behind me asked. At a sign from the head of the camp the three chairs were tipped over. . . . Then the march past began. The two adults were no longer alive. . . . But the third rope was still moving; being so light the child was still alive. . . . For more than half an hour he stayed there, struggling between life and death, dying in slow agony under our eyes. . . . Behind me I heard the same man asking: "Where is God now?" And I heard a voice within me answer him: "Where is He? Here He is – He is hanging here on this gallows. . . ."[28]

Now, crisis does not mean tragedy. The word "crisis" comes from the Greek word *krisis*, which means decision. Crises are decision points, turning points. In medical terminology, for example, to say that a patient's illness is "critical" means that the patient has reached a turning point, from which there can be either improvement or further deterioration and possibly death. The Chinese have an interesting way of writing "crisis": they juxtapose two characters, one that stands for danger and the other for opportunity. In each crisis of faith there is the danger that we shall say "No" and refuse to accept a change in our relationship with God, or give up that relationship altogether. In Elie Wiesel's story there was the danger that, in face of this horrible tragedy, some would lose faith in God ("Where is God now?"), unable or unwilling to cope with this experience. On the other hand, while there is a danger that we may say "No," we also have the opportunity to open ourselves more completely in faith and trust; we have the opportunity to renew our commitment, to see our relationship to God in a new light ("Here He is – hanging on this gallows" – the revelation of God as a God of powerful compassion), and to say "Yes."

Doubt

Saint Thérèse Martin, a Carmelite nun, died in 1897 in her convent at Lisieux, France, at the early age of 24. Her short but extraordinary life of commitment to prayer and the love of others has made her one of the great saints

---

28   Elie Wiesel, *Night* (New York: Bantam Books, 1986), pp. 61-62.

of the church. Brought up in an exemplary and loving Catholic home, one of the outstanding features of her truly remarkable faith was her sustained and persevering belief in heaven. Yet, in her last and horribly painful illness it was exactly this most consoling aspect of her faith, the real meaning and purpose of her life, that was assailed by harrowing doubt.

> During those very joyful days of the Easter season . . . He permitted my soul to be invaded by the thickest darkness. . . . The thought of heaven, up till then so sweet to me, . . . [was] no longer anything but the cause of struggle and torment. This trial was to last not a few days or a few weeks, it was not to be extinguished until the hour set by God Himself and this hour has not yet come.[29]

Thérèse knew she would not recover from her illness; she knew she was going to die. These doubts about heaven, which she described as the "thickest darkness," must have been excruciatingly painful. But through it all she never lost her faith and trust in God.

The kind of doubt that Thérèse endured has been described by theologians as "existential" doubt: doubt that can co-exist with a strong faith, doubt that does not destroy faith. This kind of doubt is a crisis leading to the opportunity to strengthen our faith. Existential doubt is a common feature of ordinary human life. Often when we make choices we cannot be certain that our choice is the correct one. Our uncertainty may produce within us some personal insecurity, some uneasiness. The decision to marry, or any important life-decision that involves personal risk, often may be accompanied by uncertainty and uneasiness as to whether we are making the right decision. As we progress through changes in our lives, most of us will have this kind of doubt concerning various aspects of our faith. Faith is always a risk, a leap in the dark. Having doubts like this does not mean that we have "lost" the faith, or that we have lost contact with God. In some cases, if the doubt is severe and very disturbing, we may need counselling or help to put us on an even keel once again. We should not be shy about seeking help.

We must distinguish between existential doubt and "skeptical" or "cynical" doubt. Skeptical doubt reveals an underlying attitude of resistance to belief. Such resistance to belief may arise from two sources. We may be unwilling to accept that there are things about God, and God's relationship to us, that must remain mysterious, beyond our capacity to fully explain or understand. We may also resist belief when we realize that faith will be costly, that it will make certain demands on our lifestyle. We cannot honestly open ourselves to the truth unless

---

[29]   From the autobiography of St. Thérèse of Lisieux, *The Story of a Soul*, translated by John Clarke, O.C.D., Washington Province of Discalced Carmelite Friars, Inc. (ICS Publications, 2131 Lincoln Rd., N.E., Washington, D.C., 1976).

we are prepared to make the sacrifices that such openness may involve. Skeptical doubt can often develop into a kind of sneering attitude towards religion. This kind of doubt is destructive of the trust in God that is characteristic of true faith. Skeptical doubt is not worthy of a true believer. True faith cannot co-exist with skeptical doubt.

Stages in the Development of Faith[30]

Our faith-expression is greatly affected by the changes that take place in our own continuing development as human persons. Taking a look at the stages of human development will help us understand some of the ways in which faith is expressed in our lives. Vital to our faith development will be our own self-understanding, our concept of ourselves, and that will depend largely on how we understand the stages of our own human development. As we consider these stages, we shall almost certainly find a little bit of each stage in our own faith-response.

1. Infancy and Childhood

The infant has all its needs taken care of: feeding, sleeping, changing of diapers. It learns pretty quickly that a few well-modulated yells will bring people running to take care of its needs for a comfortable environment. Infancy and early childhood are marked by a strong self-centredness. But that situation does not last forever. The growing child learns that it cannot always be the centre of attention. There are other people in the world, too, and they also have needs. But the discovery of otherness does not completely eradicate the ingrained selfishness of this early period. In fact, selfishness is a basic problem that remains with us, more or less strongly, throughout life. It is the root of all sin. Even as adults, our own self-preoccupation makes us tend to manipulate others to suit our own needs, whims and desires.

Applying this to our faith-response, we see that we sometimes tend to look upon God almost exclusively as someone who will satisfy our needs and desires. God is someone who will provide security against the problems and dangers of the big, wide world. God becomes the one to whom we rush when we get into trouble, or when we need something. Somehow we believe that God will manipulate the world to suit us. God, after all, is the generous giver of gifts, but God is also like the baby's pacifier. God will fix things. Take a look, for example, at how we pray. Does our prayer consist almost exclusively of asking God for things? Not that asking is wrong – Jesus himself encourages us to ask in prayer for what we need – but how often do we thank God for his mercy and

---

[30] The material here is adapted from Chapter 6 of John Powell, S.J., *A Reason to Live! A Reason to Die!* (Allen, TX: Tabor Publishing, 1975). The reader is referred to this book for a fuller treatment of the topic.

generosity? Do we ever pray just to praise God for what he is and not only for what he can do for us? Do we ever pray just for the sake of praying, just to be in God's presence, to enjoy God's company, just to allow God to love us and exercise his parental right to delight in us?

Now, we must admit that there is an element of childhood in everyone's faith; there is an element of personal selfishness, but this should not dominate our faith-response. God is our loving Father, our help and security. But if that is all we focus on, then the danger is that we will use God almost exclusively to satisfy our needs and desires. That is a sign of an immature faith.

An important aspect of the development from infancy and childhood to further maturity is taking charge of one's own moral sense. During early life, the child's parents are the external agents of discipline. The child's moral sense develops according to the positive or negative reinforcement provided by the parents or guardians. Things are right or wrong because the parents say so. The child's conduct is regulated from the outside. Gradually the child has to learn to regulate her own conduct and to take responsibility for her own actions. She must learn to interiorize her moral sense.

Taking responsibility for one's own actions can be a risky business. One can get hurt, which is why certain people choose to live their lives completely ruled by others and take little or no personal responsibility. Slavery can have the advantage of being relatively comfortable and secure! Furthermore, one can always blame others when things go wrong. In matters of faith and religion, people who have failed to develop and respect their own value systems are often over-scrupulous about following all the laws and regulations because then, they feel, God can't blame them for anything. Many people have been educated to ask a priest to make their important decisions for them. The priest becomes a sort of surrogate parent, the external guarantor of a correct moral response, the guarantor of God's approval. But, as John Powell points out, "God himself is no substitute for conscience. Things are good or bad, actions are right or wrong, because they are such in themselves, not because of a declaration by God."[31] Or, we might add, by anyone else (this question will be dealt with more fully in the chapter on morality). What we must do is pray for light to be able to see the way things really are in themselves, to determine the intrinsic morality of each situation, so that we make our own decisions and can shape our actions accordingly. Surely one of the clear duties of teachers is precisely to help their students to understand the intrinsic rightness or wrongness of their actions. Refusal to take responsibility for one's own decisions and actions can only result in the prolongation of infancy and the stunting of moral and religious growth.

---

[31]   *Ibid.*, p. 162. The general outline of this chapter follows the scheme proposed by Powell.

It is well to recognize that not many of us ever completely succeed in growing out of our need for some external approval for our actions. Infantilism has great staying power! The challenge is to become more mature, to become more and more "our own person," as the jargon would have it. A risky business, yes, but perhaps we have to take risks in order to grow in the love of God! For example, many young people move away from regular participation in Sunday Eucharist because their parents forced it on them in the early years. Perhaps this is a necessary stage in their development; they may have to break rules in order to see later that the rules were good and beneficial for their own free expression of love of God. Crisis is always a danger and an opportunity. Accepting responsibility for one's own decisions is a step in the direction of maturity.

2. Adolescence

The great struggle of adolescence is the struggle for self-identity and self-acceptance. One must become a person in one's own right. One must grow out of and away from dependence on others. Consequently, some form of rebellion against authority is a notable feature of this stage of development. At the same time, becoming independent means that one can also experience great loneliness, which is one reason why adolescents seek refuge in their peer group. The peer group, rather than parents or family, becomes the reference point for the adolescent's growing up. Also, adolescents are going through strong physiological changes, which make them awkward and self-conscious. They wonder if they will ever adjust and may feel unloved and unlovable.

How do these changes affect the adolescents' faith response? Rebelling against authority can take the form of rebellion against their parents' religion. One is reminded of the commercial advertising a new generation of cars: "This is not your father's Oldsmobile"! Adolescents often struggle for a faith-expression that is different from that of their parents. Here is how one writer especially interested in adolescent religious education puts it.

> If it is to be more than lifelong lip service, religion must come only after a quest as harrowing as the quest for personal identity. Internalized learning – even religious learning – must begin with genuine curiosity, or it will never begin at all. Authentic learning (as opposed to rote memorization) is impossible unless the learners question what they are told, try to poke holes, try to sniff for rats, challenge the validity of the shamans and all their shibboleths – till they can say, "This is not my parents' faith; this is mine."[32]

---

[32] William O'Malley, S.J., "In Praise of Doubt: Scepticism Need Not Be Cynicism," *The Living Light*, January, 1988.

Some people claim that to teach religion in such a spirit of open inquiry is a recipe for producing real cynics and non-believers. That danger does exist. There is always a danger that, when presented with the challenge of Jesus, the challenge of belonging to the church he founded, some will turn away. Questions must be asked, but a lot will depend on what questions are asked and on how they are asked. Do we ask questions with a genuine intention of seeking enlightenment and clearing up misunderstanding, or do we ask them in a spirit of rebellion and petulance in order to undermine faith? To make the point again, crisis is always a danger and an opportunity: without the danger we frequently do not grasp the opportunity to develop a more mature faith.

There is some evidence that adolescents give up on religion because they find it too "preachy." It seems to them that they are presented with ideals (love, kindness, forgiveness, obedience, sexual control) that are too difficult to attain given their own present state of angst and uncertainty. Their sense of feeling unloved and unlovable may well extend to their relationship with God. God, they may feel, is just asking too much. There are no easy solutions to these problems. What adolescents most need is someone to whom they can relate well and who will accept them, affirm them and understand them in spite of all their uncertainty and contradiction. It stands to reason that if the adolescent cannot find such a person or persons at home, the teacher must try to fill this role as far as possible. Helpful also is some sort of role model, someone who has experienced what the adolescent is presently experiencing and who has come through it with faith intact and firm.

Just as we have probably found some of the infant and the child in the expression of our faith, very probably we shall still find some of the adolescent, too. We need to ask ourselves how much of this adolescent rebellion, how much of this awkwardness, still exists in our relationship with God. How much of our present faith-stance is due to our failure to re-examine our faith-response, to learn more, to mature? As mature believers, we can never let our faith lie fallow, remain static; we should always be searching for better ways of meeting and responding to God in our life.

3. Adulthood

Two stages are significant here:

a) Early adulthood is a period of risk;

b) Later adulthood may bring on a crisis of meaning.

Risk. Early adulthood is a period when people tend to form more mature personal relationships. It is also a period in which serious life-decisions are made: for example, the choice of a career, the decision to marry and raise a family. When we express our love for someone we tend to expose ourselves to being hurt. A true love relationship cannot blossom unless the parties are prepared to share themselves fully with each other. The more personal we get, the deeper down we dig, the more we throw off our protective masks, the more we go out of ourselves, the greater the risk of suffering the hurt of rejection or misunderstanding. Some people just cannot face that risk, and retreat into a form of self-isolation which is devastating to human relationship.

And so it is also in our relationship with God. Adulthood is a time when we must formulate our own personal way of believing and of living our faith. There is always a risk of doubt and uncertainty as to whether we are doing it right. There is the risk of criticism from others, the risk of being misunderstood. We may have to throw off our childhood notions of God that gave us such security in our early years. For example, it is very possible that something like this will happen to you, the reader, as a result of reading this book. Some of the earlier ideas and images that you have grown up with, some treasured beliefs, may be shattered. Perhaps, on occasion, your questions may be answered in a way you do not expect, or in a way you do not want to hear. That may be painful, but pain is the occasion for growth. As John Powell says, "The road to firm and mature faith is strewn with many anxious moments, sudden feelings of disbelief and agnosticism, a certain loneliness." Our purpose is not to be iconoclastic, to shatter for the sake of shattering. Our purpose is to help you to a more mature faith, to develop a new, more realistic, more personally satisfying relationship with God, the God whose love is always greater and infinitely beyond our capacity to grasp.

Meaning. The problem of meaning does not only arise in later life, though it may become more prominent at this stage. In his book *Modern Man in Search of a Soul,* the famous psychoanalyst Carl Jung notes that a third of the people he dealt with were suffering not from any clearly definable neurosis but simply from the senselessness and emptiness of their lives. He calls it the "general neurosis of our time." We are all familiar with what is known as mid-life crisis – dead-end job and routine work-weariness, unfulfilled ambitions, advancing age, often complicated by traumatic physical changes such as menopause. The real crisis is often the inability to find a sense of meaning and purpose for it all. Lack of meaning and purpose contribute greatly to the human problems with which we are all so familiar: mental breakdown, alcoholism, drug abuse, and the other sorry, sordid, seamy aspects of broken human lives.

In his simple but powerful chronicle *Diary of a Country Priest,* George Bernanos remarks that "Man does not live by things, but by the meaning of things." According to Viktor Frankl in his groundbreaking book *Man's Search for Meaning,* the search for meaning is a basic human drive, as instinctual as the drive of hunger or of sex. Meaning is at the heart of what we call "human"; it is constitutive of our human personality. Meaning is what distinguishes us from the animals. As Carl Jung noted, if we are unable to make sense of life, then we become neurotic and often physically ill.

The first step in coming to faith in God is probably an inquiry into the meaning of life. We discover that God is the only satisfactory answer to the great questions about human life: Why are we here? Why do we die? What happens after death? Why do people suffer? We recall the simple but eloquent testimony of Dag Hammarskjold, former general secretary to the United Nations, in his book *Markings*: "On the day I first really believed in God, for the first time life made sense to me and the world had meaning." The Christian vision of the world is that of a world created by God who continually calls to us, who will make all things work together for good. The Christian vision is one that sees an essential cohesion and purpose in life because God is its source and its purpose. From God we came and to God we must go to fulfill the purpose of our creation. A mature faith is a faith that finds meaning in human life because God is the source of meaning.

Summary and Conclusion

Faith is not a static thing; we do not remain stagnant in any one expression of faith throughout life. It ebbs and flows, waxes and wanes, changes its perspective. Faith goes through doubts and crises. Each crisis is an occasion of and an opportunity for further growth, for further maturity. The way we live and express our faith changes with the development of our human personality. God always works in and through our human nature, not apart from it. Even though we grow and mature physically and psychologically, we shall often find in our faith response some aspects which seem to correspond more closely to an earlier stage of growth. In our faith response we shall find aspects of the infant, the child, the adolescent, the mature adult. The important point is that *we should not allow ourselves to become fixated in any of the earlier stages so that any one of them totally dominates our relationship with God.* Always we should aim at greater maturity.

> Maturing in faith is possible only if faith is integrated into the whole framework of life. All new knowledge and experience should somehow expand one's religious frame of reference. . . . For growth in faith, it is essential that we maintain some flexibility, that we possess some willingness and desire to integrate new insights and revise old positions. The danger is atrophy; and when atrophy sets in apathy is not far away.[33]

---

[33]   *A Reason to Live! A Reason to Die!,* p. 166.

As Powell says, faith must be integrated into the whole framework of life. New insights will certainly be gleaned from our experience of life, but also from study. Maturing in faith requires that we devote some time to reading and the study of matters scriptural, theological and moral. We do not consider ourselves educated in any subject if we never get past what we learned in Grade 2. The question is, how far have we progressed beyond Grade 2 in the understanding and practice of our faith? It is extraordinary how many otherwise good and "faithing" people make no effort at all to improve their knowledge of their faith. (See the quote from F. J. Sheed in Chapter 1.)

Finally, we should pray. It is prayer that puts us in touch with God and energizes our relationship with God. Our struggle is always to interpret God in every aspect of our life as a God of love. Without prayer our struggle will be infinitely more difficult.

Reflection Questions

1. Where do you find examples in your own faith life of (a) infancy and childhood, and (b) adolescence?

2. What are the signs of a maturing adult faith in your own life?

3. Explain the following quotation: "Those who have the faith of children have also the troubles of children" (Robert Hugh Benson).

4. When we say to God "Abba, Father" as Jesus did, we speak like a child. Distinguish between a faith that is childlike and one that is childish.

5. Distinguish between existential doubt and skeptical doubt. Describe a situation of existential doubt that you have experienced in your faith life.

Further Reading

Powell, John, S.J. *A Reason to Live! A Reason to Die!* (Allen, Texas: Tabor Publishing, 1975), particularly Chapter 6.

Part II

AN INTRODUCTION TO THE OLD AND NEW TESTAMENTS

6

REVELATION

"It pleased God, in his goodness and wisdom, to reveal himself and to make known the mystery of his will. His will was that men should have access to the Father, through Christ, the Word made flesh, in the Holy Spirit, and thus become sharers in the divine nature." (CCC 51; *Dei verbum* 2)

After this quote, which opens the section on Revelation, the Catechism continues, "God, who 'dwells in unapproachable light,' wants to communicate his own divine life to the men [and women] he freely created, in order to adopt them as his sons [and daughters] in his only-begotten Son" (CCC 52). God, indeed, "dwells in unapproachable light." God is mystery. Nevertheless our faith tells us that God has entered our lives, God calls to us, God reaches out to us. The only way we can come into contact with this mystery is if God initiates that contact. God must communicate with us in some way and make himself available to us. God's communication with us we call *revelation*. This word comes from the Latin *re-velare,* which means to lift the veil, to disclose, to uncover. God discloses himself, partially uncovers the mystery.

What Is Revealed?

What God reveals is nothing less than himself. God reveals himself as personal, as possessing personal qualities, after the analogy of human personal qualities. In order better to understand God's revelation, it is helpful for us to take a look at how human persons reveal themselves to one another. For example, I can tell you a lot of facts about myself. I can give you a lot of information: where I was born, where I went to school, how old I am, whether I play hockey or basketball, and any number of other trivial factors. But I really only reveal myself to you when I disclose (either by words or by the way I act) what kind of person I am, what are my true human qualities. Thus, am I kind and considerate? truthful? just? forgiving? caring? hardworking? generous? loving? Or, on the other hand, am I mean? prone to anger? hypercritical? untrustworthy? and so on. In a relationship between two people, the relationship grows deeper, more personal and more intense as each person penetrates the human qualities of the other.

And so it is with God. God does not simply reveal facts and information: that is not the major focus of revelation. It is true that God reveals several things about himself and his activity in the world that we could never have known but for his revelation. Nevertheless, such facts and information as God reveals come to us concomitantly with God's self-revelation. Principally, God reveals what kind of person he is: loving, caring, concerned and compassionate, forgiving, just but merciful, a saving God. It is these personal qualities that are important because they are the basis of the personal relationship to which God calls each one of us.

Why does God reveal? Because God has created us for himself, God loves us and begs for our love in return. "By revealing himself God wishes to make [us] capable of responding to him, and of knowing him, and of loving him far beyond [our] own natural capacity" (CCC 52).

Experience and Revelation

How, we may well ask, does God communicate with us?

The story is told of a certain rabbi in Cracow who dreamt three times that an angel told him to go to Livovna, where he would find a certain treasure. "In front of the palace there," the angel said, "you will learn where a treasure is hidden." The rabbi went to Livovna and when he arrived at the palace he found a guard near the bridge, so he told him the dream. The guard replied, "It is strange, but I too have had a dream. The angel told me to go to a rabbi's house in Cracow, where a treasure is buried in front of the fireplace." Upon hearing this, the rabbi, all excited, returned home and dug in front of his fireplace. There he found the treasure.

God, who is our treasure, is to be found within us, in our own home, in the depth of our personal consciousness. That immediately leads us to the question of how we experience God's presence. That question of experience will constantly crop up in our discussions and is at the root of the theological enterprise. Many have pointed out that theology is a journey of reflecting on our experiences, a search to discover God. It is, as St. Anselm says, faith seeking understanding.

Once we speak of experience, we must avoid certain pitfalls. We must avoid thinking of experience as something purely subjective, created entirely by the person experiencing, equivalent to feeling. If this is so, then our experience of God is entirely created by ourselves, or God made into our own image. But experience is not purely subjective, for we are always confronted with something real and objective, something that exists independently of our appreciation of it. In the course of the experience we assimilate the object we perceive into our consciousness according to our personal perceptual apparatus.

Our language, our culture, our personal history, our mindset, our prejudices and preferences, and, in the case of religion, most importantly our faith, shape the way we perceive things and integrate them into our consciousness. We forge, and mould, and configure the object of perception according to our mental "baggage" as it is being integrated into our consciousness. Thus, any experience is both objective and subjective; it is not wholly determined and shaped by the person who experiences, nor is it fully determined by the object. In the words of John Welch, "The experience of God occurs within ordinary human experience. God is so intimate to the experience that God is not a third thing, so we do not have the self, a sunset, and then God. In the interactive experience of the self and the sunset, God is co-experienced, co-present, co-known."[34]

Perhaps an example may help to make it clearer. We believe that God is revealed to us in Scripture. When we read Scripture, the objective aspect of revelation is God's act of self-communication recorded there. As we read, and pray over our reading, that act of self-communication is then filtered through our perceptual apparatus (of which faith is an important part). Thus emerges the experience through which God's self-communication is integrated into our consciousness. Therefore, the presence of God, the grace of God, shapes and moulds our experience in such fashion that we come to appreciate it as a revelation from God.

This important point is well illustrated by a conversation between Joan of Arc and Captain Robert de Baudricourt in George Bernard Shaw's play *Saint Joan*. Joan claims that she has received a commission from God to save France. She has heard God speaking to her; she has heard "voices."

Robert: How do you mean voices?

Joan: I hear voices telling me what to do. They come from God.

Robert: They come from your imagination.

Joan: Of course. That is how the messages of God come to us.[35]

We must in no way imagine that revelation is like some sort of divine dictation. Joan could only hear her "voices" through what she called her "imagination."

To repeat, revelation takes place in and through human experience, in which God is known and experienced simultaneously with something else. This point is of capital importance and we shall have occasion to return to it in other places. Theologians express this by saying that all experience of God is mediated: we apprehend God through the created universe, persons, places, events, nature, but most especially through the humanity of Our Lord Jesus Christ. There is no direct divine dictation. God does not hit us with some sort of supernatural "zap"

---

[34]   John Welch, *When Gods Die* (Mahwah, NJ: Paulist Press, 1990), p. 145.
[35]   George Bernard Shaw, *Saint Joan* (New York: Brentano's, 1924), p. 86.

that takes no account of who we are as human beings. No, God can only work in and through his creation.

Faith and Revelation

To say that revelation takes place within and through human experience does not mean that all human experience is revelation. Dermot A. Lane makes the helpful distinction between ordinary experiences, depth experiences and religious experiences.

> Ordinary experiences are concerned with the visible empirical world of objects "out there." Depth experiences bring us into the invisible but real world mediated by meaning: truth, beauty, love. Religious experiences are those moments in life when we perceive the world of meaning as grounded in that immanent and transcendent reality we call God.[36]

As we have already pointed out, for the believer, faith forms an intrinsic part of the perceptual apparatus. To perceive the world of meaning as grounded in God requires faith: the ability to "see beyond" the merely human, as St. Joan did. It is faith that makes us see, for example, that this particular human manifestation of truth or goodness or love or forgiveness is in fact the reality of God reaching out to us. Without faith, we cannot come into contact with God in the depth of our experience. At the same time, faith is a grace and a gift from God. Consequently, we should be able to see that a fundamental unity exists between revelation and faith; the two go hand in hand. We do not really receive a revelation from God until we respond in faith: a faith that is active, a faith that is a believing, trusting and doing faith, working itself into daily life.

There is another aspect of our faith-response to revelation that is worth considering. This is well illustrated by the story of Moses before the burning bush. An angel of the Lord appeared to Moses in a flame of fire out of a bush that was not consumed in the flames. Moses was curious; he was determined to see why the bush was not being burned up. As he approached, God called to him from the bush, "Moses, Moses!" And he said, "Here I am." Then God said, "Come no closer! Remove the sandals from your feet, for the place on which you are standing is holy ground." He said further, "I am the God of your father, the God of Abraham, the God of Isaac, and the God of Jacob" (Ex 3:2-6).

God calls Moses by name; he approaches Moses in a personal and intimate way. God reveals to Moses his great compassion and concern for the people of Israel enslaved in Egypt. But Moses must approach God in reverence (take off his shoes); confronted with God he stands on holy ground. Perhaps none of us

---

[36]   Dermot A. Lane, *The Experience of God* (New York: Paulist Press, 1981), p. 35. Used by permission.

will ever have the startling experience of a revelation before a burning bush. But, perhaps, if we "took off our shoes," if we approached our experience of the world and events of our own lives with a sense of reverence, we might see the whole world as revealing God.

> Earth's crammed with heaven
> And every common bush afire with God;
> And only he who sees takes off his shoes –
> The rest sit round it and pluck blackberries.

Elizabeth Barrett Browning

Yes, reverence, an attitude of reverence for the whole of creation and for our part in it: such an attitude of reverence for human life and human relationships, coupled with faith, will help open our eyes to the God who calls to us from the depth of our experience.

Avenues of Communication

God's revelation comes to us in many and diverse ways. Not all of these ways are dealt with here, but we have attempted to point out the principal avenues of communication so we can become aware of the presence of God in our lives.

1. Revelation through Creation

Chapter 3 noted that we can come to know God by contemplating the created universe. Most of us, at one time or another, have had our religious sense awakened by the beauty of nature, the stillness of the forest, the pounding of the waves, the reflection on the surface of a lake, the beauty of the aurora borealis. We believe that God is the creator and the giver of all. In the very heart of creation God's goodness and God's self-gift are revealed. Thus, through applying our faith to our experience of nature the experience becomes revelatory. "The heavens are telling the glory of God; and the firmament proclaims his handiwork" (Ps 19:1).

So many experiences open up to us the possibility of discovering the presence of God. For example, as we take a look at creation, we see how marvelously balanced and ordered it is. We begin to understand how all things in the universe are related, how we ourselves are part of an eco-system, linked in the deepest way to the environment. The balance and order in nature could only have come from a supremely intelligent and loving being. That very fact tells us something about who God is. Even the most prosaic soul can be moved by poetry such as that of Gerard Manley Hopkins:

The world is charged with the grandeur of God.
It will flame out like shining from shook foil;
Gathered to greatness like the ooze of oil
Crushed. Why do men then now not reck his rod?

2. *Revelation through History*

That God should be revealed in the sweep of history follows naturally from our understanding that God is revealed in creation. God does not simply create the universe and leave it unattended in much the same way that we might construct a building which can then stand on its own. No, God's creation is ongoing. Should God cease to create continuously, the universe would cease to exist, for everything depends on his sustaining power. God is intimately concerned with the whole evolution of the universe and with our part in it (CCC 301).

In order for the events of history to become revelatory we must take a faith view of them. It is part of the religious genius of the Jewish people that they understood God as intimately concerned with the ordinary events of their life, not aloof from them. They applied this faith to their understanding of their own history, national as well as personal. They understood their history as meaningful, as giving evidence of a divine plan with a promise for the future. God was the guiding principle for their history. Thus what for us might be a purely secular event in history (such as a battle, or a plague, or a drought, or a plentiful harvest) is interpreted as God speaking to them, God intervening in their life, God revealing. The question for us is this: can we adopt this faith view of history? Can we discern what God is saying to us in what might be considered purely secular events?

The people of Israel have given an account of how they understood God as intervening in their lives and history. This account we call the Hebrew Scriptures, the first part of the Bible. Their faith story has become our faith story, for it is against the background and in the context of Jewish history and faith that Jesus Christ entered the world, Jesus who is the ultimate and complete statement of God's revelation. The story of God's revelation through history is further written down in the Christian Scriptures, the second part of the Bible, the story of the life of Jesus and of the early Christian communities.

From the story of world history we come to our own personal history. There can be no question that God's loving communication comes to us through the ordinary events of our life. In other words it comes to us through the daily grind of living: the happiness, the joys, the suffering, the boredom, the drudgery and tiredness, the moments of triumph and the moments of failure, the illness and the certainty of death. It takes the genius of faith to see God in all this and to interpret what God is saying to us. In particular it takes faith to interpret God's message as one of care and compassion, nearness and forgiveness, a message of love.

In order to help us understand God's personal message to us, we turn for inspiration and insight to the Bible. We draw on the revelation story of the Jewish people and the early Christian communities, helped in our interpretation by the teaching of the church. The Jewish people and the early Christian communities wrote down their faith-interpretation of their experiences; can we do the same thing with our lives? It is a very useful exercise for us to write an account of our own faith-journey. We need such a reflection to enable us to understand better our present relationship with God and also to see where we must go and how we can improve that relationship. Teachers of religion can use the strategy of writing down one's faith journey with students to help them clarify their own faith development.

3.   Revelation through the Prophets

To understand what God is saying to us in history and in the events of our life, we need prophets. A common misunderstanding of the role of a prophet is that a prophet is someone who predicts the future. Prophets may predict the future, but this is incidental to prophecy and not its main focus.

Prophet* comes from the Greek *prophetes* (*pro* – for, on behalf of, and *phetes* – speaker): thus, "to speak on behalf of someone." The prophets speak on behalf of God, they tell us God's message. They interpret the signs of the times so that we may understand what God is saying to us in these events. Thus, simply telling the story of a historical event does not constitute revelation; some prophetic interpretation is necessary in order to understand the message that God is giving through that historical event. It is for this reason that the Jewish account of some event in history recorded in the Bible might well be different from a secular historian's account of the same event.

The Bible is insistent that God has spoken to us through the prophets. In many places in the Christian Scriptures we are told that the life of Jesus is a fulfillment of the ancient prophecies. The Letter to the Hebrews begins as follows: "Long ago God spoke to our ancestors in many and various ways by the prophets, but in these last days he has spoken to us by a Son . . ." (Heb 1:1). The prophets referred to are the ancient Jewish prophets whose works are recorded in the Hebrew Scriptures and whose names are familiar to us – Isaiah, Jeremiah, Amos, Ezekiel, Daniel and others. Are these the only prophets that we must pay attention to who have given us the message of God? Has God stopped speaking to us through the prophets? Is what is recorded in the Bible God's final say-so? The answer to that is partly "Yes" and partly "No." The "Yes" part we shall deal with presently; let us first deal with the "No" part.

God still does speak to us through the prophets; the message of God to us is still being honed and clarified and applied to different circumstances. Modern-day prophets exist because God still continues to speak to us through people who live today, or who have lived in recent times, such as Jean Vanier, Mother Teresa of Calcutta, Mahatma Ghandi, Pope John Paul II, Martin Luther King, and many others. How can we know that their message is from God? Go back to the Bible. Is there a message of care for the poor and abandoned (Mother Teresa)? Is there a message of justice (Mahatma Ghandi, Martin Luther King)? Is there a message of care for the weak, the needy and disabled (Jean Vanier)? In the message of these modern prophets, God is revealing himself as caring for the poor and abandoned, bringing justice to those who seek it, concerned and compassionate with the weak and disabled. All this, we might object, is not a new message. It is all there already in the Scriptures. In the life and ministry of Jesus, God has already said it. True, but in large part we seem to have forgotten it; we need to be reminded of it time and time again, we need to be awakened from our lethargic response to God's revelation. That is the work of the modern-day prophets.

But the work of prophecy is not confined to a few very special people. To a certain extent, all of us have been given this gift of prophecy for building up the church. All of us, by the example of our lives, can serve as prophets to those who have forgotten God's message, or perhaps have never heard it. This is particularly true of those who have been called to the teaching ministry. More than any other the teacher is called, in the words of John Paul II, "to put people not only in touch, but in communion, in intimacy with Jesus Christ." The teacher is the modern prophet *par excellence*.

How can we discern a modern prophet? How can we know whether someone is genuine? This is no easy matter; the signs of prophecy are not always clear. Theologians have suggested some criteria for judging who might be regarded as a prophet:

1. The prophet never claims to speak on his or her own behalf, but always on behalf of God (it is God's message, not the prophet's).

2. The prophet's message will, in the long term, make for unity in the church ("that they all may be one"), promote the reign of God, even though in the short term the prophetic word may bring discord and pain. Jesus said that he had come to bring fire on earth and that his message would set brother against brother.

3. The example of the prophet's life must be part of the message. They must live by the words they speak; otherwise they are suspect.

4. True prophecy is never for show, for display, or for personal gain.

5.   Prophecy must be clear enough to be understood by the majority of people, not so esoteric as to be available only to a few.[37]

4.   Revelation through Jesus Christ

The greatest of all the prophets, the perfect revelation of God to us, the definitive Word of God spoken to us in history, is Our Lord Jesus Christ. Jesus speaks God's word to us in a language we can understand, a human language. The gospels show him as growing up in a human way and, as a human being, learning more and more the meaning of human existence and sharing that vision and knowledge with his associates and followers. By reading the Scriptures, with help from the teaching church to interpret them, we too can share in this vision and knowledge and learn how to live in union with him.

5.   Revelation through the Church

Jesus' chosen apostles, the twelve, together with some others, lived constantly in his company. They reflected on his words, they came to appreciate and copy his way of life as meaningful for them, and thus they received his revelation. The preaching of the apostles was, in fact, a prophetic interpretation of the life and words of Jesus. After the resurrection the early group of Jesus' followers formed themselves into a community, a community which was the beginning of what we now call the church. This early community in time generated other communities and so, finally, the church as we know it today.

In the church today we have a life, a culture and traditions based on the life of Jesus, and an interpretation of that life by succeeding generations. We have statements of belief (creeds), we have prayers and ways of praying (e.g., liturgical ceremonies), we have sacraments, and we have a code of moral behaviour. All of these take part in revelation. God speaks to us in and through the whole life of the church. God speaks to us through the lives of holy people who have evidently taken Jesus' message to heart and serve as an example to all. As we participate in the life of the church we participate in revelation. We believe that Jesus is still speaking and acting through the church, through us and through our participation in the life of the community. We believe that we, as church, continue Jesus' preaching and mission to the world.

When the earliest disciples of Jesus passed on his message, it was not passed on as a detailed theology. A theology of Jesus and his message, a codification of what is called "revealed truth," came later after much reflection and prayer. What was first passed on then was not dogma, not theological assessment and theological statements, but a way of life learned from Jesus and rooted in the belief that God had raised Jesus from the dead. Each succeeding generation in

---

[37]   See Richard P. McBrien, *Catholicism*, p. 262.

the church must strive to do the same. The word of God is not static. The word of God lives and grows as we constantly struggle to live the life that we learned from Jesus within the changing times and circumstances of our world. What this means is that revelation is not a once-and-forever thing, but is ongoing. It might be compared to a conversation that is always going on between God and us, with Jesus as the centre of that conversation. He is always present in the church to *be* revelation, opening us up to new ways of understanding and acting on God's message to us.

The Transmission of God's Revelation

The Catechism deals with the question of precisely how God's revelation is transmitted from generation to generation (CCC 74-79). It points out that after the death of Jesus, this task fell first to the apostles, who lived with Jesus and heard his message first hand. The Pope and bishops, who are the successors of the apostles, now carry on that task. The whole church, by living the life that Jesus taught, also transmits revelation from generation to generation. The gospel message was handed on orally, and in writing. "This living transmission, accomplished in the Holy Spirit, is called Tradition" (CCC 78). (Tradition will be dealt with in detail in the next chapter.)

The Bible and Revelation

Christians believe that the Bible is the inspired word of God. The Bible, therefore, contains God's revelation. Because that revelation is written down, it is clearer and more pointed than revelation that may come to us from other sources. It follows that one of the most significant places where God's revelation is to be found is in the Bible.

Earlier we asked if revelation had been completed. As we pointed out, the answer is partly "No." Revelation, we said, is ongoing, a continuing conversation, as it were, between God and ourselves. But principally, the answer must be "Yes." Jesus Christ, or what we might call "the Christ-event," is God's final and definitive word to us; there will be no other (CCC 65, 66). The authentic source of the life and message of Jesus, that definitive word, is the Bible. True enough, that message may undergo further explanation and adaptation to changing circumstances in human life, but its authentic heart, its core, is the Bible.

Let us now make two statements about revelation and the Bible.

1.   *Not Everything in the Bible Is Revelation*

We pointed out earlier on that the essence of revelation is that God reveals himself. God is personal. While it is true that the whole Bible is the word of God, there are things in the Bible (facts, sayings, recordings of history, obiter dicta) that tell us absolutely nothing about the kind of person God is. For example, in the book of Tobit, twice there is mention of a dog that seems to have been Tobias's pet: "And," the Bible says, "the dog came out with him and went along with them" (Tob 6:2, and again in 11:4). Scripture commentators think that the dog is a survival from the folk tale from which this story is taken. In the original folk tale the dog may have had a specific role. In any case, in the biblical tale mention of the dog serves no revelatory purpose at all. The dog tells us nothing about the kind of person God is; mention of the dog is not revelatory.

2. *Not All of Revelation Is Contained in the Bible*

God, as we have pointed out above, does communicate with us in other ways. Nevertheless – and this is important – since the Bible is certainly the most significant place where revelation is to be found, and since it is the inspired word of God, the Bible, and particularly the Christian Scriptures, is normative for understanding and interpreting all of revelation. Normative? What does that mean? It means that no subsequent revelation of God can contradict the biblical revelation. The Bible is the norm, the rule and the measure by which we assess and interpret all revelation. In the Christian scheme of things, the Bible has pride of place in our efforts to develop a personal relationship of faith with God.

Private Revelation

The Catechism notes that "Throughout the ages, there have been so-called 'private' revelations, some of which have been recognized by the authority of the Church. They do not belong, however, to the deposit of faith. It is not their role to improve or complete Christ's definitive Revelation, but to help live more fully by it in a certain period of history" (CCC 67).

By definition, private revelation is given first to an individual or small group and therefore is not immediately available to the public in general or to the church in particular. It comes after the revelation of the whole of the Christ-event. All that we need to know about God is already there. Nothing completely new can or will be added to this revelation. But, as we pointed out, revelation is ongoing; God continues to speak to us whether as individuals, or as groups (such as the church), or to the world in the ways we have outlined above. Down through the centuries many have claimed to have had special and personal revelations from God: charismatics (such as St. Joan of Arc, who always referred to her "voices"); leaders of groups that subsequently developed into sects; mystics (such as St. Catherine of Genoa, St. Teresa of Avila, St. John of the Cross). Perhaps the private revelations most prominent in the minds of many today are the "apparitions" of the Mother of God and the accompanying mes-sages that she has given at these apparitions. Some of these are the Miraculous Medal revelations to St. Catherine Labouré (Paris, 1830); revelations to St. Bernadette Soubirous (Lourdes, 1858); revelations to three Portuguese children

(Fatima, 1917); revelations to a group of children at Beauraing in Germany (1932–1933); and many others, including some very recent ones that have not yet been approved by the church (such as at Medjugorje in Croatia).

Since revelation occurs in and through human experience, even with the very best of intentions there is the strong possibility of mistaking what is in fact a very human experience for one of God. Consequently, we cannot rule out the possibility of delusion, distortion and misunderstanding, even when the private revelation is genuine. It pays to be extremely cautious in dealing with private revelation; indeed, caution is the watchword of the church's approach. Before any private revelation receives church approval, there is a prolonged and thorough investigation by a church-appointed commission.

Thus, while many private revelations are of importance to the church, everyone is not bound to have faith in them. All that we need for our personal salvation is already there. Private revelations may indeed focus our attention on some aspect of God's revelation that needs to be emphasized, but they do not add anything new to this revelation.

Finally, when the church gives approval to some private revelation, this approval means a) the revelations are consistent with Sacred Scripture and with the official teaching of the church; b) there is no fraud or deception on the part of the visionaries; c) the revelations may be published for the benefit of the faithful; d) the church's liturgy may be celebrated in honour of the event. Church approval emphatically does not mean that there is an obligation on every one of the faithful to believe the revelation.

Reflection Questions

1. What is the relationship between revelation and faith?
2. If someone were to confide in you that they had received a personal and private revelation from God, what attitude would you adopt?
3. What is the meaning of prophecy? To what extent are we all prophets? Pick out some prophetic words and/or actions relevant to our times.
4. What do we mean by saying that the Bible is normative for understanding and interpreting revelation?
5. Describe an event or time in your life when you felt that God was revealing something of importance to you.
6. The story is told of a temple that was built on an island and which held a thousand bells. When the wind blew or a storm raged, all the bells would peal out in symphony and would send the heart of the hearer into raptures. But over the centuries the island sank into the sea and, with it, the temple bells. An ancient legend said that the bells continued to peal and

could be heard by anyone who would listen. Inspired by the legend, a young man traveled thousands of miles, determined to hear the bells. He sat for days and weeks on the shore facing the vanished island, but all he could hear was the sound of the sea. Finally, he decided to give up the attempt. Perhaps he was not destined to hear the bells. Perhaps the old legend was false. On his final day he went one last time to say good-bye to the sea and the sky and the wind and the coconut trees. He lay on the sand and for the first time listened intently to the sound of the sea as the waves broke on the shore. Soon he was so lost in the sound that he was barely conscious of himself. And in the depth of that silence, he heard it! At first a tiny bell, then the thousand bells were pealing out in harmony, and his heart was rapt in joyous ecstasy.[38]

What does this story say to you about God's revelation?

Further Reading

Hellwig, Monika. *What Are the Theologians Saying?* (Dayton, OH: Pflaum, 1971). A concise and excellent summary of some modern thought on certain theological themes. See particularly Chapter 2, "What Did God Really Reveal?"

Lane, Dermot A. *The Experience of God: An Invitation to Do Theology* (New York: Paulist Press, 1981). Not only deals with experience but also with the nature of revelation and the activity of faith. A short and excellent synthesis.

---

[38] Adapted from Anthony de Mello, S.J., *The Song of the Bird* (New York: Doubleday, Image Books, 1984), pp. 22-23.

7

TRADITION AND SCRIPTURE

Many of us have seen that wonderful musical *Fiddler on the Roof.* It is the story of how a little group of Jewish people in a small corner of Russia held on to its religious and cultural traditions despite being immersed in a much larger and hostile culture. In the show's opening lines the principal character, Tevye, says,

> In our little village of Anatevka, you might say everyone of us is a fiddler on the roof, trying to scratch out a pleasant, simple tune without breaking his neck. Why do we stay here if it's so dangerous? We stay because Anatevka is our home. And how do we keep our balance? That I can tell you in one word – tradition! . . . Here in Anatevka we have traditions for everything – how to eat, how to sleep, how to wear clothes. For instance, we always keep our heads covered and always wear a prayer shawl. This shows our constant devotion to God. . . . Because of our traditions, everyone knows who he is and what God expects him to do.[39]

By hanging on to their traditions, this group of Jewish people kept memories alive, and memories helped keep the group together. But more than that, traditions helped everyone to know who they were, what were the influences that formed them, and what were their obligations to God. It can hardly be better put.

We all have family stories that we tell and retell at family gatherings. Families have customs and ways of doing things that are peculiar to themselves. We strengthen our family bonds by keeping these memories alive. In this way we help one another cope with the stress of life through the support we receive from our own close community. Traditions are also an important part of our cultural heritage. It is these traditions that have helped shape us, helped define us, helped us to understand ourselves. However, traditions sometimes overpower us. We continue to live out of them even though, in the light of new circumstances, we realize that the old traditions are not helpful to our present-day conditions. This is true of many of the less-important traditions concerning our religious expression, which we shall deal with shortly.

---

[39]   *Fiddler on the Roof,* lyrics by Sheldon Harrick.

Now, just as we belong to a natural human family and to a cultural group, we belong to a religious family, which has also helped shape our personality and make us who we are. Our religious traditions are a definite part of our cultural milieu. This religious family we call "the church"; it, too, has memories and experiences that it wants to keep alive so that we may keep our faith, remain united and serve God. Its memories are those of the deeds and words of God in history, "spoken," as we have seen in the chapter on revelation, in many different ways. In the words of the Catechism, "God graciously arranged that the things he had once revealed for the salvation of all peoples should remain in their entirety, throughout the ages, and be transmitted to all generations" (CCC 74). *Religious traditions are witnesses to faith.* It is this faith of the people and the way it is lived out that is to be passed on to succeeding generations.

The word tradition itself is derived from the Latin *tradere*, which means to hand on. It can refer either to the *content* of what is passed on or, in wider meaning, to the *process* by which it is passed on. It is useful to bear this in mind because sometimes the word is used in one sense only, though clearly both aspects are necessary (see CCC 76–79). Perhaps tradition is most clearly defined as a process: "the Church, in her doctrine, life and worship perpetuates and transmits to every generation all that she herself is, all that she believes" (CCC 78). And this process is accomplished by the power of the Holy Spirit acting in the church (CCC 78).

In practice, how does this handing on, this transmission, take place? It started with the preaching of the apostles and is now continued in the life of the church through 1) preaching; 2) teaching; 3) religious services and customs; 4) personal and communal prayers and devotions (e.g., devotion to the Mother of God); 5) special days of feast and remembrance (e.g., Easter, Christmas); 6) religious laws and obligations (e.g., the obligation of praying with the community at the Eucharist); 7) sayings and catch phrases (e.g., Christ has died, Christ is risen, Christ will come again); and 8) story telling (telling and retelling the story of Jesus and of our Jewish ancestors in the faith through the Bible).

Traditions Written Down

This same process of tradition was in operation among the Jewish people. At first, all the traditions were oral, passed on from one generation to the next by word of mouth and by stories. But, as Scripture scholars now believe, some of these traditions began to be written down around 1000 B.C.E.[40] Gradually, over

---

[40]   B.C.E. (Before the Common Era); C.E. (the Common Era). These designations are now often used in preference to A.D. (Anno Domini – the Year of the Lord), and B.C. (Before Christ). The latter designations look at history as revolving round the coming of Jesus Christ. This is a specifically Christian look at history. Many of the non-Christian religions, particularly Judaism, feel that the designations A.D. and B.C. cannot represent their view of history: hence the attempt to find designations that are not offensive to anyone.

a great number of years (right down to just before the Common Era), these written traditions were formed and shaped, edited and added to as the life of the Jewish people progressed. The Jewish people had the particular genius of seeing and understanding their whole life – history, literature, stories, religious observances, customs – in relation to God. A collection of these traditions came to be written down and has given rise to what we now call the Hebrew Scriptures, or the Old Testament.

The same process was at work among the early Christian communities. These communities wished to preserve their memories of Jesus and their response to his message. Some of these traditions were written down within 30 to 70 years of Jesus' death. It is this writing that we call the Christian Scriptures, or the New Testament. The Hebrew and Christian Scriptures together make up the Bible.

Three points are worth making here.

1.   The Bible Does Not Contain the Whole of Tradition

When people write down their traditions, they obviously make a selection. They generally do not wish to preserve the trivial and unimportant things that will not help the faith of succeeding generations. Thus, not everything was written down by the Jewish and Christian authors. A selection of the more important traditions was made.

Scripture itself attests to this process. Thus, St. John writes at the end of his gospel: "Now Jesus did many other signs in the presence of his disciples, which are not written in this book. But these are written so that you may come to believe that Jesus is the Messiah, the Son of God, and that through believing you may have life in his name" (Jn 20:30-31).

2.   Scripture Comes from Tradition

Tradition is the prime witness to God's revelation. But the Church "'does not derive her certainty about all revealed truths from the holy Scriptures alone. Both Scripture and Tradition must be accepted and honoured with equal sentiments of devotion and reverence'" (CCC 82).This, as can be readily recognized, is a major point of difference between Catholicism and many other Christian denominations who hold that all of God's revelation is contained in the Bible. Since not all of tradition was written down as Scripture, there are aspects of God's revelation that exist in the church as *unwritten tradition*. The discernment of this unwritten tradition can be a difficult and controversial process. To help us in the discernment, we turn for guidance to the teaching authority of the church. Consider, for example, the question of the ordination of women to the priesthood. The present position of the teaching authority of the church is that women's non-admission to the priesthood (certainly unclear from Scripture alone) is part of the unwritten tradition and intrinsically and essentially part of God's revelation to us.

3. *Tradition Does Not Stop When It Is Written Down*

The tradition continues, but now with the added advantage that it can draw on the writings already there as it is formed and shaped in the life of the church (CCC 80). The advantage of having texts is that they are much clearer, more pointed and precise, more condensed, and therefore easier to interpret than oral tradition with all the various nuances associated with storytelling. These writings have shaped the present faith of the Christian community, and so we say that they are normative* for understanding God's revelation to us. If we want to interpret revelation, we always have to take into account what is said in Scripture. Other traditions in the church cannot contradict what is in Scripture; otherwise God would be self-contradictory.

Large *T* and Small *t* Traditions

As we have said, tradition is not a static thing; we well know from our own experience and history that traditions grow and develop. We have already noted in the chapter on revelation that revelation is not static, but ongoing and developing. In order to understand this point, it is helpful to make a distinction between Tradition (with a large T), and tradition (with a small t). Tradition "comes from the apostles and hands on what they received from Jesus' teaching and example and what they learned from the Holy Spirit" (CCC 83). Thus, Tradition has to do with matters *essential* to the faith that, if not present, would represent a distortion of the gospel message. Such Tradition, for example, would concern the doctrine that Jesus is God and man, Christ's resurrection from the dead, the real presence of Jesus in the eucharist, and many others. This Tradition cannot change, even though our understanding of it may undergo development.

There is only one Tradition, but there are many traditions. These traditions – theological, disciplinary, liturgical or devotional – have arisen at various times and in various places, often to take into account local conditions and in many cases to safeguard, promote and enhance Tradition. They do not belong to the essential deposit of faith and therefore are subject to change or even elimination, under the guidance of the teaching church. An example of one such is the requirement of celibacy for the Roman rite clergy.

Tradition refers to the great and essential mysteries of religion (such as Jesus Christ, God and man, the real presence of Christ in the Eucharist). Because people find it difficult to relate directly to these mysteries, traditions develop which help put people in touch with them. Examples of such traditions would be genuflection, bowing, the sign of the cross, holy water and other forms of reverence to Christ in the eucharist. There is no doubt that such traditions can be invaluable aids in safeguarding Tradition. Nevertheless, it happens that the faithful people of God often confuse traditions with Tradition. Mere traditions in the church sometimes come to be seen as essential to faith. As a result, people cling, sometimes obsessively, to the externals (traditions), so that often the external form itself becomes the main focus of faith. A good example of this is what happened at the time when Friday abstinence from meat was a general rule of the church. For many, the whole of Catholicism became associated with Friday abstinence; it was the distinguishing mark of being a Catholic. Some years ago a group of people in Nova Scotia, Canada, who fervently believed in the apparitions of the Mother of God at Bayside, New York (declared to be fraudulent by the church), insisted that they receive communion kneeling down because the Virgin Mary had said that this is what should be done. When the pastor of the church refused to allow it because it was disruptive to the majority of churchgoers, the group took the church to court on the grounds that it was interfering with their freedom of religion! The case eventually reached the Supreme Court of Nova Scotia on appeal, where it was finally thrown out. This is the kind of thing that happens when a misguided faith cannot distinguish between Tradition and tradition, in this case with tragic results for the peace and unity of the church.

In order to guard against disunity and damage to the faith, from time to time the church must go through the process of sorting out Tradition from traditions. There is a constant need to clarify what is authentic Tradition and distinguish it from the many accretions and misunderstandings that tend to creep in. This is part of the renewal process in the church that must always go on under the guidance of the Spirit of God. The sorting-out process is one of the major reasons that the church holds Ecumenical Councils (such as Vatican II*) and synods (meetings of bishops and other people).

Inspiration

Christians believe that sacred Scripture is inspired by God (CCC 105). Faith in the divine inspiration* of Scripture dates back to Old Testament times. There was the conviction, even then, that certain parts of the scriptural writings were inspired by God. The New Testament, or Christian Scriptures, takes this inspiration of the Hebrew Scriptures for granted, making it clear that Jesus himself, who was a faithful Jew, believed it. In the Second Epistle to Timothy we read, "All scripture is inspired by God and is useful for teaching, for reproof, for correction, and for training in righteousness . . ." (2 Tim 3:16). It is also clear that the earliest Christian writers believed in the divine inspiration of the Christian Scriptures as well. This faith has been passed on to us as an essential Tradition in the church.

But what is inspiration? How are we to understand it? We can do no better than to quote Vatican Council II:

For holy mother church, relying on the faith of the apostlic age, accepts as sacred and canonical the books of the Old and the New Testaments, whole and entire, with all their parts, on the grounds that, written under the inspiration of the holy Spirit. . . . God chose certain men who, all the while he employed them in this task, made full use of their powers and faculties so that, though he acted in them and by them, it was as true authors that they consigned to writing whatever he wanted written, and no more.[41]

From this statement certain points emerge.

1. The writers were human authors. This means that they went through the same process of research and composition as any human author, and they wrote in their own particular style and with the linguistic tools available to them as products of their own particular culture and circumstances of life.

2. The Holy Spirit acted in and through the authors' own natural human powers and abilities. God did not *dictate* what to write, in the sense of putting words into their minds. The Holy Spirit made sure that in their choice of words and forms of expression they were conveying the message God wanted.

Thus, the Holy Spirit is the principal author of Sacred Scripture (CCC 304), but the message God wanted is couched in human language that corresponds to the intention of the author. *It is what the author intended to write that contains God's message, not the simple face value of the words.* Let us now elaborate further on this very important point.

Interpretation of Scripture – Exegesis

It should be clear that the Bible is both the word of God and a human word. In order to understand what God is saying to us, we must get at the proper meaning of the human word (CCC 104, 109). We call this process "interpretation."

Many Christians claim that since God is the prime author of the Bible, we must take the word of God literally: the words mean exactly what they say. If the Bible says that God took six days to create the world, then that is factually and historically true. We call such persons literalists, or biblical fundamentalists.* Many of the so-called T.V. evangelists are of this stripe. This is not the position of most of the mainline Christian churches, which hold that the Bible needs to be properly interpreted.

What, then, is the major principle of interpretation? In order to get at the proper meaning of the text, we must try to get into the mind of the author and ask

---

[41] *Vatican Council II, Constitution on Divine Revelation (Dei verbum)*, No. 11.

this question: What did the author intend, or mean, when he wrote those words? Surely, this is not such a difficult process to understand! People constantly have to ask one another, "What do you mean?" The actual spoken word often does not immediately convey the meaning intended by the speaker. Sometimes students have to explain to professors what they really meant by a certain passage in an assignment or paper (with or without success!). Literary critics have made a profession out of trying to explain what famous works of literature mean. Many passages of Shakespeare, after 400 years of literary criticism, are still somewhat mysterious.

In order to get at the meaning intended by the author, we must delve into the history of the writing, the language used, the style (e.g., historical, poetic, metaphorical), the cultural norms that influenced the author, and so on (CCC 110). This process of getting into the mind of the author to discern proper meaning is called *exegesis** (from the Greek, meaning to explain, to lead out).[42]

Many of the passages of Scripture are very clear and can be taken at their face value, but many are not. We often need the help of Scripture scholars who are experts in exegesis to help us understand what the text is really saying and hence what is God's message to us.

Authoritative Interpretation

Since Scripture is the norm and touchstone of our faith, if we all are to have the same faith and hold to the same truths, then we must be sure that we have God's message correct. In order to assess the relative importance of various interpretations, we need some kind of authoritative decision. We need a central authority that will determine what is and what is not a correct interpretation. This authoritative interpretation* is provided by the teaching authority of the church under the guidance of the Pope and bishops (CCC 119). In order to have some advice and guidance in the interpretation of Scripture, the Pope has established the Pontifical Biblical Commission. This international Commission consists of a group of the pre-eminent Catholic Scripture scholars of the day. From time to time they issue statements of what, in their opinion, is the correct interpretation of disputed passages in Scripture. Their decision, of itself, does not constitute an authoritative statement, but in practice the Pope and bishops usually follow the advice of these scholars.

---

[42]   The Catechism, quoting Vatican II, gives three criteria for interpreting Scripture. 1) Be especially attentive "to the content and unity of the whole Scripture." 2) Read the Scripture within "the living Tradition of the whole Church." 3) Be attentive to the analogy of faith. For further elaboration of these points, see CCC 112-114.

That some authoritative interpretation is needed is the position held by Roman Catholics, but not by some Protestants. One of the touchstones of the Protestant Reformation was that each person should interpret Scripture in his or her own personal way because the Holy Spirit speaks to each person in the depths of his or her heart and reveals God's message. It is probably this one factor, more than any other, that has brought about the fragmentation of the Protestant denominations. Any group can claim it has an authentic interpretation of God's message that is different from the others and therefore it can form its own church. The fact that the Roman Catholic church has held to the necessity of having a central authority for interpreting Scripture is something that is sometimes much admired by Protestant scholars who have to struggle along on their own.

The Senses (Meaning) of Scripture

As a glance at any manual of theology will show, we can approach this topic in many ways. Sometimes the divisions and subdivisions become detailed and complicated. In the interests of simplicity and brevity we shall identify only two ways in which we can understand what Scripture is saying.

1.   The Literal Sense (Meaning)

The literal meaning* of Scripture can be taken in two ways.

a)   What the words mean at their face value.

People who understand "literal" in this sense would hold that, when the Bible says that Noah was in the Ark (Gen 7:24–8:19) with a pair of every species of animal, this is factually true. (The staggering logistics of this feat do not seem to bother the literalists!) One is reminded of the story of the religion teacher who, having done the Noah story with her students, asked, "And what do you think Noah did all those days in the Ark? Did he, perhaps, fish?" One student piped up, "What, with only two worms?!"

b)   What the author intended the words to mean.

If the author did not intend us to take the story of Noah literally, what did he intend? He intended to convey a religious message, a message about God and God's relationship to us. The best understanding that we have at present is that the author used an ancient and traditional story about a universal flood "as a vehicle to express a fundamental theme of Israelite faith: God's judgment in the affairs of history. . . . The boat into which he [Noah] takes his family and the pairs of animals was a sign of Yahweh's intention to deliver a remnant with which to make a new beginning in history. . . . and that even though 'the imagination of man's heart is evil from his youth' Yahweh would never again curse the ground with such severe judgment."[43] So, from this story we learn that God does enter the affairs of human history, expects us to follow what is right and will judge us if we don't; and God is merciful and his salvation is always available despite the fact that "the imagination of man's heart is evil from his youth."

When we talk about the Literal Sense of Scripture, what we are looking for is the latter sense: the meaning the author intended in writing those words (CCC 116).

2.   *The More-Than-Literal Senses*

The meaning of the Bible may go beyond the literal sense. Even though we may not be able to say with certainty that this or that is the true literal sense intended by the author, the meanings that we derive from our reading of the Bible may well be to our spiritual benefit. The question we can ask is this: How does the message I perceive God to be conveying affect my life today? I may be able to read into the Bible a meaning that is particularly significant for my faith today, even though this meaning may not be what the author intended to convey. This happens frequently enough when we read Scripture for our own personal benefit, and for prayer. We call this the Spiritual Sense of Scripture.

A certain bishop tells the true story of how, as a young priest, he returned to his diocese after having done advanced Scripture studies in Europe. Some years later, his father was diagnosed with a painful form of cancer. On one of his visits home, the priest found his father reading the Book of Job in the Bible. His father thought that Job was a real man, that Job was cursed by God, that Job actually sat in a dungheap and disputed with his friends about whether God was merciful, that Job showed patience and finally accepted his lot. The young priest admitted that he could have told his father that the whole Book of Job is a folk tale, possibly borrowed from Babylonian writing, an elaborate parable, but related in the Bible for a religious purpose. He could have enlightened his father as to the place of Job in the Wisdom literature of the Bible and that the story of Job is the story of every one of us. He could have told his father many other scholarly things about the Book of Job, but his father's simple faith helped him to derive great consolation from reading the book as though it were factually and histori-cally true. His father was gleaning a deep spiritual sense from the Book of Job that was probably not what the author intended when the book was written.

---

[43]   Bernhard W. Anderson, *Understanding the Old Testament*, 3rd ed. (Englewood Cliffs, NJ: Prentice-Hall, 1975), p. 214.

Truth in Scripture

In the words of the Catechism, "The inspired books teach the truth" (CCC 107). But often enough we hear the complaint that Scripture is not "true." Since the Book of Job is only a story, it is not "true": the events described did not actually happen. The same thing can be said about the story of Jonah and the whale. Again, did a universal flood cover the whole earth, and did Noah really survive it by going into the ark? Is this true? Did it really happen as described? Well, it all depends on what we mean by "true."

When we ask questions like these, we are showing ourselves to be authentic children of our culture. Ours is a culture browbeaten by science, by newspaper and television reporting. We are excited by "investigative reporting" or the digging up of the true facts, facts that correspond to reality. We want to know all the details, often for no other reason than to be titillated. Our equation of truth with what can be clearly demonstrated is a legacy left us by the French philosopher René Descartes, one which has profoundly affected our thinking. But the Scriptures were not written in that way; the writers were not investigative reporters. Scripture was written to convey a religious message about God seen through the eyes of faith. What is true in Scripture is the religious message, not necessarily the scientific details or the stories in which that message is couched.

Let us use as an example one of Aesop's fables. A dog with a fine, meaty bone in its mouth was crossing a bridge over a small stream. As the animal reached the middle of the bridge, it looked down and saw its own reflection magnified in the water. Thinking that the dog in the water had a larger bone, the animal on the bridge leaped into the water to grab the larger bone. Not only did the dog lose its own bone but it was drowned. What is true in this story? Is it the actual passage of the dog over the bridge? Or rather is it the very deep human truth that we all know and experience within ourselves: namely, that greed kills?

Inerrancy* in the Bible

Some people claim that, since the Bible is written under God's guidance, it cannot contain error. Well, that depends on what you mean by "error."

If it is a question of scientific, historical, factual errors of reporting, then the Bible has several of these. For example, there are contradictions in the Bible. Genesis 7:17 has it that the Flood lasted 40 days, while Genesis 7:24 has it lasting 150 days. There are errors in science. In Joshua 10:13 the sun is said to have stood still, an observation that comes from the understanding that the earth is the centre of the universe and does not move. When Galileo proved to his own satisfaction that the earth did indeed move, he got into trouble with the church authorities for denying the truth of Scripture. There are moral misunderstandings in the Bible. In war, the total destruction of everyone, even those not actually engaged in the fighting, is seen as good because it is God's will (Josh 11:14-15).

How Do We Account for These Errors?

The errors in the Bible may be accounted for in a number of ways.

1. Human authors make human mistakes; their knowledge of science (cosmology,* for example) was primitive. The Bible does not set out to teach these errors. The Bible cannot be used as a textbook of science, or history, or geography. The point we must stress is that the religious message of the Bible is not affected by the errors.

2. Biblical writers use all the common literary devices, such as poetry, figures of speech, paradox, approximations, folklore, legend, myth, song. No one has ever accused the poets, for example, of being scientifically correct; that is not their intention or purpose, nor is it the intention of the biblical writers. We must sift through these literary devices to get at the intended message.

3. The writers did not belong to our present-day Western culture. Their thought patterns, modes of expression, and philosophical presuppositions are different from ours. For example, they were not infected with our passion for logic and detail. In no sense can we take the Bible in the same way as we take newspaper reporting.

4. It is certain that one single individual did not author all the books of the Bible. The writings were developed and edited over a long period of time and often represent a compilation of traditions from different sources. That there will be variations in these traditions is understandable and may well account for some of the seeming contradictions we find in the Bible.

When it is a question of the religious message of the Bible, we can say that the Bible contains no error. The Bible is free from error in those religious affirmations that are made for the sake of our salvation. Vatican Council II states it this way:

> We must acknowledge that the books of scripture, firmly, faithfully and without error, teach that truth which God, for the sake of our salvation, wished to see confided to the sacred scriptures.[44]

Thus, we may conclude that the Bible contains error, but teaches no error.

Conclusion – Scripture and You

The words of Scripture are God's word to us, God's invitation to us, God's message of love. It should be unnecessary to say that we are encouraged to read the Bible. But reading the Bible, for some people, is a real chore. What possible significance can the stories of Noah and Moses and Abraham (to take just a few)

---

[44]   *Constitution on Divine Revelation (Dei verbum),* No. 11.

have for my life? Their lives seem wrapped in the miraculous, which does not at all relate to what I experience in mine. In their lives, God seems to be acting all the time, but where is God now? Why doesn't God intervene in my life in the same tangible ways God intervened in theirs? We must not forget that the Bible is written through the eyes of faith. It is a faith look at history and human events, a faith look that sees the hand of God in what, for other people, would be merely a human event. The Bible should encourage us to take such a faith look at our own life and times. Étienne Charpentier puts it beautifully:

> To read the Bible should lead us to reread our existence with the eyes of the believer. If we do, we shall discover that God continues to speak to us as he spoke to the prophets, and he continues to act. And the whole of our life will appear to us to be a history full of miracles.[45]

When we take up the Bible to read it, we should remember that, through these pages, God is really speaking to us. Furthermore, as Charpentier reminds us, we should read ourselves into the Bible stories and ask what these stories are saying to our own personal life. God is trying to communicate with us; we should do our utmost not to put roadblocks in the way of this communication. We should have reverence and respect for these writings. There is tremendous power in the word of God. Through the power of the Holy Spirit, God will speak to us, if we properly dispose ourselves to listen. Lots of people read the Bible because they find that it is just good literature. For us it is that, and much more.

The Bible should have an honoured place in every Catholic home; it should have an honoured place in every Catholic classroom. We must teach children respect and reverence for the Bible from their very earliest years. While the Bible cannot be called a sacrament in the true sense, it certainly participates in the general principle of sacramentality (see Chapter 16). The Bible may be a human book, written by human authors for human readers, but it is also God's book, given to us in love.

Reflection Questions

1. What is religious tradition? How is it handed on?

2. What memories do you have of non-religious traditions that have helped to shape your personality and your self-identity? Can you say something similar for some religious traditions?

3. Have any of your family traditions and memories been written down? If you have access to this written account today, review how the account has influenced your life. Can you verify these memories from other sources? How accurate are they?

---

[45] Étienne Charpentier, *How to Read the Old Testament* (London: SCM Press, 1982), p. 10. CCC 129 also gives us some advice on reading the Old Testament.

4. Give some examples of Traditions as distinct from traditions, other than those given in the text of this chapter.

5. If God did not actually dictate to the Scripture writers what to write, how can we call the Bible "the word of God"?

6. How would you answer someone who claims that there are several errors in the Bible, and that therefore it cannot be the word of God?

Further Reading

Flannery, Austin, O.P., Ed. *Vatican Council II: The Basic Sixteen Documents* (New York: Costello Publishing, 1996). A standard reference text of the Conciliar documents, which should be in every Catholic library.

Harrington, Wilfred, O.P. *Record of Revelation, Vol. 1 of Key to the Bible* (New York: Doubleday, Image Books, 1976). A compact, clear, easy-to-understand guide to the Bible that deals with many of the questions raised in this chapter. Inexpensive paperback.

Kealy, John P., C.S.Sp. *The Changing Bible* (Rockaway, NJ: Dimension Books, 1977). Deals with modern methods of biblical study by which scholars attempt to discover in the text the meaning intended by the author, which is God's revelation to us. Short and easy to read.

8

THE HEBREW SCRIPTURES: OLD TESTAMENT

As we have said before, Christianity cannot escape its Jewish roots. Our Lord Jesus Christ was a Jew, and all the very early Christians were Jews. Like other Jewish children, Jesus was taught the Hebrew Scriptures. He loved and revered them and used them in his own teaching. His teaching, he said, is meant to fulfill the Hebrew Scriptures, not abolish them (Mt 5:17). It is in these ancient Hebrew writings that we find the expectation and promise of a Messiah. The Christian Scriptures, or New Testament, give clear evidence that Jesus is the promised Messiah, the anointed of God. The new law, the new covenant initiated by Jesus, has its origin and root in the Hebrew Scriptures.

Without doubt the Bible is the bestseller of all time. Since the advent of printing, more copies of the Bible have been printed than any other book. It has had an enormous impact on the moral codes by which we live today and on the spiritual life of the vast majority of people (the Koran of Islam was deeply influenced by the Bible). Even George Gallup informs us that his polls indicate the Bible is the most significant source of today's moral and social behaviour (in the Western World, at least). But the Bible is much more than a source book of moral behaviour. The Hebrew Scriptures are God's word to us, a valid source of God's revelation, and therefore merit to be read, studied and prayed over. Pope John XXIII has the truth of it when he says, "Today for a self-respecting Christian, ignorance of the Bible is unpardonable. Ignorance of the Scriptures is, in fact, ignorance of Christ." In this chapter, we aim to offer a simple introduction to the first part of the Bible: the Hebrew Scriptures, or Old Testament.

What Is the Bible?

The word "Bible"* comes from the Greek *ta biblia*, which means "the books," or "the writings." The Bible came to be referred to in the singular as The Book. As we have mentioned, it is composed of two parts: the Hebrew Scriptures* (or Old Testament*) and the Christian Scriptures* (or New Testament*), with the Hebrew Scriptures being much longer.

The word "testament"* in Scripture means "agreement," "covenant,"* and should not be confused with the more popular modern usage, as in "last will and testament." The Old Testament writings refer to several mutual agreements made by God with the Jewish people. Most particularly, however, it refers to the one entered into by Moses on behalf of the people, from which we have the Ten Commandments. With the advent of Jesus, with his life, death and resurrection, we have now entered into a new agreement, a new covenant with God through Jesus: hence, the New Testament. The record of this new covenant is found in the Christian Scriptures. The Old and the New Testaments together make up the Bible.

We would be less than honest if we didn't admit that the terminology could be confusing. Calling the first Testament "Old" does not mean that now it is useless and of no consequence and has been completely supplanted by the "New." We must not allow ourselves to fall into a mode of thinking that is fuelled by the commercialism to which we are subjected in modern times. We often get caught up in this commercial language, which tells us that things are no good unless they are "new and improved." Young is good; old is passé, no good. It is also somewhat insulting to our Jewish brothers and sisters who still order their lives according to the "Old" Testament. By saying that their Testament is "Old," we may well be perceived as telling them that their religion, their expression of how God works in their lives, is no good. We "New" Testament followers have the truth; they do not! That kind of arrogance does not become true followers of Christ. For these reasons, many scholars prefer to talk about the Hebrew Scriptures and the Christian Scriptures. However, the terminology Old and New Testament is still widely used and we shall continue to use it in this book. As we shall see, the terms Hebrew Scriptures and Old Testament do not mean exactly the same thing.

The Hebrew Scriptures are a compilation of traditions ranging over a wide spectrum of the life of the Jewish people: their history, poetry, story, folk wisdom, religion and theology. But, and most important, it is the life of a believing people who understood that God had entered their lives and was calling them to a special relationship, to which they had agreed in the covenant. The Scriptures are inspired by God, and are documents of faith (CCC 121).

History of the Israelite People – Clarification of Terminology

We should begin our look at the Old Testament with a review of the history of Israel for, as we have said, these written traditions span the whole extent of the life of the Israelite people, and we should know something about the background against which these traditions developed. A short summary of this history is provided in the accompanying tables. Please study these tables carefully.

Before proceeding, let us attempt to clear up a source of confusion. Sometimes the people are referred to as Jews,* or Jewish. At other times they are referred to as Israelites,* and the nation as Israel,* or we talk of the Hebrew people. It seems that these terms are used interchangeably. As is indicated in the historical table, the best evidence we have at the moment (from the Bible, from archaeology and from secular history) indicates that the family of Jacob entered Egypt at the time of a famine in the land where they lived. In Egypt, they prospered and multiplied under the Semitic rulers of Egypt at that time, the Hyksos. This group of Jews in Egypt, therefore, are considered to be descendants of Jacob. The Bible contains a rather mysterious account, difficult to explain, of Jacob wrestling with an angel (Gen 32:23-31). He is told that from then on his name shall be "Israel," which means "he contended (or fought) with God" (CCC 2573). Although the name "Israelite" clearly comes from "Israel" (i.e., Jacob), the name more properly refers to the people united by the covenant after the Exodus. It refers particularly to the tribes that constituted the Northern Kingdom after the breakup in 922 B.C.E. (Refer to the historical table.)

Date B.C.E.	History of Israel	Oral and Written Traditions
ca. 1800	Abraham, first true believer. Migrates from Ur (in modern-day Iraq) to Canaan (modern-day Israel and Palestine). (Genesis 12 ff.)	Oral tradition begins
ca. 1700	Family of Jacob (Abraham's descendent) go into Egypt. Egypt under the control of a Semitic group, the Hyksos, who usurped power from the Egyptians. Jacob's family, being Semites, well treated. They prosper (Genesis 36 ff.)	
ca. 1300	Egyptian revival, Hyksos lose power. Descendants of Jacob (Semites) fall into disfavour – oppression and slavery. Source of cheap labour (Exodus 2).	
ca. 1290–1250	The advent of Moses. Brought up in the court by Pharaoh's daughter after he had been abandoned. He experiences God at the burning bush. After the plagues, leads a group of Israelites out of Egypt. The Exodus experience of crossing the Sea of Reeds – God the Saviour. Wanderings in the desert, a nomadic people. COVENANT with God – The Ten Commandments. God's demands – THE LAW (TORAH). Israel a people (Exodus 2 ff.).	
ca. 1250–1200	Moses dies on Mt. Nebo east of the Dead Sea (Dt 34:1-8). Israelites enter the land of Canaan, led by Joshua, from east of the Jordan River, through Jericho. Begin conquest and infiltration of Canaan (Joshua 1–12).	

Date B.C.E.	History of Israel	Oral and Written Traditions
ca. 1200–1000	Israelites solidify their conquest of Canaan. Israel not yet a united nation but a loose confederation of tribes (extended families descended from the 12 sons of Jacob). Period of Judges. Chief judge Samuel anoints the first king of Israel, Saul (ca. 1000) (1 Samuel 1–11). Saul's downfall and the rise of David (1 Samuel 12–31).	The story of Israel fairly well shaped and put together.
ca. 1000–922	Kings David (1000–965) and his son Solomon (961–922). Greatest extent of Israelite hegemony. Israel rich and strong. Building of the first temple in Jerusalem by Solomon. Solomon imposes taxes and forced labour to maintain powerful infrastructure. People's freedom curtailed by oppressive government – the beginnings of government bureaucracy.	Traditions begin to be written down. Oral tradition continues together with written.
922	Upon his death, Solomon's sons fight over the kingdom. Country divided into a Northern Kingdom (Israel – by far the larger portion) and a Southern Kingdom (Judah – land around Jerusalem). Succession of kings in each kingdom (Books of Kings and Chronicles).	
721	Northern Kingdom overthrown by the Assyrians from the north.	
587	Southern Kingdom overthrown by the Babylonians from the east (Iraq).	Pentateuchal traditions completed and written.
587–538	Exile in Babylon. Most of the important people in Judah taken into captivity by Nebuchadnezzar. Jerusalem sacked and burned. Temple, centre of Jewish worship, destroyed. Many precious artefacts, such as the books of the Law, lost.	
538–400	Rise of the Persians. Persians gain control of Babylon. King Cyrus of Persia allows the captured Israelites to return home. They begin to restore their shattered lives. Slow rebuilding of Jerusalem. Israel under Persian control. Ancient book of the Law discovered in the ruins. Restoration of Jewish worship (Books of Nehemiah and Ezra).	
400–200	Egyptians from the south overthrow the Persians and gain control of Israel.	Collection of Psalms and Wisdom writings
168–63	Israelites rebel under the leadership of the family of the Maccabees. Attain a partial and uneasy independence (Maccabees 1 & 2).	
63	Roman conquest. Israel a colonized and subjugated people again. Into this political milieu Jesus is born.	

The word "Jew" is a derivative of "Judah," meaning the Southern Kingdom after the breakup in 922 B.C.E. This is the area in the south traditionally occupied by the descendants of Judah and Benjamin (sons of Jacob), an area much smaller than the Northern Kingdom (Israel). Jews/Israelites are often referred to as the Hebrew people because Hebrew is the language of the original written traditions that are derived from both the Northern and Southern Kingdoms.

If all this sounds somewhat confusing, it is. The terms are, to a certain extent, interchangeable. "Israelite" is certainly the more ancient term, "Jew" the more recent (though recent, of course, is relative).

The Books of the Old Testament

First, more terminology! The books of the Bible are often referred to as canonical* books. *Canon* is the Greek for "rule" or "norm." The canonical books form the rule, or norm, of faith; they are recognized and accepted as inspired by God. The word "canon" also came to mean "list." The canon is the list of books that the church recognizes as inspired. So, a canonical book is recognized by the church as inspired by God and necessary to our faith. (If all this terminology – and there is more to come – is confusing and difficult, please don't despair! There is a summary at the end of the chapter.)

The Old Testament is not a single book but rather a collection of books – a whole library, in fact. The Scriptures contain historical writings, stories, poetry, songs, writings on human wisdom, writings on prophecy. As we have said – and it is worth repeating – the Old Testament is, in fact, a collection of the written traditions that span the whole extent of Jewish life. A people rereads its life in the light of faith, a faith that saw God's rule extending to every aspect of that life, and in the light of the covenant they made with God. There are many things in these books that today may offend our moral sense and put some people off reading the Bible. These faults and failings, the sinfulness, are part of an honest record of the life of the people, but they are not condoned; we are not encouraged to copy them. As has been mentioned, the Bible offers us a moral code second to none that is the basis of most moral behaviour today.

Different Versions of the Scriptures

Just before the turn of the era, around 250 B.C.E., an event of great importance in biblical history took place: the original Hebrew of the Old Testament was translated into Greek (the most commonly used language of the time). This work was done by a group of Jewish scholars in and around Alexandria, in Egypt. The scholars were traditionally thought to be 70 in number; hence the Greek version came to be known as the Septuagint.* In making their translation, the scholars added other well-known books that were not originally written in Hebrew but in Greek, or possibly Aramaic (a dialect of Hebrew that Jesus spoke). The Catholic church has accepted all these books of the Septuagint as canonical; they constitute the Old Testament (CCC 120). Strictly speaking, therefore, the Hebrew Scriptures constitute only those books originally written in Hebrew. As we said, the terms "Old Testament" and "Hebrew Scriptures" do not mean exactly the same thing.

Towards the end of the first century (66 C.E.), the Jews rebelled against the Romans, who occupied what today we call Israel and Palestine. The rebellion was crushed with the greatest severity, finally resulting (in 70 C.E.) in the sacking of Jerusalem and the destruction of the temple, centre of Jewish worship. Some Pharisees, afraid of the possible destruction of the entire Jewish religion, gathered at Jamnia (modern Jabneh, south of Tel Aviv) for a religious revival conference. This group of hard-liners drew up a Jewish canon of Scripture that contained only those books originally written in Hebrew – 40 in all. They excluded from their canon the following books of the Septuagint: Wisdom, Ecclesiasticus (Sirach), Baruch (Chapters 1-15), Judith, Tobit and parts of Daniel that they considered non-canonical. This is still the canon accepted by Jews today. When in the 16th century the Protestants started making translations from the original Hebrew, they used the Jewish canon and left out of their translations the books listed above, declaring them to be not inspired. Thus, in many Protestant editions of the Bible, these books are listed at the end under the name apocrypha*: that is, of doubtful authenticity. As we shall see, a similar process operated in the drawing up of the New Testament writings. I am happy to report that in modern times there has been a great convergence of Scripture scholarship, and Protestants and Catholics for the most part accept the same canon of Scripture.

Basic Division of the Books

There are 46 books in the Old Testament. In order to make the Scriptures easier to study and refer to, the books have been grouped together according to different schemes. In the Jewish tradition, there are three basic divisions: The Law, The Prophets, and The Writings. Christian Bibles, following the grouping in the Septuagint, add a fourth division, separating the historical books from the Prophets. Refer to the contents page in your Bible for a full list of all the books in the Hebrew Scriptures. The four main divisions are The Pentateuch, the Historical Books, the Wisdom Writings, and the Prophets.

1. The Pentateuch

The word Pentateuch* literally means "five containers." The first five books of the Bible are specially revered by the Jewish people as containing those traditions that have substantially descended from Moses, the hero of the Exodus. In particular, these books deal with the covenant between God and the Jewish people given through Moses, the central event affecting all Jewish life. Scrolls of the Pentateuch are kept in a prominent place in the synagogue; it is read from at Jewish religious ceremonies. It plays a key role in the Bar Mitzvah ceremony, in which Jewish boys are considered to have reached religious maturity. For the Jewish people, the Pentateuch is also known as the Torah.* Torah means "teaching" and is revered as God's special teaching to the people of Israel. Torah represents the divine guidance that God gives to the people for their pilgrimage on earth.

Torah is sometimes called the Law.* The whole notion of Law is sacred to the Jews. In our Western democratic culture we often have a negative view of law, seeing it as something that restricts our freedom, that forces us to do things we would prefer not to do, that we obey only because of what might happen to us if we don't. The Jews, on the other hand, understand that God's law is for their guidance, a help given them in keeping their side of the covenant. For the Jews, the Law is the act of a loving God who asks us to respond. The great book of the Law is Deuteronomy, the fifth book of the Pentateuch. Indeed, this book is frequently quoted in the New Testament. As reported in the gospels, Jesus affirmed that the whole teaching of the Torah could be fulfilled in two commandments found in Deuteronomy: "The first is . . . 'you shall love the Lord your God with all your heart, and with all your soul, and with all your mind, and with all your strength.' The second is this, 'You shall love your neighbour as yourself.' There is no other commandment greater than these" (Mk 12:29-31; see also Mt 22:37-40 and Lk 10:27; the reference is to Deut 6:5).

The book of the Law, therefore, is really an expression of the faith of the Israelites: God has intervened in my life; here is how I shall respond to God's goodness. The Torah is not to be thought of as a mass of demands made by God to limit freedom. Rather, it must be looked upon as an instrument of freedom, an expression of God's love. It is God's instruction on how to live in order to be faithful to the covenant. Christians would do well to adopt this attitude towards the demands that the new covenant makes on us. The requirements of that covenant, to which we agreed at our baptism, are fulfilled in and through our membership in the church, just as the Jews fulfilled the old covenant by being part of the people of Israel.

2. *The Historical Books*

These books give us a history of how the people lived out the demands of the covenant as they infiltrated, conquered and spread through the promised land of Canaan. The major theme of these books is the ups and downs Israel experienced as the people lived out the promises they made in the covenant. It is primarily a story of infidelity. The sufferings and setbacks that afflict the people are understood as punishments for not obeying the covenant. The books frequently

issue the warning of a final disaster, which will be the result of this wayward-
ness. This disaster was the final defeat of the kingdoms of Israel, the destruction
of the temple, the central place of worship, and the exile in Babylon (586–538
B.C.E.). Several books written after the exile are included in this section, such as
the books of Ruth, Esther, Judith, and Tobit. While not strictly historical, these
books relate stories of Jewish piety that probably bolstered the spirits of the
people trying to rebuild their shattered lives after the return from exile in
Babylon. The historical section closes with the books of the Maccabees that tell
the story of the partially successful Jewish revolt for independence from their
Greek colonial masters (168–164 B.C.E.).

3. The Writings

In these, Israel reflects on human life in the light of its faith. The book of
Psalms, for example, is a collection of hymns and prayers expressing the central
themes of Israelite faith. The Wisdom literature (Wisdom, Sirach, Qoheleth,
Proverbs) offers us religious insights into human behaviour. The book of Job
wrestles with a deep human question – the problem of suffering.

4. The Prophets

Scholars divide this section into the Major Prophets and the Minor Prophets,
probably for no better reason than the size of the books. The writings associated
with the Major Prophets, such as Isaiah, Jeremiah, Ezekiel, are substantial. The
Minor Prophets, such as Amos, Micah, Joel and Malachi, are no less important in
what they have to say, but their writings, or the written record of their utterances,
are shorter.

Chapter and Verse

The Bible was originally written without any divisions into chapter and
verse. It was not until the thirteenth century that a British scholar, Stephen
Langton (who later became the Archbishop of Canterbury), conceived the idea
of dividing the material into chapters. It was not until the sixteenth century that
a printer, Robert Estienne, decided to divide the material into verses, thus
making it easier to refer to specific passages by using a combination of chapter
and verse. The result is that today we have an internationally recognized method
of quoting Bible passages. First, the name of the book is abbreviated (for
example, Gen for Genesis, Jn for the Gospel of John, 1 Cor for the first letter to
the Corinthians). The chapter and verse are then written in number form, such as
12:2-4 (chapter twelve, verses two to four inclusive).

Basic Experience of the Jewish People

What might be called the bedrock experience of the Jewish people is that
God is a saving God. God saves his people from disaster but above all saves them

from the pernicious effects of their own folly and sinfulness. God saves because God loves. God is *for* us. The great saving event, which sets the tone for all future relations between God and the people, is the Exodus.* It is of fundamental importance for us, if we want to understand the Old Testament, to realize that the Scriptures were written in the light of the religious faith born of the Exodus experience. They were written in order to preserve the traditions growing out of this event and the subsequent covenant with God.

Up to about 1300 B.C.E., the Jews were not a people or a nation, as we understand these terms. They were a motley collection of Semites with loose family ties (the tribes of Israel) living in slavery in Egypt.[46] In the Bible, these people are the descendants of Abraham, the first true believer. And God must be faithful to the promises he made to Abraham that his descendants would be a great nation, a great people (see Gen 12:1-3; 15:13-15).

Moses

The central figure in the Exodus event is Moses. The story of Moses is related in the Book of Exodus, Chapter 2 and following. We shall not go into its details here. Moses had an intense religious experience as related in the story of the burning bush (Exodus 3).

READ: Exodus 3:1-15.

Moses asked God his name. In Jewish culture the name was terribly important, for it told who the person was and what the person was like. (For example, Jesus means "God saves," Jehosaphat means "God is judge.") Furthermore, knowing someone's name gave one a certain power, a certain control, over the person. Moses was anxious, and probably just plain curious, to find out who was talking to him. And God said to Moses, "I am who I am," an enigmatic saying that could mean several things. It could mean, for example, "My name is no business of yours; just pay attention to what I have to say." The name given to God in certain parts of the Hebrew Scriptures is YAHWEH – he/she is, or he/she who is. Bernhard Anderson comments: "Thus the name God signifies God whose being is turned toward his people, who is present in their midst as deliverer, guide, and judge and who is accessible in worship."[47] In a word, God is *for* the people. A religious Jew, however, would never utter the name of God for, as mentioned above, this would imply some control over God, and that would be blasphemy. Therefore, when they read the Scriptures they substituted

---

[46]   As noted in the table of the history of Israel, the Israelites, being Semites, were at first well treated by the then rulers of Egypt (the Hyksos, a semitic people), but were later enslaved as a source of cheap labour when the native Egyptians regained power.

[47]   Anderson, *Understanding the Old Testament*, p. 55.

the term *Adonai*,* meaning Lord, for the name Yahweh. Many editions of the Bible retain the title Lord in place of Yahweh.

The Bible story says that, as instructed by God, Moses went to Pharaoh and asked him to let the Jews go. Pharaoh refused, probably because he did not want to give up an easy source of cheap labour. "But the king of Egypt said to them, 'Moses and Aaron, why are you taking the people away from their work? Get to your labours!'" (Ex 5:4).

Then we are told about the plagues of Egypt – the Nile runs with blood, frogs, mosquitoes, gadflies, death of the Egyptians' livestock, boils, hail, locusts, darkness. According to the Bible, all these came about as a direct result of God's action to punish Pharaoh for not letting the Jews go. But these plagues could have been natural events. We have, even in contemporary times, experienced many of these ourselves when the climatic conditions are right – locusts, for example, mosquitoes, gadflies, hail, the prolific growth of a red alga that might turn the water a blood colour. The important point, though, is that the people, looking at these events with the eyes of faith, understood these plagues as God's way of persuading Pharaoh to let them go. It is a faith perception of what could have been natural events.

The Sea of Reeds

Not all the descendants of Jacob left Egypt. We do not know how big the band was. No doubt by this time, despite the oppression of the Egyptians, many of them had done reasonably well in life. They were not about to give up the "fleshpots" of Egypt for an uncertain future in the desert.

This motley group of people, the ones who followed Moses, travelled east and came to a marshy area called the Sea of Reeds, probably in the area of what is now the Suez Canal. It is often referred to as the Red Sea, but this has been shown to be a misreading of the text. The Sea of Reeds is not a continuous body of water but rather an area that may have been seasonally swampy. At this point Pharaoh's army seems to have caught up with them. Obviously, Pharaoh had not pursued them immediately when they departed. We do not know how long it took them to reach the Sea of Reeds. Some scholars have suggested that the Israelites arrived there during the dry season when the area was not very swampy. Pharaoh's army, on the other hand, arrived when the weather had changed, and the area was now really swampy. The Bible account of what happened there is somewhat confused. There can be little doubt that it is a compilation of traditions from different sources that developed in the course of Israel's history. It is almost impossible to reach an accurate historical appraisal of what happened. The most popular account, taken from a literal reading of one part of the text and depicted in the movie *The Ten Commandments,* is that God parted the waters to allow the people to cross and then allowed the waters to flow back and engulf Pharaoh's army. It is worth quoting a long passage from Anderson because he seems to have captured the real essence of the event:

> The account of the miraculous opening of a path through the waters (Ex 14:15-31) belongs to the *poetry* of Israel's faith. The event constitutes, in the language of Emile Fackenheim, a "root experience" which to the present day is celebrated in the Passover Service as the sign of "a saving Presence" in history. Even historians who are skeptical about many of the ancient Mosaic traditions admit that at this point we strike "the bedrock of an historical occurrence," an event "so unique and extraordinary that it came to constitute the essence of the primary Israelite confession and was regarded as the real beginning of Israel's history and the act of God fundamental for Israel." Undoubtedly the story of the Event at the Sea is not pure fiction; it rests upon something that actually happened, something that aroused ecstatic jubilation and became the undying memory of the people. Yet it is almost impossible to penetrate behind the faith-language of the account and to deal with the inevitable question of the modern reader: what really happened at the Reed Sea?[48]

Thus, the "bedrock experience" of this band of escaped slaves is that God delivered them, saved them and liberated them because God loves them.

For many years this band of people wandered around the deserts of the Arabian Peninsula. During their time in the desert God gave many signs of his presence with them (e.g., the pillar of fire at night, a cloud during the day). God fed them with manna (probably a sticky secretion of insects – see Anderson p. 76), and birds (probably migratory birds too exhausted to fly). To us these may well have been natural phenomena, but for the Jews their faith made them see God as providing for his people. God continues to *save*.

The Covenant

A covenant, as we have seen, is a mutual agreement whereby each party to the covenant agrees to do something for the other party. The Hebrew Scriptures record several covenants: covenants of peace between nations, marriage covenants, covenants of friendship. Also recorded are several religious covenants entered into by God and various individuals representing the people: for example, with Noah (Gen 6:18) and with Abraham (Gen 17:9-10), of which circumcision was to be the outward sign. The biblical covenant, while having many of the elements of a contract, is not a strict contract. In a contract, if either party reneges on the deal then the other party is freed of all obligations. God, however, initiates the biblical covenant as a free gift of love. God is always faithful to the covenant and will not renege on the covenant promise even when we are unfaithful to our

---

[48]   *Ibid.,* p. 70; emphasis added.

part of the bargain. In other words, God's fidelity is not dependent on our fidelity. The covenant we want to focus on particularly is the covenant entered into by God and Moses that sprang from the great Exodus experience.

READ: Exodus 19:1-8.

In this account of the establishing of the covenant, we should note a couple of important points:

1. It is God who takes the initiative; it is God who calls; it is God who first promises, "you shall be my treasured possession out of all the peoples . . . a priestly kingdom and a holy nation." It is God who first reaches out to us, asking us to respond to this offer of love and care and salvation (Ex 19:5-6).

2. God requires that the people keep their part of the bargain. And so, "all the people answered with one voice, and said, 'All the words that the Lord has spoken we will do.'" The people agreed to the covenant and ratified it by a religious ceremony (Ex 24:3-7).

READ: Exodus 20:1-17.

The heart of the covenant is what has come to be known as the Ten Commandments; it is the Israelite side of the bargain made with God. (We shall deal with the Ten Commandments in more detail later on in the section on morality). In his teaching Jesus clearly ratified that covenant, and so the code of behaviour enjoined by the Ten Commandments is now a Christian code of behaviour.

Not all of God's requirements were given on Mt. Sinai. Over the centuries, as the people reflected on the original covenant, they began to see more clearly how they should be faithful to God. Other laws and requirements developed in the course of history. This process of developing a code of behaviour over time and as society evolves is something that is very familiar to us. For example, in the time of Christ, slavery was acceptable. Jesus only condemned it obliquely, never openly and directly. Yet in our time we have come to see it as a gross infringement of the rights of any human being and in conflict with Jesus' teaching on human dignity and freedom.

The Great Legacy of Faith Left Us by Moses

The faith of the Israelites is *our* faith; Christianity cannot escape its Jewish roots. Here are four key elements of that faith that we can and should apply to our own response to God.

1.   There Is But One God (Yahweh – He Who Is)

As we shall see, it was this aspect of the covenant that gave Israel the most trouble. Living as they did among pagan polytheistic peoples, the temptation to worship other gods, which seemed to make these peoples successful and strong, was ever present. But the covenant clearly says that God cannot be likened to "anything that is in heaven above, or that is on the earth beneath, or that is in the water under the earth" (Ex 20:4). The only exception to this is *adam* (human being) – male and female – who is created in the image and likeness of God.

And so there are some questions for us: Who, or what, are the other gods we serve apart from, and perhaps in place of, Yahweh? To which gods do we pay allegiance; what gods rule our life? Money? Power? Pleasure? Material success? Self? Sex? We must be aware of the tremendous dignity that is ours, the only creatures created in the image and likeness of God, who calls to us in love.

2. Yahweh Is a Saving God Who Enters Our History

According to the first commandment of the covenant, there is to be no more polytheism. Pagan gods were concerned with nature – the rain, the sun, movements of the earth, and so on. Yahweh, on the other hand, is concerned with people. In their writings the authors of the Bible say that Yahweh sometimes uses the powers of nature in order to be *for* the people. For example, in the Exodus Yahweh controls the power of the sea in order to rescue the people. The point is that Yahweh acts in human history, and the history of Israel is a history of God acting in the world.

Now, some questions for us. How do we look at history, particularly our own history? Do we take a faith view that tries to see how God is acting in our life, how God is concerned with our welfare? Or do we simply take a natural, scientific, psychological view of things? When there is tragedy in our life can we see God as living through the tragedy with us, helping us to derive meaning, always acting in love? Do we perhaps see God as a capricious god who causes suffering and pain when we are bad and is not much concerned with our problems?

3. Yahweh Has Taken the Initiative to Establish a Personal Relationship with His People

The mighty, the holy, the creator God has taken the initiative to enter into a covenant with the people. The Israelites are not to be God's slaves, only doing what they are told. They (and we) are God's children, who freely enter into a covenant. "Thus says the Lord: Israel is my firstborn son" (Ex 4:22). It is our choice; God will not do violence to our free will.

The notion of a covenant with God is basic to Israel's faith. Israel is formed into a community, a people. Can we see ourselves in the same way, formed into a community that is the church, in and through which we encounter the living God? Are we committed to this church, loyal to it, suffering with it, contributing to its mission to be a light to the world?

4. The Law of God Is Essential to the Covenant

The ratification of the covenant by the Israelites meant that they agreed to the conditions set down by God, that they should keep the divine law. This law is not to be seen as something that only imposes burdens and obligations and restricts personal freedom. God's law is a law of love; it is a law of divine guidance, showing us how to live in order to make a success of our life in society. In other words, God is giving us good advice for our own benefit. The demands of the law "are really a divine favour; for their intent is to make Israel a wise people (Deut 4:5-8) and to put them in contact with the will of God."[49]

Some questions for us. What is our attitude towards God's law? Do we see it as restrictive of our freedom, or beneficial to our life? Can we appreciate the laws and regulations of the church as being ultimately for our own good? Is criticism our first reaction?

Summary and Conclusion

The Old Testament forms the basis of our Christian faith. Because of this we cannot remain ignorant of its message, which is God's revelation to us. The New Testament has not supplanted or superseded the Old; the Old is the basis and root of the New.

The Old Testament is not a single book but rather a whole library of books, ranging over every aspect of the life of the Jewish people. The Jewish people reread their whole life with the eyes of faith, seeing in what we might call natural events the work of God. Also, the Old Testament was written in the light of the great covenant made through Moses. They form a record of how the people responded, or did not respond, to this covenant initiated by God. In particular, the Pentateuch (often called the Law) is revered by the Jewish people as God's divine guidance for the ordering of their lives in relation to the promises they made in the covenant.

The bedrock experience of the people arising from their miraculous experience at the Sea of Reeds is that God is a saving God, a God who is *for* them, a God who loves unconditionally. It is this basic idea of what God is like that runs through the whole tradition of the Jewish people, tradition that was put in writing in the Old Testament. The Pentateuch is most particularly a record of the traditions that were most closely associated with Moses, a figure deeply revered by the Jews as being at the foundation of their covenant and their faith. From this Mosaic faith have come important principles that apply to our own faith in the Christian era. And so, there is but *one* God, and no other shall we serve; this God

---

[49] Xavier Léon-Dufour, *Dictionary of Biblical Theology* (London: Geoffrey Chapman, 1970), p. 265.

has entered our lives and history in a particularly intimate way; this God wishes to establish a close, personal relationship with us; this God has left us guidelines on how to live so as to preserve this relationship and thus make a success of our lives.

We can conclude by repeating what was said about the Bible in the chapter on tradition. The Old Testament is as much a part of God's revelation for us as is the New Testament; God speaks to us through them both (CCC 128-130). We must honour, revere, read and pray these Scriptures, for they speak to our own needs, show how God intervenes in our life, show that God is a saving God, a God of love. The Bible may be a human book, written by human authors for human readers, but it is also God's book, given to us in love.

Reflection Questions

1. What do we mean by the "Old Testament," as distinct from the "New"?

2. What are canonical books?

3. When the Jews speak of "the Law," what do they mean?

4. In her religious education class, a certain teacher told the story of the crossing of the Sea of Reeds. Upon returning home, one of the students was asked by her mother what she had learned in religious education class that day. "Well," said the student, "the Jews were racing to the Red Sea, pursued by Pharaoh and his army. When the Jews reached the Red Sea they did not know how they would get across. But Moses had an idea, and they built a big bridge over the sea and the Jews crossed over. When the Egyptians came to the bridge Moses called out the Air Force and they bombed the bridge and the Egyptians were drowned." The astonished mother said, "Did your teacher really tell you that?" "Well, not exactly, Mom, but if I told you what she really said you'd never believe it!"

   What do the Jews (and we ourselves) believe about the crossing of the Sea of Reeds, and why is it so important in Jewish history?

5. How does the great legacy of faith left by Moses affect us Christians today?

6. "We need to free ourselves from the idea of God's law as a statute imposed upon us from without, and to substitute that of his spirit as a principle governing life from within" (William Adams Brown). Comment on this quote.

Further Reading

Anderson, Bernhard. *Understanding the Old Testament*, 4th ed. (Englewood Cliffs, NJ: Prentice-Hall Inc., 1986). This book is a standard reference on the Hebrew Scriptures. Clearly and interestingly written, it will repay study even though it is long and fairly detailed.

Boadt, Lawrence. *Reading the Old Testament: An Introduction* (New York: Paulist Press, 1984). A standard introduction to the Hebrew Scriptures, highly recommended for all introductory classes.

Charpentier, Étienne. *How to Read the Old Testament* (London: SCM Press, 1981). An excellent, simply written introduction to the Bible and the Hebrew Scriptures. Can also serve as further reading for Chapter 9.

9

THEMES IN THE HEBREW SCRIPTURES

In the last chapter, we provided an overview of the history of Israel in table form, compiled from the best biblical, historical and archeological evidence available to us. In order better to understand some of the religious themes in the Old Testament, we need to know something about the political, cultural and social background of the scriptural writings. The writers wrote in the light of the great covenant made through Moses that affected every aspect of their life. In what follows we shall say something about 1) Canaanite religion and culture, 2) the political situation, and 3) the great demand of fidelity to the covenant. But first, a short review of Israelite history.

Israelite History – A Review

The Israelites escaped the wrath of Pharaoh and were saved miraculously at the Sea of Reeds. They received the covenant from God. There followed a period of wandering around in the desert on their way to the land that God had promised them. Eventually they arrived at Mt. Nebo, on the eastern side of the Jordan river where it empties into the Dead Sea. There Moses died (Deut 34:4-6). On the western side of the Jordan at this time lay the town of Jericho. The Israelites were led across the Jordan into Jericho. The Bible relates the miraculous fall of Jericho and the triumph of the Israelites (of which speaks the beautiful Negro spiritual "Joshua Fought the Battle of Jericho") (Josh 1-6).

From Jericho the Israelites fanned out to the west and north, and there they began the slow infiltration, conquest and settlement of the land of Canaan* (modern-day Israel and Palestine). This was by no means a triumphant war campaign, as one is led to believe from reading the book of Joshua (1–12). The process went on gradually over a period of 150 to 200 years. In the early stages of the conquest, the Israelites only managed to occupy the high ridge of mountains in the centre of modern-day Israel (part of the Rift Valley system). These hills were rocky, devoid of sufficient topsoil, barren in many spots (as anyone who visits modern Israel can easily see). The fertile lower land to the west, the plain of Esdralon, which supported a rich agriculture, was probably not fully conquered till the time of King David (1000 B.C.E.).

Canaanite Religion and Culture

It often happens in history that the victorious nation imposes its culture on the defeated one. But the opposite is also true: the victors sometimes get absorbed into the culture of the vanquished. This latter was probably the case with Israel and the Canaanites. Consider the situation. The Canaanite religion, as described in the Bible, was one of worship of the Baals and their female counterparts, the Astartes (see, for example, Judg 2:13, 10:6; 1 Sam 7:4). The names are used in the plural, for there were many such gods associated with different regions. The Baals and Astartes were fertility gods concerned with the productivity of the soil and the control of climatic factors (the sun and the rain) that made for good agriculture. Sacrifice was offered to these gods; fertility rituals were enacted in the temples. We find the Israelites being specifically warned against these rituals and particularly not to give themselves up to sacred prostitution (Deut 23:17-18).

The Canaanites were successful farmers on the rich bottom land of what is modern-day Israel. The Israelites who entered the land had no experience of agriculture. For a long time (probably a couple of generations) they had been nomads in the desert, and before that they had been slaves in Egypt. The productive farming of the Canaanites was attributed to the intervention of the Baals and the Astartes, and the Israelites wondered if their God, Yahweh, could compete with the obviously successful Baals. Their persistent temptation was to give up worship of Yahweh and turn to the Baals and Astartes. The Bible is full of instances where the Israelites erected altars to worship Baal. Usually these were on mountaintops referred to in the Bible, with derision and scorn, as "the high places." Of course, such worship is a fundamental violation of the covenant: "You shall have no other gods before me" (Ex 20:3).

This is but one example of the persistent struggle of the Israelite people to keep the requirements of the Law. It is this battling with the covenant, as it were, in many other fields as well, that occupies so much of the writing in the Old Testament. In the perception of the sacred writers, the pattern goes something like this: Israel reneges on the covenant; they are "punished" by God (e.g., lose a battle); they repent; and they are received by God once again. Always the emphasis is on a God who loves and forgives.

The Political Situation

In the early years of the conquest of Canaan, Israel was not a nation in the political sense, even though in the covenant God had drawn them together as a "people." For a very long time they remained only a loose confederation of tribes – extended families named after the twelve sons of Jacob. In time, these tribes came to occupy specific parts of the conquered land. So, for example, the tribes of Judah and Benjamin occupied the area around Jerusalem. At this period the people were ruled over by a succession of judges. These were not judges in our legal sense; rather, they were charismatic leaders who rose to lead the various tribes in times of war and then carried on as tribal heads. Their exploits are written of in the Book of Judges. The last, and one of the greatest of the judges, was Samuel. It was during Samuel's tenure that Israel decided to become a kingdom.

As time went on, and the Israelites settled more and more of the land, they became envious of the surrounding peoples who were ruled by kings. Why this envy? What does a king do for the people? First, the king is a visible sign of unity that makes for a closer-knit group and therefore a stronger group. Second, while formerly Israel was a loose confederation of tribes, with a king they saw themselves becoming a nation in the true sense, a nation like any of the other peoples of the region. The king would lead them in war and fight their battles for them. Third, the king, with a court, would give the nation a certain prestige. Now there would be an elite to admire (an aspect of social life that is still with us) and, in their eyes and the eyes of other peoples, they would become more important in the reflected glory of the king.

The people asked Samuel to anoint someone as king. Samuel was a prophet and, as the Bible tells it, consulted with God as to whether he should give in to the people's request. God instructed him to anoint Saul as the first king of Israel (see 1 Sam 10:1 ff). Saul was followed by David, and then David's son Solomon. But kingship, as God had predicted, was a mixed blessing. Together with certain advantages (Israel achieved its greatest political hegemony under kings David and Solomon) came many abuses, and these provide fertile ground for the strictures of the prophets.

Fidelity to the Covenant

The covenant that God made with the people through Moses is central to the whole of Jewish history (CCC 62). In fact, one could say that to follow the history of the Israelite people is to follow a history of the covenant. The major theme in all the writings in the Old Testament is the working out of the covenant in the lives of the Israelite people. Theirs is a story looked at through the eyes of faith, a story that details their relationship with God in all aspects of their life. It is a deeply religious story. God is understood to be working in and through the political fortunes, the economic progress, the social life and the personal relationships of the people. What God requires above all is fidelity to the covenant. God's fidelity never wavers, God's love is ever constant. What God says is this: I have been, and will be, faithful to my promises; please keep your side of the bargain, as you promised (see Ex 24:3-7).

The classic biblical tale of fidelity and sincerity is the story of Ruth, proposed as a paradigm of fidelity to the covenant. The book of Ruth is a literary masterpiece. The story is crafted with simplicity and beauty in the best storytelling fashion and conveys a deep and purposeful religious message. We cannot relate the whole story here, but the book is not long and should be read in its entirety.

The fidelity of Ruth is a paradigm of the fidelity that God requires in the covenant. The story also shows how God cares for those who love and trust him and are faithful to him. God is intimately concerned with and acts through every aspect of human life, even the simple family life of very ordinary people such as Ruth.

The Bible is often lyrical in its use of images to portray God's love and fidelity. The Song of Songs, for example, is a love poem, full of the wild exaggerations of two people madly in love. It is the love story of God and his people written in openly sexual language. It is but a small indication of the lengths to which God will go to show his love for us. Scripture commentators have always seen this poem as an image of God's love for the church.

The Bible frequently compares the covenant to a marriage (e.g., Ezek 16:1-63). The greatest sin in marriage is infidelity. When Israel is unfaithful to the requirements of the covenant (such as the worship of the one true God), she is accused of being a harlot, a prostitute who has given herself away to another. Thus, for example, speaks the prophet Jeremiah: "The Lord said to me in the days of King Josiah: Have you seen what she did, that faithless one, Israel, how she went up on every high hill and under every green tree, and played the whore there?" (Jer 3:6). (The high places – hills and mountain tops – were always associated with the worship of false gods.)

With this background, let us now say something about the prophets.

The Prophets

The story of prophecy and the background to the development of prophecy as a mode of revelation in the history of Israel is a complicated one. Any kind of detailed treatment is well beyond the scope of this book. However, writings about the prophets, and by the prophets themselves, occupy a large portion of the Hebrew Scriptures and they cannot be ignored. The importance of the biblical prophets for us today is that they address problems concerning the fidelity of Israel to the covenant which are still our problems more than two millennia later. Therefore, they speak to us in the same way they spoke to the people of their time. The effects of original sin are very much still with us – the more things change, the more they remain the same! The best we can do here is to select but a few of the major themes of prophecy in the Old Testament. We shall try to indicate how much they still apply to our present-day life and how, therefore, God still speaks to us through the biblical prophets. As one author put it, the Bible lives; God's message to us has not changed.

Prophecy

We have already seen in the chapter on revelation that the major work of prophecy is to remind us of God's message (CCC 64). The prophets speak on behalf of God. The prophet interprets the signs of the times in human life (persons and events) and indicates what God is saying to us through those signs. Much of the Bible is, in fact, a prophetic interpretation of the history of the Jewish people. It carries a religious message, a message that God wants us to hear. Looked at from another point of view, we can say that the work of the prophet is to inform, and form, the conscience of the people, to call them back to God when they have strayed from God's will. Therefore, what prophecy does is to criticize the present. It offers a critique of what is wrong with our present life, how we have taken the selfish road of our own will and desires rather than the one God wants from us. In other words, prophecy calls us to make a decision for the future, to change our life; it calls us to conversion.*

We have noted that foretelling the future is incidental to prophecy; nevertheless, the future is a factor in prophecy. Thus, the prophet may indicate to us what will happen if we do not seek the opportunity to change. In this sense prophecy may be said to predict the future. It is much the same, for example, as when a doctor makes a prediction that a patient has only a short time to live. The doctor's purpose is not prediction (which, we know from experience, may be notoriously inaccurate), nor is the doctor's purpose to frighten the patient. The doctor's purpose is to allow the patient realistically to assess his or her position and to make the patient's last days more precious and serious. In the same way, God is calling to us to change in the light of his great redemptive purpose.

Let us now take a look at a few of the major themes of prophecy in the Hebrew Scriptures. As we go through these themes, we shall see how well they apply to our present-day situation. The ancient prophets still speak to us today, they bring God's message to us in our time. How well do we listen?

Some Major Themes of Old Testament Prophecy

1.   The Holiness and Greatness of God

As we have seen, one of the perennial temptations for the Israelite people was idolatry, the worship of false gods. It would seem that they had a very tenuous hold on the first of the Ten Commandments, especially if worship of false gods promised some kind of material benefit.

The prophets are dismayed at this behaviour. They continually stress the holiness, the greatness and the uniqueness of God.[50] Consider Isaiah's vision of the majesty and the splendour of God:

In the year that King Uzziah died, I saw the Lord sitting on a throne, high and lofty; and the hem of his robe filled the temple. Seraphs were in attendance above him; each had six wings: with two they covered their faces, and with two they covered their feet, and with two they flew. And one called to another and said: "Holy, holy, holy is the Lord of hosts; the whole earth is full of his glory." (Isa 6:1-3)

Often the prophets interpret tragedies that befell Israel as punishment for their infidelity to the covenant.[51]

Because of their innate sense of the holiness of God, the prophets speak out against formalism in worship. Formalism means going through the outward exercise of worship without the corresponding dispositions of heart (i.e., practising the externals of religion without the internal disposition of love and obedience).

The prophet Amos lashes out against the Israelites for their formalistic worship. They openly worshipped Yahweh but were filled with hypocrisy because they still practised injustice to others: "[God says] I hate, I despise your festivals, and I take no delight in your solemn assemblies. . . . But let justice roll down like waters, and righteousness like an ever-flowing stream" (Am 5:21-26).

2. *Justice – Oppression of the Poor and the Dispossessed*

Under kings David and Solomon, Israel became a relatively wealthy and powerful nation. The ethos that developed in Israel at this time was simply carried on when the country was divided upon the death of Solomon (922 B.C.E.), which is why the prophets in the Northern Kingdom and those in the Southern often have substantially the same message. Often it is a message directed against the injustices that seem to be endemic in an affluent society. Here are a few examples:

a)   Development of a government bureaucracy with all its attendant evils that we know so well today – influence-peddling, pork-barrelling, favouritism, bribery. Unbridled wealth-seeking almost inevitably breeds injustice, and it is the poor who get hurt. In forceful language the prophet Micah goes after the leaders, who should be giving good example but who are steeped in injustice. (The words are spoken as though God were saying them.)

---

[50]   For the Catechism's treatment of the holiness of God see CCC 2807-2809.
[51]   We should note that God does not punish us directly. If we understand some event as punishment, then it is not vindictive but rather corrective. This question will be more fully dealt with in a subsequent chapter.

And I said: Listen, you heads of Jacob and rulers of the house of Israel! Should you not know justice? – you who hate the good and love the evil, who tear the skin off my people, and the flesh off their bones; . . . Then they will cry to the Lord, but he will not answer them; he will hide his face from them at that time, because they have acted wickedly. Thus says the Lord concerning the prophets who lead my people astray, who cry "Peace" when they have something to eat, but declare war against those who put nothing into their mouths. (Mic 3:1-5)

And the prophet Amos is no less pointed:

Hear this, you that trample on the needy, and bring to ruin the poor of the land, saying, "When will the new moon be over so that we may sell grain; and the sabbath, so that we may offer wheat for sale? We will make the ephah small and the shekel great, and practise deceit with false balances, buying the poor for silver and the needy for a pair of sandals, and selling the sweepings of the wheat. (Amos 8:4-6; see also Amos 2:6-8; 5:7, 10-12)

b) Israel always had a system of fairly even land distribution, for the land had been promised by God to all the people. Now, as some became richer they were able to acquire the land of the less well off, enslaving them as tenants on their own land – the birth of the rich landowner and the absentee landlord.

Hence the prophet Isaiah's complains:

For the vineyard of the Lord of hosts is the house of Israel, and the people of Judah are his pleasant planting; he expected justice, but saw bloodshed; righteousness, but heard a cry! Ah, you who join house to house, who add field to field, until there is room for no one but you, and you are left to live alone in the midst of the land! The Lord of hosts has sworn in my hearing: Surely many houses shall be desolate, large and beautiful houses, without inhabitant. (Isa 5:7-9)

The huge problem of uneven land distribution is still very much with us (especially in the developing world), a source of much misery and hardship to the poor. The prophets call for justice; so should we.

c) In order to satisfy his huge thirst for grandeur, Solomon undertook many expensive building projects. The opulence of his own personal house is described in 1 Kings 7:1-8. For these building projects, Solomon used slave labour drawn from the peoples who had been conquered by Israel (1 Kings 9:15-20). This prescription went directly against the very thing that the Lord had freed the Israelites from: namely, their days of slavery in Egypt.

Forms of slavery still exist in many parts of the world today, which is another aspect of the deep injustice the prophets condemn. How far do we ourselves tend to enslave others to achieve our own selfish ends? Even today it is not as fanciful as it sounds.

There are many evils that are endemic to an abuse of the capitalist system – greed, a large gap between rich and poor, unjust trading practices, oppressors and oppressed. This is not to say that the socialist system is free of all evil; it too is full of injustices. The crime of Israel (and surely our crime, too) is that they were willing to sacrifice fellow Israelites for material gain. The possibility of money and power makes us disregard the human rights of others. These evils fly directly in the face of the covenant. We are not slaves but free people. There are no preferences with God. Justice and love for one another are the true marks of the people of God. The prophets call for repentance and a return to the true ideals of the covenant.

3.   Trust and Fidelity

The prophets constantly call on the people to have trust in God; God will look after them because he has promised to, and God is always faithful to his promises. From the very first, the history of Israel was a shameful story of betrayal of God's love. The prophets call for a return to steadfast love and kindness, trust and fidelity. God is always faithful; God will not let his people go, even in face of their fickleness and harlotry. Thus the prophet Hosea laments that though God is full of fidelity and loving compassion, the people do not respond.

> Hear the word of the Lord, O people of Israel; for the Lord has an indictment against the inhabitants of the land. There is no faithfulness or loyalty, and no knowledge of God in the land. Swearing, lying, and murder, and stealing and adultery break out; bloodshed follows bloodshed. (Hos 4:1-2)

Hosea complains that there is no knowledge of God. Clearly he is not referring to mere cognitive knowledge; rather, he is referring to relationship, to the deep experience of and response to God in the heart, a real in-depth knowing with one's whole being.

God is revealed as freely giving a total love and fidelity, not because of any legal obligation but out of complete goodness, graciousness and generosity. As God speaks to us through the prophet Hosea, his words are full of tenderness, compassion, forgiveness and deep pathos.

> How can I give you up, Ephraim? How can I hand you over, O Israel? How can I make you like Admah? How can I treat you like Zeboiim? My heart recoils within me; my compassion grows warm and tender. I will not execute my fierce anger; I will not again destroy Ephraim; for I am God and no mortal, the Holy One in your midst, and I will not come in wrath. (Hos 11:8-9)

The Hebrew word used to describe God's love is *hésed*. It is a difficult word to translate, but what it means is the faithfulness and the loyalty that bind two parties together in a true relationship of love and self-giving. It could aptly be used of the ideal marriage relationship. God has *hésed* for us; he begs us to have the same for him. And through the prophet, God pleads with us: "For I desire steadfast love [*hésed*] and not sacrifice, the knowledge of God rather than burnt offerings" (Hos 6:6). (The New Testament has a strong echo of Hosea's words as Jesus indicts the hypocrisy of the Pharisees: "Go and learn what this means, 'I desire mercy, not sacrifice.' For I have come to call not the righteous but sinners" Mt 9:13. And again, "But if you had known what this means, 'I desire mercy and not sacrifice,' you would not have condemned the guilt-less" Mt 12:7.)

Nowhere are these two themes of justice and the love and fidelity that God asks of us better summarized than in the prophet Micah. The prophet presents a beautiful, plaintive, heart-rending plea by God to the people of Israel (and to us). It seems that God is almost begging us to listen and respond.

> *Hear what the Lord says: . . . "O my people, what have I done to you? In what have I wearied you? Answer me! For I brought you up from the land of Egypt, and redeemed you from the house of slavery; and I sent before you Moses, Aaron, and Miriam." . . . He has told you, O mortal, what is good; and what does the Lord require of you but to do justice, and to love kindness, and to walk humbly with your God? (Mic 6:1-8)*

"To do justice" – a plea not only to act justly and with sincerity and integrity in our own lives but also to help to eradicate injustice in all its forms, injustice which most injures those who are poor and powerless.

"To love kindness" – to reach out to others, to spend ourselves in the service of others, to "do" our faith.

"To walk humbly with your God" – to recognize God, who is always with us, to accept in our hearts that this God loves us, to trust our God and to live humbly in this faith and trust.[52]

Surely this must be one of the most beautiful and moving of all revelations of what God is for us. The God of power, the God who created us, the God who sustains us in being, is the one who seeks us, who begs us to love him, who pleads with us to trust, to be faithful, to come back when we stray. God never abandons us; God is always faithful. How tremendously touching! How tremen-

---

[52]   This passage from Micah is beautifully linked to religious education in Walter Brueggemann, Sharon Parks and Thomas Groome, *To Act Justly, Love Tenderly, Walk Humbly* (New York: Paulist Press, 1986).

dously humbling! How tremendously consoling and inviting! How shall we respond?

4.   *Messianism*

The word "Messiah" means "anointed," "specially chosen," "specially designated." "Anointed" means anointed with oil, a ceremony reserved for the crowning of kings and the installation of the high priest. Such a person is "set apart," viewed as specially designated by God. The Greek form of the Hebrew word is *Christos*, from which we get the English "Christ."[53]

The coming of a Messiah was a deep and constant theme of the prophets. These prophecies are of great importance because of our Christian faith that Jesus is the promised Messiah of God – God's specially chosen one.[54] At the time of Jesus, the hope for a Messiah who would deliver the people from the misery of colonial and pagan exploitation was a strong one. In a sense we may say that the whole of the Old Testament is messianic, in that it looks forward to the coming of Christ (CCC 711-716). The whole Old Testament is a preparation for the New. But we need to say more than that.

As we have mentioned, the history of Israel as perceived by the biblical writers is one that revolves around the theme of Israel as a kingdom. Specifically, it revolves around King David, for it was under him that Israel became united as a nation and that it achieved its greatest hegemony. True enough, as the Israelites understood it, this was the work of God but was accomplished through the king. The king, therefore, was seen as God's instrument for fulfilling his promises to make Israel a great nation.

Out of the history and experience of kingship arose the notion of a messianic kingdom. It would be a kingdom that God would use to accomplish his promises. Such a kingdom would be one of peace and prosperity, a kingdom in which God's law would be respected and followed, a kingdom in which the covenant would be faithfully kept; all enmity would disappear and all living things would dwell in perfect harmony on earth. The prophet Isaiah provides us with an idyllic view of this kingdom:

> *The wolf shall live with the lamb, the leopard shall lie down with the kid, the calf and the lion and the fatling together, and a little child shall lead them. The cow and the bear shall graze, their young shall lie down together; and the lion shall eat straw like the ox. The nursing child shall play over the hole of the asp, and the weaned child shall put its hand on the adder's den. They*

---

[53]   The meaning and significance of anointing are dealt with in CCC 695.

[54]   CCC 840 notes that in many ways the expectation of a Messiah in the New covenant is similar to that in the Old. Just as the Jewish people awaited the arrival of the Messiah, we now await the return of the Messiah who died and rose from the dead.

will not hurt or destroy on all my holy mountain; for the earth will be full of the knowledge of the Lord as the waters cover the sea. (Isa 11:6-9)

That the kingdom of God has arrived and therefore we live in the "last times" is one of the major themes of the preaching of Jesus.

Over a number of years, the kingdom of David was divided and finally destroyed. How would the reality of a messianic kingdom be accomplished now? Here we have a clash of faith and experience. Israelite faith in the messianic kingdom remained strong, but the inability of the Davidic line to establish this kingdom was painfully evident. Out of this clash is born a new faith, a new way of looking at things. A new king would come, born of the line of David, filled with the power of God, who would personally bring about the fulfilment of God's promises. (The New Testament takes pains to point out that Jesus is descended from King David.) The prophets Jeremiah and Ezekiel, who flourished at the time of the final dissolution of the Davidic kingdom (586 B.C.E.), are particularly associated with this new approach. (For example, see: Jer 23:1-8.)

As the years and centuries went by, Israel continued to be under the domination of other nations (see the historical table in the previous chapter). Faith in a personal messiah gradually became loaded with political overtones. The messiah came to be understood as some sort of militaristic political leader who would restore the fortunes of Israel, much as they had known in the time of David and Solomon. It was this attitude that made it most difficult for the Jewish leaders to understand that Jesus was the promised Messiah of God.

Conclusion: Jesus Christ – the Messiah

The Catechism deals extensively with this topic (CCC 436-440, 528-529, 535, 540, 590, 674). What follows is but a summary of some of the more important points. The authors of the New Testament understand Jesus to be the promised Messiah of God, and that also is our faith. In him all the messianic prophecies are fulfilled.

1. Jesus comes from the Davidic line.

2. Jesus admits that he is a king, though not a political king. He is king over the hearts and minds of those who believe in him and accept him as Saviour.

3. The New Testament writers, particularly the writer of the Gospel of Matthew, which was written for a newly converted Hebrew community, frequently indicate how Jesus is the fulfilment of the Old Testament prophecies.

4. One of the prophetic characteristics of the messianic kingdom was peace among nations, the absence of enmity. Jesus has given us the wherewithal to

achieve "a peace that the world cannot give," an interior peace, peace of mind and heart, peace of conscience, which can be achieved even amid the most disturbing external circumstances.

5.   Israel expected that the reign of God would extend over all the earth, that the world would be filled with "the knowledge of God." We Christians believe that the church is the presence of Jesus on earth and that the church is bent on extending the reign of God over all the earth. "And he said to them, 'Go into all the world and proclaim the good news to the whole creation. The one who believes and is baptized will be saved; but the one who does not believe will be condemned'" (Mk 16:15-16).

6.   The kingdom of God would be one in which there would be a renewed relationship between God and the people, a renewal of the covenant: "I shall be your God and you shall be my people." Jesus calls us to a renewed relationship with God in and through him. How can we help to bring about the messianic age? By living the gospel message. If we wonder why the messianic age still seems far away, we should pay attention to the words of that great Englishman G. K. Chesterton: "Christianity has not failed; it has just not been tried"!

Reflection Questions

1.   Briefly describe the effect Canaanite religion had on the Israelites who came into the land of Canaan.

2.   Why did Israel choose kingship as a form of government? What effect did that choice have on the recording of Israelite tradition in the Bible?

3.   What does it mean to say that the biblical story of the Israelites is a story told through the eyes of faith?

4.   A prophet once came to a city to convert its inhabitants. At first the people listened, but they gradually drifted away until no one listened to the prophet when he spoke. One day a traveller said to him, "Why do you go on preaching?" "In the beginning I had hoped to change these people," said the prophet. "If I still shout it is only to prevent them from changing me."[55]

     What does this story say about prophets, prophecy, and ourselves?

5.   Explain the meaning of *hésed* as exemplifying God's relationship to us and our relationships to one another.

6.   What is the meaning of messiah? Why is Jesus called the Messiah?

---

[55]   Adapted from Anthony de Mello, S.J., *The Song of the Bird* (New York: Doubleday, Image Books, 1981).

Further Reading

Breuggemann, Walter, Sharon Parks, and Thomas Groome. *To Act Justly, Love Tenderly, Walk Humbly* (Mahwah, NJ: Paulist Press, 1986). A short, very readable little volume on the famous passage from Micah specially applied to religious educators.

La Sor, William, David Hubbard, and William Bush. *Old Testament Survey: The Message, Form and Background of the Old Testament* (Grand Rapids, MI: Eerdmans, 1987). A somewhat detailed treatment of important facts and themes in the Hebrew Scriptures. A useful reference.

10

THE CHRISTIAN SCRIPTURES: NEW TESTAMENT

As we have seen, the Jewish people expected a Messiah, the specially anointed one of God, who would bring about the reign of God on earth and restore the covenant and the political fortunes of Israel. (Modern-day Jews still are waiting for the advent of the Messiah.) The early followers of Jesus, who were all Jews, saw him as the promised Messiah for, after all, had not all the ancient prophecies of the Old Testament been fulfilled in him? As well as saying so himself (Mt 4:17), had he not given clear evidence by his life and work that the kingdom of God was at hand? And so, one of the most important factors in the development of the New Testament is that the writers understood Jesus to be the promised Messiah. Therefore, they interpreted his life in terms of the revelation of the Messiah in the Old Testament. Throughout the New Testament writings, reference is made to the fact that Jesus was "fulfilling" the prophecies and promises made about the Messiah in the Old Testament. In fact, Jesus cannot be understood except in the light of what went before in Jewish history and of the Jewish expectation of a Messiah. The Old Testament is the base and foundation of the New (CCC 128-130).

There are some references to Jesus in the secular history of the time, for example in the writings of the Latin historian Tacitus and the Jewish historian Josephus. But our real knowledge of Jesus, his life and his teaching, comes mainly from the four gospels and some other works of the New Testament. In order to understand Jesus and his message, it is essential that we understand how these writings of the New Testament came into being.

The Formation of the Christian Scriptures

Let us first identify some very basic elements, or realities, which underlie everything written in the books.

First Reality: The Resurrection

The resurrection of Jesus from the dead is the key event in our understanding of the New Testament writings. Faith in the resurrection is essential to

Christian life, to Tradition. The Christian life cannot be understood without faith in the resurrection (CCC 651). St. Paul leaves us in no doubt on this point :

> *If there is no resurrection of the dead, then Christ has not been raised; and if Christ has not been raised, then our proclamation has been in vain and your faith has been in vain. If Christ has not been raised, your faith is futile and you are still in your sins. If for this life only we have hoped in Christ, we are of all people most to be pitied. (1 Cor 15:13, 17, 19)*

Not only is there a statement here that Jesus was raised from the dead, but a clear indication that we too shall rise from the dead if we are faithful to him.

What Happened?

Jesus died a criminal's death on a cross and was buried in a tomb. We are told that all his chosen apostles deserted him in his last hours, with the exception of the "beloved disciple," traditionally identified as St. John. When Jesus was apprehended in the Garden of Olives the apostles fled in fear, undoubtedly thinking that the authorities would come after them next. Tragically, even after living with him for three years, they had badly misunderstood the true meaning of his mission. Their understanding of a Messiah was clouded by the political ideal, current at the time, that the Messiah would "restore the kingdom to Israel" (Acts 1:6), and make Israel as politically great as it was under King David and King Solomon. Jesus' death shattered their hopes; it was a crushing defeat. In fear and trembling they locked themselves in a room in the city.

In this locked room they had an experience of Jesus that convinced them he was still alive, and therefore, that he had risen from the dead. The account of this experience is given in all the gospels – Matthew 28, Mark 16, Luke 24, John 20 and 21. These accounts should be read. But scholars warn us that as with the crossing of the Sea of Reeds in the book of Exodus, the account of the resurrection is couched in a faith-language that defies scientific analysis. We are warned not to fall into the error of "over-belief," that is, a fundamentalist* interpretation of every fact related by the gospels.[56] Nevertheless, the modern reader will inevitably ask: How exactly did the resurrection take place? We really cannot answer this question unless we go into the realm of speculation. We should not concern ourselves with trying to solve the mystery of how exactly the resurrection took place. In this regard, Charpentier gives us some timely advice. "It is useless and impossible," he says, "to imagine how the resurrection took place. The only certainty the believer can have is to hold on to two things: Jesus is risen

---

[56]   See Gerald O'Collins, S.J., *What Are They Saying about the Resurrection?* (New York: Paulist Press, 1978), pp. 46 ff.

and glorified and we shall be with him."[57] What is certainly crucial, however, is this: just as faith in the Reed Sea salvation is the basis for understanding the Old Testament, so also faith in the resurrection is the basis for understanding the New Testament.

There is no doubt that the apostles had an actual experience of Jesus: it was not mere fantasy, nor an overactive imagination, nor a hallucination. They experienced him "in the body," a body which was his but not quite the same as the body they knew had died on the cross. Let us be very careful here – we should on no account confuse resurrection with resuscitation. Resuscitation means the mere revival of someone who was dead, such as Lazarus (Jn 11:17 ff.) or the son of the widow of Naim (Lk 7:12 ff.). It means a return to the same body they had before death. But Jesus rose to a new and different life, a life of which we can have little or no experience. The apostles understood Jesus to be alive, but transformed into a new mode of existence, an existence that transcends and is different from the former mode but is continuous with it. Jesus had conquered death (CCC 645-646).

This experience completely transformed the lives of the apostles. They began to reflect on the life of Jesus from a totally new perspective. As a result of memory, reflection and prayer, they came to realize that this man Jesus was different – not just a charismatic figure but someone in whom the power and presence of God had been expressed as never before. They reinterpreted his life in the light of this new and stunning eye-opener. Incidents in his life that before had seemed rather prosaic and ordinary now took on a new meaning when understood as part of the life of God's chosen one.

Jesus was raised from the dead by the power of God, for only God can conquer death and give new life. How does this supreme event fit into our lives? What does the resurrection mean for us?[58]

1.   *Jesus' resurrection from the dead is a statement by God that the effects of sin have been conquered.*

Suffering and death, we are told in the Bible, are the result of sin. Jesus conquered both, but it doesn't mean that now we cannot sin, or suffer, or that we won't die. Rather it means that now we have the help of God's power and presence to deal with these realities and to overcome them. As St. Paul reminds

---

[57]   Étienne Charpentier, *How to Read the New Testament* (London: SCM Press Ltd., 1982), p. 43; see also CCC 647.

[58]   CCC 651-655 makes the following further points about the effects of the resurrection. (1) It is a confirmation of Christ's works and teachings. (2) The truth of Jesus' divinity is confirmed by it. (3) By it Jesus opens to us the way to new life, a life that reinstates us in God's grace and brings about our adoption as God's sons and daughters.

us, sin is the "sting" of death (1 Cor 15:56); it is our guilty conscience that makes us fear death. Freed from that burden of guilt by the power of Christ's resurrection, death will hold no terror for us. We are no longer slaves to sin, we are no longer trapped in fear by suffering and death; we can rise above sin and death to a new life. This is a tremendously liberating experience.

2. *Jesus risen from the dead, Jesus alive, means that he is continually present with us.*

"And remember," Jesus said to his apostles, "I am with you always, to the end of the age" (Mt 28:20). Jesus is our friend and companion throughout life, someone who shares our human nature, someone who knows the meaning of suffering, someone who loves and understands us. Jesus is God with us – Emmanuel – in every aspect of our life. Again, this a very consoling and liberating experience.

3. *The resurrection transforms our understanding of human life.*

Human life has meaning and dignity; human life is worthwhile. If we live according to the teachings of Jesus, we shall experience the effects of the kingdom he came to bring – justice, love, peace, liberation from evil and the slavery of sin. But more than this, God's salvation, given to us in Jesus, is continued and completed in and through our working and living in the world. We are the church, and it is through us that Jesus continues his work in the world.

4. *We can expect to share in this resurrection, to rise to a new and better life.*

As we have seen, St. Paul leaves us in no doubt that there is a resurrection from the dead. It is crystal clear from our own experience that our human desires and aspirations are never perfectly fulfilled in this life. No joy or happiness ever totally satisfies us, for we experience them as transitory, ephemeral. Because Jesus was raised from the dead, we are filled with hope that we shall experience this fulfillment after death.

This is the basic faith in the resurrection that transformed the lives of the first apostles, the first believers in Jesus. It is because they believed that we believe. We were not there, but we believe their testimony to the resurrection. It is a belief that has been the bedrock of Christian faith from its inception, a belief that has never varied down through the centuries.

Second Reality: Christian Scriptures Are Rooted in the Hebrew Scriptures

We can only understand the New Testament writings if we understand that they were written in the light of what went before, that is, the Old Testament writings that were accepted by all religious Jews. The apostles, as good Jews, were steeped in the idea of the coming of a Messiah, and Jesus seemed to fulfill all the messianic promises. It was important for them, in their early preaching to mainly Jewish audiences, to point out that Jesus was indeed the fulfillment of what the Scriptures had spoken about; the messianic age had indeed arrived. And here we have a most important principle of scriptural interpretation: if we have difficulty understanding what the New Testament writings mean, we must go back to the Old Testament. As the Catechism reminds us, "The New Testament has to be read in the light of the Old. . . . As an old saying [from St. Augustine] puts it, the New Testament lies hidden in the Old and the Old Testament is unveiled in the New'" (CCC 129). And again, "The unity of the two Testaments proceeds from the unity of God's plan and his Revelation. The Old Testament prepares for the New and the New Testament fulfills the Old; the two shed light on each other; both are true Word of God" (CCC 140).

Third Reality: The Influence of the Early Christian Communities

From the very beginning, the first converts to Christianity formed themselves into small groups, or communities, after the example of the apostles and close followers of Jesus. Some aspects of the birthing and teething pains of these early communities are related in the Acts of the Apostles, and are well worth reading. It was in these early communities that the memories of Jesus were most specially preserved. How do we know that the traditions were faithfully preserved? How do we know that what we have today are authentic presentations of the memories of Jesus from the earliest times? In his book *The Making of the Bible*, William Barclay points out that stories about Jesus became stereotyped because they were constantly repeated in the communities and were used for preaching and teaching. In fact, a community is the best place to preserve unvarying memories. We have only to recall how children always seem to want the same story read in exactly the same way, the way they learned it first. Parents reading stories to their children have often been surprised when they try to abbreviate a story or change it. "No, Mom, that's wrong!" they cry, or "You left out part of it." Barclay quotes F.C. Grant as follows:

> This has most important consequences. It means that the Gospels are in fact the possession of the church; it means that they embody a social tradition, which was the common property of all the churches, and which did not rest on the recollections of a few individuals. . . . The memories of a few individuals might be mistaken – since human recollection is notoriously fallible – but the testimony of a group, even if anonymous, is more likely to have been verified, criticized, supported, culled, and selected during the first generation of early church evangelism.[59]

---

[59]   William Barclay, *The Making of the Bible* (Edinburgh: St. Andrew Press, 1979), pp. 51-54.

The gospels, therefore, developed out of the early Christian communities. They were influenced by the expressions of faith, the meditations, the prayers, the desires and aspirations, the myths*[60] and the recollections of these communities.

Having explained some general matters concerning the Christian Scriptures, now let us take a look at the books themselves.

The New Testament

As is the case with the Old Testament, the New Testament is not a single book but a collection of books and letters: 27 in all. Take out your Bible and look at the table of contents, where these books are listed, and use it with the table provided.

The books are:

1. **The Four Gospels**: Matthew, Mark, Luke and John. The word gospel* means "good news." They are concerned with the story of Jesus and the good news of salvation offered by him.

2. **The Acts of the Apostles**: the second volume written by Luke. It comprises a history of the early church, with special reference to the missionary journeys of Paul, whose disciple Luke was.

3. **The Pauline Epistles (Letters)**: There are 13 letters attributed to St. Paul, but by examining the texts scholars are certain that he did not personally write all of them. The letters were written to the early churches that Paul founded. We may divide them as follows:

    a) **Genuine Writings of Paul**: 1 Thessalonians, Galatians, Philippians, 1 and 2 Corinthians, Romans, Philemon.

    b) **Probably Not Genuine Writings of Paul** (probably written by disciples but imbued with Pauline teaching): 2 Thessalonians, Colossians, Ephesians.

    c) **Not Written by Paul**: Titus, 1 and 2 Timothy.

These letters are not listed in chronological order in modern editions of the Bible. Almost certainly, the earliest of the letters was 1 Thessalonians. Written between 50 and 55 C.E., it is the earliest written document in the Christian

---

[60] It is important to understand the proper meaning of myth. Too often we tend to take myth as meaning "not true," "pure imagination," or suchlike. In fact, myth means an attempt by us humans to express in human language something which is essentially beyond our present understanding (such as the transcendent) but which we experience as true deep within ourselves. That Jesus, and some incidents in his life, were beyond the full understanding of the early communities should come as no surprise. In situations like this, we tend to create myths so that we can live with our non-comprehension, making meaning out of things that seem to have no obvious meaning.

Scriptures. The other letters were written by Paul before his death in Rome in 64 C.E. Scholars vary widely in their opinions of when the other letters were written, although they were almost certainly written before 150 C.E.

4. **The Letter to the Hebrews**: author unknown.

5. **Seven Letters to All Christians**: one by James, two by Peter, three by John, one by Jude. Opinions as to date of writing again vary widely from about 60 C.E. to early in the second century.

6. **The Book of Revelation (Apocalypse)**: Apocalypse* means extraordinary, cataclysmic, mystical revelation not normally seen or heard by human beings. It is a visionary book, a book most difficult to interpret. The opening verse refers to John as the author, but scholars are not convinced that the John referred to is the apostle John, the author of the gospel. The book dates from the end of the first century.

The New Covenant

At the Last Supper with his disciples, Jesus proclaimed a new covenant,* a new agreement between ourselves and God which Jesus had come to announce and initiate. He took the cup of wine and said, "This cup which is poured out for you is the new covenant in my blood" (Lk 22:20; Mt 26:28; Mk 14:24). As we have already noted, it is impossible to understand the Jewish relationship to God unless we understand the central place the covenant had in their thinking, their traditions and their way of life. We have already dealt with the fact that Jesus does not abrogate the old covenant made through Moses; rather he enhances it and fulfills it. God's promises to the Israelites still stand, but now God has come directly to us in Jesus, not through intermediaries such as Moses. "Do not think that I have come to abolish the law or the prophets; I have come not to abolish but to fulfill" (Mt 5:17). God renews the old agreement but proposes a new and enhanced way of life that is a completion of the old way; we call this the Christian way. The old covenant was sealed and signed in the blood of animals (Ex 24: 5 ff.); the new covenant is sealed and signed in the blood of Christ.

The book of the new covenant, containing Jesus' message and promises, is what we call the New Testament, the second part of the Bible. Let us now see how this book came to be written.

The First Century		
Roman and Jewish History	**Christian History**	**History of New Testament Writings**
Emperor Augustus	5 B.C.E. Birth of Jesus	
4 B.C.E. Death of Herod the Great		
14 C.E. Emperor Tiberius		
	c. 27/28 Jesus begins public ministry	
	c. 30 Death of Jesus	
	c. 33 Conversion of St. Paul	
37 Emperor Caligula		
41 Emperor Claudius		Early Christian communities
49 Claudius expels Jews and Christians from Rome		
54 Emperor Nero	Christian persecution	Paul's letters written
	Paul imprisoned in Rome	
64 Great fire of Rome		
66–70 Jewish rebellion		
70 Emperor Vespasian	Destruction of Jerusalem	Mark's Gospel written
81 Emperor Domitian		Matthew's Gospel written Luke's Gospel and Acts of theApostles written
96 Domitian persecution	Severe persecution of Christians	John's Gospel and Book of Revelation written

The First Century: The Emergence of the New Testament

As we have already indicated, the books of the New Testament emerged over a period of time. The following schema will help us to understand the steps in this process and so serve as a basis for better understanding the Good News of Jesus Christ.[61]

---

[61]   Not all writers follow the schema given here, though they deal substantially with the same stages. For alternate arrangements, see CCC 126; Leonard Foley, "How the Gospels Were Written" in *Catholic Update* (Cincinnati, OH: St. Anthony Messenger Press, 1983); Thomas Zanzig, *Jesus is Lord* (Winona, MI: St. Mary's Press, 1982); Donald Senior, C.P., *Jesus: A Gospel Portrait* (Dayton, OH: Pflaum Press, 1981). In the schema presented here we take for granted what some writers prefer to call the "first stage," namely, the life and teaching of Christ himself. It is from his life and words that the Christian Scriptures originate and on which they depend.

Stage 1: The Development of an Oral Tradition

An oral tradition about Jesus began to emerge after the resurrection, as the disciples proclaimed and celebrated their faith in early community settings.

a) Proclamation

The disciples of Jesus who had experienced the resurrected Christ had a tremendous desire and urge to share this experience with others. From the start, they took seriously Jesus' command to preach the gospel to everyone (Mk 16:15).

At first their preaching was very simple: they proclaimed the Lord Jesus. The English word "proclaim" comes from the Latin *proclamare*, meaning "to cry out." In other words, the disciples did not simply preach, but they preached boldly, fearlessly, with enthusiasm, with joy, probably with lots of body language. They left no one in doubt as to their own faith and their desire to share the knowledge of the Lord Jesus with others. (As an aside, we may note that this is a great model for Catholic teachers to follow. Students must be able to see them as proclaimers – enthusiastic about their faith, caught up in the excitement of knowing the Lord Jesus, anxious to share this great gift with others. All educational research shows that teacher behaviour is one of the most crucial factors in learning. If the teacher shows himself or herself to be enthusiastic, dedicated, obviously in love with a subject, students will pick up this enthusiasm and their learning will be greatly enhanced. How many times, for example, have we heard sermons in which, though we might not remember everything that was said, we certainly remember being mightily impressed by the sincerity and enthusiasm of the preacher! The stirring of emotions certainly helps the process of learning. All the great demagogues of the world have understood this very well.)

And, in its simplest form, what is this good news that is worth proclaiming? Peter put it well in his very first sermon to the crowd in Jerusalem (Acts 2:14-36): this Jesus, whom you crucified, is indeed Lord because God has raised him from the dead. No greatly sophisticated theology, just fairly simple, straightforward statements about Jesus and his message.

The core content of this early preaching is often referred to as the *kerygma*.* By careful study of the Christian Scriptures, we can pick out several passages that represent some of this content. Here are some examples:

> *For since, in the wisdom of God, the world did not know God through wisdom, God decided, through the foolishness of our proclamation, to save those who believe. (1 Cor 1:21)*

> *If you confess with your lips that Jesus is Lord and believe in your heart that God raised him from the dead, you will be saved. (Rom 10:9)*

For Christ also suffered for sins once for all, the righteous for the unrighteous, in order to bring you to God. (1 Pet 3:18)

Not only did the apostles preach, but they gave witness with their lives: they were prepared to suffer and die so that the good news could be proclaimed. Their deaths are a powerful testimony to their faith. When one is prepared to suffer greatly and die for one's beliefs, people sit up and take notice. Their message was not mere empty words meant to deceive their listeners.

b) Celebration

The early Christians celebrated their faith. In particular, they gathered together for the Eucharist, a re-enactment of the Last Supper and of Jesus' sacrifice on the cross, as he had instructed them to do (Lk 22:19). For these celebrations they made up prayers, hymns, slogans, greetings and creeds. An example of an early hymn is found in Philippians 2:6-11.

Slogans are short, punchy, easy-to-remember rallying cries that stir up emotions. Every group that wants to stick together and be identified as a group makes up slogans. For example, a modern-day Christian slogan is "The family that prays together stays together." Early Christian slogans proclaimed the essence of their faith: "Jesus is Lord," "God lives," "Christ has died, Christ is risen, Christ will come again."

An example of a Christian greeting is "God be with you" (corrupted in English to "good-bye") or "God and Mary be with you" (in Ireland they add "and Patrick"!).

As Christianity spread, creeds* were composed. Creeds are simply lists of beliefs that probably originated as prayers or slogans. As we know, the creeds carry for us the beliefs of the community and hold for us many of the Traditions of our faith. Possibly the earliest creed we have can be found in 1 Cor 15:1-11, which contains the essence of the basic *kerygma*. The Apostles' Creed, which we still use today, is believed to go back in its essence to apostolic times. The version we have today was constructed in the second century. The Nicene Creed, which we sometimes use at Sunday Eucharist, originated from the Council of Nicea (325 C.E.). It is an expansion and development of the Apostles' Creed.

Stage 2: Early Letters and Writings

In the early period of apostolic preaching and celebration, nothing was written down; everything was passed along orally so that after some years there had developed a strong oral tradition about Jesus and his teaching. This oral tradition was not immediately written down. Why? First, as long as the apostles were alive, there was no need to write anything down; they were living eyewitnesses to Jesus and his message. Second, in the early church there was a powerful belief that the Second Coming of Jesus was imminent. St. Paul puts it succinctly: "I mean, brothers and sisters, the appointed time has grown short . . . . For the present form of this world is passing away" (1 Cor 7:29, 31). The early Christians felt that, since the world might only last a few weeks, or perhaps months, there was no need to write things down because it would serve no purpose. But fairly soon it became clear that the end of the world was not imminent. Then the eyewitnesses, the apostles, began to die out. There was need for some written record so that the message of Jesus would not be lost or become corrupted by purely oral tradition. Furthermore, as William Barclay points out, "there was need for something written, something concrete to which one could refer, to settle disputes and heresy. And again, as the church expanded beyond the confines of Palestine, there was need for something that would appeal to the more literate world of the Roman empire."[62]

The Earliest Writings

The earliest writings that we have in the New Testament are some of the letters of St. Paul. Paul was the great missionary of the early church; Luke chronicles his missionary journeys in the Acts of the Apostles. He travelled all over Asia Minor and Greece, establishing Christian groups, or churches, wherever he went. As he moved on to a new place, he wrote letters to the communities he had founded. These letters aimed to strengthen the faith of the Christians, to remind them of his preaching, and to provide them with practical rules for the conduct of their lives (for example, the famous passage on love in 1 Cor 13). The first letter we have from Paul is the letter to the Thessalonians, written shortly after 50 C.E. These letters were read and re-read in the churches. They came to be revered, and in time people came to believe them inspired by God. They are still read in our churches today as part of God's revelation to us.

The Sayings of Jesus

Some material concerning Jesus' life and preaching began to be written down, very probably in the form of short tracts. In addition, collections were made of the sayings of Jesus. Texts from the Old Testament that were fulfilled in the life of Jesus also came to be included. How do we know this? We cannot be absolutely certain, but scholars doing painstaking work on the texts believe they are able to discern passages that are his actual words, rather than an early community interpretation of what he said. Throughout his preaching, Jesus used many enigmatic sayings – little catch phrases, gems of wisdom, which often formed a sort of summary of his teaching. For example:

---

[62]   See Barclay, *The Making of the Bible*, pp. 41-51.

Whoever is not against us is for us. (Mk 9:40; see also Mt 12:30)
The measure you give will be the measure you get back. (Lk 6:38; see also
Mt 7:1-5)
It is more blessed to give than to receive. (Acts 20:35)
In everything do to others as you would have them do to you. (Mt 7:12 –
later known as the "golden rule" of life.)

Such sayings are easy to remember; they would have been common currency in the early communities. Recalling them would spark further memories of the time and the event at which Jesus uttered them, thus providing a basis for the ongoing tradition on which the gospel writers drew. From a study of the actual texts of the gospels, scholars think that the writers, particularly of the Synoptics* (Matthew, Mark and Luke), had access to such an early document. However, if an actual manuscript of these sayings ever existed, it has now been lost. Scholars have given the name Q (after the German *quelle*, meaning "source") to this hypothetical document.[63]

Stage 3: The Actual Gospels

As we have noted, the word "gospel" (derived from the Old English *God-spell*) means "good news," "glad tidings." This good news of God's salvation in Jesus Christ was first proclaimed in words by preaching. It was witnessed to by the lives of the early disciples; as St. Paul tells the Corinthians, "You yourselves are our letter, written on our hearts, to be known and read by all" (2 Cor 3:2). We have also dealt with why the gospel was eventually committed to writing.

Mark is generally thought to be the earliest of the gospels, written about the year 70 C.E. Matthew comes next, written in Aramaic in the mid 70s C.E. for an Aramaic-speaking community. Luke is the most literary of the gospels, probably showing Luke's superior education. It was written in Greek towards the end of the 70s or early 80s C.E. John, the most mystical of the gospels, also written in Greek, was written for a Christian community at the end of the first century. The major witness of the tradition from which this gospel arose is identified as the "Beloved Disciple" (Jn 23:24). Scholars are uncertain if this Beloved Disciple is John, one of the apostles named as the son of Zebedee. John's gospel gives internal evidence (i.e., from the text itself) that it is probably not the work of a single author, but came from a community of which John was the leading personage.

Each of the four gospels has its own peculiar "stamp" or "fingerprint," its own theological approach to the life of Jesus developed from the faith life of the

---

[63]   An excellent collection of the sayings of Jesus (*Quelle*, or Q) is to be found in John S. Kloppenborg, Marvin W. Meyer, Stephen J. Patterson, and Michael G. Steinhauser, *Q Thomas Reader* (Sonoma, CA: Polebridge Press, 1990).

particular community from which it came. The gospels, in fact, probably say as much about the community and its faith life as they do about the main subject matter. Matthew, for example, was clearly writing for a community of recent Jewish converts, so careful is he to link every aspect of the life of Jesus with prophecies and sayings in the Hebrew Scriptures. The Gospel of Luke, written in Greek, was aimed at a community of Gentile (non-Jewish) converts, for whom Jewish customs would have been a non-issue.

Of all the scriptural writings, the gospels hold pride of place. As the Catechism points out, "The *Gospels* are the heart of all the Scriptures 'because they are our principal source for the life and teaching of the Incarnate Word, our Saviour'" (CCC 125). And so, "The fourfold Gospel holds a unique place in the Church" (CCC 127). Taken together, the gospels provide a rich mosaic rather than a one-dimensional view of Jesus and his life. It is from this richness that we can nourish our own faith and foster our personal relationship with him.

The Gospels Are Not Biographies

Something of crucial importance follows from the above. The gospels are in no sense biographies, as we understand that word today. For example, we have no record of what Jesus looked like, how tall he was, whether he wore his hair long, and so on. We know virtually nothing about his life before the age of 30. All the gospels tell us is that he was obedient to Mary and Joseph. We have no clear indication of his education; we simply surmise that he must have been educated in the same way as any Jewish boy his age. But the purpose of the gospels is not to give accurate historical detail. In no way should they be taken as similar to newspaper reports. No one followed Jesus round with a notebook and tape recorder. *The gospels are statements of faith written to strengthen the faith of the early Christian believers.* They are written by believers for believers in a faith-language appropriate to the community from which they arise. As one writer puts it, "The material in the gospels was chosen primarily for what it had to say about the meaning of the Christian life. Almost everything said about Jesus in the gospels ultimately is a statement about what a Christian is to be."[64] The gospels are substantially historical in that they are based on historical fact, but the historical life of Jesus is much obscured in them. We must not let our passion for accurate historical detail cloud our minds and make us look in the gospels for things that are not there, things which the gospel writers had no intention of addressing. We cannot ask the gospels questions the writers never intended to answer.

---

[64]   Donald Senior, C.P., *Jesus: A Gospel Portrait* (Dayton, OH: Pflaum Press, 1981), p. 51.

The Words of Jesus

If the gospels are not biographies, how can we be sure, for example, that the words of Jesus recorded there were actually spoken by him and are not the result of interpretation and elaboration by the early communities? The answer, in short, is that we cannot be absolutely certain. The gospel writings are a mixture of fact and interpretation. The historical fact of Jesus is indisputable, but he did not write anything himself (that we know of); his life was his message. Again, this is not such a difficult process to understand. The only reason that we have some of the philosophical thought of the great philosopher Socrates, for example, is that his disciple Plato wrote it down. Socrates was a great teacher, but he wrote nothing (that we know of). If we want to learn from Socrates, we have to study Plato. Similarly, if we want to learn about Jesus, we have to be content with what his disciples, or others near him, wrote down of the early Christian traditions.

The gospel writers themselves were interpreters – they wrote from a certain point of view (as do all people who write history). They would not deliberately distort what Jesus said (if they *knew* exactly what he said), but it is quite understandable that they selected from the memories of the early communities and interpreted this material to suit their purpose. To repeat, their purpose was not to write accurate history or biography but to bolster the faith of the early communities. Even if Jesus' words are not recorded exactly as he spoke them, the writing in the gospel conforms to the faith of his early followers, the beginning of Christian tradition. As we have said before, their faith is our faith. Jesus' message has not been substantially distorted. That some of Jesus' words recorded in the gospels are the actual historical words he spoke is also beyond doubt, but to discern which these are is a difficult problem of historical and textual reconstruction. Many Scripture scholars have made this their main area of ongoing research.

The Synoptics

The gospels of Mark, Matthew and Luke are very similar in content and arrangement, which is why they are referred to as the Synoptics. So similar are they in content and arrangement that the various incidents in Jesus' life can be put side by side in parallel columns.[65] Such an arrangement has the advantage of making comparisons easy. To be able to compare one gospel with another is a great help in determining the theological stance of the authors, as it lets us see easily how each author approaches the event described. The relationship of the

---

[65] An arrangement first undertaken by Johann Griesbach (1745-1812). An excellent modern version is provided by Burton Throckmorton Jr., *Gospel Parallels,* 4th edition (New York: Thomas Nelson, 1979).

Synoptic gospels to one another is a complicated one that we shall not go into here.

The Emergence of the Canon

Let us first refresh our memories. The canon of Scripture is the list of books accepted as being inspired by God, offering a rule of life, and thus authentic revelation. The establishment of which books were canonical and which were not was not an easy process and did not take place in one single act or declaration. There were many books and letters circulating in the early church, such as The Gospel of Thomas, The Gospel of Philip, The First Letter of Clement (who was Bishop of Rome at the turn of the first century), and The Epistle of Barnabas (written towards the middle of the second century). Why did they not become canonical? What was, and is, the criterion of canonicity?

For Roman Catholics, the criteria for canonicity is clear and simple: tradition, and the authority of the believing and teaching church. Thus, the books are canonical because the church says they are, and that is the faith of the whole church. Certain books were regarded from the beginning as having come from the apostles or from their immediate associates. In other words, they were apostolic. They contained first-hand evidence of Jesus and his message; they were used in church worship; they were read at the eucharistic gatherings; they served as sources for prayer. That fact alone served to bring them to the attention of everyone in the church; they became canonical almost by acclamation. These books had about them what William Barclay calls a "self-evidencing" quality. "To read them," he says, "is to be brought into the presence of God and truth and Jesus Christ in a unique way. They have always exercised, and still exercise, a quite unparalleled power on the lives of men."[66]

All the original manuscripts of these writings have been lost. What we have to go on today are copies of the originals, or rather, copies of copies. We do have pieces of papyrus with some texts from the Christian Scriptures on them that date back to the second century; however, the earliest complete text we have dates from the fourth century. How can we be sure that these are, indeed, faithful copies of the originals? In truth, we cannot be absolutely certain. There is ample evidence that, as copies were made, the copiers, or editors, made changes when either the text was not clear or they did not perfectly understand the original. Sometimes they made marginal notes, and in some cases these notes found their way into subsequent copies.

Now, this is a perfectly normal process that operates in secular history. For example, many of the texts of the early Greek philosophers, which form the basis

---

[66]   *The Making of the Bible*, p. 74.

of modern thought, only exist as copies. Yet, we do not throw them out as non-authentic. On the contrary, we accept them because we can recognize their value for human thought and human living. In a similar way, when it comes to the biblical texts, we rely on the continuous faith and teaching of the church. That these texts have been accepted by the believing church, and so declared by the teaching church, is our guarantee of authenticity. And so, when the writers in the early church made a selection of books that they regarded as canonical, they were not doing so in an arbitrary fashion. They were simply stating that these books were the ones that were already accepted in the church as being apostolic, as teaching about Jesus and his message, and as nourishing the faith life of the people.

The four gospels, the letters of Paul and the book of Acts came to be regarded almost from the beginning as authentic revelation. It took more time for the other writings to be accepted as canonical. As time went on, more and more books were understood as meeting the criteria for canonicity. The first list of the canonical books that we have dates back to the middle of the second century. It did not contain all the books we now accept. Other lists followed in the third and fourth century until, in 367 C.E., St. Athanasius, Bishop of Alexandria, listed all the 27 books we have today. The Council of Trent in 1546, acting against the Protestant reformers, declared that anyone who did not accept these 27 books as authentic and canonical was "anathema," that is, separated from the church, excommunicated. The canon of Scripture was officially closed.

Summary and Conclusion

Since the gospels are such an essential part of our faith, since from them we draw most of our understanding of Jesus and his message of salvation, let us repeat the major principles that affect their writing and our understanding.

1. *The gospels are not biographies; they do not pretend to be accurate history.*

The purpose of the gospel writers was to present the Good News, to proclaim Jesus and his message of salvation. As a result, we can expect that the details of the historical person of Jesus will be somewhat obscured. Many of his speeches and sayings were edited, worked over and interpreted so as to present the sense of what he said.

2. *The gospels were written in the light of the resurrection experience.*

The life of Jesus is re-interpreted, newly understood, because of the resurrection experience. The apostles understood things about Jesus and his life they had not understood before. They now try to explain things that before had not been a problem for them: for example, the early life of Jesus, his origins, how God had come to be born on earth.

3.   *The early Christian community, the church, is an important factor in the production of the gospels.*

The church came before the gospels; the communities of believers were there before the gospels were written. It is these communities that preserved the memories and traditions about Jesus. The church enabled the gospels to be written. As we have seen, Scripture comes from tradition. The gospels come from the church, not the other way around.

4.   *Each gospel bears the distinctive mark of its human writer – a distinctive theology, a distinctive style, a distinctive agenda.*

The writers were writing to nourish and develop the faith of Christian communities with which they were involved. We can expect, therefore, that the different gospel portraits reflect the different traditions and understandings of Jesus that developed in the different early communities. When we put the four accounts together, the portrait of Jesus that emerges is far fuller and richer than if there had been only one writer.

It should be quite unnecessary to say that we should read the Christian Scriptures, particularly the gospels. Everything that we said in a previous chapter about reading the Bible applies here. To quote the Catechism:

> The Church "forcefully and specifically exhorts all the Christian faithful . . . to learn 'the surpassing knowledge of Jesus Christ', [Phil 3:8] by frequent reading of the divine Scriptures. 'Ignorance of the Scriptures is ignorance of Christ.'" (CCC 133)

But let us ask ourselves an honest question: When did we last pick up the Bible and read passages from it? If someone asked us if we had read the details of our insurance policy and we admitted that we hadn't, then it should not surprise us that, if we have to make a claim, we may not get what we expect. While it may be inappropriate to look upon the Christian Scriptures as our insurance policy for salvation, they do contain the living Word of God; they do contain Jesus our Saviour and his promise of eternal life. We shall get to know and understand him better, to live more closely in his presence, to know and understand how we can better live in obedience to his teaching, if we read and pray the Scriptures.

Reflection Questions

1.   Someone once remarked that "the gospel is not good advice but good news." Comment on this statement.

2.   "The gospels are not biographies." Explain this statement carefully and draw from it some important conclusions for teaching.

3. "The New Testament writers were not writing just for the sake of writing, nor even to leave a literary monument to posterity. . . . They were writing to nourish, safeguard and develop the faith of fellow Christians."[67]

What does this statement say about a) the interpretation of the Christian Scriptures and b) our approach to reading and teaching the Christian Scriptures?

4. "Reflection on and conclusions from the Jesus stories began early in the church. We see this in the church's earliest writings, the epistles of Paul. When you reflect on story, make associations, and draw conclusions, you have a theology."[68] The Christian Scriptures are said to contain many theologies; what does this mean? How can the above quote help us to understand?

5. What does the resurrection of Jesus mean to you personally?

6. What criteria were used in choosing the books to belong to the canon of Scripture? What guarantee do we have that these are, in fact, canonical books?

Further Reading

Barclay, William. *The Making of the Bible* (Edinburgh: St. Andrews Press, 1979). A compact and inexpensive little book containing a simple but excellent treatment of several key points in the development of the Bible. Well worth reading.

Brown, Raymond E. *Responses to 101 Questions on the Bible* (New York: Paulist Press, 1990). This pre-eminent New Testament scholar provides a goldmine of information on current problems affecting biblical interpretation asked by audiences who have heard his lectures. Should be in every school library.

— —. *The Virginal Conception and Bodily Resurrection of Jesus* (New York: Paulist Press, 1973). Though rather theological in its treatment and therefore requiring careful reading, Brown gives us a clear and thorough account of the present theological understanding of these somewhat difficult questions of faith.

Charpentier, Étienne. *How to Read the New Testament* (London: SCM Press, 1981). A companion volume to *How to Read the Old Testament* and, like it, presents a readable and interesting introduction to the Christian Scriptures aimed at helping the reader understand the background from which the writings developed.

---

[67] Pheme Perkins, *Reading the New Testament: An Introduction* (New York: Paulist Press, 1978), p. 7.

[68] William J. Bausch, *Storytelling: Imagination and Faith* (Mystic, CT: Twenty-Third Publications, 1986), p. 198.

Perkins, Pheme. *Reading the New Testament: An Introduction* (New York: Paulist Press, 1978). An easy-to-read presentation by one of the foremost Catholic New Testament scholars in the United States. A little more detailed and theological than Charpentier, but well worth studying whether individually or in groups.

Senior, Donald. *Jesus: A Gospel Portrait* (Dayton, OH: Pflaum, 1981). Contains a first-class treatment of the development of the New Testament.

11

JESUS OF NAZARETH

The Christian Paradox

At some time or another all of us have been faced with the paradoxes that seem to be an integral part of our religious faith. For example, how can we reconcile a loving creator with the existence of evil in the world and the suffering of the innocent? How can we reconcile the mercy of God with his justice? How, in the words of the gospel, can we find life by losing it? (Mt 10:39)

The dictionary defines paradox as a statement or sentiment that is seemingly opposed to common sense and yet perhaps true in fact. William Bausch talks about paradox as "expecting one thing and being caught off guard with another. . . . it will unsettle our common conventions and make us see reality anew."[69] For G.K. Chesterton, paradox is "truth standing on her head to attract attention."[70] There is deep truth buried in paradox, but until it "stands on its head" and affronts our common sense we shall not appreciate it. Our psyche does not like things that are opposed to common sense; we tend to feel ill at ease, out of sorts. Often in order to maintain our personal equilibrium and not become neurotic, we try to solve paradoxes. Generally, we do this by emphasizing one side of the paradox at the expense of the other. It is a futile pursuit. We do not solve paradoxes, we learn to live with them, for, as we have said, at the heart of paradox there is deep truth, truth that can only be experienced and penetrated in the very teeth of the tension.

Why, you may ask, this rather long excursus on paradox? The answer is that Jesus Christ is the central paradox of Christianity. Christianity has, from its very inception, wrestled with the problem posed by Jesus himself: "Who do people say that the Son of Man is?" (Mt 16:13) Christians believe that the human Jesus, a Jew who lived in a specific time and place in history, is also God, fully human yet fully divine. This, of course, is a faith statement that cannot be proved empirically. Theologians speak of this phenomenon as the Incarnation* (from the Latin *in* and *caro* meaning "flesh") – God became enfleshed as a human being like us in everything but sin (CCC 464, 479-483).

---

[69] *Ibid.,* See especially Chapter 4.
[70] G.K. Chesterton, *The Paradoxes of Mr. Pond* (London: Cassell, 1937), p. 71.

The people who lived with Jesus experienced him as human (CCC 470, 476)[71] but, particularly after the resurrection, they came to the strong realization that he was more than human. They realized that in this man God dwelt in a special and unique way. Therefore, and most importantly, they came to know his divinity through his humanity. In Jesus, God speaks to us in a language that we can understand. It is by studying Jesus' words, his actions, his values, his approach to life, his love for us, that we shall begin to grasp and enter into the love of God, which surpasses all knowledge, wisdom and understanding (see Eph 3:16-21).

Down through the centuries many explanations of this central Christian paradox have been offered; none of them is completely satisfactory because we are dealing with a deep mystery.[72] Almost from the beginning the early church struggled with this problem. Attempts to solve the paradox by overemphasizing the divine Jesus or the human Jesus were not lacking. These early heresies* affronted the faith of the church and were all condemned.[73] True Christian faith has always insisted that Jesus Christ is fully human and fully divine, with everything that those terms imply; not one iota of either the humanity or the divinity must be removed or diminished. Sadly, however, because of our dislike of paradox, we still in small but real ways harken back to the early heresies. Our inner psyche is more comfortable with either the divine Jesus or the human Jesus; sometimes we switch from one to the other to suit our purposes. We must come back to our original point: we don't solve paradoxes, we learn to live with them. By accepting both sides of the paradox "at white heat" (the words of F.J. Sheed), by not in any way diminishing one or the other, we shall find a reconciliation taking place deep within us; we shall experience the emergence of truth, which will transform us.

Jesus in His Time

Most of the information we have about Jesus comes from the New Testament, particularly the four gospels. However, there are several references to him in secular literature: for example, in the writings of the Jewish writer Josephus and the Roman authors Suetonius, Tacitus and Pliny. It is unchallenged historical fact, therefore, that Jesus was a real human being, a Jew who lived at a specific time in history and in a specific place. He was influenced by the people, the politics, the culture, the religion of the land in which he lived. It will be helpful for us to take a brief look at the influences that shaped the human Jesus.

---

[71]   CCC 472-475 deal with Jesus' human and divine knowledge and will.

[72]   The presence of mystery at the heart of the human experience of paradox is dealt with in an enlightening way by John Shea in *Stories of God: An Unauthorized Biography* (Chicago: Thomas More Press, 1978), Chapter 1.

[73]   CCC 465-467 give us a good summary of some of the principal heresies.

The Political Situation

Palestine was a vassal state of the Roman Empire. Though maintaining a presence in the territory, the Romans did not govern Palestine directly but selected a family of Idumean Jews, the Herodians, to look after the internal running of the state. The most famous of these was Herod the Great; he ruled from 37–4 B.C.E. (Idumea is a territory to the south of Palestine that had been conquered by the Israelites in their brief period of independence, 142–63 B.C.E., and the inhabitants had been forced to accept the Jewish religion.) By Roman permission Herod had great internal power in Israel: for example, he could impose taxes and could even remove the high priests, thus directly interfering in Jewish religion.

While Herod was cruel and arbitrary, he did make many material improvements in the country. His greatest achievement was the building of the magnificent temple in Jerusalem (begun in 26 B.C.E.), referred to in the gospels (e.g., Mk 13:1-2). This temple became the centre of Jewish worship and the great pride and joy of the Jewish people. As a result of a Jewish uprising against their colonial masters, the Romans destroyed the temple in 70 C.E. (foretold by Jesus in Mk 13:2) in order to wipe out all vestiges of Jewish rebellion centred on their religious attachment to the temple.[74]

Herod the Great died in 4 B.C.E., and on his death the territory was divided between three of his sons. Herod Antipas was given the territory of Galilee. He was the Herod that Jesus knew and in whose territory Jesus lived and did most of his ministry. The Roman procurator at the time of Jesus' ministry was Pontius Pilate, who lived in Caesarea Maritima on the Mediterranean coast just north of present-day Tel Aviv. He visited Jerusalem from time to time, particularly on the days of Jewish festivals. The Romans kept a garrison of soldiers in Jerusalem precisely to guard against any Jewish unrest; they lived in the Antonia fortress at the northwestern corner of the temple. It was in the courtyard of this fortress that the scourging of Jesus and his crowning with thorns took place.

The land of Samaria lay to the north of Jerusalem, with the principal city Sechem (modern-day Nablus) a scant 50 kilometres from Jerusalem as the crow flies. The Samaritans figure prominently in the gospels, but the history of Samaria and the evolution of its religion is a complicated one that we cannot go into here. In short, most Jews regarded the Samaritans with a deep suspicion which, at the time of Jesus, had hardened into real hatred. The Samaritans had retained some of the Jewish religious observances and Scriptures, and this hybrid religion made them anathema to true religionists. The Samaritans were

---

[74] All that remains of the temple today is the Western Wall. The courtyard near this wall has been excavated and serves as the main place of prayer for Jews in Jerusalem today.

also regarded as a backward and somewhat rebellious people. We are cryptically told in the gospel, "Jews do not share things in common with Samaritans" (Jn 4:9). Jesus was taunted with being a friend of Samaritans and even a Samaritan himself, which was the meanest form of insult (e.g., Jn 8:48).

The Jewish Religious Leaders

The scribes, the Pharisees and the Sadducees duck in and out of the gospel narrative with regularity – mostly, it seems, in opposition to Jesus. Who were they, and how did they affect the ministry and teaching of Jesus?

As with many religions today, various sects and groups existed in the Judaism of Jesus' time. The *Sadducees* were the priestly class, the ruling overlords of religion. The gospels report their theological arguments with Jesus, such as on the question of resurrection, which the Sadducees rejected (Mk 12:18-27). Being priests, their main focus was the temple and the acts of worship performed there, which Jesus saw as nothing more than empty ritual (see Jesus' rebuke, Mt 15:6-9). Because of its prime importance in the religion of Israel, the temple was in many ways the central rallying point of Judaism. The gospels often link the Sadducees with the Pharisees as though all Sadducees were Pharisees; however, the two groups were not the same. The head of the Sadducees, the High Priest, was a political appointee. He had considerable prestige and influence, and was regarded by most Jews as the symbol of true religious observance and hence a unifying force in Judaism. The *scribes* have been called the "jurists" of Israel. They studied the Pentateuch (the Law) and wrote legal opinions about its proper interpretation. They were also teachers who, because of their learning, were often called "rabbi" (teacher) or "doctor of the law."

Along with the Sadducees, the *Pharisees* also were sticklers for the observance of the law but were much more conservative in political matters than the former. They had considerable influence among the people. They are portrayed in the gospels as the "bad guys," seemingly always in conflict with Jesus, who treats them to some of his most condemning and vituperative language (see Mt 23:23-24). It was true that, because of their attachment to the Law, many Pharisees became overly legalistic and hypocritical about its observance. It was this lack of integrity and honesty that angered Jesus the most. Perhaps the Pharisees have had a bad press, so to speak. The gospels, remember, were written more than 30 years after the death of Jesus and reflect much of the thinking and experience of the early church. By that time, the young Christian church had come into conflict with various Jewish groups bent on maintaining strict observance to the Law as advocated by the Pharisees. The so-called "Judaizers" wanted all new Christians to be first and foremost Jews; hence they opposed the admission of Gentiles* to Christianity unless they were prepared to accept all Jewish legal and religious observance (such as circumcision and the laws governing eating). The gospels, therefore, reflect an attitude of conflict with the Pharisees that may not have existed in the time of Jesus. An even more unfortunate result of this quirk of history is that those who were depicted by the gospels as opposed to Jesus came to be identified as "the Jews" (particularly in the Gospel according to John), thus stigmatizing the whole Jewish people. Many scholars believe that this unhappy circumstance has been the source of much of the undenied Christian anti-semitism down through the centuries.

The *Sanhedrin* plays an important part in the last days of Jesus. Literally translated, the word means "senate" or "assembly." The Sanhedrin, composed of 70 members drawn from the various parties and the important people (the elders) of the land, should not be identified as a body totally opposed to Jesus. There is some indication that, in fact, some members of the Sanhedrin may well have been secret disciples of Jesus, or at least admired his teaching. The Sanhedrin was the main governing body of the Jews and through control of all matters religious it regulated every aspect of Jewish life. The Romans accepted this state of affairs and generally did not interfere in the decisions of the Sanhedrin.

Finally, the *tax collectors* turn up regularly in the gospels. They are portrayed as "sinners," outsiders with whom Jesus seems to have associated rather freely, much to the anger and dismay of many Pharisees. The Jewish people, as with many oppressed people even today, were overburdened with various forms of taxation: Herod's taxes, the religious tax (called the temple tax), and the Roman taxes. The tax collectors referred to in the gospels were Jews who agreed to raise taxes from their own people for the Romans. They were given a tax quota, and anything they could extort beyond this quota they could keep. It is not difficult to understand why they are referred to in the gospels with such scorn and were viewed by their fellow countrymen as extortionists, thieves and sinners, not to mention being Roman "toadies." It was such sinners that Jesus was often accused of favouring and to whom he said he had been sent by his Father.

The Birth of Jesus

Factually and historically, we know hardly anything about the birth and childhood of Jesus. We do know that he was born to a poor family and in very humble circumstances (CCC 525). Later in his life he seemed to associate (by choice) with the poor and the humble, those on the fringes of society. Nevertheless, the gospels give us extraordinarily little to go on. We do not even know with certainty the year or the actual birthdate of Jesus. We know that he was born in the reign of Herod the Great (who is referred to in the Gospel according to Matthew) and therefore that he must have been born before 4 B.C.E., which we know from other sources was the year of Herod's death. For many this may indeed be a surprise. Why not 0 C.E.? The simple answer (though it is far more historically complex) is that when the calendar was being developed in the sixth century, a mistake was made and never corrected. Why December 25 (for those who follow the Julian calendar) or January 6 (for those who follow the Gregorian calendar)? The best answer seems to be that this is the date of the winter solstice, after which the sun begins its return to the northern hemisphere, thus symbolizing the rising light of Christ returning to the earth and shining on the darkness.

It might surprise us to find that only two of the four gospels – Matthew and Luke – have anything to say about the birth and childhood of Jesus. On the other hand, all four gospels contain long and detailed accounts of the passion, death and resurrection of Jesus. That fact alone should indicate that the gospel writers saw the passion, death and resurrection as far more important for preserving the faith of the early church. It is the events of the last days of Jesus' life that set the seal on his whole message. The church's curiosity about the origins of Jesus only came as a result of the realization of who he was and the importance of his message. Thirty or 40 years after his death, Matthew and Luke try to satisfy that curiosity in the context of their own Christian communities. It is entirely possible that similar concerns did not greatly occupy the energies of the communities of Mark or John. Therefore, we must emphasize that the major point at issue is always the faith needs of the early communities; the stories are little preoccupied with historical fact.

The Infancy Narratives

The accounts of the birth and early childhood of Jesus in the Gospels according to Matthew and Luke are often referred to as the "infancy narratives" – the announcement to Mary that she was to be God's mother, the visit to her cousin Elizabeth, "there was no place for them in the inn," the shepherds and angels and the birth of Jesus in Bethlehem, the visit of the wise men from the east, the moving of the holy family to Egypt to escape Herod, the return to Nazareth, the finding of the child Jesus in the temple among the teachers and doctors of the law.[75] These are very familiar and much-loved Christian stories that never fail to touch us each year at Christmas-time. But are they historical and biographical?

The simple answer to that question is: minimally so. The important thing to remember about the infancy narratives is this:

They were not intended as mere factual narrations but as proclamations of the birth of the Messiah. The details surrounding the story point to a

---

[75] CCC 527-530 mentions some of these stories as well as their theological and spiritual significance.

specialness, an extraordinary birth, a divine event. The truth is a deeper truth; it is the witness of believers who joyfully tell of the nativity of God's own son.[76]

These stories were never intended to be biographical; their purpose is theological and faith-inspiring. The infancy stories in the Gospels according to Matthew and Luke are there to complete the main theme of the gospels: the salvation brought by Jesus Christ. Therefore, the theological tone of these stories is that of the marvellous work of God in accomplishing our salvation, the major event of which was the passion, death and resurrection of Jesus. In these stories, it is almost impossible to separate fact from imaginative projection. According to the best interpretation of Scripture scholars today, the stories may be understood as theological meditations arising from the prayers, the questions, the surmises and the poetry of the early Christian communities.

We can see this process at work in our very own times. Folk wisdom today has it that three wise men visited Jesus from the east for the event of the Epiphany. However, the gospel account does not in fact mention any specific number – it simply specifies that "wise men" (some translations call them astrologers) came from the east. But because three gifts are mentioned we have associated each gift with a distinct person, hence three wise men! (We are not even sure that they were all men!) What's more, modern folklore has made these three "wise men" into kings! So now we have it that three kings visited Jesus. We sing the Christmas carol "We Three Kings of Orient Are." Not satisfied with this, we have developed the tale even further. We have now given these three kings names (not found in the gospels) – Melchior, Balthazar and Caspar – which are enthusiastically taught to children! What is happening here? What is happening is that our own prayers, meditations and poetic insight are at work developing the gospel story. This is a good example of a process that almost certainly took place in the early Christian communities and so is reported in the gospels.

As a help to understanding how the infancy narratives developed, let us consider just one important factor among many others. We have already mentioned in the chapter on the Christian Scriptures that the Old Testament had an important part to play in their writing. And so, for the early church and the New Testament writers, if Christ was the Messiah mentioned in the ancient Scriptures, then whatever was understood as applying to the Messiah should be applied to Jesus. Annunciation stories appear regularly in the Old Testament. These stories are a literary device to introduce the birth and development of important scriptural figures and the part they will play in the history of salvation.

---

[76]   Eileen Flynn and Gloria Thomas, *Living Faith: An Introduction to Theology* (Kansas City, MO: Sheed & Ward, 1989), p. 69.

(For example, there is the birth of Isaac [Gen 18:1 ff.]; the birth of Samuel [I Sam 1:1 ff.]; the birth of Samson [Judg 13:1 ff.]; and the birth of John the Baptist [Lk 1:5-20].) And so, Jesus' birth – there is no one more important than he – is heralded by an annunciation story. In many cases, the announcing of important news was associated with the intervention of angels (in the case of the Annunciation to Mary, the angel Gabriel).

As far as the annunciation of Jesus' birth is concerned, therefore, rather than emphasizing the historical details, we must emphasize the indication given of the importance of the person to be born and the creative power of the Spirit of God. The important points for our faith clearly indicated by the infancy narratives are these. First, Jesus comes from God, not from any human power; the presence of Jesus on earth is entirely the work of God acting through the power of the Spirit. Second, God's power and presence are expressed in a special, unique and intimate way in Jesus. Third, it is through Jesus that God, and God alone, accomplishes our salvation.

The fact that the stories cannot be shown to be primarily biographical and historical should not cause us to become completely skeptical about their content. Even though not historical in every detail, the stories are undoubtedly based on historical fact. Therefore, they are valuable witnesses to Christian faith. Down through the centuries they have been a key element in helping Christians to come to a realization of who Jesus is, and an appreciation of his person and his message.

The Ministry of Jesus

The best historical evidence we have seems to indicate that Jesus began his "public" life at about the age of 30. It is from this point that the bulk of the writing in the gospels begins. What went on in his life before that time is open only to surmise and conjecture. We can simply presume that he was educated and grew up as would have any normal Jewish boy from small-town Galilee. Within the limited confines of this chapter, we can only barely scratch the surface of Jesus' ministry. The reader is urged to fill in what is missing by further research and reading. We can never know enough about the person of Jesus and his message.

For about three years after his baptism in the Jordan by John the Baptist, Jesus assumed the life of an itinerant preacher and teacher. It was not uncommon for teachers to wander from place to place, accumulating students and followers who chose to study under them. There were many different kinds of itinerant teachers: the philosopher types (called sages), who taught about human wisdom; the scribes and rabbis, who taught about Jewish law and custom; and the prophets and visionaries. Jesus' teaching perhaps combined some of the characteristics of all these types, and he too attracted followers. The first group of followers was the apostles, some of whom were chosen by Jesus to join him (for example, Andrew, Simon Peter, Philip and Nathanael – Jn 1:35-51), but the gospels report that great crowds seemed to follow him everywhere (see, for example, Mk 3:9).

What, we might ask, was so attractive about Jesus? There is little doubt that Jesus was a charismatic figure of immense fascination. He is described by one of his own disciples as one "who was a prophet mighty in deed and word before God and all the people" (Lk 24:19). He was mighty in deed, for he did things that no one had ever done before. His miraculous cures of the sick attracted great crowds of people. He was mighty in word for he taught with great sincerity and persuasion, and "with authority." "Now when Jesus had finished saying these things, the crowds were astounded at his teaching, for he taught them as one having authority, and not as their scribes" (Mt 7:28-29). When the scribes and rabbis taught, they generally offered confirming evidence for their teaching from their interpretation of Scripture or from the teaching of other rabbis. Jesus, on the other hand, taught on his own authority without having to appeal to the opinions of other rabbis or prophets (see, for example, Mt 5:20-48). Furthermore, Jesus showed himself to be truly a man of the people, for he addressed his words to everyone, not merely to special groups of scholars, as might happen in the rabbinical schools.

We speak of Jesus' teaching and his deeds as his "ministry." Ministry, as we have already seen, means service – Jesus served the needs of the people of his time and he still serves our needs. As he serves our needs, so must we serve one another's needs and carry on his work in the world. After Jesus had washed the feet of his disciples at the Last Supper, he said to them, "Do you know what I have done to you? You call me Teacher and Lord – and you are right, for that is what I am. So if I, your Lord and Teacher, have washed your feet, you also ought to wash one another's feet. For I have set you an example, that you also should do as I have done to you" (Jn 13:12-15).

Teaching

a) The Kingdom of God

Without question, the notion of the kingdom of God is absolutely central to Jesus' teaching (CCC 541-546). One cannot pick up any of the gospels without being struck immediately by the importance that Jesus gave to it. It is not the easiest of realities to understand, but we must make some attempt to do so if we are to enter deeply into the teaching of Jesus.

Central to Jewish faith was the belief that in due time God would overcome all the forces of evil that beset the world and thus bring about the total triumph of good. With the evolution of the political fortunes of Israel and their decision to adopt kingship as their form of government, the king became the symbol of the presence of God among the people. Thus, the kingship of God is a common enough theme in the Old Testament. Although Jesus speaks of the kingdom, it would perhaps be better to speak of the reign of God, a period in which, according to the prophet Isaiah, "the earth will be full of the knowledge of the Lord" (Isa 11:9). As the forces of evil and sin are overcome, everyone will observe God's will and live according to his ordinances. Thus, an era of peace, justice, harmony and proper human development will be established everywhere; all hostility will cease, all enmities disappear, all pain, sorrow and suffering be assuaged. In brief, the world will be saved. Belief in the reign of God was the result of the Jewish people trying to balance their own difficult and painful experiences (e.g., the division of the kingdom, war and defeat) with their faith in the goodness and love of God. For them God had made a promise in the covenant; therefore he could not allow evil to triumph, which so often seemed to be the case. The reign of God is opposed to the reign of evil, or sin. Eventually God will fully triumph over the forces of evil.

This hope and expectation of the final triumph of good is shaped and moulded by the key factor in the whole of Jesus' life, namely, his own understanding of God as a loving Father, his "Abba." The whole matter is extremely well put by Thomas Zanzig, and it is worth quoting him:

> The key to understanding Jesus' teaching about the Kingdom of God is his conviction of the passionate, unrestricted, and unconditional love of God which is everywhere available to all people, and the power of that love to release and free people to love one another unconditionally, without restrictions. The kingship of God becomes real when God reigns over the hearts of people, and God rules over our hearts when we are in tune with his will. . . . when people conform their lives to God's will there will be peace, joy, and love for all – that is, the Kingdom of God will be fully realized.[77]

We believe that the kingdom of God has come in Jesus; the kingdom is established in the world. But the evidence of our experience seems to indicate otherwise. There is still hatred among peoples; there is still war and tragedy and pain and suffering. Where, then, is the kingdom?

The Greeks have two words for time: *chronos* and *kairos*. *Chronos* (from which, for example, comes the English word "chronometer") speaks of hours and days and years; it speaks of clocks and calendars. It means time as a measurement of succession, of change. *Kairos*, on the other hand, means time

---

[77]   Thomas Zanzig, *Jesus Is Lord! A Basic Christology for Adults* (Winona: MN: St. Mary's Press, 1982), pp. 118, 119.

now, as in "this is the time," "the time has arrived"; time, therefore, as an event, time as present. The kingdom of God is in both kinds of time. It is the time (*kairos*) but not yet the time (*chronos*). The kingdom is *kairos* because it is present in Christ, present to me now. But the kingdom, clearly, is not fully present, not fully complete; it will only be completed in the future, at the end time, in God's good time. We measure the future by *chronos*. Here, once again, we are faced with a deep Christian paradox – the kingdom is simultaneously a present and a future reality. Once again, we don't solve paradoxes; we learn to live with them. Thus, during our lifetime, we have the obligation to work for the establishment of the kingdom, which is what Jesus did. Like him, we try to make peace, heal wounds and sickness, promote justice and integrity, heal brokenness and alienation, live according to the law of love. At the same time, we must realize that we cannot bring about the kingdom on our own; we need God's help. The full establishment of the kingdom is ultimately a work of God that will be accomplished in God's own good time – "you know not the day nor the hour."

But, after all, is there any concrete evidence that the kingdom of God has arrived? In other words, has Jesus made a difference? That very same question was asked even in Jesus' time:

> *The disciples of John reported all these things to him. So John summoned two of his disciples and sent them to the Lord to ask, "Are you the one who is to come, or are we to wait for another?" When the men had come to him, they said, "John the Baptist has sent us to you to ask, 'Are you the one who is to come, or are we to wait for another?'" Jesus had just then cured many people of diseases, plagues, and evil spirits, and had given sight to many who were blind. And he answered them, "Go and tell John what you have seen and heard: the blind receive their sight, the lame walk, the lepers are cleansed, the deaf hear, the dead are raised, the poor have good news brought to them. And blessed is anyone who takes no offense at me." (Lk 7:18-23)*

In other words, the kingdom of God has arrived (CCC 547).

But what about our time? Look around you. Are the sick being tended to and cared for? Are there people trying to make peace? Are there people who promote justice and are prepared to die to see it accomplished? Are there people and institutions committed to healing brokenness and alienation? In other words, are there people today trying to carry on the work of Jesus? If the answer to that question is "yes," then the evidence is there that the kingdom is present among us. The major question that Jesus' teaching addresses to me personally is: How complete is the kingdom in my own life? How do I measure up now to the demands of the kingdom as outlined above? The kingdom demands a personal conversion; it must begin in my own heart. To quote Archbishop Oscar Romero, the martyr of El Salvador, "If I want to change my world, it must begin with an urgency to change my own heart first." We cannot teach the demands of the kingdom to others if we ourselves are making no effort to live by its principles. We shall be constantly in need of conversion because, being subject to sin, we constantly reject the demands of the kingdom in our own lives.

Before completing this section on the kingdom of God, we should note one little anomaly in the Scriptures. Instead of calling it the kingdom of God, the Gospel according to Matthew calls it the "kingdom of heaven." Without going into the historical reason for this, we should note that this usage has had the unfortunate result of making some people think that the kingdom of God can only come in heaven. (Scripture scholars assure us that this interpretation is not what the author intended.) As we have seen, it is true that the kingdom will only be completed when we experience the fullness of eternal life, but that is only one side of the paradox. The other side of the paradox must be given equal emphasis.

b) The Primacy of Love

For Jesus, love is the pre-eminent Christian virtue, the virtue in which "the whole law and the prophets" is contained. We have seen in the previous section that Jesus' teaching on love is also the basis of his teaching on the kingdom because of his own intense conviction of the uncompromising love of God his Father for everyone. The reign of God means the reign of God's love in the world. The love that Jesus teaches is love of the most radical kind (radical, from the Latin word *radix*, meaning root). Many other religions teach that we must love one another, but none goes so far as the teaching of Jesus.

The radical nature of the love Jesus teaches is graphically expressed, particularly in the Gospels according to Matthew and Luke, where Jesus asserts that we are to "love our enemies." How literally are we to take such exhortations as to "turn the other cheek" if we are beaten or insulted? Should we also give up our shirt if someone grabs our coat? How realistic is it for us to bless those who curse us and pray for those who abuse us? (Lk 6:27-31) Many Scripture scholars admit the paradoxical nature of these recommendations by Jesus, but they point out that Jesus may be giving such advice simply to prod us into a better understanding of how we must love others. We should never completely cut off any chance of forgiveness and reconciliation, even though in many cases it may well be impossible to take these recommendations literally.

The great example that Jesus gives of loving one's enemies is in the parable of the Good Samaritan (Lk 10:30-35). The parable clearly asserts that our love for others should know no bounds; it should even override such open hostility as the Jews had for the Samaritans, and vice versa. Love recognizes only the need in the other person; love calls forth compassion and generosity.

c) Parables – How Jesus Taught

The limitations of time and space do not allow us to go into a detailed examination of all aspects of how Jesus taught. For example, he used parables*; he used proverbs; he used pronouncement stories (a story leading up to a concise and easily-remembered punch line); he uttered many prophetic statements; he sometimes used apocalyptic images. Here we can only say something about his use of parables since the parables occupy a good part of the gospels and frequently appear in the readings at Mass on Sundays.

The word "parable" comes from the Latin *parabola*, meaning a comparison. Parables invite us to make comparisons between a story drawn from familiar everyday life and some other less evident, perhaps hidden, reality. Educators today recognize that storytelling is a powerful means of teaching. The story is a good way of conveying deep truths that are difficult to describe directly. A good story always makes us wonder; there is often an air of mystery that makes us question. Stories should never be too obvious. Fully explaining a story tends to destroy it, which is probably why so few parables in the gospels are explained. The educational process at work (and indeed it is a powerful one) is that of discovery – we discover for ourselves the truth that is conveyed in the story; it is not fed into us or forced on us. We must put our imaginations to work and try to see ourselves as part of the story. We must try to identify with one or another of the characters in the story in order to discover ourselves and how we would react in similar circumstances.

Thus, the parables are not meant to supply us with concrete answers to particular problems. Rather, they are meant to make us examine our own life in light of the story and in light of our Christian duty, and to question our assumptions, our attitudes, our way of acting (CCC 546). And so, after telling the parable of the Good Samaritan, Jesus said to the one who had asked him the question, "Which of these three, do you think, was a neighbour to the man who fell into the hands of the robbers?" (Lk 10:36) Jesus puts the onus on the listener to make the decision; he does not himself tell the questioner what to think. When we hear the parable of the Good Samaritan, we should ask ourselves: How would I react, faced with a similar situation? How many times have we passed by the scene of an accident without trying to help, using such excuses as "I don't want to get involved" or "I'd better get out of here before I get hurt myself"? The parables invite us to make adult decisions about our own lives. It is up to each one of us to make the kingdom of God a reality for ourselves.

Healing

a) *Outreach to Sinners and Social Outcasts*

There is suffering in every life; it is an intrinsic part of the human condition. When we really love someone, we grieve with them as well as laugh with them, we reach out to them in empathy, we show compassion. Compassion literally means to "suffer with." We show our concern for others by being prepared to suffer with them, knowing that often this will make their own suffering easier to bear. Often we tend to confuse pity and compassion. Pity comes from a position of favour, of being better off than the other; we can "look down" on the other with a certain sorrow. Compassion, on the other hand, is born of vulnerability, because we share the same fragile nature. We can pity someone, feel for them, but pity will only become compassion if, as the old saying goes, we are prepared to "walk a mile in someone's moccasins." That Jesus was a deeply compassionate person shines through the gospel story; in fact, he has been called "the compassion of God." His compassion reaches out to any situation where he perceives human suffering or even discomfort. The great miracle of the multiplication of the loaves is introduced in the gospels in the following way: "I have compassion for the crowd, because they have been with me now for three days and have nothing to eat. If I send them away hungry to their homes, they will faint on the way – and some of them have come from a great distance" (Mk 8:2-3). Jesus' concern is not restricted to material discomfort; he felt deeply also for people's spiritual need. "When he saw the crowds, he had compassion for them, because they were harassed and helpless, like sheep without a shepherd" (Mt 9:36). Jesus spent himself in caring for others, in giving himself. We are told that often he suffered from lack of sleep because of the demands that were made on him by the crowds. He had no fixed address, no home to go back to for rest and relaxation.

Jesus seemed to seek out the least fortunate in society: the prostitutes, the dishonest and despised tax-collectors, the sinners – in other words, the people whose company others shunned. Many times the accusation was thrown at him that he "ate with sinners and tax collectors," for he visited their homes. His excuse? "Jesus answered, 'Those who are well have no need of a physician, but those who are sick'" (Lk 5:31). Again, he said his mission was to the "lost sheep of the house of Israel" (Mt 15:24). Never is it recorded that Jesus pointed an accusing finger at these people; he seems to make no moral judgment on their lifestyle. To the woman who was brought to him after having been caught in the act of adultery (for which by Jewish law she deserved death), all he said to her was, "Sin no more." Jesus only asks that sinners change their way of life. His major concern is that these people were "suffering," from qualms of conscience or because they had been rejected by society, or both. They were the "little people," without power or prestige, and he empathized with their plight. Many of the people Jesus had to deal with in these situations were women; we are dramatically reminded in the gospels of the oppression that the female sex has suffered at the hands of males down through the centuries. The very way that Jesus acted towards women says that any such oppression is evil.

That Jesus was making a social statement that we can well apply to our own time is so evident as to hardly need affirmation. Evil, anything that contributes to human suffering in all its forms, must be tackled purposefully and energetically. "You help a person who is down. You do not keep a set of books on people. You have the loser uppermost in your thoughts. Suffering is to be found everywhere in life. The work that should compel your highest energies is to relieve it."[78]

b) Cure of Diseases

Jesus not only taught about the kingdom of God, but he also worked actively to bring it about in his own time and in the circumstances in which he lived. He did this especially by his works of mercy and healing.

Jesus went throughout Galilee, teaching in their synagogues and proclaiming the good news of the kingdom and curing every disease and every sickness among the people. (Mt 4:23)

In Jesus' time, disease and sickness were considered evil. The sick person was thought to be in the grip of the power of evil because of some sin, or perhaps because of someone else's sin. We have lots of evidence for this in the gospels. For example, as he walked along, he saw a man blind from birth. His disciples asked him, "'Rabbi, who sinned, this man or his parents, that he was born blind?'" (Jn 9:2) Thus, the belief was there that sin deserved punishment and that punishment could be visited even on another generation. The point is that, in curing illness and disability, Jesus was overcoming the power of evil, a clear sign of the arrival of the kingdom of God. Thus, Jesus reveals God's power to heal and to save.

The gospels tell us that Jesus also calmed storms, that he walked on water, that he multiplied loaves and fishes to feed the people, that he raised people from the dead. The same principle applies: anything that adversely affects humans is evil – to overcome evil is to establish the reign of God and thus usher in an era of peace and freedom. Therefore, what is very important for us is that Jesus' teaching and ministry clearly indicate that we should see healing (in all its forms) as one of the most important works of the Christian life.

---

[78]   Gerald S. Sloyan, *Jesus in Focus: A Life in Its Setting* (Mystic, CT: Twenty-Third Publications, 1983), p. 106.

Miracles

The Jewish writer and historian Flavius Josephus, born a few years after the death of Jesus, testifies that Jesus was a "worker of wondrous deeds." There can be no doubt at all that the gospels attest to a strong and authentic tradition about the miraculous power of Jesus. In fact, so pervasive is the account of miraculous intervention that it is clear that the very earliest traditions considered Jesus' miracles* as important as his actual teaching. But for the modern reader schooled in the scientific method, there is a problem of credibility. Can miracles take place? Does God suspend the laws of nature that he himself created, or does God, in order to be true to himself, respect those very laws? There is a serious theological problem here for which there is no easy solution.

The tendency of most of modern science is to discount all miracles. Most scientists start with the premise that miracles just can't happen. Working from that premise, all so-called miracles are just unexplained scientific events. If we are unable to explain certain occurrences, it is just because the state of our scientific knowledge does not presently allow it. People who think this way try to find natural explanations for the gospel miracles. But to start from this premise is to miss the point. That type of thinking betrays a particular scientific worldview, a worldview that did not exist in the time of Jesus. Whether or not God can, or does, suspend the laws of nature is certainly not a question that would have occurred to the gospel writers. It is hardly likely that the gospel writers even understood that there were laws in nature as we understand them today. The gospel accounts are not aimed at answering such a question, they are aimed at bolstering faith. Therefore, when we consider Jesus' miracles, we have to adopt a theological worldview, which is the worldview of the gospel writers. The gospel miracle stories are woven into the whole scheme of Jesus' teaching on the reign of God; they are signs of the breaking in of God's power to overcome evil, which is the firm basis for our faith.

The word "miracle" itself is misleading. The word derives from the Latin *mirare*, to gaze at, to stare fixedly at, to wonder at. The inference is that a miracle is something spectacular, sensational, akin to magic. In the original Greek, however, the word used by the synoptic gospels is *dynameis*, meaning "works of power." The gospels are speaking of works of God's power, which is greater than the power of evil. Miracles are not magic; they have little in common with sensationalism. The problem is that we are fascinated by magic; we are always on the lookout for the sensational (in our day, strongly bolstered by the media). Unfortunately, if we keep looking for the sensational, for magic, we shall miss the workings of God's power in our lives.

God's power is ever active in the world, but it takes faith to see it. *Miracles are for believers*. Miracles confirm and strengthen the faith of those who already believe. The gospel miracles are not there merely for their apologetic* value. Jesus refused to work miracles just to convince unbelievers (see Lk 23:8; Mt 27:39-40). In fact, Jesus' miracles are almost always associated with faith. He often demands faith before he will work a miracle (Mk 9:23-24). After a miracle he proclaims that he did it because of the person's faith (Lk 8:48), and we are told that he did not work many miracles in his home town of Nazareth "because of their unbelief" (Mt 13:58). Miracles are signs of God's love, a love to which we respond by faith. We must not forget that Jesus' miracles did not convince everyone; in fact, the evidence seems to be that Jesus did not make many converts in his lifetime. The gospels seem to make it plain that on many occasions the crowds that followed Jesus were more on the lookout for the sensational than interested in their own conversion. Miracles will not convince us if we don't want to be convinced.

We may have heard it said that in this modern scientific time, the age of miracles is over; this is patently not so. Apart from the many cures attributed to prayer, for which the scientific community has no explanation, there are many other examples of the working of God's grace and power on earth today. The point is that, if we keep looking for the sensational, we shall miss them. We can still make miracles happen by our faith. Jesus even tells us that we can and should make exaggerated requests in our prayer. For example, he says, "Truly I tell you, if you say to this mountain, 'Be taken up and thrown into the sea,' and if you do not doubt in your heart, but believe that what you say will come to pass, it will be done for you" (Mk 11:23). Faith can accomplish the seemingly impossible.

Because of our inquiring scientific minds we are always asking the question *how* do miracles take place, which is the same question we were concerned with about the crossing of the Reed Sea or Christ's resurrection. As Étienne Charpentier reminded us in the previous chapter, instead of asking how, let us rather have faith in the fact that Jesus did accomplish many works of power as signs of the inbreaking of God's kingdom.

Let us close with the following story. Owing to the excitement caused by several alleged miracles in the St. Medard cemetery in Paris in 1732, Louis XV had this sign placed on the locked gates: "By order of the King, God is hereby forbidden to work miracles in this place." With similar arrogance, the "I" on the throne of our unsurrendered hearts forbids God to work miracles within us.[79]

---

[79] Tony Castle, *More Quotes and Anecdotes* (Leominster, UK: Fowler Wright Books, 1986), p. 229.

Jesus the Saviour

The Meaning of the Word

In the prayers used in the liturgy, there is constant and consistent reference to salvation and redemption. We pray that God may "accomplish in us salvation of mind and body," and again, "Strengthen us by this Easter sacrament; may we feel its saving power in our daily life" or "Lord, watch over those you have saved in Christ." Salvation is a major theme of Christian theology, but what does it mean and how does it affect us in living our daily life?

The word "salvation" has the same root as the word "salve" (for example, a medical substance we apply to the skin to soothe and assuage some injury, such as sunburn). A salve is used to heal, to cure some hurt, to relieve pain. In the same way, salvation means being saved from some evil that threatens us or has affected us. Salvation heals us, assuages the pain, and makes us whole and healthy again.

Experiencing the Need

At the purely material level, we are all searching for salvation – we are all searching for a salve to assuage the painful and embarrassing aspects of our earthly existence. Each of us experiences the whole catalogue of evils that affect us as human beings, not only the evils that threaten us from outside but the ones that come from deep within our own personality. Our desire for perfection is one such. We want to be good and generous, but instead we are often petty, hostile and demanding. We lie to excuse ourselves and to get away from embarrassment but then feel guilty about subverting the truth. We read about some politician who, because of weakness and greed, has been caught with his hand in the cookie jar, and we feel smug that we are not like that. In similar circumstances, we assure ourselves, we would have been honest and unselfish! We are all conscious of the bad habits that we have allowed to control us – overeating, overdrinking, anger, vanity, laziness, and so many others. What is perhaps more debilitating is the fact that deep down inside we don't want to be like this, but we are. Consider the words of St. Paul:

> *For I know that nothing good dwells within me, that is, in my flesh. I can will what is right, but I cannot do it. For I do not do the good I want, but the evil I do not want is what I do. Now if I do what I do not want, it is no longer I that do it, but sin that dwells within me. (Rom 7:18-20)*

We are trapped by the evil that is so evident in our own lives; we feel the need for freedom, for healing. Nor should we be smug that at least we are not like the real monsters, the murderers, the torturers, the child molesters and other really evil people. Sometimes we try to console ourselves that, after all, our transgressions are only small things compared with the truly big evils of the world. But if we have contributed to the evil in the world in any way, then we have hurt others, we have hurt ourselves, and we have no business being smug. We need to experience healing, wholeness, integrity, and that is what we call salvation.

Jesus Saves

Frequently, when we talk about salvation, what we are thinking about is heaven. We shall be saved when we experience eternal life. Well, that certainly is part of it, but definitely not the whole of it. There are three aspects to salvation that are dealt with in the New Testament: the salvation of the world (cosmic salvation); the salvation of the whole of humanity; and personal salvation.

Cosmic salvation is referred to in the letters of St. Paul. Paul sees the whole world, the material universe, as being affected by evil and therefore in need of redemption and wholeness. In God's good time, the salvation brought by Jesus will restore the world to its original created state (which God saw was "good"), before it was scarred by human evil. All of us today experience the disastrous results of our greedy exploitation of the earth. In our pursuit of the good life, we have wasted the earth's natural resources and caused environmental disasters and ecological imbalances; the world itself is in need of healing and restoration.

As far as the whole of humanity is concerned, it is God's desire that all, absolutely everyone, should be saved and come to knowledge of the truth (1 Tim 2:4). One of the ways in which we frequently speak of salvation is that "by his death on the cross Jesus has saved us." Mary Ann Fatula puts it well:

Jesus' death on the cross was the ultimate act of love and self-giving. It was in stark   contrast to the basic selfishness which characterizes our own life and which is the cause of all the evil in the world. On the cross, love itself absorbs the world's hatred and evil in its vast embrace, and here, in this embrace, the chain of hurting passed on throughout all of history is broken.[80]

God's grace and favour have affected the whole universe and are available to all who freely wish it.

But perhaps the most important aspect of salvation is its healing of human sin, which is the cause of the moral evil of which we are so conscious. We should note that Jesus does not solve the problem of evil (which is indeed a deep mystery); he himself was subject to suffering, and he died. But he does, by the help of his grace, offer a way of handling evil so that we are not defeated by it

---

[80]   Mary Ann Fatula, O.P., *The Triune God of Christian Faith,* The Order of St. Benedict, Inc. (Collegeville, MN: The Liturgical Press [Michael Glazier], 1990), p. 44. Used with permission.

and do not ourselves contribute to its growth. Jesus offers us an answer to the major problems and mysteries of human life. What are some of these?

1.   Jesus saves us from meaninglessness

As we have already pointed out in the chapter on the development of faith, human beings live by meaning; we need to find meaning in what we do or we become neurotic. In fact, finding meaning may well be the pre-eminent crisis of our age. There is nothing so sad as watching people go to their death not having found any real meaning in life and with nothing to look forward to but nothingness itself. Jesus assures us that human life has real meaning. That God should choose to be one of us should be evidence enough. By his presence and his teaching, he shows us how to make a success of our human life; he assures us of resurrection to eternal life. Because of him we can hope.

2.   Jesus saves us from the evil of sin

On the cross Jesus took unto himself our entire sinfulness, that we might be saved from the effects of sin. "For our sake he made him to be sin who knew no sin, so that in him we might become the righteousness of God" (2 Cor 5:21) (CCC 602-604). As we shall see in more detail in a subsequent chapter, sin ultimately means personal alienation and self-destruction. Sin enslaves us – we become slaves to our own passions, desires and selfishness. Jesus does not prevent us from committing sin (God will not interfere with our free will), but he does three things: he suffered and died on the cross to redeem us from sin; by his grace and goodness he forgives sin; and he gives us the example of how to live so as to free ourselves of the alienation that is sin. Jesus saves us from ourselves; he frees us.[81]

3.   Jesus saves us from the evil of suffering and death

Jesus himself suffered and died in the same way we do, and in his suffering and death he gives us a way of handling these experiences of evil. As for suffering, we can unite our suffering to that of Jesus, thus making it meaningful. As for death, we have already seen that what gives death its "sting" is sin. (The "sting" of death is also the pain, fear, hurt, and worry that are associated with it.) Often it is not so much death we fear but the whole process of dying. We need not be afraid of death if we arrive at it having honestly tried to live out the message

---

[81]   Please note that we are talking here about the correct understanding of freedom. People generally understand freedom as freedom from outside coercion and control. But true freedom comes when we are no longer slaves to our passions, our desires, our selfishness. We are truly free when we control our passions and desires and they don't control us. If we have this kind of freedom, then it is something that no amount of outside coercion can take from us. We can be free even behind prison bars or in the face of imminent death.

of Jesus and having asked forgiveness for our failings. It is the burden of an uneasy conscience, a lack of meaning, that will make death painful and scary.

Finally, it is worth emphasizing again that salvation is *now*. Too much of our teaching seems to point only to salvation as a next-life phenomenon, which we cannot really experience in this life. No, salvation is also for this life. It is our duty, therefore, to work for the accomplishment of such salvation for all peoples: for example, by eliminating poverty, injustice and oppression, enslavement of peoples by war, exploitation of the powerless by the greedy. St. Augustine reminds us that "God who created us without ourselves will not save us without ourselves." We have to make the salvation offered by God now a reality. Jesus has brought salvation; we are living in the new age of salvation. We should be experiencing its effects now; otherwise, how could we possibly experience the grace of Christ, which makes our life better now?

The Hebrew name *Jesus* means "God Saves."

The Death of Jesus

As we have already pointed out, it is quite clear from the gospels that Jesus' passion, death and resurrection were of far greater importance to the gospel writers than his infancy and childhood. But even though the passion narratives are more historically detailed than many other parts of the gospel, they are still very much theological reflections. History tries to get at accurate detail and fact; theology tries to understand the working of God in human experience. The gospel writers were less interested in accurate fact than in what the events meant as a fulfillment of the Scriptures and a revelation of God. It was as a result of the death and resurrection experience (historical fact) that the apostles came to a clearer realization that Jesus was indeed the chosen one of God, the Messiah (theological reflection). Thus, God had set a seal on the life and message of Jesus. This faith was the basis for the formation of the church.

It is evident from the gospels that, in his inner human consciousness, Jesus understood that he had a mission from his Father to preach the good news of God's reign and to work for the establishment of that reign. He was totally faithful to that vision. He understood that his mission was to do the will of God, and he pursued that goal with a single-minded fidelity that he foresaw would bring him into conflict with the secular and religious powers. It was this deep human integrity that brought about his destruction. He was not the first or the last person to suffer for his integrity and principles. Therefore, it would be wrong for us to regard the death of Jesus as some form of martyrdom, that is, some form of "dying for the faith." It was more an example of how the forces of evil in the world, working through the selfishness of people bent on preserving their own privileged positions, can, for a time at least, overcome the forces of good.

The gospels portray Jesus as coming into conflict with the religious powers for the following reasons:

1. *He associated with outcasts and sinners (such as tax collectors and prostitutes) and therefore, by insinuation, was a sinner himself.*

Jesus' understanding of his mission brought him into closer and closer contact with the poor, the powerless, the most despised, the sinners, whom he saw as needing his help and the mercy and forgiveness of God. Inevitably he came into conflict with vested authority, who saw him as a threat to their authority and their vision of religion. Nothing seems to have changed, even in our time. In many countries in the recent past, those who worked for the poor and therefore challenged established patterns of society were called "communists" (i.e., despised and evil people).

2. *He was accused of not observing the law of Moses; for example, he healed the sick on the Sabbath day.*

Jesus indicated that such criticism was hypocritical because it did not recognize that there is a higher law of charity that takes precedence over the ritual law of the Sabbath. Punctilious observance of positive religious law can make one proud, smug, heartless and hypocritical, which, Jesus indicates, is very far from true religion.

3. *He spoke of God in the most intimate terms as his Father, his "Abba."*

That, in the eyes of the Jewish leaders, was blasphemy because he "made himself equal to God." According to Jewish custom, the name of God was so sacred it was never openly uttered. And so, the fact that Jesus called God his Father and spoke of this Father in the most intimate way possible was just one more strike against him. He defied the religious customs of the time, thereby challenging those who interpreted the law from the safety of their privileged positions.

4. *He was accused of being a threat to the security of the nation.*

There may have been some merit in this charge because the Jewish leaders were fearful that the Romans would do as they had done before and crush any opposing movement with great cruelty (Acts 5:34 ff.). But it seems certain that the Jewish leaders used this as an excuse to be rid of Jesus, whom they saw as a threat to the establishment. If we think about it, isn't that what our reaction might be if we found someone threatening our national way of life? We too might find it expedient that "it was better to have one person die for the people" (Jn 18:14). Many spies, when caught, have been abandoned by their country precisely on this pretext. The death of Jesus is the age-old story of human sin: the destruction of the powerless by the powerful.

Historically speaking, Jesus was executed by the Romans with typical Roman cruelty. If we are to take the account in the Gospel of Luke as accurate (Lk 23:2), we see that the Sanhedrin persuaded the Romans that they had ample reason for executing Jesus, citing three counts: he was perverting the nation, he refused to pay taxes, and he made himself king, thus defying the power of the emperor. We can see that, once again, what is at work is a power play, the power of Rome against someone perceived as a threat to that power. The drama is acted out against the weakness of Pilate, who is determined to save his own neck, even at the expense of going against his conscience. How very typical this is of so many human tragedies which are still played out today! (One can think of the murder of Archbishop Oscar Romero and the Jesuits of El Salvador.) As Gerard Sloyan astutely observes, "The deep desire to remain in power met a man who said, 'No.' That man had to die."[82]

The message comes through loud and clear: Jesus was the most honest, integral and straightforward of persons. He understood what was his duty and, in obedience to his conscience, was prepared to carry it out, even if it meant death. Integrity and honesty and dedication are the human virtues *par excellence*. That is our example, a thoroughly human and humane life through which shines God's expectation for us all, God speaking to us through the human Jesus. But there is more. What the passion and death of Jesus say to us is that, if we dedicate ourselves to establishing the reign of God on earth, we can expect to face powerlessness, misunderstanding, persecution and even death. The story of the passion, death and resurrection is portrayed in the gospels as the age-old battle between the forces of evil and the forces of good. The forces of evil prevail to bring about the death of an innocent man, but they prevail only for a time. The resurrection represents the triumph of the forces of good and, therefore, the resurrection is the centre of our hope that God, in his goodness and love, will not abandon us to a pointless death and the power of "the evil one."

Conclusion

In the last chapter of the Gospel of Luke, an incident is related which can serve as a fitting conclusion to this section on Jesus. It is a very beautiful story and should be read in its entirety (see Lk 24:13-35). After the resurrection, two of Jesus' disciples were walking along the road to Emmaus, a village near Jerusalem. They were discussing the momentous events of the previous days and as they walked along, Jesus joined them but they did not recognize him. Jesus quickly determined from their conversation that they had not understood the significance of his death and resurrection, so "beginning with Moses and all the

---

[82] Gerard S. Sloyan, *Jesus in Focus: A Life in Its Setting* (Mystic, CT: Twenty-Third Publications, 1983), p. 144.

prophets, he interpreted to them the things about himself in all the scriptures" (Lk 24:27). Fascinated, the disciples asked Jesus to stay with them for supper. "When he was at the table with them, he took bread, blessed and broke it, and gave it to them. Then their eyes were opened, and they recognized him; and he vanished from their sight" (Lk 24:30-31).They recognized him when he repeated what he had done at the Last Supper: his gift of himself in bread and wine. "They said to each other, 'Were not our hearts burning within us while he was talking to us on the road, while he was opening the scriptures to us?'" (Lk 24:32) They then set out immediately for Jerusalem to share this wonderful experience with the other disciples.

We must do as the disciples did on the road to Emmaus; we must come to "recognize" Jesus in all our human vicissitudes, to believe that he is indeed risen from the dead, that he is alive and with us at every step of our journey through life. In one short statement we have touched the core of the Good News that Jesus came to bring – the Good News that God has indeed come among his people, bringing us a message of salvation. Thomas Zanzig has a beautiful comment on this Gospel story.

> The story has tremendous insights to offer each of us in our personal struggles to come to terms with Jesus. The story tells us that God always meets us on our own terms, that he "walks with us" in our journey through life, and that he is sensitive to our own story and our unique needs. If our need is to question, to doubt, and to search, it is our responsibility to do that honestly and without guilt. Jesus and his message can offer each of us an understanding of life that can "burn within our hearts" if we choose to accept it. But each of us, like the two disciples on that dusty road long ago, needs to open our heart to God, just as those two men invited Jesus into their home.[83]

Faith in Jesus is the centre point of the Christian life, the energizing core that gives meaning and purpose to life. Jesus' whole desire for us is that we should come to know God through him; "And this is eternal life, that they may know you, the only true God, and Jesus Christ whom you have sent" (Jn 17:3). Christians have always believed that this "recognition" of Jesus, this faith in Jesus, comes best and most easily within a Christian community, which we call church. It is by sharing with one another in the church our faith in Jesus and our own experience of him that we shall come to know him better. And an essential aspect of hearing and accepting the Good News is that we tell others about it, that we do not keep this wonderful experience to ourselves but share it with others and become true missionaries of Jesus' message.

---

[83]   Thomas Zanzig, *Jesus Is Lord!* p. 197.

Reflection Questions

1. What story about Jesus in the gospel appeals to you most? Why? What does this say about your own relationship to Jesus?

2. Take any one of the gospels and write down some of the questions Jesus asked of various people: the apostles, the scribes and Pharisees, the centurion with the sick child, etc. Many of these questions are also addressed to us. How would you answer them?

3. Jesus is said to have "saved us." What is the meaning of "salvation," and what does the salvation of Jesus mean to you personally?

4. What does it mean to say that Jesus came to establish the reign of God on earth? Have we any part in this?

5. Humpty Dumpty sat on a wall:
   Humpty Dumpty had a great fall.
   All the King's horses and all the King's men
   Couldn't put Humpty Dumpty together again.

   Upon hearing his mother recite this nursery rhyme, a young child is said to have remarked: "Jesus could have done it!" Comment, and explain the purpose of Jesus' miracles.

6. Write a parable set in modern times to illustrate some aspect of Jesus' teaching.

7. It is said that Jesus came to "comfort the afflicted and afflict the comfortable." Explain what this means. How does Jesus challenge you?

Further Reading

Brown, Raymond E. *The Virginal Conception and Bodily Resurrection of Jesus* (New York: Paulist Press, 1973). Already recommended for the chapter on the Christian Scriptures.

Senior, Donald. *Jesus: A Gospel Portrait* (Dayton, OH: Pflaum, 1981). A fine work of theology and Scripture scholarship that is simple enough not to demand specialist knowledge. First-class material for those beginning a study of Jesus. Already recommended for the chapter on the Christian Scriptures.

Sloyan, Gerard. *Jesus in Focus* (Mystic, CT: Twenty-Third Publications, 1983). An approach to Jesus specially designed for the unbeliever but highly recommended for the believer as well. A new and refreshing treatment that will hold the reader's attention.

Zanzig, Thomas. *Jesus Is Lord! A Basic Christology for Adults* (Winona, MN: St. Mary's Press, 1982). One of the best books available in non-technical theological language on the background to Jesus' life, his teaching and its meaning for us. Highly recommended as a source book for teachers.

— —. "Who Is This Jesus We Are Teaching?" *P.A.C.E.*, No. 13, 1983. A very useful summary of his more detailed treatment of the state of christology in *Jesus Is Lord!*

Part III

CHURCH AND SACRAMENT

12

THE CHURCH

The Origins

Nero punished, with exquisite torture, a race of men detested for their evil practices, by vulgar appellation commonly called "Christians." The name was derived from Christ, who in the reign of Tiberius, suffered under Pontius Pilate, the procurator of Judea. By that event the sect, of which he was the founder, received a blow, which, for a time, checked the growth of a dangerous superstition; but it revived soon after, and spread with recruiting vigour, not only in Judea, the soil that gave it birth, but even in the city of Rome . . . . Nero proceeded with his usual artifice. He found a set of profligate wretches who were induced to profess themselves guilty, and, on the evidence of such men, a number of Christians were convicted, not, indeed, upon clear evidence of having set the city on fire, but on account of their sullen hatred of the whole human race. They were put to death with exquisite cruelty, and to their sufferings Nero added mockery and derision.[84]

Thus does the Roman historian Tacitus (78–112 C.E.) describe in his *Annals* how the Emperor Nero instituted a persecution of the Christian community in Rome. According to Tacitus, Nero persecuted the Christians on the pretext that they were the ones who had set the great fire of Rome (64 C.E.), which destroyed three-quarters of the city. In this persecution perished the apostles Peter and Paul, the leaders of the infant church. Tacitus' writing provides us with evidence, from a secular and pagan historian, that the Christian church had spread to Rome a scant ten years from its beginnings in Jerusalem after the death of Christ.

Jesus attracted bands of followers during his lifetime. His chosen group of apostles, and some others, particularly some women, travelled with him as he went about preaching the message of the kingdom of God throughout Judea and Galilee. This little band of Jesus' followers would not have known the word "church" or the word "Christian." The appellation "Christian," as we are told in the book of Acts, was first given to the infant church in the city of Antioch (in modern-day Turkey) years after the death of Christ. Nevertheless, it is this

---

[84]   Cornelius Tacitus, *The Annals,* translated by John Jackson, (Cambridge MA: Harvard University Press, 1986-1992), No. 15,4.

particular communal lifestyle that sets the tone for the development of other communities that are the building blocks of the Christian church.

Despite the fact that early bands of followers attached themselves to Jesus during his lifetime, the day that traditionally marks the beginning of the Christian church is the day of Pentecost (CCC 1076). Pentecost, the Jewish Feast of Weeks, is one of the three great feasts of the Jewish law and is kept on the fiftieth day after the feast of Passover (hence the name Pentecost). The first Christian Pentecost thus occurred 50 days after the resurrection, which is why today we celebrate Pentecost 50 days after Easter.

The twelve apostles, and some of the early band of followers, including Jesus' mother, Mary, were gathered together in a house in Jerusalem. Here is how Luke, in the Acts of the Apostles, describes what happened:

> *When the day of Pentecost had come, they were all together in one place. And suddenly from heaven there came a sound like the rush of a violent wind, and it filled the entire house where they were sitting. Divided tongues, as of fire, appeared among them, and a tongue rested on each of them. All of them were filled with the Holy Spirit and began to speak in other languages, as the Spirit gave them ability. (Acts 2:1-4)*

From being a rather insignificant and somewhat frightened group, the apostles were transformed by the power of the Holy Spirit and boldly preached the message they had learned from Jesus. Wherever they preached, those who came to believe in Jesus and who accepted baptism formed themselves into small communities. These communities would meet for prayer and particularly for the celebration of the Eucharist. They also supported and helped one another, and shared their goods in common (see Acts 2:42-47).

The early communities ultimately came to be called *ecclesia*, the Greek word for church, which means a grouping or assembly of people. In most northern European languages, the word "church" comes from the Greek *Kyriake oikia*, meaning "the family of the Lord." Always, therefore, the essence of church is a gathering, a family, a close-knit group. Sometimes the word was applied to a small house gathering, or to Christians in a specific locality; sometimes it was applied to the whole group of Christians everywhere. So, even today, a small gathering for celebration of the Eucharist can be called church; so also can all the Catholics in a local area such as a diocese (e.g., the church in Toronto). Catholics all over the world constitute the Universal Church.[85] Such a diverse use of the word is obviously confusing, and so, when we use the word today, we must be well aware of the context. Only much later in history did the

---

[85]   CCC 834-835 deals with the relationship of local churches to the church of Rome which, being the seat of the Roman Pontiff (the Pope), "presides in charity" over all the churches.

word "church" come to be applied to the building where the *ecclesia* worships and celebrates the Eucharist.

From this somewhat sketchy summary of the beginnings of the church some important points emerge. From its very origin, church means people: people who believe in Jesus, who come together to profess their faith, to worship and celebrate together, to commemorate the Lord's death and resurrection and to help one another. Therefore, one of the salient features of the early Christian church was a sense of community, a sense of togetherness. Community – a helping, sharing, caring community – is the bedrock principle on which the church is built. The human race was meant to live in harmony and peace with God, with one another, and with the earth, but sin changed all that. Jesus Christ came to re-establish our true unity with God and with one another; his work was to overcome the destruction and alienation of sin. His instrument for accomplishing his purpose is the church built on the ideal of community, a community centred in the Eucharist where it experiences Christ's unifying presence.[86]

However, as time went on, the church became more and more institutionalized and defined in legalistic terms. The sense of church (community) was to a large extent lost; the church became an "it," not a "we." This loss of the sense of being church, of our own personal involvement in church affairs, is truly a tragic quirk of history that has had the effect of altering our whole thinking and our whole theology of church. One effect, for example, is the way we think about and participate in the sacraments. We too often tend to view sacraments as "things" done to us, "things" that we "receive" from the ministers of the church, rather than actions we do. Another effect of the legalistic definition of church is that the word "church" came to be applied almost exclusively to the leaders of the church: the Pope, bishops and clergy. The general tendency of those who write or speak about the church today is to identify the church with its leaders. It is true that these leaders are an essential part of the church; however, they belong to the whole people of God and are not separate and apart from this people. They should not, and do not, form a special caste, though this is often the common perception.

The Church Is a Mystery

The church is a mystery of faith[87] – faith in the continuing presence of Jesus among us, faith in "the purpose of God's plan: 'to unite all things in him'" (CCC 772). As we have pointed out, the church is not an "it"; we are the church, and it is through us that Jesus continues his work in the world today.

---

[86] CCC 946-953 deals with the meaning of "communion" in the church, that is, the common life of the people of God and the various ways in which they are united to form one body, sharing their faith, charisms, goods and love. It is a stirring and wonderful ideal.

[87] The church as mystery is beautifully expressed in CCC 770-773.

We continue his priestly work by offering worship to God. We do this not only in a formal way, by participating in the liturgy, but also by living a life of faith, by obeying God's will and by imitating Christ's love for us as we love one another in a practical and giving way. "Little children, let us love, not in word or speech, but in truth and action" (1 Jn 3:18).

We continue his prophetic work by doing our part to hand on his message (CCC 571). We do this not only by talk, persuasion and teaching, but also by the example of our lives. "By this everyone will know that you are my disciples, if you have love for one another" (Jn 13:35).

We continue Jesus' work in our efforts to help those who are in need, those who are sick and suffering, as well as those who need guidance, counselling, commiseration, encouragement. We are Christ's body; it is through us that he acts in the world. The story is told of a soldier in Europe during World War II who came with his battalion to a bombed-out church. Among the ruins was a statue of Jesus with no hands. Etched in the base of the statue was the request of an unknown soldier: "He has no hands but yours. Will you give him your hands?"[88] Will we give Jesus our hands, our whole self, to carry on his work in the world?

Since the church is essentially a mystery, we cannot fully understand the church any more than we can fully understand God. We must be prepared, in our own minds, to accept this fact. But mystery does not mean mystification. As was pointed out in Chapter 3, we may lack full understanding, but that does not mean that we cannot know anything at all. It simply means that we cannot find a full and complete explanation; there will always be aspects of church that elude our grasp. We shall always be searching for new ways that lead to better understanding.

Models of the Church

Some Preliminaries

In order to help us understand better some of the mysterious reality that is the church we use images, or models. Scientists have long used models to help explain complex realities not immediately available to the senses, such as for the structure of the atom. Since Jesus was a teacher *par excellence*, it should be no surprise to us that he used everyday images to try to explain the mysterious reality of the kingdom of God. And so, for example, Jesus says that the kingdom is like the many fish that are caught in a fisherman's net. The fisherman rejects the bad ones but keeps the good (Mt 13:47-48). The kingdom is like a merchant

---

[88] Adapted from Eileen Flynn and Gloria Thomas, *Living Faith: An Introduction to Theology* (Kansas City, MO: Sheed & Ward, 1989), p. 173.

in search of fine pearls. When he finds one he sells everything in order to buy it (Mt 13:45-46). And Jesus also uses the beautiful image of the vine and its branches to indicate the unity that should exist between him and all people (Jn 15:1-6). To find images for the kingdom of God is also to find images for the church, for it is the church that carries on Jesus' work of establishing the kingdom on earth.[89]

But before we go on to describe some of the images of church that are in use in current theology, there are some preliminary points to which we need to pay attention.

1. An image, or model, is in fact an analogy. It tells us what the church is like by using experiences with which we are familiar. What it does, therefore, is provide a point of view; it indicates a way of looking at the church. Our point of view dictates what we see, and how we see it. We get different impressions when we look at the same thing from different angles. Thus, if we were to look at a football game from the Goodyear blimp, things and their relationship to one another would look quite different than if we viewed the game from inside the stadium itself.

2. Each image is limited in what it enables us to grasp and understand. No image or model is completely adequate in explaining the phenomenon, for the truth is greater than any one of them. This is why Jesus, in his teaching, used so many images of the kingdom and why we need several images to try to capture as much of the reality of the church as possible. One of the dangers in using models is precisely that when one model becomes popular, perhaps because it responds to a particular social or theological teaching currently in vogue, some people tend to overplay it as the only way to look at the church.

3. If we are to find helpful images of the church, then each image must take account of two important factors: (a) the church is divine, has come from God and exists only through the power of God's gift of the Spirit; and (b) the church is also human, made up not of disembodied spirits but of persons who are sinful human beings (CCC 779).

And so,

(a) The church is a eucharistic community brought together and held together by the power of God's Spirit and attempting to live the life of Christ on earth;

---

[89]   CCC 753-757 deals with various symbols (images) of the church: the sheepfold, the cultivated field, the building of God where God's family dwells, the temple, the Jerusalem above.

(b) This community is a human community and is sinful; people are not perfect. In order to realize God's will, the church needs structures – human structures – and the authority to make these structures work. Structures generate rules and regulations aimed at keeping the community together, a necessary factor in any grouping of people who want to stay together, even such mundane groupings, for example, as a literary society or a stamp club.

Some Models [90]

A. The Church as the Body of Christ

The image of the church as the Body of Christ is spelled out very clearly in Paul's First Letter to the Corinthians (1 Cor 12:12-30); it is, therefore, a quintessentially scriptural image. This passage from Scripture should be read and studied in its entirety; its richness can only be adequately appreciated and savoured by careful meditation. The passage from 1 Corinthians makes no mention that Jesus is the head of the body that is the church. We find this in other parts of the New Testament that should be taken as completing the image given in 1 Corinthians. It would take too long to provide a detailed analysis of the image of the church as the Body of Christ, but here are some of the points that are worth noting:

1. The church is the body of Christ and he is the head of the body, giving life to the whole (CCC 669, 792, 805). The whole church community lives with the life of Christ (see also Jesus' own image of the vine and its branches – Jn 15:1-6). Jesus continues his work through the church – worshipping, preaching, teaching, healing, counselling, forgiving and working for justice.

2. Each part of the body (that is, each one of us) is unique and has a specific work to do (if the body were all eye, how would it function?). The diversity of parts, and the diversity of work, enables the body to function as a whole. The individual parts work for the good of the whole, not exclusively for their own good (CCC 791).

3. If one part is sick, or dead (the effect of sin), the whole body is weakened. If all parts are healthy, the whole body is healthy (CCC 953).

4. Each part lives with the life of the whole: that is, the life of Christ. Separated from the body (from Christ), the parts cannot have any existence of their own; they will die.

---

[90] A standard theological work on models of the church is that by Avery Dulles, S.J., *Models of the Church* (New York: Doubleday, 1974). In what follows we shall take Dulles' book as our guide.

B. The Church as the People of God

Vatican Council II, in Chapter 2 of its Dogmatic Constitution on the Church *(Lumen gentium)*, a landmark document of the Council, proposed an image of the church as the People of God. This is a strongly community-oriented image. As we have pointed out above, the notion of community is basic to any understanding of the church. However, the church is more than a mere sociological community in which there is human caring and helping fellowship among the members. The church owes its inner life to the Holy Spirit who, in fact, is the true source of the communion that exists among its members (CCC 739). It is for this reason that we refer to the church as a mystical communion.

As with the Body of Christ image, the People of God image is community-oriented, focusing on the interrelationship and mutual helpfulness of the members. However, it provides us with a slightly different point of view from the Body of Christ image – and the more points of view we have, the better. Some of its features are as follows:

1. Ideally, all should work for the good of the whole community and this work should operate on the principle of shared responsibility. The ideal proposed is that of service – service to one another and service to the whole body. This model fosters a more democratic approach to church and church governance than some others.

2. Some structure, some form of authority is necessary but, again ideally, authority will be based on true leadership and not merely on rank and position.[91] Also, authority is based on service; the Pope refers to himself as "the servant of the servants of God." While possessing the authority to lead and guide the church, the leaders are the signs and centres of unity – the Pope for the whole church and the bishops for their individual churches in union with the Pope.

3. The Holy Spirit pervades the whole church. All members receive and possess the Holy Spirit, who fosters a true relationship of love among the members. God's Spirit, therefore, is not only given to the leaders of the church.

---

[91]   A true leader must (a) show personal competence, (b) give good example, (c) lead by persuasion and by education rather than by raw authority and power, (d) be able to recognize and sharpen the talents and responsibilities of those led so as to be able to delegate authority and decentralize the structure.

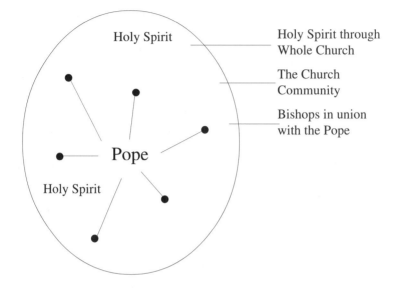

The People of God Model

1. Pope, bishops, priests, people form one community.

2. The Pope is the centre of unity for the whole church. Bishops in communion
   with him are centres of unity for their respective areas.

3. The Holy Spirit pervades the whole community and inspires all in virtue of
   their baptism.

4. Holy Spirit given especially to office holders because of their special duties.

As we have already mentioned, no model is of itself adequate to fully
explain the mystery. Each model has its strengths and its weaknesses that must
be taken into account in assessing the value of that particular model or image.
What, then, are the strengths and weaknesses of the People of God model?

Strengths

1.   This model has a better basis in Scripture than many others. In the Old
     Testament Israel is constantly referred to as God's chosen people, while in
     the New Testament the church is often referred to as the People of God of
     the new covenant (see, for example, Rom 9:23-26, Heb 8:10). Furthermore,
     if we look at the descriptions of the early Christian communities found in
     the Acts of the Apostles, we can easily see how well they realize the ideal of
     the communal model of church.

2. This model helps us to understand the historical nature of the church as a community that persists through history and is incorporated in many different cultures. We must be open to change, flexible, willing to study the signs of the times and to constantly reassess our understanding and practice of Christ's teaching.

3. This model is particularly well-suited to the contemporary social scene when the ideal of democracy and close interpersonal relationships is being promoted everywhere. It is a time when, as Avery Dulles, S.J., remarks, "large institutions are accepted as at best a necessary evil. They are felt to be oppressive and depersonalizing."[92] Generally, too, people want to have a say in the important things that affect their lives. A more democratic approach to church (for example, in the appointment of bishops) should allow for this.

Weaknesses

1. The model tends to be somewhat amorphous and idealistic. All of us are searching for the ideal human community that will meet all our needs for love and understanding. But the ideal is too often clouded over by the reality of sin and selfishness. Human experience gives clear signals that structure and authority, rules and regulations, which somewhat curb our individuality and freedom, are necessary if the community is to survive. The early church quickly realized this, as reported in Acts 15:19-21.

2. Ideally, the notion of *koinonia** which is proposed by this model can and should be applied to both the horizontal dimension (helping, caring fellowship, union) and to the vertical dimension (communion with God). Unfortunately, in many presentations of this model, the two aspects are not seen as necessarily going together. As Dulles wisely remarks, "it is not clear that outgoing friendliness in point of fact leads to the most intense experience of God. For some persons, perhaps, it does, but not for all."[93]

3. Some people have pointed out that this model does not sufficiently give Christians a clear sense of their own identity.

C. The Church as Institution

The church as institution is outlined by Vatican Council II in Chapter 3 of *Lumen gentium*. This model is a fairly late development in church history. The institutional notion of church developed in the late Middle Ages, particularly in the Counter-Reformation period when the church was intent on responding to the attacks of the Protestant Reformers. Its first precise formulation is generally

---

[92] Dulles, p. 55.
[93] *Ibid.*, p. 56.

attributed to St. Robert Bellarmine, S.J. (1542–1621). Insistence on the institutional model reached its zenith around the time of Vatican Council I* (1871). For all practical purposes it is the model that seems to be the one most favoured by church leaders at the present time.

1. The model is based on the ideal of the secular state, which has a constitution, government and laws to help it achieve its proper end. Just as the secular state operates by a chain of command through legislation (prime minister, cabinet, parliament, people), so does the church (Pope, bishops, priests, people). The church differs from the modern state in that it is not a democracy, its rulers are not elected by popular vote, and the church is hierarchical* in nature. This hierarchical structure derives from St. Peter (who represents Christ) and the apostles (whose successors are the bishops) and was therefore instituted by Christ (CCC 874, 880-887). The Pope, it is true, is elected, but elected by cardinals who have been appointed by previous popes; bishops are appointed by the Pope.

2. The major functions of the church are to teach, to govern and to sanctify. The hierarchy controls each of these functions. Thus, the hierarchy issues authoritative interpretations of revelation, from which they derive decrees and directives. The people respond by respectful obedience, secure in the knowledge that they are "doing the will of God." The hierarchy also controls the very prayer life of the church, the sacraments and the liturgy, by controlling how, when and in what form these channels of sanctification are to be used.

3. As can be seen from the above, there is a clear distinction between the clergy and the people: that is, those who teach, govern and sanctify and those who are taught, governed and sanctified. The tendency is to make the clergy a separate caste within the church. This distinction between clergy and people was clearly expressed in a schema prepared for Vatican Council I (but never debated because the Council was interrupted): "among the faithful some are clerics and some are laymen, . . . there is in the church the power from God whereby to some it is given to sanctify, teach, and govern, and to others not."[94]

4. In this model the members of the church are clearly visible. The members can be distinguished as those who accept the doctrines taught by the magisterium (i.e., the official teaching arm of the church), who participate in the sacraments and who submit to the legitimate governing authority. This point is made in opposition to the Protestant position that the church is essentially invisible, existing in the hearts and minds of its adherents.

---

[94] Quoted by Dulles, p. 35.

5.   The Holy Spirit, though present in the whole church and in each member, is more powerfully present in the hierarchy because of their office.

This model can be represented in a diagram as a pyramid.

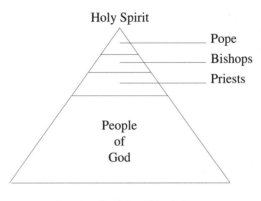

The Institutional Model

1. Pope and bishops are the authentic (so designated by Jesus Christ) teachers and interpreters of revelation. Because of this duty they have a special claim to the inspiration of the Holy Spirit in performing their duty for the whole church.

2. The clergy, who form a separate group distinct from the rest of the church, control all aspects of church life, teaching, governing and sanctifying.

3. The people, who support the pyramid, are instructed by the leaders of the church in how to live the gospel. They accept and obey these instructions as God's will.

Strengths

1.   This model bears the strong weight of tradition since the 16th century. Since that time this model has been taken for granted in several church documents, which affirm it as being divinely revealed. Undoubtedly, it is the model that most dominates the present-day church.

2.   It points to the continuity of the church from Jesus and the apostles as seen in the Pope and bishops in unbroken succession.

3.   The tight hierarchical structure of the church and the method of governance are a strong force promoting unity and acting against fragmentation, which is so characteristic of other Christian bodies. This model, with its clearly defined authority structure providing authoritative interpretations of the message of Christ, is often much admired by those who belong to churches based on looser-fitting models.

4. The relatively clear definition of membership, and the centralized authority, provide Catholics with a certain sense of identity, and a certain sense of security that they are in the "right place." As Dulles points out, "They knew clearly who they were and what they stood for, when they were succeeding and when they were failing."[95]

Weaknesses

1. In a now-famous speech at Vatican II, Bishop Emile De Smedt of Bruges, Belgium, criticized the institutional model as prone to three serious defects.

The first of these is what he called clericalism: everything in the church is controlled by the clergy – teaching, sanctifying and governing. The clergy thus form a separate caste, and lay people are not given their rightful place in church ministry.

The second defect is that of juridicism, which is the tendency to exaggerate the role of human authority in the church. We become overburdened with church law and regulations which, as with secular states, in turn tend to breed a bureaucracy to administer these laws. Furthermore, it fosters legalism: an undue preoccupation with the letter of the law. Particularly distressing is the tendency to apply this legalistic approach to the sanctifying power of the church such that "spiritual ministries are not regarded as effective unless they conform to the prescriptions of canon [i.e., church] law."[96]

The third defect of this model, according to Bishop De Smedt, is that of triumphalism. This model tends to foster the idea that we are better than others, that we belong to the "*true* church" and therefore have an inside track on salvation. The leaders of the church, the bishops, are often referred to as "princes" and, indeed, sometimes move with a pomp and circumstance modeled on secular potentates. We might well ask: is this what Jesus envisaged for his humble flock of followers?

To these three defects from the debates at Vatican II, the modern concern with the rights of women encourages us to add a fourth: the continuing scandal of sexism (though this may not be a defect inherent in the institution model itself). This defect is no doubt fostered by the fact that the clergy, in whom all power is concentrated, is exclusively male. To date, insufficient attention has been paid to the proper position of women in the church. Though much more effort is being presently made to correct this defect, much still remains to be done.[97]

---

[95]   *Ibid.*, p. 39.
[96]   *Ibid.*, p. 36.
[97]   See John Paul II in his exhortation to the laity, *Christifideles laici* (1989), and his letter on the dignity and vocation of women, *Mulieris dignitatem* (1994).

2. This model has little support in Scripture, which portrays the church in a much more communitarian and mystical form. Jesus himself criticized the institutionalized religion of the Scribes and Pharisees; his authority did not come from any institutional appointment but from God his Father, in whose name he spoke.

3. Vatican Council II encouraged us to take account of the "signs of the times" in our interpretation and understanding of God's revelation. There is little doubt that one of the pre-eminent signs of the times is the spread, and almost universal acceptance, of the democratic ideal by which all the governed should have a say in how they are governed. It seems that the institution model of church is out of step with this ideal.

D. Some Other Models of Church

There are many other models of church than the ones described above. The more models we can develop, the better, for they enable us to delve deeper into the mystery. Let us, therefore, take a very quick look at two more: the church as sacrament and the church as servant to the world.

The Church as Sacrament

A sacrament is an external sign of an interior grace, the mystical presence and power of God. A sacrament effects, or brings about, what it signifies. Jesus is the primary sacrament, for in him God is revealed in a tangible and sense-perceptible way. "Whoever has seen me," he said, "has seen the Father" (Jn 14:9). It is only in and through Jesus that we can go to God. But, as we have seen above, the church is the body of Christ. Through the church, Jesus is made actively present in the world; the church continues Jesus' ministry to the world. Therefore, the church is a tangible, sense-perceptible sign of Jesus' presence to the world. Not only is it a sign, but it is an efficacious sign which actually accomplishes what it signifies (i.e., the presence of God in the world); hence, it can well be called a sacrament (CCC 775-776). As God is present in Jesus, so Jesus is present in the work and ministry of the church. A strength of this model is that it shows us how, through the church, we encounter Jesus in a very real way in the world, and particularly through participation in the sacraments.

The Church as Servant to the World

If we study the life of Jesus we find that he spent a considerable amount of time ministering to the ordinary human needs of people. He ministered to the sick, he comforted the sorrowing, he calmed consciences by forgiving sin, he promoted justice and integrity, he was a peacemaker: in other words, he worked for the establishment of God's kingdom. As he said himself, he came to serve, not to be served; service was the keynote of his ministry. In a phrase made famous by Dietrich Bonhoeffer, Jesus was, in the truest sense, "a man for others." This model of church claims that the principal mark of the church should be that of service to the world, that the primary work of the church is to promote everything that makes for the betterment of humankind. Indeed, the 1971 Synod* of Bishops stated that work for justice was "constitutive" of preaching the gospel. This model of church is often promoted by those (such as the liberation theologians) who claim that Christ's promise of salvation cannot be only for the next life, it must apply also to this life. We must work for the human betterment of everyone, but particularly the poor and the destitute and those suffering from injustice. It is not sufficient only to preach to them that they must accept their sufferings in this life in view of a better life to come.

There is no doubt that a strength of this model is that it focuses on an important aspect of the work of the church which we should constantly keep in mind: namely, service to justice and to the poor and disadvantaged. However, a definite weakness, as Dulles points out, is that there is little backing for it in the New Testament. Here the church is portrayed "as existing for the glory of God and of Christ, and for the salvation of its members in a life beyond the grave. It is not suggested that it is the church's task to make the world a better place to live in."[98]

Synthesis of Models

We have already mentioned that none of these models captures the full reality that is the church. Each gives only a partial glimpse of the truth. The church is a mystery greater and more transcendent than any model that attempts to explain it. Therefore, it would be wrong for us to say that this image, or that one, is the image we should fully adopt. It would seem that the way forward is by a synthesis of the various models. In the process we should aim to heighten the strengths and reduce the weaknesses of the various models.

One of the criticisms levelled at church leaders today is precisely that they seem to espouse only one model of church, namely, the institution model. It is the model which is largely operative at present and seems to dominate much of the thinking and theologizing about the church. This model has been dominant for so long that it has, more than any other, determined what the church looks like today and how it is conceived in the minds of members and non-members alike.

Since Vatican II, there has been an effort to give more prominence to the People of God model, that is, a more community-oriented view of the church. That there should be some tension among supporters of the various models is

---

[98]   Dulles, p. 95.

only to be expected. But, almost certainly, the tension is in many ways healthy, for it serves as a spur to greater research and the progress of knowledge and understanding of church.[99] We are a pilgrim people, a people on a journey of self-understanding, seeking how we can best express and respond to God's presence in our lives. That self-understanding, the search for truth, can only progress through research, questioning and scholarly argument.

Church Teaching

Doctrine/Dogma

Two terms that are associated with church teaching, sometimes used synonymously and frequently confused, are *doctrine* and *dogma*. A doctrine (from the Latin *docere*, to teach) is a teaching that has received the official approval of the church coming through the Pope, or a general council, or a group of bishops in union with the Pope. An example is the inviolability of conscience, taught by many theologians but also strongly emphasized by Vatican II.[100] A dogma (from the Greek *dogma* meaning decision, ordinance) is a doctrine that is definitively (that is, infallibly) taught by the church as explicitly revealed by God and which therefore must be believed with religious faith. Thus, all dogmas are doctrines but not all doctrines are dogmas. A dogma is usually promulgated with great solemnity, most often in clear and succinct written form, such that to deny it would constitute heresy and involve separation from the church (e.g., the dogma of Mary's assumption into heaven). Many dogmas already exist in clear form in Sacred Scripture (e.g., the dogma of the resurrection of Jesus) and so do not have to be restated by the church.

The Magisterium

"Magisterium" is derived from the Latin word *magister,* meaning "teacher," and is the word used to designate the teaching authority of the church. Roman Catholics believe that the right and duty of authoritatively teaching the true gospel of Jesus Christ belongs to the Pope and the bishops in union with him. They are the successors of the apostles, and to them Jesus gave the duty of helping God's people to understand and live the gospel message (CCC 890). To

---

[99]   It is interesting that an attempt has recently been made to reconcile somewhat the differences between the People of God model and the Institution model. See, for example, "Letter to the Bishops of the Catholic Church on Some Aspects of the Church Understood as Communion issued by the Congregation for the Doctrine of the Faith" (*L'Osservatore Romano*, English Edition, June 17, 1992). This letter attempts to explain that the communion model, when properly understood, is adequate for explaining all aspects of church, including its hierarchical structure. Again properly understood, the model also helps to promote ecumenism, that is, the union of all the Christian churches.

[100]   See, for example, the *Declaration on Religious Liberty (Dignitatis humanae)*, Nos. 2-3; *Pastoral Constitution on the Church in the Modern World (Gaudium et spes)*, No. 16.

them is given the duty of preserving intact the true teaching of Jesus Christ. Vatican Council II expresses it this way:

> The bishops, in as much as they are the successors of the apostles, receive from the Lord, to whom all power is given in heaven and on earth, the mission of teaching all peoples, and of preaching the Gospel to every creature, so that all may attain salvation through faith, Baptism, and the observance of the commandments.[101]

Such a teaching authority is a necessary bulwark against false teaching that may lead the faithful people of God astray, as has happened many times in history to those who have refused to accept this teaching authority. Indeed, the acceptance by the people of God of a central teaching authority is one of the great strengths of the Roman Catholic Church.

Sometimes we come across the terms "ordinary magisterium" and "extraordinary magisterium"; it will be useful to note briefly what these terms mean. The "extraordinary magisterium" is exercised when the Pope and bishops together (as in an ecumenical council such as Vatican II), or the Pope alone in solemn definition, declare certain teaching to be binding in faith and to be believed by the whole church. This manner of teaching does not occur frequently. The "ordinary magisterium" is exercised when the Pope and bishops, in the course of their ordinary pastoral responsibilities, teach on matters concerning faith or morals. In the strictest sense, therefore, the term "magisterium" refers to those who teach authoritatively in virtue of their office: that is, the Pope and bishops. However, as a result of the deliberations at Vatican II, the term is beginning to assume a broader meaning. Thus, the faithful "who by Baptism are incorporated into Christ . . . have been made sharers in their own way in the priestly, prophetic, and kingly office of Christ, and play their part in carrying out the mission of the whole Christian people in the church and in the world."[102] And so, the whole church has the duty and privilege of participating in the threefold work of Christ in the world: his prophetic work (his work as teacher), his priestly work (his worship of the Father) and his kingly work (his shepherding or service to the world). In the context of teaching, therefore, we must teach one another; we must help one another to better understand and live our life of faith. Furthermore, in their teaching the Pope and bishops must take account of the *sensus fidelium,* that is, the "instinctive sensitivity in matters of faith exercised by the whole body of believers whose appreciation and discernment of revelation is guided by the Holy Spirit."[103] The faithful people of God have also received the gift of the

---

[101]   *Dogmatic Constitution on the Church (Lumen gentium)*, No. 24.

[102]   *Ibid.*, No. 31.

[103]   Gerald O'Collins, S.J., and Edward Farrugia, *A Concise Dictionary of Theology* (New York: Paulist Press, 1991), p. 219.

Holy Spirit and therefore can have something to say about the living out of Christ's message in their own social context. They, too, should contribute to the teaching of the whole church.

Infallibility

Closely connected with the teaching function of the church is the question of infallibility. Infallibility means "cannot fall into error" (from the Latin *in* and *fallere*, to deceive). It is a gift of the power of God's Spirit "with which the divine redeemer wished to endow his church."[104] If the true church of Jesus Christ subsists in the Catholic Church, as taught by Vatican II, then that church cannot fall into error and thus cease to be the church of Jesus Christ. The gift of infallibility ensures that, in teaching on matters pertaining to faith and morals affecting the Christian life, the church cannot be wrong. Thus, to say that a certain teaching is infallible means *that by the grace of God this teaching is free from error and therefore must be accepted and believed with religious faith by the whole church.* Put another way, it means that this truth clearly belongs to the deposit of revelation; *God has spoken.*

The Pope, in his position as head of the universal church, possesses that same infallibility that belongs to the church as a whole. Similarly, the ordinary magisterium (as defined above) also possesses the gift of infallibility. "The infallibility promised to the Church is also present in the body of bishops, when, together with Peter's successor, they exercise the supreme Magisterium, above all in an Ecumenical Council" (CCC 891). This certainly does not mean that the Pope can wake up one morning and, while having his morning coffee, decide to make this or that infallible declaration! Infallible pronouncements are only made after a prolonged process of consultation with the world's bishops, theological research and sounding out the beliefs and practices of the faithful people of God: the church.

The gift of infallibility is probably one of the most misunderstood character-istics of the church. Faithful Catholics have a tendency to develop an "infallibil-ity mentality" by which they tend to view every statement coming out of Rome as being infallible. Teachers have often encouraged Catholics to accept every papal statement as if it were infallible. For such people the test of one's orthodoxy is, as Dulles says, "a readiness to believe whatever the church might teach for the very reason that the church was teaching it."[105]

Infallibility is not that difficult to understand and accept if we keep in mind the following points.

---

[104]   See *Dogmatic Constitution on the Church*, No. 25.
[105]   Dulles, p. 168.

1.   First, the fact that a statement is infallible does not mean that it necessarily is the best and only way to formulate that particular truth. In other words, there may well be better and clearer ways of saying it, remembering that all language is historically and culturally conditioned and also (particularly in the case of theological statements) conditioned by its underlying philosophy. All that is guaranteed by infallibility is that, *as formulated*, the teaching is not erroneous.

2.   Second, certain rather stringent conditions apply before a papal definition can be considered infallible.

(a) The statement must concern faith or morals. Thus, the Pope is not infallible when speaking on other matters, such as science, politics, world peace or social questions.

(b) The teaching must be given in an official, formal and unambiguous manner such that there can be no mistake that infallibility is intended and that the definition applies to the whole church. When the Pope speaks this way, he is said to speak *ex cathedra* (literally, "from the chair," the chair representing his position of authority in the church).

(c) The definition must reflect the faith of the whole church. Generally, the Pope ascertains the faith of the church by consulting with bishops all over the world. However, actual consensus of all the bishops is not necessary for infallibility.

3.   Third, if the whole church is united in believing and teaching a certain doctrine, even though the Pope has made no formal pronouncement on the matter, the doctrine can be said to be infallibly taught and requires the assent of religious faith. The reason is that by the power of the Holy Spirit the gift of infallibility is given to the church as a whole.

Encyclical Letters

The teaching of the church comes to us in many different forms, such as Encyclical Letters, Decrees of Ecumenical Councils, Instructions, Exhortations, Letters to individual bishops, papal homilies and many others, not all of which carry the same weight of authority. Individual bishops may also write pastoral letters to the people of their diocese on matters of local importance or to emphasize certain aspects of church teaching.

Of all the statements issued by the teaching authority of the church, Encyclical Letters are probably the most frequently used and therefore deserve to have something more said about them. "Encyclical" literally means "circular letter"; the Pope uses these letters as the most common means of exercising his ordinary teaching authority (CCC 2034). They are written by the Pope, or under his direction, on matters of doctrine, morals or discipline, and are addressed to the whole church.

Because these teachings emanate from the supreme teaching authority of the church they must be received with respect and with "internal and religious assent of the mind." Vatican II points out that "The Catholic Church is by the will of Christ the teacher of truth. It is its duty to proclaim and teach with authority the truth which is Christ . . ."[106] However, even though we should give religious assent to the teaching contained in encyclicals, it should be noted that the teaching there does not carry the same authority as teaching given by the extraordinary magisterium (see above for the difference between the ordinary and extraordinary teaching authority). These letters do not normally carry the weight of infallibility; they are not normally a *definitive* statement (that is, that the matter is officially "closed") on moral or dogmatic matters. It follows that while such teaching should always be an essential ingredient in the forming of one's conscience, "the authority of the Church when she pronounces on moral questions, in no way undermines the freedom of conscience of Christians."[107]

Our Response to Official Teaching

As we pointed out above, because of the responsibility given them by the Holy Spirit, the Pope and bishops must be listened to attentively when they teach on matters of faith and/or morals. Due consideration and respect must be given to such teaching even if it does not carry the weight of infallibility. Nevertheless, we should realize that most of the teaching in encyclicals, for example, is a practical application of infallible teaching carried out by the ordinary magisterium. And so, we cannot and should not dismiss non-infallible official teaching as of no consequence. The matter is succinctly put by the Congregation for the Doctrine of the Faith: "Such teachings are [however] an authentic expression of the Ordinary Magisterium of the Roman Pontiff or of the College of Bishops and therefore require religious submission of will and intellect. They are set forth to arrive at a deeper understanding of revelation, or to recall the conformity of a teaching with the truths of faith, or lastly to warn against ideas incompatible with those truths or dangerous opinions that can lead to error."[108] As the Catechism expresses it, we should adhere to such teaching with "religious assent, which, though distinct from the assent of faith, is nonetheless an extension of it" (CCC 892).[109]

---

[106] *Declaration on Religious Liberty, No 14.*
[107] Pope John Paul II, Encyclical Letter *Veritatis Splendor,* No. 64.
[108] Congregation for the Doctrine of the Faith, *Doctrinal Commentary on the Concluding Formula of the Profession Fidei* (Libreria Editrice Vaticana, 1998), p. 19.
[109] See, in this context, the Apostolic Letter of Pope John Paul II *Ad Tuendam Fidem* (*Origins,* July 16, 1998). In this letter the Pope emphasizes that all teaching that is necessary for the "holy keeping and faithful exposition of the deposit of faith" must be firmly accepted and held.
See also the *Instruction on the Ecclesial Vocation of the Theologian* of the Congregation for the Doctrine of the Faith (*Origins,* July 5, 1990), especially numbers 27–31.

Therefore, we shirk our responsibility if we shrug and say, "I disagree!" or "That's only their opinion!" when the teaching does not happen to suit us, or because we have some emotional reaction against it. To set ourselves up as equal to, or better than, the Pope and bishops in matters pertaining to the Christian life is a particularly objectionable form of arrogance. It is possible, however, that after studying, praying, and seeking advice, someone can remain perfectly loyal to the church and yet may be sincerely unable to accept non-infallible teaching. Such a person should not be considered to have rejected the respect and submission due to such teaching. Everyone is bound to follow their conscience, providing it has been properly formed; the church does not advocate blind obedience in non-infallible matters.

Early Church History and the Modern Church

This chapter has not dealt at any length with church history. Before we conclude, let us summarize some of the points made above and connect them with the early history of the church.

1. The church is a *missionary* church dedicated to spreading the message of Jesus everywhere. The tremendous enthusiasm of the early Christians for telling the Good News should still be ours today.

2. Christianity is primarily a way of life. The formulation of beliefs came *after* a dedication to a way of life that Jesus taught. Religion is never simply a system of beliefs. We cannot divorce our way of acting from our faith. We express our faith by acting it out in our daily lives. Faith is a verb, not a noun. There is no such thing as a non-practising believer.

3. The early church soon discovered that "love" and "togetherness" and "*koinonia*" were not enough. Faced with the common experience of sin, they soon realized that, to keep the church together as a community dedicated to the ideals of Jesus, *rules and discipline were needed*. Some of these early rules are mentioned in Acts 21:17-35. The church today needs organization and discipline, no matter how distasteful such discipline may be to some people. If we wish to be identified as belonging to a community we must observe the "rules," which are there for the good of the whole community.

4. The early church soon came up against the secular arm. For example, an early Roman court ruled that Christianity was tantamount to an attack against the Roman way of life. Christianity still remains profoundly *counter-cultural*. Jesus did not bless any culture, form of society or social system. All these are flawed, subject to sin and in need of redemption. In our time, we as church have to consistently expose the false values that are pervasive in our culture. To be a Christian may often require heroic resistance to these false values. A great turning point came for the church in 313 C.E. with the

conversion to Christianity of the Roman Emperor Constantine. As a result of this conversion it became popular, or just politically expedient, to become a Christian. The church now faces a new danger, that of being too closely allied with the secular arm, with politics and power in high places. The modelling of the church on the secular state (see above) is perhaps the greatest barrier to it becoming the humble flock of Jesus.

5. Given the previous point, the church *can expect to be persecuted* as it was persecuted in the early years even if in more subtle ways than the violent persecution suffered in those times. The church has always produced martyrs who are prepared to die for their Christian beliefs and for their commitment to the way of life taught by Jesus. Persecution takes different forms in different times, but a Christian community genuinely trying to live by the ideals of the gospel can expect opposition that may call for some form of heroism.

6. The sweep of church history proves conclusively that Jesus is faithful to his promise to be with the church to the end of time. No other group, organization or community has survived over the past two thousand years as well as the church has. This gives us great cause for optimism for the future, as well as confidence in the abiding presence of Christ in our lives.

Conclusion

There are two things that we should always bear in mind about the church: (1) the church is *divine*, instituted by Jesus Christ, manifests his presence to the world and is held together by the power of the Holy Spirit; and (2) the church is also *human*, made up of fallible, sinful human persons who stumble along in their attempt to live up to their exalted calling. It is this split personality that often is so troubling to many people.

Because the church is divine, people expect it to be free from all the ills that affect other societies. And so, its ministers are expected to be perfect and virtually sinless; its leaders are expected to make the right decisions and say the right things; it must stick to the pulpit and not meddle in secular affairs. In other words, many people simply will not make allowance for the fact that the church, including its leaders and special ministers, is also human and therefore flawed, always in need of reform and conversion. Particularly distressing is when the whole church is judged by the fallibility of a few of its members and by the very human mistakes of some of its functionaries. People sometimes give up the practice of their faith just because they have had some altercation with a priest or bishop. Jesus is always present in the church and that presence is always open to the sincere seeker. Unfortunately, his presence is often masked by the church's all too human face. We are called, above all, to love the church and be loyal to it, in spite of all its defects and deficiencies. In so doing we are loving Jesus and, ultimately, loving ourselves, for the great truth that we must burn into ourselves is that *we* are the church. When Pope John Paul II visited Peru in 1985, a spokesperson from one of the very poor areas of the country read to him the following beautiful statement, so expressive of the ideal of church we have been trying to inculcate:

> We are hungry, we live in misery, we are sick and out of work. Our women give birth in tuberculosis, our infants die, our children grow weak. . . . But despite this we believe in the God of life. . . . We have walked with the church and in the church, and it has helped us to live in dignity as children of God and brothers and sisters of Christ.[110]

Our weaknesses, the difficulties and troubles in life, can be overcome by the meaning and comfort we shall find by participating fully in the life of the church. By our lives of commitment to the ideals of Jesus we make the church live, for we make Christ present to the world. In turn, our faith and our deep relationship to Christ are nourished in and through the church community.

Reflection Questions

1. Why do we use models to help us understand something about the church? Why is it important to develop as many models as possible?

2. The church is the Body of Christ. What does that statement mean to you personally and to your Christian life?

3. Explain carefully the difference between doctrine and dogma.

4. What do you understand by the Magisterium?

5. What is the meaning of infallibility? Under what conditions is the Pope infallible?

6. A man who took great pride in his lawn found himself with a large crop of dandelions. He tried everything he knew to get rid of them but failed. He then wrote to the Department of Agriculture, enumerating all the things he had tried to be rid of the dandelions. He closed his letter with the question, "What should I do now?" Back came the reply from the Department: "Learn to love them!"[111] What does this story say to you about the church? Evaluate your own attitude toward the church.

7. How should we respond to authoritative church teaching?

---

[110] Quoted by Mark Link, S.J., *Path Through Catholicism* (Allen TX: Tabor Publishing, 1991), p. 79.

[111] Adapted from Anthony de Mello, *The Song of the Bird* (New York: Doubleday, Image Books, 1984).

Further Reading

Donovan, Daniel. *The Church as Idea and Fact* (Wilmington, DE: Michael Glazier, 1988). A slim introductory volume on the church which presupposes no special theological training on the part of the reader.

Dulles, Avery, S.J. *Models of the Church* (New York: Doubleday, 1974). A standard work on the church used in many theological schools. Requires careful reading but is highly recommended.

Orsy, Ladislas, S.J. *The Church: Learning and Teaching* (Wilmington, DE: Michael Glazier, 1987). Deals with the foundational and much-discussed question of the teaching authority of the church, the forms it takes, and our obligation to respond to it.

Sullivan, Francis A. *Magisterium: Teaching Authority in the Catholic Church* (Dublin: Gill and Macmillan, 1983). This book, by a former professor at the Gregorian University in Rome, offers a systematic presentation of modern Catholic thinking about the nature and function of teaching authority in the church. Can serve as a useful reference.

13

MARY, MOTHER OF GOD

Introduction

It is perhaps stating the obvious to say that Vatican Council II (1962–1965) was a watershed for the Catholic church. Its decrees have affected all aspects of Catholic life, and certainly one of these is Catholic theology. One area of Catholic theology that has undergone a substantial change in orientation as a result of recent advances in Scripture scholarship is the theology of Mary, the Mother of God. As a result of this "new-think," which was evident in the discussions at Vatican II, popular devotion to the Mother of God has gone through an acute metamorphosis. From being one of the central figures occupying a privileged place in Catholic practice and prayer, Mary now appears to be relegated to some sort of "back bench," out of the limelight – a once-prominent icon now forgotten by many and to many others hardly even known. We have moved from a pre-Vatican II era in which the watchword concerning Mary was "we can never say enough" to a time, it seems, when we have little enough to say.

The reasons for these changes stemming from Vatican II are complex. In short, the Council members who voted for a change in the theological approach to Mary in no way intended that this change should lead to a virtual devastation of popular devotion to her; in fact, that was the furthest thing from their minds. Pope Paul VI, aware of what had happened to Marian devotion and determined to reinstate it as an integral part of Catholic practice, produced his Apostolic Exhortation *Marialis cultus* in 1974, a scant nine years after the Council ended. We shall have something more to say about this document.

Whichever way we approach it, Mary, the Mother of God, is an essential part of the teaching of the Catholic church. "She is hailed as pre-eminent and as a wholly unique member of the church, and as its exemplar and outstanding model in faith and charity"[112] (CCC 967). It is because of the present theological emphasis on Mary as a pre-eminent member of the church that our consideration of her follows the chapter on the church. If we want to know what it is to be loyal, devoted and productive members of the church, we must look to Mary.

---

[112] *Dogmatic Constitution on the Church*, No. 53.

Since Mary is the mother of Jesus, she is also the mother of the church (CCC 963).[113] We have already seen that the church is Jesus carrying on his mission on earth to teach, to heal and to give glory to God. We are the church, we live with the life of Christ, we carry on his mission to the world. Therefore, Mary is our mother also, and that fact alone should serve as a source of great devotion to her.

In what follows we shall first take a look at Mary in Scripture, and then summarize the history of devotion to Mary in the church, tracing many of the titles by which she is known to Catholics. The following section will deal with Catholic dogma concerning Mary, and present a summary of Paul VI's suggestions for a proper integration of Marian devotion in the church today.

Mary in the New Testament

As far as the search for the historical Mary is concerned, we get little or no help from the New Testament. If the material in the Christian Scriptures is not strictly biographical for Jesus, it is even less so for Mary. When we read the scriptural texts about Mary we should be far more concerned with Mary as a symbol, a symbol of obedience and fidelity to God, a symbol of true faith and devoted discipleship, a symbol of motherhood and self-giving. Can we not say the same about many other women in history? Yes, we can. Then what's different about Mary? What is different is that she is the mother of God, the mother of Jesus, and it is from this unique fact that she is pre-eminent in the church. Everything wonderful that we can say about Mary is derived from this singular privilege and from her closeness to Jesus. In no way should devotion to Mary take away from, or distract us from, devotion to her son, Jesus. On the contrary, it should lead us to a greater understanding of and intimacy with the one who gave his life for us.

Let us now take a look at some of the texts in the New Testament concerning Mary.

1. Paul in his letters does not mention Mary by name but he makes several important, if indirect, references to her. In his letter to the Galatians, for example, he says, "But when the fullness of time had come, God sent his Son, born of a woman, born under the law" (Gal 4:4). God is born on earth of a woman just as other humans are; Jesus is a real human being like us, and Mary is his mother.[114] If Mary is the mother of Jesus, then she is the mother of the church, our mother.

2. We have already dealt with the infancy narratives in a previous chapter. Most of what we know about Mary comes from these stories. She is the first

---

[113]   An entire section in the Catechism, CCC 963-970, deals with the question of Mary's motherhood of Jesus and of the whole church.

[114]   This fact was asserted by the church against what was probably the first christological heresy (Docetism) which claimed that Jesus, being God, did not have a true body but only the appearance of one.

Christian, the first to have faith in Jesus. She is the model disciple, for she hears the word of God and keeps it. She is devoted to the interests of her son, learning from him, often not understanding his words or actions but pondering the wondrous events of Jesus' birth "in her heart" (Lk 2:19). In the singular and most beautiful prayer attributed to her by Luke, the Magnificat (Lk 1:46-55), she evokes a major theme of the gospel: that God has exalted the humble, the "little ones," the *anawim* (the poor who look to God) and those who hunger and thirst for justice. She is already identifying with the mission of her son; she is a prime example of faith. She is our great example, for we too must accept this same identity and work with that same faith to complete Jesus' mission on earth.

3.   In the Gospel according to Mark, Jesus is told that his mother and brothers had come looking for him. While we have no real historical evidence that Mary followed Jesus around during his active ministry, this incident related by Mark may well have been inserted in order to teach an important lesson, a lesson on which the early church frequently would have meditated.

A crowd was sitting around him; and they said to him, "Your mother and your brothers and sisters are outside, asking for you." And he replied, "Who are my mother and my brothers?" And looking at those who sat around him, he said, "Here are my mother and my brothers! Whoever does the will of God is my brother and sister and mother." (Mk 3:32-35)

The lesson is that if we do God's will, we belong to the family of Jesus; we are his brothers and sisters.

4.   There is mention of Mary in the Acts of the Apostles. She is with the apostles in the early days of the church, joining them in prayer (Acts 1:14). It is only natural that she should have been present on the day of Pentecost, when they received the gift of the Holy Spirit. She is at the heart of the church, its first and pre-eminent member.

5.   There are two incidents about Mary related in the Gospel according to John: the marriage feast at Cana when Jesus turned water into wine, and the words of Jesus on the cross. At Cana the wine runs out and, in order to avoid embarrassment to the newly married couple, Mary asks Jesus to perform a miracle. "And Jesus said to her, 'Woman, what concern is that to you and to me? My hour has not yet come'" (Jn 2:4). Jesus indicates that he is not yet ready to take on the ministry of which miracles will be an important part. But Mary's faith is supreme; she is ready to believe that Jesus will begin his public ministry right then and there by performing the "first of his signs" (Jn 2:11). At the foot of the cross, Mary is given to the "beloved disciple" as his mother. Anthony Tambasco comments: "Now, as Jesus moves from death to resurrection he leaves in the symbol of the beloved disciple a community

of faith. John also wants to say that Mary relates to Jesus primarily in that same faith relationship, so Mary is given as mother to the community symbolized by the beloved disciple."[115]

From these scriptural references, this portrait of Mary emerges:

1.   She is the mother of God, mother of the church and our mother.

2.   She is the perfect example of the true disciple learning from the master and keeping his words, therefore the first and pre-eminent member of the church.

3.   She is the prime example of faith – the faith that is required of all true followers of Jesus, faith that is a condition of discipleship.

Historical Development of Mary in the Church – Her Titles

When we study the historical development of devotion to Mary in the church, we see immediately how, as time went on, it strayed from its scriptural base. In the course of history, the love people had for her resulted in more and more names. Love, as everyone knows, is prone to exaggeration, and exaggeration is certainly characteristic of devotion to Mary down through the centuries. Nevertheless, we must concede that this exaggerated development is a healthy sign of the faith of the church. It is faith that determines all our relationships in the church, but even fulsome faith needs to have a solid theological foundation (CCC 971).

It would be impossible to trace the development of all the titles by which Mary is known. The best we can do is to take a look at how some of the more prominent ones still in use in the church originated.

1.   For the first 300 years, there is hardly any mention of Mary in writings attributed to that period. She was given minimal attention, and no special devotion seems to have arisen in those early years. The reason for this may well be that at that time the church was struggling with its theological understanding of Jesus. Also, the cult of the martyrs in the early church provided the great heroes and heroines of faith. When the persecution of the church ceased under the emperor Constantine, the cult of the martyrs became less prominent, and monasticism became the new pathway to holiness.

2.   Around 400 C.E. we have the beginnings of monasticism. The movement was started by men who withdrew from active life in the world to devote their time to prayer. They took the vow of celibacy as a way of showing that in the completed kingdom of God "they neither marry nor are given in

---

[115]   Anthony J. Tambasco, *What Are They Saying About Mary?* (New York: Paulist Press, 1984), p. 30.

marriage" (Mk 12:25; Mt 22:30). It was not long before women followed the example of men into the monastic life. It seems that women, having vowed themselves to celibacy, chose Mary as their model because she was a virgin. In the theology of the time, Mary's sinlessness was seen as closely linked to her virginity. It is because she was a virgin that she lived a life of total perfection and obedience to the will of God and could serve as a model for the monastic life. It is from that time that the title "the Blessed Virgin" came to be applied to Mary, a title we still use today. Mary is described as a pure person, submissive (after the ideal of the monastic vow of obedience), prayerful, careful about her possessions, pious. She is an exemplar of what a good monastic woman is expected to be, but virginity is the key to understanding her specialness.

3. The year 431 C.E. saw the great Council of Ephesus and the culmination of many theological battles about the divinity and humanity of Jesus. Its champion was St. Cyril of Alexandria, who led the council in declaring, against Nestorius the Patriarch of Constantinople, that Mary was the Mother of God and not merely the mother of the human Jesus. This declaration led to universal recognition of Mary and the devotion to her that erupted in special prayers, liturgies and feasts.

4. One of the outstanding characters of the twelfth century was St. Bernard, a doctor of the church and abbot of the great French Cistercian Abbey of Clairvaux. In his preaching he championed devotion to Mary as a personal closeness, an emotional attachment. Mary is *my* mother, not merely our mother. We look to her for the same protection, the same warmth, the same understanding and love as we expect from our own personal mothers. While we may sometimes have a little fear of God, we should never fear Mary because Mary is one of us; we can feel safe in her care for she speaks to God for us.

5. In the Middle Ages, Europe was losing the faith that had previously been so strong. The complex reasons for this are beyond the scope of this book.[116] The re-evangelization of Europe was entrusted to the Franciscans and the Dominicans, two of the most ancient religious orders in the church. Their main instrument for accomplishing their mission was prayer to Mary in the form of the rosary. The rosary consists of 15 "mysteries" or meditations on various events in the life of Christ. Each has attached to it ten Hail Marys, thus bringing the total number of Hail Marys to 150. The number 150 corresponds to the 150 psalms from the book of Psalms in the Bible, which

---

[116] If readers are interested in learning more about this period, they should consult some history of the church, such as Thomas Bokenkotter, *A Concise History of the Catholic Church* (New York: Doubleday, 1977).

were recited by the clergy. Thus, the rosary was considered to be a simplified form of monastic prayer for uneducated lay persons. Down through the centuries to the present time the rosary has remained the prayer to Mary most favoured in the church. Many, many times have people attested to its power to re-focus their Christian life.

The Middle Ages was also the era of chivalry and the romantic notion of love much associated with the royal courts of Europe. Women were exalted, honoured and protected (one can think of Sir Walter Raleigh spreading his cloak over a muddy puddle so that the queen would not have to get her feet dirty). It was from this time that the designation "Lady" came into use, with all the nuances that we generally apply to the terms "ladylike" and "feminine." The husband refers to his wife as "My Lady"; women of noble birth were also called "Lady." This cultural preference was in turn transferred to Mary, the Mother of God, who came to be called "Our Lady" (still one of our favourite titles for Mary). She is the most "ladylike" of women; she is to be loved, honoured and respected by all. And so, the title "Our Lady" is added to many Marian devotions: she is Our Lady of the Rosary, Our Lady of Sorrows, Our Lady of Good Hope, and many others.

6. In the fifteenth and sixteenth centuries, devotion to Mary deteriorated, the result of bad theology and superstitious practices prevalent at the time (for example, "Mary can make God change his mind"!). Pious practices, such as wearing a scapular or medal of Mary, were often endowed with almost magical powers. The Reformers of the early sixteenth century denounced these practices as excessive pietism. Even today, some Protestants accuse Catholics of "worshipping" Mary. Martin Luther advocated that Christians should praise Mary but not pray to her. Muslims also honour and respect Mary as the mother of the prophet Jesus, but do not pray to her. From this time on, devotion to Mary became an exclusive Roman Catholic practice; in fact, it became distinctive of Roman Catholicism.

7. What might be called "the era of the two dogmas" runs from 1850 to 1950. The dogma of the Immaculate Conception was defined in 1854 and the dogma of the Assumption in 1950. During this period, devotion to Mary reached its highest peak – special prayers, sodalities, feasts, special times of the year (e.g., the months of May and October), processions, rosary crusades, sermons, many religious orders (both of men and of women) dedicated to Mary, and so on. It was the period when we could not say enough about Mary.

Vatican II and Mary

As a result of the deliberations of Vatican II (dealt with above), we now live in a time of reaction to this period of what some would call "excess." In an attempt to return to a more balanced and theologically correct devotion to Mary, the Council makes some very general suggestions.

The Protestant position has always been that in praying to Mary and the saints we are, in fact, taking away from God. God (the Trinity) is the only one to whom prayer should be directed. Vatican II points out that whenever we honour Mary we also honour her son, Jesus Christ. Thus, in our devotion to Mary the Council suggests the following:

1. "Let them rightly illustrate the offices and privileges of the Blessed Virgin which always refer to Christ . . . ."

2. "Let them carefully refrain from whatever might by word or deed lead the separated sisters and brothers . . . into error about the true doctrine of the church."

3. Let them remember "that true devotion consists neither in sterile or transitory feeling, nor in an empty credulity, but proceeds from true faith, by which we are led to recognize the excellence of the Mother of God . . ." and be moved to filial devotion.[117]

As a follow-up to these exhortations and to clear up any misunderstanding of the Council's position on Mary, Pope Paul VI published in 1974 his Apostolic Exhortation *Marialis cultus* on devotion to the Mother of God. The exhortation warns against a narrow-minded elimination of devotion to Mary as the opposite extreme of exaggerated devotion to her. The aim should be to achieve a happy medium. While avoiding the excesses of the past we must, at the same time, give devotion to Mary a prominent place in the church and in our own personal lives. The Pope suggests the following:

1. We should re-focus our devotion around the liturgy, from which it had become somewhat divorced during the era of the two dogmas. This will ensure that the cult of Mary is always related to the cult of Christ within the church. She is deeply involved in three aspects of the liturgy: commemoration, invocation and imitation.

2. Mary is also an intimate part of the cult of the saints, for she is the pre-eminent saint. The tradition in the church has always been that some people lived their Christian lives in a special and heroic way. These people are enjoying the total vision of God and are God's special friends. If we pray to them they can intercede with God on our behalf. Precisely how this

---

[117] *Dogmatic Constitution on the Church*, No. 67.

intercession takes place is a somewhat difficult theological problem, but it is certainly the traditional faith of the church. Mary is the pre-eminent saint who intercedes with God on our behalf.

3. Pope Paul VI suggests that personal devotion to Mary should be centred on the rosary. The praying of the rosary is a well-established tradition in the church and has been proved extraordinarily effective both in preserving and enhancing faith and as a powerful means of evangelization.

4. True imitation of Mary will be centred on her perfect discipleship. She was willing to "listen to the word of God and to keep it." She attuned herself to receive God's revelation and did God's will in her life. In this she is the perfect model for every Christian.

Major Dogmas About Mary

Strange as it may seem, there are only three dogmas about Mary, the mother of God, which are clearly defined.

1. Mary is the Mother of God (Council of Ephesus, 431).

2. The Immaculate Conception – she is conceived in the womb of her mother without original sin (defined by Pope Pius IX in 1854).

3. The Assumption of Mary into heaven – on her death she went directly to God and enjoyed the beatific vision (defined by Pope Pius XII in 1950).

Before we say something about the latter two of these dogmas we need to mention one belief and teaching about Mary which, while not being specifically defined as a dogma, is central to all the definitions, and taken for granted in them: the perpetual virginity of Mary.

The Virginity of Mary

Belief in the perpetual virginity of Mary arises from the belief that Jesus was conceived and born of a virgin. It can best be stated in the words of the Apostles' Creed: Jesus was "conceived by the power of the Holy Spirit and born of the Virgin Mary." In other words, Jesus had no human father; furthermore, the constant tradition of the church has always been that Mary remained a virgin, even after the birth of Jesus. Belief in the perpetual virginity of Mary was already entrenched and unquestioned in the church from very early on. Early witnesses to this faith, such as Ignatius of Antioch, go back as far as 117 C.E. As we see, the doctrine appears in the Apostles' Creed, the date of which is uncertain but which is one of the earliest summaries of Christian faith. Again, it is stated in the Nicene Creed (the creed that came out of the Council of Nicea, 325 C.E.), and therefore we are led to conclude that already from the fourth century it was a universally accepted doctrine. Again, it is included in the Athanasian Creed (end of the fifth century). There are further references to it in several councils of the church. There can be no doubt that it is revealed by God and belongs to the essential Tradition of the church. Only in very recent times has this belief been challenged. The challenges run along these lines.

1. Scripture scholars argue that the accounts in the gospels cannot be taken as historically accurate, and even if they were historical, there is no way we could verify this historicity. A point to note also is that the doctrine of Mary's perpetual virginity is virtually never referred to in other parts of the Christian Scriptures. If the belief were factual and historical, other references would likely occur.

2. Since Jesus is truly human, then would it not be far more in keeping with his human nature that he should be born of the union of man and woman in the normal way? Furthermore, would it not be far more in keeping with ordinary Jewish behaviour that Mary and Joseph should have had other children?

In reply, let us first note that, if we could prove beyond doubt that Mary was a virgin, then it would not be a matter for faith. It should be clear that the gospels tell us nothing about the biology of Jesus' conception and birth. It was not their purpose to answer scientific questions such as this. The purpose of the gospels is theological and religious. How a virgin could conceive and give birth we simply don't know, and probably cannot know. Nor should we think of the Holy Spirit, as it were, supplying the male element in the conception of Jesus; that is clearly not what the gospels are saying. In point of fact, the issue cannot be satisfactorily settled from Scripture alone. But our faith is not based on Scripture alone. Our faith is based on the whole tradition of the church that has never wavered in its assertion of Mary's perpetual virginity. What the gospels are trying to tell us is that the presence of Jesus on earth is entirely the work of God, a work of power expressed though the Holy Spirit, and something no human power could accomplish. That is a theological assertion, not a biological or scientific one.

Secondly, while it may seem more fitting that Jesus (in accordance with his true human nature) should have been conceived and born in the normal way and that Mary and Joseph should have had other children, that is not what the constant faith tradition of the church tells us (CCC 499-500). It would be wrong to try to force our purely human way of thinking onto an event that is essentially mystical and mysterious. While it may seem more "fitting" or more "human," we cannot force God into our mould and demand that God act in accordance with what we think.

The Immaculate Conception

The Immaculate Conception is hinted at in many places in Scripture, but there is no clear statement about it in the written text. Therefore, we cannot look to Scripture alone to prove the Immaculate Conception. In defining the dogma, the church has drawn on its tradition, a tradition for which there is ample evidence and which in this case has existed at least since the sixth century. A dogma is true not because it has been defined; it is defined because it is true.

Though it is difficult to know why, there is a quite common misunderstanding, often promulgated by teachers who should know better, that this dogma refers to the conception of Jesus in Mary. It does not. The dogma is about the conception of Mary in her mother's womb. What the dogma says is that from the very first moment of her existence (human life begins at conception) Mary was, by the special grace of God and in view of the merits of Jesus Christ Saviour of the world, preserved from original sin. Therefore, she was not entrapped by the sin of the world, by the evil tendencies that we all inherit by being enmeshed in a sinful world. During her life she did not sin (CCC 411). But she was not preserved from the consequences of the human condition – namely, sickness, suffering, death – nor was her son, Jesus.

Now, this may be all very nice for Mary, and we can all rejoice with her for the special privilege she received from God, but is the pronouncement of this dogma of any use to us in our own struggles to do God's will? Here is what one writer has to say:

> The heart of the doctrine of the Immaculate Conception is not in Mary's being different from the rest of humanity, *but in her being the prototype of all humanity redeemed from original sin.* Mary is from the very first moment of her existence what we hope to become . . . a new creation. What God did for Mary offers promise to the church and to each member.[118]

Therefore, the Immaculate Conception invests us with a huge boost to our hope. She is what we hope to become. We look to her and realize what a marvellous thing humanity would be without sin, and we are drawn to try to seek out that perfection in our own lives, even though we know we shall not achieve it fully. By the gift of the Immaculate Conception, God has opened to us the immense possibilities of human life – union with God, devotion to God's will and work, not immersing ourselves in the sin of the world and the evil that surrounds us.

The Assumption

The dogma of the Assumption of Mary states that, "The Most Blessed Virgin Mary, when the course of her earthly life was completed, was taken up body and soul into the glory of heaven" (CCC 974).

---

[118] *What Are They Saying About Mary?* p. 50; emphasis added.

The dogma of the Assumption is not a biological statement but an eschatological one. What does eschatological mean? The word is derived from the Greek *eschata,* meaning the "last things." Eschatology, therefore, is the study of the "last things," the final in-breaking and full establishment of the reign of God, the final manifestation of God's love both for each individual person and for the whole world. In Catholic theology the *eschata* or "last things" refers to death, judgment, heaven, hell, purgatory, and the second coming of Christ. To say that the dogma of the Assumption is an eschatological statement means that it refers to the "end time." It means that Mary experienced what it is to be fully redeemed, to share in the glorified life of her son. Hence, the dogma does not state that Mary did not die, and for this we have no scriptural evidence one way or the other. However, we can only presume that, since Jesus, her son, suffered death, it would be most fitting that Mary should have had the same human experience.

Again, as we noted for the Immaculate Conception, this is very nice for Jesus' mother and we rejoice with her for the favour granted her, but what does it say to us? How can we benefit from this dogma? First, the Assumption is a sign and a pledge of our final glorification: what was granted to Mary will also be granted to us. It is an affirmation of human destiny and therefore sets a seal on our hope. Second, as with the Immaculate Conception, the dogma opens to us the possibility of being transformed even in the present. Should we choose to live a life in tune with God's will, then we are already participating in the final reward promised by Jesus; we already "have" eternal life. Third, the dogma states that she was assumed "body and soul into heavenly glory." What this says to us is that our whole person will share in the glory of the resurrection, and not merely the spiritual part of us. It is an assertion of the basic goodness and importance of the body as an integral part of our personality. Fourth, in the words of Anthony Tambasco, "The Assumption . . . reminds us that death need not be punishment. It need not be escape from material reality. It need not be the end but the beginning. Mary stands again as the perfect Christian, reminding us that in Christ life and death are not undone by sin. What God has begun in the church he will complete in final glory."[119]

The Apparitions of Mary

Mary, the Mother of God, is believed by many to have appeared to certain persons at regular intervals throughout history. The frequency of these apparitions seems to have increased markedly in the past 150 years (although this may simply be a function of the rapid expansion of communication technology). In practically all cases the Virgin has left messages and advice on how to live the

---

[119] *Ibid.*, p. 53.

Christian life, sometimes even confiding special "secrets" to the visionaries. Many of the places of these apparitions have become major Catholic shrines (such as Lourdes and Fatima), attracting great crowds of the faithful who come to pray, where the sick are comforted or cured and where many genuine conversions have been reported – the so-called miracles of grace.

Enough has already been said about private revelations, and the meaning of church approval of such revelations, in the chapter on Revelation. The reader is urged to review that section. In the discussion on miracles (in the chapter on Jesus), it was pointed out that we seem to have an insatiable appetite for the marvellous, the spectacular and the mysterious. It is precisely this type of mentality that attracts so many to private revelation. Now, in no way do we wish to disparage the many people who derive real spiritual benefit and experience a renewal of their faith when visiting the shrines associated with private revelation, but certainly, a word of caution is in order. We can do no better that to quote the words the Bishop of Tours spoke at the major Marian shrine of Lourdes in 1986:

> The best antidote for this appetite for the marvellous and for revelation is the direct and effective participation in the mission of the church. A Christian who studies the teachings of the church, for example, shares in the solemnity of the transmission of the Christian mysteries and in the education of the faith, and will not be encumbered with new revelations; the gospel and the Creed are enough for such a person.[120]

We already have all we need in order to make a success of our Christian life and participate in the establishment of the reign of God. While private revelation may remind us of certain things in our life that may need correcting – things that we may have forgotten and need to have emphasized again – it will add nothing new to God's message to us.

Reflection Questions

1. In Michelangelo's masterpiece of sculpture, the *Pietà* (Mary receiving the body of her son taken down from the cross), the Mother seems far too young to be the Mother of the dead Son. Someone said this to Michelangelo, and he replied, "You don't know anything. Chaste women retain their fresh looks longer than those who are not chaste. The Madonna was without sin, without even the least unchaste desire, and so she was always young."[121]

---

[120] Quoted by Jean-Pierre Prévost in *Mary, Mother of Jesus* (Ottawa: Novalis, 1988), pp. 95-96.
[121] F. W. Drinkwater, quoted by Tony Castle, *Quotes and Anecdotes: An Anthology for Preachers and Teachers* (London: Kevin Mayhew Publishers, 1979), p. 160.

What does Michelangelo mean that Mary was without sin? Why was she without sin?

2. What does the church's tradition teach us about the virginity of Mary?

3. At the great Marian shrines (such as Lourdes and Fatima), fewer miraculous cures are being reported now than in previous times. Why do you think this is so?

4. Why is Mary frequently called "Our Lady"? Trace the historical origin of this title.

5. Vatican Council II calls Mary "an outstanding model" for us. What, in your opinion, is the key ingredient in her life that makes her a model for us?

6. Suppose a Protestant friend of yours said to you that in praying to Mary you were doing a disservice to Jesus, who should be the true object of devotion. How would you answer?

Further Reading

Brown, Raymond E., et al., *Mary in the New Testament* (New York: Paulist Press, 1978). A detailed examination by a group of eminent Scripture scholars of all the scriptural texts pertaining to Mary in the Christian Scriptures. Rather detailed and unashamedly theological; serves as a good resource.

Macquarrie, John. *Mary for All Christians* (Grand Rapids, MI: William B. Eerdmans Publishing, 1990). Mary has traditionally been regarded as a sign of separation, not to mention a bone of contention, between Catholics and Christians of other denominations. This book, by an outstanding Anglican theologian and spiritual writer, provides an excellent ecumenical approach to the question and shows how much common ground there is between believers on the question of Mary. Has an excellent chapter on God and the Feminine.

Tambasco, Anthony J. *What Are They Saying About Mary?* (New York: Paulist Press, 1984). Summarizes the writing and teaching of contemporary theologians on the subject. A useful reference.

14

PRAYER

We have already noted that one of the distinguishing features of the very early Christian communities was that they gathered together for prayer (Acts 2:42 ff.; see also Acts 1:24 ff., 4:24-30). In the New Testament, the letters of Paul to the early communities founded by him are also full of references to prayer as an essential aspect of the Christian life. This tradition of prayer has been passed on through the centuries to the present day. Prayer was an integral part of Jesus' life, and he himself gave this example to his followers. The gospels are full of accounts of Jesus at prayer. He often went off to a lonely place to pray (Mk 6:46). He spent whole nights in prayer (Lk 6:12). Then there is the famous incident when his apostles, obviously impressed by his prayerfulness, asked him to teach them how to pray. He taught them that most basic of all Christian prayers, the Our Father (Mt 6:9 ff.; Lk 11:2 ff.).

There can be no question, therefore, that if we are to be true followers of Christ we must follow him in his dedication to prayer. For Christians, prayer is not an option; it is a necessity and an obligation. In the Christian church, prayer is Tradition, belonging to the essence of what it means to be Christian (CCC 2744).

What Is Prayer?

Prayer is an effort to recognize the presence of God in our life. It is an attempt to establish conscious contact with God, to attend to God, to enter into a personal relationship with God. "Prayer is the raising of one's mind and heart to God or the requesting of good things from God" (CCC 2590).

We need to pray because we have a basic need and duty to recognize God in the midst of life and to respond to God's gift of himself. But, as Leonard Foley remarks, "Prayer can hardly be called a commandment. If husband and wife have to be commanded to talk to one another, they are nowhere near being candidates for the Couple of the Year award."[122] No, we pray because we are in love with God, because we want to communicate with God and respond to his love for us. The primary focus of prayer, therefore, is to allow ourselves to be loved by God.

---

[122] Leonard Foley, O.F.M., *Believing in Jesus* (Cincinnati, OH: St. Anthony Messenger Press, 1985), p. 152.

But it is not we who initiate dialogue with God. God is already present to us, continuously, intimately. God constantly seeks to make his presence known and felt; God continually calls to us. Prayer is not the attempt to make present an absent God, but rather the growing in awareness of a God already present. Prayer is a response to this presence, to this call. Prayer is a gift of God. It is God who first speaks to us by his revelation; our response is also his gift to us, for we pray only under the influence of the Holy Spirit: "No one can say 'Jesus is Lord' except by the Holy Spirit" (1 Cor 12:3). St. Paul further emphasizes the work of the Holy Spirit in prayer in these words: "Likewise the Spirit helps us in our weakness; for we do not know how to pray as we ought, but that very Spirit intercedes with sighs too deep for words" (Rom 8:26).

Mary O'Hara, an Irish songwriter, ballad singer and harpist, gives this beautiful testimony to the work of the Holy Spirit in prayer:

> One day last summer, after I'd been working on some songs, I left the harp before the open window. Suddenly I heard the sound of a distant and very lovely music. It lasted only a few seconds and left me very puzzled. When it happened again I noticed that the sound came from the instrument and was caused by the gentle breeze from the open window playing on the harp strings.

> At times of prayer we can be like that harp, by allowing sufficient calm to gather around us so that the Holy Spirit, the Breath of God, may play music on us. But remember, it was a very gentle breeze and the music could be heard only because of the surrounding stillness.[123]

It is not enough to know intellectually that we must pray; it is not enough to convince ourselves of its necessity; it is not enough simply to know that prayer is essential to the Christian life. Knowledge is necessary, yes, but to this knowledge we must add the honest desire to pray. We may know, for example, all about the medical importance of quitting smoking, but unless we really want to quit, our knowledge won't help us. The story is told of a young man who visited a monastery. He was very impressed by the prayer of the monks and later asked one of them to become his spiritual director and to teach him to pray. The monk looked straight into the eyes of the young man for a long while then, without warning, he put a cloth over the young man's face and held it there. The young man finally broke loose and sputtered, "What did you do that for?" The monk said, "You've just had your first lesson in prayer. When you want to pray as much as you wanted to breathe just now, only then can I teach you to pray."

---

[123]   Quoted by Tony Castle, *More Quotes and Anecdotes*, p. 212.

The desire to pray, to want to meet and communicate with God, is the product of a strong faith, a faith that believes that the God who loves us is always present and waiting for our loving attention.

Forms of Prayer

We may make a simple division of prayer into a) personal prayer, in which we spend time, however short, alone with God, and b) common, or public prayer, in which we share our prayer time with others. This is not a hard and fast division (sometimes personal and common prayer tend to shade into one another), but it is helpful as a guide to further study.

A. Personal Prayer

The following story, from a Chicago high school student, illustrates well three styles of personal prayer.

> One day, after playing a hard game of basketball, I went to a nearby fountain for some water. The cool water tasted good, and I felt refreshment enter my sore, tired body. Suddenly, I began to think: we need water for refreshment and strength. "But where does water come from?" I wondered. "Clouds," I thought. "But where do clouds come from?" "Vaporized air." This went on until I got no answer. Or rather, I was left with only one answer: God! For the next couple of minutes, I just lay on the grass, looking up into the sky, marvelling at what God must be like. Then I prayed to God (I forget what I said) and started for home.[124]

(a) Meditation[125]

We try to become aware of God's presence in the midst of life: the water, the clouds, the stars, the rolling waves, the forest, fields of grain, music, the rhythm of poetry. A student once told the author that he could become aware of God's presence on the highway amid the concrete, tarmac, exhaust fumes and flying steel, to which we say "Bravo!" The story is told of Pope Pius XII, who, while suffering a very painful death, asked that a recording of Beethoven's first symphony be played for him. Clearly, this music helped him to come into closer contact with God. In praying by meditation we focus on the universe and on our place in it. Then our mind is raised to God, for God is the only answer to the mystery that we meditate upon. Another way to meditate is by creative use of the imagination. We pick a scene from the gospel – the crucifixion, let us say – and imagine ourselves to be present there, perhaps identifying with one or another of the characters, in order to bring ourselves into God's presence. Many are the

---

[124] Quoted by Mark Link S.J., *You: Prayer for Beginners and Those Who Have Forgotten How* (Allen, TX: Tabor Publishing, 1976), Used with permission.

[125] This style of prayer is extensively dealt with in the Catechism, 2705-2708.

techniques we can use to help us to meditate; these techniques can be found in any book on meditation.

(b) Contemplation[126]

Contemplation means "marvelling at what God must be like." It means focusing our attention on God and not on ourselves, turning Godward, not selfward. We allow the idea and the experience of God to take hold of us so that we are "spellbound." In contemplation, we remain quietly in the presence of God and allow the Holy Spirit to play on us, as the wind played on Mary O'Hara's harp. We listen to the promptings, the inspiration (literally, the in-breathing) of the Holy Spirit, not with our ears but within the depths of our heart. This form of prayer was often practised by the great mystics (such as St. Teresa of Avila, St. John of the Cross, Julian of Norwich, St. Catherine of Genoa). Often they report themselves, or were seen by others, as being in ecstasy (from the Latin *ex-stasis*, "standing outside of"), a state in which they experienced being "taken outside of themselves," "taken up" by God. This style of prayer may seem to us to be rather esoteric and beyond the reach of ordinary working people caught up in the daily grind for survival. Not so. Resting quietly in the presence of God is a form of prayer open to anyone who can spare a few moments for quiet solitude. The trouble is that not many of us ever try, and we excuse ourselves by saying that we can't find the time.

(c) Conversation[127]

We speak to God, either with actual words formed by the lips or with words formed in the heart. Conversation is by far the most frequent form of prayer for most of us. Often enough we don't even think we are praying unless we are saying something. Notice how in the story above the student only talks about praying when he speaks to God. But conversation must be just that, a conversation; both parties must speak. We speak, but we must also listen. Part of our conversation involves listening to God in the depths of our heart. Prayer must not be a monologue. We remember the injunction of Jesus: "When you are praying, do not heap up empty phrases as the Gentiles do; for they think that they will be heard because of their many words" (Mt 6:7).

We can also speak of prayer as mental prayer or vocal prayer. In the above schema, meditation and contemplation are mental prayer, while conversation is vocal prayer.

---

[126]   This style of prayer is extensively dealt with in the Catechism, 2709-2719.
[127]   The Catechism deals with this style of prayer in the section on Vocal Prayer, 2700-2704.

B. Public or Common Prayer

It is not enough to pray privately. We are also a church, a community gathered in the name of the Lord. The whole church must pray, because the whole church lives with the life of Jesus on earth. When the assembly of the people of God prays together with the properly appointed ministers to lead them, and in forms approved by the church, we call this prayer "liturgy." Such liturgical celebration has existed since the time of the apostles (CCC 2178). The word is derived from the Greek *leitourgia*, meaning "the work of the people." The central act of the church's liturgy is the community celebration of the Eucharist. The gathering together for the ritual meal was, from the very beginning, the rallying point for the Christian community, the celebration that most expressed the presence of the Lord among them and gathered them together as church. If liturgy is "the work of the people" then it is not only the priest's work. Liturgy means that the people must be actively part of the prayer and the ceremonies that mark this form of public worship. They are not to be simply spectators at a liturgical "performance." The matter is clearly put by Vatican II in reference to the Eucharist, but applies equally well to all liturgical celebration.

> The church, therefore, spares no effort in trying to ensure that, when present at this mystery of faith, Christian believers should not be there as strangers or silent spectators. On the contrary, having a good grasp of it through the rites and prayers, *they should take part in the sacred action*, actively, fully aware, and devoutly.[128]

As with private prayer, public worship is also a Tradition in the church; it is an essential aspect of the church's life. A believing Christian cannot opt out of community worship and honestly still claim to be a Christian. One's faith must be expressed in "doing"; to say one has faith and do nothing about it is a form of self-delusion. In other words, as with private prayer, prayer with the community is not an option for believing Christians: it is a necessity and an obligation. The Catholic church has insisted that this obligation be fulfilled by active participation in the eucharistic liturgy on Sundays. "The Sunday celebration of the Lord's Day and his Eucharist is at the heart of the Church's life. . . . and is to be observed as the foremost holy day of obligation in the universal Church" (CCC 2177).

We shall have more to say about the liturgy when we consider the sacraments.

Reasons for Prayer

There are four purposes of prayer, or reasons why we pray. These reasons fit any form of prayer, private or public, mental or vocal: (a) Adoration, (b) Contrition, (c) Thanksgiving, and (d) Supplication.

---

[128] *Constitution on the Sacred Liturgy (Sacrosanctum concilium)*, No. 48; emphasis added.

(a) Adoration

Adoration means true worship of God for what he is in himself, not merely for what God can do for us. "Prayer is no mere compass for our activity. God comes first and is to be adored for his own sake; He is not to be reduced to the state of a helper in our work."[129] God is the transcendent mystery at the heart of all being, but God is also the infinite and consummate lover. In adoration we "fall down" before God, as the apostle Thomas did, and say, "My Lord and my God!" (Jn 20:28). Adoration means recognizing and accepting the infinite difference between God and every creature (CCC 2628). We rejoice in God's sanctity and glory – "Holy, holy, holy is the Lord God of hosts"; "Hallowed be thy name."

(b) Contrition

We pray to God because we want to express sorrow for our sins. We have all sinned; we are all conscious of having failed, in one way or another, to live up to the promises we made at baptism. We all need to say "I'm sorry" and to seek conversion with the help of God's grace (CCC 2631). Echoing the New Testament (1 Jn 1:10) someone once said, "Show me someone who says that he/she does not need conversion and I will show you a liar." To pray because we are sorry is to recognize and accept the mystery of God's mercy and compassion, a mercy that reaches out to us in every circumstance no matter what we have done.

(c) Thanksgiving

Praying to thank God for his goodness to us is one of the great characteristics of the prayer of the church. In the Eucharist the church celebrates the great prayer of thanksgiving (CCC 2637). Thanksgiving is a common human need that makes for good human relationships; so also must it be part of our relationship with God. We need to thank God for all that he has done for us and continues to do for us. Everything that we have, all that we are, has come from God. "Thanksgiving is essential . . . because it is a fundamental religious reaction of the creature who discovers, in a tremor of joy and veneration, something of God, of his greatness, and of his glory. The capital sin of pagans, according to Paul, is this: "For though they knew God, they did not honour him as God or give thanks to him" (Rom 1:21)."[130]

---

[129] Aloysius Cardinal Ambrozic, "General Observations on the Canadian Catechism," (manuscript, 1973), p. 11.

[130] Xavier Léon-Dufour, S.J., ed., *Dictionary of Biblical Theology* (Montreal: Palm Publishers, 1967), p. 525.

[131] Prayer of Petition is extensively dealt with in the Catechism, 2629-2633.

(d) Supplication

The word is derived from the Latin *supplere*, "to beg, to ask insistently." Supplication, or asking, is surely the most frequent form of prayer; it is also called the prayer of petition (from the Latin *petere*, meaning "to ask").[131] We ask God for what we need because we know that God loves us and is concerned about us, that God is a God of compassion (that is, God suffers with us). Jesus taught us to pray this way. He taught us the Our Father, most of which is a prayer of asking. In his teaching, he also told many stories to illustrate the need for asking prayer: the story of the importunate widow (Lk 18:1-5); the story of the insistent and demanding friend (Lk 11:5 ff.; Mt 7:7-11). Every petition we make must be made with the understanding that it is God who grants the favour, it is his will that we seek. And so, we pray as Jesus prayed, "Not my will but yours be done" (Lk 22:42).

The reasons for prayer are given in the above fashion because it forms a useful mnemonic or memory aid: **A**-doration, **C**-ontrition, **T**-hanksgiving, **S**-upplication – ACTS.

We may be motivated to pray for any or all of the above four reasons. For example, we may participate in the Eucharist because on a particular occasion we want to express our gratitude for favours received, or because we want to express our sorrow for having sinned. In fact, focusing on some specific reason for eucharistic participation is a good way to motivate ourselves to be coopera-tors in the liturgy and not simply spectators. Sharing in the ceremony of baptism may motivate us to worship the God who expresses his love by receiving us into his church. Praying with a group of people, we may ask for some special favour, and so on.

The Whole Person Prays

Prayer is not simply a function of the mind. We are body-persons, not disembodied spirits, and much as we may sometimes like to, we can never totally divorce the mind from the body. Taking account of the fact that we are body-persons is a basic and extremely important principle in all of Roman Catholic theology. And so, in prayer, even though we may sometimes speak of mental prayer, it is always the whole person who prays. Failure to take account of this fundamental principle of who we are is the rock on which many an effort to pray has foundered.

Since prayer involves the body as well as the mind, it follows that we should aim to dispose the body to pray. There are, for example, many techniques for putting the body into a favourable state for prayer. Some of these are silence, various yoga positions, deep and regular breathing, uttering a mantra. The purpose of all these is to help us to lose contact with the outside world and attend more closely to God, whose Spirit speaks to us like the movement of a gentle wind. Again, because prayer is a function of the body as well as of the mind, it is something that can, to a certain extent, be taught. A very sound educational principle is that we learn best by doing (we learn to pray by praying); nevertheless, a good teacher and adviser who will instruct us in the various prayer techniques can be a great help.

As with many things, praying becomes easier and more spontaneous if we can make it a habit. Here are some common-sense suggestions for developing a good habit:

a) Constant Repetition

Practice, practice, practice, even when we don't feel like it. No artist, athlete or performer, even those at the very top of their profession, can escape without hours and hours of practice. Their bodies need to be trained to respond, almost instinctively, to the demands of their art. While we are not required to spend hours in prayer every day, the more often we pray the more natural it becomes, and the easier it becomes. This is particularly true of participation in Sunday Eucharist. To set ourselves to pray even when the distractions are great and when we "get nothing out of it" requires great faith, but the mere effort to be in the presence of God is itself prayer (CCC 2731).

b) Set Times

Having set times for doing things (e.g., brushing one's teeth, taking care of personal hygiene) facilitates what we want to do. Again, this is but a natural effect of the way the body works. Even though it is true that we can pray at any time of the day, in any event of our lives (CCC 2660), having set times for prayer is helpful. Many people find that the morning or evening (or both) are good times for prayer. As Mahatma Gandhi said, "Prayer is the key of the morning and the bolt of the evening."

c) Work

To pray well involves some work; it requires dedication, a certain conquest of self, going against one's natural inclination, and overcoming one's lazy tendencies (CCC 2725). Nothing worthwhile comes easy. St. Paul makes an apt comparison: "Athletes exercise self-control in all things; they do it to receive a perishable wreath [the laurel wreath given to athletes], but we an imperishable one" (1 Cor 9:25).

When prayer becomes second nature to us, then it is easier to pray in times of crisis, when we may not even be able to think straight.

The Separation of God from the World

It is true that we often think of prayer as some sort of private experience that we do not share with others. It is more a matter between ourselves and God alone. We have already pointed out in the chapter on faith our strong tendency to separate the spiritual from the material, God from the world, our prayer from our moral life, as though these exist in different spheres and "never the twain shall meet." Kathleen Fischer expresses it well: "This sense of prayer as intrinsically isolated from life stems in part from the split we have established between God and world. Seeking the face of God means turning away from the world." But, in reality, she continues, "Prayer, no matter what its mode, is in fact the path to increased awareness of our oneness with God, with one another and with the world. Prayer does not take away from action and from other people. . . . Prayer opens to us the ground of love through which all things find their identity and uniqueness."[132] There are some who criticize the contemplative religious orders of men and women because they are not "doing their share" in making the world a better place. Their "withdrawal from the world" becomes a sort of escape from responsibility. But, the truth is that even when we engage in such prayer as contemplation, where we seem to be totally alone with God, we are still very much in touch with the world and are led by our prayer to serve the needs of others in imitation of Jesus' service of us. Contemplative prayer brings many blessings on the church and our work in the world as we try to establish the kingdom of God. In effect, therefore, prayer does not isolate us from others, it does not isolate us from "the world," it does not isolate us from our everyday duties; on the contrary, prayer provides us with the energy and dedication we need to do God's will in our everyday life. Prayer puts us more in touch with ourselves so that we can see and appreciate how best to direct our life to serving God and our neighbour.

Participation in the Liturgy

It should go without saying that active participation in the celebration of the liturgy is required, particularly in the Eucharist and the other sacraments. In no sense should we be onlookers, bystanders, part of the audience, while the sacraments are "done" or "administered" by a priest or deacon. We do not go to the liturgy to be entertained but to meet the Lord. Therefore some effort on our part is required to bring about this meeting with God. The liturgy is our work, too.

---

[132] Kathleen Fischer, "Prayer in a Relational World," *Catechist's Connection* (Vol. 8, May 1993).

Here are some fairly simple and common-sense observations:

1. We must know and, as far as possible, understand what is going on in the liturgy; we may need to undertake some study and reflection on this.

2. We should know something about the symbols used in the celebration and their significance (e.g., the baptismal candle and white garment, the flowing water, the oil of Confirmation and the laying on of hands). The same applies to the actual ritual of the celebration; it is not haphazard, it has meaning and purpose.

3. A conscious effort to participate will mean

    a) joining in the common prayers and the singing;

    b) listening to the readings and their explanation;

    c) trying to focus our minds and hearts on the celebration.

The rule is quite simple: we shall get out of the liturgy what we put into it.

Spontaneous Prayer, or Prayer Formulas?

All prayer should be spontaneous in the sense that we should come to God freely and willingly. Also, prayer is often a conversation, and conversation is best carried on in a spontaneous fashion. We should speak openly, from the heart, and in our own words. God is interested in every aspect of our life. We can speak to God about anything, at any time, treating him as a real friend, a friend who truly loves us.

Many claim that using set prayer formulas (such as the Our Father, the Hail Mary, the I Believe, the Gloria) tends to be mechanical and repetitious and does not readily engage the heart and emotions. While all this may be true to a certain extent, the use of set formulas for prayer is a strong tradition in the church, starting with the Our Father, which Jesus taught to his disciples. Is there any advantage in using set formulas, particularly those we have learned by heart? The answer is, unequivocally, Yes.

a) Set formulas give our prayer content, direction and a certain self-discipline. They help us avoid self-pitying introspective individualism, which may creep into purely spontaneous prayer.

b) Many of the set prayer formulas in general use in the church have a long and deep tradition as expressions of faith. For the most part they are trans-cultural and therefore help to keep us in touch with the faith tradition of the whole church.

c) Prayer formulas learned by heart, and often repeated, come more easily to mind in times of sudden crisis, when spontaneous prayer may desert us.

Does God Answer Our Prayers?

The easy answer to this question is yes, always, but not necessarily in the way we may want or expect.[133] We need never fear that any prayer is ever "wasted," because all prayer puts us in touch with God, and that is always the final purpose of prayer. Only God sees the whole picture, only God sees how our prayer fits into the whole providential scheme of things. Therefore, we must accept that sometimes God will not directly grant us what we pray for. The story is told of two children who were arguing over whether God answers prayers or not. One of them vehemently declared that God really did not answer prayers. "For example," he said, "you remember the time you asked God to get you a bicycle; did he answer your prayer?" "Yes," replied the other, "he answered. He said 'No!'"

But the matter is not that simple. What's involved here is the whole question of God's Providence, as well as the question of evil in the world, both of which are mysteries that give rise to thorny theological problems. When, for example, we pray to be rid of a certain illness, does our prayer make God change the natural scientific course of events? When we pray for a safe journey, does this mean that God will suspend the forces of nature that may otherwise cause us to have an accident?

There are two extremes we must avoid. One is to think that by prayer we can induce God to change his mind and thus re-order the direction of his Providence. The other is to think that prayer is of no use at all, or just some sort of "positive thinking" that makes us feel better. These two extremes give rise to a deep paradox that is inherent in all prayer; it is well expressed by the Danish proverb "Pray to God in the storm – but keep on rowing!" St. Augustine puts it this way: "Pray as though everything depended on God, but work as though everything depended on you!" As has been said already, we don't ever solve paradoxes; we have to learn to live with them. Overstressing one side of the paradox at the expense of the other will not, in the long run, solve the problem. Therefore, by all means pray for miracles (Jesus would have us do no less), but work as hard as you can to accomplish miracles of your own.

Something we should always keep in mind is this: our aim should not be to "get something" out of prayer. It is because this "getting something" is too often our main motivation for praying that we are disappointed and give up. "God is not listening," we argue, "so what's the use?" (Recall the story of Tommy from Chapter 2.) Prayer is a "surrender" to God, a giving of oneself in return for God's love. The real purpose of prayer is to develop intimacy with God. In the words of Mother Teresa of Calcutta, "Prayer enlarges the heart until it is capable of

---

[133] See CCC 2735-2737 on "Why do we complain of not being heard?"

containing God's gift of himself." The purpose of prayer is not to bend God's will to ours, to make God do what we want, but rather to bend our will to God's, to help us accept what God wants. It is the prayer of Jesus in the garden of suffering: "Father, if you are willing, remove this cup from me; yet, not my will but yours be done" (Lk 22:42).

Reflection Questions

1. A football team from a Catholic high school was about to play an important game. A newspaper reporter came up to the coach and said, "I understand that you have a chaplain to pray for the success of the team. I should like to meet him." "Which one," said the coach, "the offensive chaplain, or the defensive one?" What does this story say to you about the coach's attitude to prayer?

2. Does God answer our prayers? Can you recall a time when your prayers were answered? What about a time when they were not answered? What does this say to you about God?

3. Why is participation in Sunday Eucharist so important for us?

4. When we pray, the whole person prays. Explain this carefully. What consequences for our prayer follow from this?

5. Two friends walking along a road in winter came upon a man who had slipped on the ice and injured himself badly. While one ran to call an ambulance, the other asked the man if he believed in God. "Yes," replied the injured man. So he said the words of the Our Father slowly, asking the injured man to repeat them after him.

   If you were the person who came across someone who was badly injured, what prayer might you say and ask the injured person to repeat? Why is this prayer important for you? Why is it important to have some prayer formulas that we know and can repeat by heart?

6. It is a fact of sociological experience that when there is a natural tragedy affecting many people (such as an earthquake or a flood), church attendance rises dramatically. Why do you think this is so? What does this tell us about faith and prayer?

Further Reading

There have been dozens and dozens of books written about prayer, particularly in recent years. Prayer is such a personal thing that it is hard to recommend reading material that will suit everyone. Here are four of the author's personal favourites.

Caulfield, Sean, O.C.S.O. *The Experience of Praying* (New York: Paulist Press, 1980). "These pages," says the author, "tell of the pain and joy in praying, and in discovering within it the meaning of life. They suggest that what is experienced by the mystics of an earlier age is available to all of us."

De Mello, Anthony, S.J. *Sadhana: A Way to God* (New York: Doubleday, Image Books, 1984). Makes insights from Eastern spirituality available to the Western world. An excellent little book which helps us to reach out to God through concrete things and stories of life. Contains many gems of wisdom.

De Mello, Anthony, S.J. *The Song of the Bird* (New York: Doubleday, Image Books, 1984). An incomparable collection of very short stories, reflections and helpful hints that can serve as the basis for intimate prayer and reflection on life.

Link, Mark, S.J. *You: Prayer for Beginners and Those Who Have Forgotten How* (Allen, TX: Tabor Publishing, 1976). A short, simple, excellent little volume that could become one of your bedside books. Has a useful section at the end on how to organize a meditation group in a secondary school.

15

SACRAMENTALITY AND SACRAMENTS

Section 1 – Sacramentality

We must not forget that for religious man the supernatural is indissolubly connected with the natural, that nature always expresses something that transcends it.[134]

The Principle of Sacramentality

For people who believe in God, all the world's a symbol pointing beyond itself to the uncreated, unseen God. As we have already seen in Chapter 3, *God's presence and action in our lives are always mediated through the created universe, through people, events and things. For us there is no other way.* We ourselves are persons created by God, both body and soul, intimately connected with the universe, through which we experience everything and relate to everything. God can only be co-experienced and co-known at the heart of some human experience. This reality is of fundamental importance for a truly Catholic understanding of our religious response to God. It cannot be stated too often or too strongly. We call it the principle of sacramentality. It is a principle that is absolutely central to Catholicism and to its identity and self-understanding (CCC 1147-1148).

The principle of sacramentality follows naturally from the fact of the incarnation (from the Latin *in* and *caro* meaning flesh). God, the Second Person of the Blessed Trinity, took human flesh and became man. As a religion, Catholicism is deeply incarnational, following its founder Jesus Christ. Jesus is the true and essential sacrament of God, for in him God comes to us in created human form. The church, which continues Jesus' life on earth and which is made up of enfleshed human beings, is the next important sacrament of God, mediating God to us. Thus, for Roman Catholics, religion is an earthy thing, very much tied up with our being fleshy, earthy people, not disembodied spirits. We relate

---

[134] Mircea Eliade, *The Sacred and the Profane* (New York: Harcourt, Brace & World, 1959), p. 117.

to God as whole human persons, body and spirit together. We have already mentioned, for example, in the chapter on prayer, how important it is for us to realize that the body has an essential part to play in any consideration of how we reach out to God in prayer.

Other Christian denominations have given varying importance to the principle of sacramentality. In general, Protestantism has been far less insistent on it than has Catholicism. Protestantism tends to urge rather that the central principle of religion is God's word, a word which God's Spirit speaks directly to our spirit in a very non-bodied way. For this reason, Protestantism has been somewhat suspicious of material symbolism and bodily participation. The difference between the Protestant and the Catholic approach to religion is extremely well enunciated by the well-known University of Chicago Baptist theologian Langdon Gilkey.

> There is, especially to a Protestant, a remarkable sense of humanity and grace in the communal life of Catholics. Compared to Protestants, Catholics seem to be far less "uptight" about the moral rules their grandfathers held . . . . Consequently, the love of life, the appreciation of the body and the senses, of joy and celebration, the tolerance of the sinner – these natural, worldly, and "human" virtues – are far more clearly and universally embodied in Catholics and in Catholic life than in Protestants and Protestantism.[135]

For Catholics, human life in all its manifestations, drama, art, dance, celebration, images and symbols, is the way in which we appreciate and relate to God in life. Michael Novak, writing on the anniversary of the publication of that English classic, Hilaire Belloc's *Path to Rome*, touches the heart of the matter.

> Catholicism, G.K. Chesterton once said, is a steak, a cigar, and a glass of stout: a sacramental religion that sees the presence of God in every concrete, created thing. [Hilaire] Belloc shared this enthusiasm for cigars, for ale, for vivid and singular humans and created things. . . . He gloried in the concreteness of the Catholic faith, its stimulation of the senses through colour, incense, and the sonorous variety of ringing bells. The more he believed in spirit and transcendence, the more tightly he held to the joy of physical things, so as to approach God, until the end, as flesh and spirit both, awaiting the resurrection of both.[136]

---

[135] Langdon Gilkey, *Catholicism Confronts Modernity: A Protestant View* (New York: Seabury Press, 1975), pp. 17-18.

[136] Michael Novak, "July's Child: Hilaire Belloc's Path to Rome," *Crisis* (January 1988), p. 32.

Pantheism

To say that we relate to God through the material universe does not mean that God is identified with the material universe. To hold that would be to hold that all things are God. That is a heresy called pantheism.* Some forms of religious expression do suffer from pantheistic limitations, and God tends to be worshipped in material things such as the sun and the moon. For example, when Moses descended from the mountain after having received the Ten Commandments he found the people worshipping a golden calf (Ex 32:1-24), a practice which, as we have seen, is directly forbidden by the First Commandment. The material universe reveals God's presence but is not itself God.[137]

Sacramentality and Human Life

There are three important factors that are integral to our life and self-understanding as human beings and therefore integral to the working of the principle of sacramentality. If our relationship to God is to be truly sacramental, then this relationship is going to be entered into and expressed by (1) symbols and symbolism, (2) celebration and (3) ritual.

1. Symbols and Symbolism

That symbols are important in human life is a truism. In fact, some anthropologists go so far as to define humans as "symbol-making beings." We only have to think about what life would be like without such things as flags, statues, medals, wedding rings, mascots, uniforms, the language of art and architectural design, to realize that our whole life is governed by symbols and symbolism. Probably the most important of all symbols is language. It is by language that we communicate our hidden thoughts to one another; it is by language that we develop our consciousness and ability to relate to the world around us. The fact that we use and, in truth, need symbols tells us that we do not simply live in a world that is immediately evident to our senses. There is something beyond, something that is not easily defined, something that engages our consciousness but cannot easily be put into words, something that we can only reach by using metaphorical or symbolic language. For example, it is not easy to describe the feelings of patriotism, unity, loyalty and togetherness we experience when we salute the national flag or sing the national anthem, particularly on such special occasions as the Olympic games. Symbolism reaches deep down into us and stirs emotions that we find difficult to express openly. Applying the above to religion, it should not be difficult to see that, in our approach to the unseen God, symbols are absolutely essential (CCC 1146).

---

[137] CCC 285 develops further the notion of pantheism.

All symbols are, in fact, signs (from the Greek *symbolon*, meaning token or sign). What a sign does is to point beyond itself – it indicates something more than itself. A red traffic light indicates that we must stop; smoke generally means that there is fire (or at least some form of combustion); the rising sun is a sign of the beginning of a new day. But symbols differ from signs in that they do not merely indicate something other than themselves; they engage our consciousness more deeply. Symbols stimulate us to think, to imagine. They stir our emotions, they enter our dreams. Thus, for example, the warm embrace of family members, the horror of the Holocaust, the singing of birds in the spring, are symbols that speak deeply to all of us, but speak differently to each of us.

But there is more. "Symbols," says Bernard Cooke, "do more than express *how* we think and feel; they are a powerful force in shaping *the way* we think and feel."[138] Furthermore, as Paul Tillich reminds us, symbols "not only point beyond themselves to something else; they also participate in the power of that to which they point."[139] Very importantly, therefore, symbols are able to "make present" to us the reality they point to. Adolf Hitler and Josef Stalin, for example, have become symbols of ruthlessness and human evil. The very thought of people like this brings us into existential contact with evil; we shudder, we cringe, we are disturbed. Similarly, the good Mother Teresa of Calcutta brings us into contact with human goodness and compassion for the most unfortunate of our brothers and sisters. We feel our hearts warmed, uplifted. She is a symbol of human goodness and love.

All these qualities of symbols are of paramount importance when we come to consider the sacraments of religion. Sacraments bring us into contact with that which they symbolize; in fact, they "make present" the unseen God. Thus, for example, the washing with water at baptism symbolizes our dying to the old life of sin and our rising to a new life of goodness and holiness. This death and rising to life brings us into the presence and grace of Jesus, who died for our sins and rose to a new and eternal life. It is the power of God that touches us through the symbolism of our very earthy and material passage through water.

Roman Catholic worship is redolent with symbols and symbolism, which engage the whole person – body and mind, senses and emotions – in reaching out to God and making God present to us. We know many of these symbols well: candles (that symbolize Christ, the light of life, and burn themselves out in the service of God); vestments of different colours (that symbolize the seasons of the year, dedicated to different aspects of our relationship with God); holy water

---

[138] Bernard Cooke, *Sacraments and Sacramentality* (Mystic, CT: Twenty-Third Publications), p. 45; emphasis added.

[139] Paul Tillich, "Theology and Symbolism," in F. Earnest Johnson, ed., *Religious Symbolism* (Port Washington, NY: Kennikat Press, 1955), p. 109.

(that symbolizes the blessing of God in all our endeavours); the smoke of incense (that symbolizes our prayer of worship rising to the unseen God), and many others. *If we are to participate fully in our worship – the prayer of the Christian community – then we must commit ourselves to knowing what these symbols mean, and particularly what they mean for us personally.*

Let us summarize what we have said about symbols.

1.   Symbols are signs that point beyond themselves to an unseen reality.

2.   Symbols engage our consciousness deeply; they stir our thinking, imagination, emotions; they shape the way we think and feel.

3.   Symbols not only point beyond themselves but share in the power of that to which they point, and thus "make present" that reality. Symbols make us present to one another in human communication and make God present to us in the depth of religious symbolism.

2.   Celebration

If we can say that humans are symbol-making beings, we are equally justified in saying that humans are celebrating beings. None of us has to look too far to realize that celebration is a natural and basic aspect of human living.

Without some form of celebration, human community would be impossible. It is so much part of us that some people even regulate their lives by looking back to the last celebration and looking forward to the next one. During the summer, some people live from one baseball game to the next, or from one party to the next! Even an insignificant celebration such as T.G.I.F. can add meaning to our week and assuage the boredom of work.

When we celebrate, we celebrate a life experience that we have in common with many others: a shared story, if you will. Festivity, or celebration, is born of our community experience and further enhances our community togetherness. We rarely, if ever, celebrate alone; attempting to do so is often less than satisfying. The most meaningful celebrations take place on special occasions – the "key experiences" of life. By sharing these occasions with others, we make them more significant for ourselves. Baptisms, birthdays, and wedding days are obvious special occasions, but so are those other occasions, such as Thanksgiving, Christmas, and Easter, when the family gets together to support one another and to share their love and appreciation for one another.

These points are well illustrated by the following story. One busy Christmas Eve, a businessman hurried to the butcher. "A Christmas turkey?" enquired the butcher. "No, hot dogs," replied the businessman. Then he told the story of how he had been financially ruined in the Great Depression and one Christmas had only enough money to buy hot dogs for the family Christmas dinner. His wife decorated the wieners with toothpicks to make them look like real dogs. This so delighted their young daughter that her infectious merriment soon spread to them all. After dinner they gave thanks to God for this most loving and especially happy time they had shared together. "So now," said the businessman, "even though we can once again afford turkey, it's hot dogs for Christmas to remind us of that happy day when we realized that we still had one another and a God-given sense of humour."[140]

In keeping with the principle of sacramentality, it should be evident that because celebration is so much part of us as human beings, then it should also be an important aspect of any human response to God in our life. We reach out to God as celebrating beings, and celebrations are an essential aspect of our communal response to God in prayer. We have already seen that prayer in common, prayer as a church, is an obligation for us if we are to be true Christians. Our prayer must be celebratory. As church, as a community dedicated to God, we celebrate the divine presence in our lives through the sacraments, through the prayer of the liturgy. In its root meaning from the Latin, celebrate means to "make famous," "to announce," "to honour." Thus in religious celebration we "announce," we "place front and centre," the wonderful God who does such marvellous things in the world.

But in that very liturgy there sometimes surfaces a certain tension. We speak of the liturgy as a celebration; thus we speak of "celebrating the Eucharist together." But we also speak of the liturgy as the "worship of God," we talk about "sharing in Sunday worship." In the minds of some people, worship and celebration just don't mix. If we have celebration, then it seems to take away from worship. Singing and dancing and noisy expressions of joy seem superficial and lacking a sense of awe. Celebration seems "secular," "worldly," while worship seems "holy." The fact is that celebration and worship are word-symbols that engage different human emotions and evoke different sets of human responses. If we ask ourselves what we think about when we hear these words, something like the following might emerge:

Worship	Celebration
Reverence, adoration	Having a good time
Seriousness, awe	Laughter
Abstinence	Eating and drinking
Meditation	Activity, dancing
Silence, peace	Noise

---

[140] Adapted from Tony Castle, *More Quotes and Anecdotes*, p. 155.

All of the right-hand column sounds somewhat worldly, and therefore removed from God. It could be, perhaps, that we think that too much pleasure is a little sinful! All of the left-hand column we associate with the presence of the all-holy God, an attempt to reach out to the transcendent One. What we have here is, in fact, an example of the age-old division of the material from the spiritual. The material/spiritual dichotomy is a true paradox that exists at the very centre of who we are as human beings, body and soul, in the world but not of the world, having the Spirit of God and destined for eternal life.

Celebration is a human activity, as is worship; therefore, if we are to be true to our sacramental principle, celebration is something that can put us into the presence of God. It is true that if we push celebration too far it can end up in excess and vulgarity. The presence of God is not the product of mere enthusiasm, it is a gift of the Spirit. There is room for enthusiasm in the celebration of Christian liturgy. After all, the very term "enthusiasm" comes from the Greek, meaning "filled with God" or "possessed by God." Nevertheless, celebration should always be tempered by reverence; there must always be room for a sense of mystery, of awe. There must be room in the liturgy for silence, too. One of the valid criticisms of the modern post-Vatican II liturgy is precisely that it is too wordy and sometimes leaves little room for silent prayer. Good liturgy should leave room for both celebration and worship. Liturgy must be celebratory so as not to be dull, but it must not degenerate into mere vulgar effusiveness.

Let us summarize what we have said about celebration:

1. Celebration is an integral part of being human, hence an integral aspect of our approach to God. We share the important moments of life with others to enhance our community togetherness, to add meaning to life and to bring us into contact with the living God.

2. Celebration and worship are different facets of our human approach to God. They are not at odds with each other but are complementary. Good liturgy must be a delicate balance of celebration and worship.

3.   *Ritual*

The third aspect of sacramentality that we must consider is ritual. As with symbol and celebration, ritual is a normal part of human life. We have rituals about the way we eat, how we dress, how we attend to personal hygiene, how we behave in the presence of others, and the thousand and one other things that make up our daily life. Rituals are repetitive – we keep doing the same things, in the same way, time after time after time. Why is this? Because it makes us feel comfortable, at ease with ourselves and with others who accept our rituals. Thus, for example, we don't have to sit and think every time we want to tie a shoelace.

And so, we may define rituals as set patterns of ordering our lives that give us a sense of security and comfort and thus make life easier and more meaningful.

Rituals are particularly important in celebration. In every celebration there are agreed-upon actions which everyone recognizes and associates with that particular type of celebration (for example, baseball and football games, or the Olympics). Sometimes we tend to think that a true celebration should be by nature free-wheeling. There should be no structure, no bosses, no one saying "we must do this now," nothing that would take away from the spontaneity of the occasion. Unfortunately, as we know from experience, that kind of celebration frequently develops into chaos and into excesses that tend to expose the seamier, more vulgar side of human nature. The central ritual event should always be there to bring the people together. Even at the most spontaneous and raucous of birthday parties the candles are blown out, the cake is cut, gifts are given, "Happy Birthday" is sung.

As ritual enters into most human celebration, so also does it enter into religious celebration for, as we have noted, religious celebration is but an extension of human life. In fact, some authors have called rituals the "primary stuff" of religions. Rituals, in fact, put us in touch with the transcendent. They lead us out of ourselves, out of the confining limits of this time and space. Being familiar with the ritual actions, we do not have to concentrate on the actions themselves; they fit us like a comfortable pair of shoes. For example, at a liturgical service with a familiar ritual (such as at Mass), actions are repeated and done in a familiar sequence. When the familiar ritual is broken, there is surprise, anxiety that something is wrong; the transcendent moment is lost. When, for example, the priest at Mass does something out of the ordinary, off-beat, "unconventional," some people start wondering if this is a Catholic Mass they are celebrating! The focus is put on the ritualizer instead of on the ritual.

In Catholic worship there is a liturgical leader. That person is generally a priest, but the celebration belongs to everyone; all must participate. The tendency in contemporary society, as in religion, is to have "professional" ritualizers (often very highly paid, such as baseball players) to do our ritualizing for us. We contribute little or nothing, apart from passive attendance. For this reason, many people, and perhaps rightly so, are wary of ritual. They find it repetitive, deadening, lacking in opportunity for personal participation – in a word, boring.

One of the serious problems confronting organized religion today is the rapid pace of change in society. Anthropologists have pointed out that rapid change, and an indifference to tradition, is the great enemy of ritual; we become less attuned to and less sensitive to symbolic behaviour. Also, today's culture (in the Western world, at least) is oriented towards the here-and-now, the pragmatic, the scientific. In very large part because of their secular upbringing, people are not able to respond to the symbolic. Because we lose this sense of the symbolic, ritual is torn from its mooring and becomes empty of meaning and purpose. Boredom is often the result. We tend to go through with ritual just because it has always been done. Many will remember the well-known story of the young woman who was asked by one of her friends why she always cut off the end of a roast before putting it into the roasting pan. Did this somehow enhance the flavour? The young woman replied that she did not know why she did it but that her mother had always done it that way. Curious, she called her mother and was told that she did it that way because her mother had always done it. Curiosity now thoroughly piqued, the young woman called her grandmother and was told, "I always had to cut off the end of the roast because my roasting pan was too small!"

Ritual that is emptied of meaning just becomes magic; it enters the realm of the superstitious. It is indeed tragic that this is precisely what many religious practices have become for many people. Medals or crosses are worn to ward off the evil spirits or to gain special favours. Baptism must be given because it "frees the child from the grip of the devil," or is simply the occasion for a party. Going to church on Sunday is what the family has "always done." Marriage in the church is the "thing to do" because society usually expects it. God has little or no part to play in these dead rituals.

Let us summarize what we have said about ritual:

1. Rituals are integral to who we are as humans; they are set patterns of ordering our lives which give us a sense of security and comfort and thus make life easier and more meaningful.

2. Rituals are integral to celebration; they "regulate" celebration. In religious celebration they lead us out of ourselves and put us in touch with the transcendent.

3. We must actively participate in ritual, not simply be passively led by someone.

4. Ritual that has lost its roots in the symbolic, that is emptied of meaning, becomes mere magic.

Revitalizing our Symbols and Rituals

We pointed out in the chapter on faith that faith is a natural human phenomenon. Faith is an attitude to life that makes us see beyond the immediate scope of the senses; it is the "conviction of things not seen." It is faith that leads us to "see" beyond the symbol to that which is symbolized. Lack of faith will lead to a lack of symbolic sense. Recall the story of Mark Twain and his mastery of the scientific routine of piloting a boat down the Mississippi (see Chapter 3). When he became professionally proficient, he lost the sense of faith that made him grasp the symbolic beauty of that magnificent body of water. In order to revitalize our symbols, we need to revitalize our faith; we need to be a more faith-oriented people, and faith-oriented particularly with respect to our own life-story. In the light of our religious faith, we must be able to look beyond the immediate experience of life and see its greater significance. "The faith of the church begins with the conviction that the story which we live and share is God's story as well as our own. There is hope, there is a future, and the story is not finished. . . . It is all a story about God and ourselves in this world."[141] If we can look beyond the confining circumstances of our own life and see ourselves re-enacting God's story on earth, then the whole of life becomes a symbol that reaches out to the transcendent. If we are only prepared to operate our life at the purely scientific, pragmatic, nuts-and-bolts, one-thing-after-another level and never practice the "looking-beyond" of faith, our life-symbols will not speak to us and enrich our lives. It is within the very stuff of life, through our faith, that we shall experience the God who is mystery present.

Sacramentality and Religious Education

The principle of sacramentality should be the basis of all good religious education. There are many practical things we might do to enhance an appreciation of the principle of sacramentality and open up the realm of the symbolic. Here is a short list.

1. The teacher should be a sacrament to the students. If the students can see goodness, compassion, fairness, a sense of faith and commitment to the church in the teacher, they can see God working in a human context.

2. The school environment is of particular importance in promoting this principle.

    a) Are liturgical services proper and well-prepared?

    b) Are things that open up the symbolic, such as sacred plays, drama, artistic presentations, and liturgical dance, given a place in the teaching of religion?

    c) Does the very construction of the school provide for such things as a chapel, niches for statues, stained glass, religious art and religious symbols? Does every classroom have a crucifix and an open Bible, nicely presented, and does the teacher inculcate reverence for these things?

    d) Are there public reminders (e.g., a bulletin board) of the different liturgical seasons: Advent, Christmas, Lent, Easter?

    e) Do the teachers develop para-liturgical services* for all or some groups of students (for example, the para-liturgical ceremony of salt ["You are the salt of the earth"], or light ["You are the light of the world"])?

---

[141] Tad Guzie, *The Book of Sacramental Basics* (New York: Paulist Press, 1981), p. 30.

The whole school environment could be arranged in a way that reminds students of their religious heritage and history, and of the all-pervasive presence of God.

3.   Do teachers inculcate an appreciation of the world, that all of God's creation is good? Hence, a care for the environment (cleanliness? garbage? graffiti?) and a reverence for nature, which speaks to us of God.

Section 2 – Sacraments

In a book of this size it is impossible to give a full treatment of all the sacraments. Only the sacraments of Eucharist and Reconciliation are dealt with in any detail, they being the sacraments that most frequently affect the lives of Catholics. However, a general overview, in summary form, of all the sacraments is given below. Such an overview could be approached in many ways. What follows is only one way.

From sacramentality we come to sacrament. But before we go into any consideration of the sacraments, we must repeat – Jesus Christ is the fundamental and primordial sacrament. In the flesh and blood of his human person, Jesus reveals God to us, brings us into contact with the mystery of God.

In Malaya during World War II, a native was helping an escaping prisoner to reach the coast and be rescued. After days of walking through almost impenetrable jungle without the slightest trace of a trail of any kind, the escapee was worried that they were lost. "Are you sure that this is the way?" he asked the native. In hesitant English came the reply: "There is no way . . . I am the way." Jesus is our way to God. He continues to live, to lead and to guide us through the impenetrable jungle of life. He does this in and through the church, which provides us with the sacraments as occasions of privileged encounter with him.

What Is a Sacrament?

There are many definitions of sacrament. The deceptively simple one that many of us learned from the early catechisms is that a sacrament is an outward sign, instituted by Christ, to give grace, or, simpler still, an outward sign of inward grace. Thus, by enacting and participating in the outward, sense-perceptible sign, through which the special grace of Christ is given, we are united with God. To this definition we should perhaps add that sacraments are ritual actions and celebrations of the church; they are community celebrations in the midst of which community we meet the Lord (CCC 1131). From this definition we can see that the basic elements of sacramentality – symbol, celebration, and ritual – are all present. Emerging from this definition, also, are some general points that apply to all sacraments.

1. Sacraments Belong to the Church

They are enacted in the church, and by the church: that is, by Jesus Christ, who continues to live in and through the church (CCC 1118). Since in the church Jesus is simply carrying on the work he started during his life on earth, it is true to say that the sacraments are instituted by Christ. Consequently, a sense of being church, a sense of belonging to a worshipping community and celebrating with that community, is essential to a proper understanding of and an "entering into" the sacramental celebration. Too frequently we tend to regard the sacraments as things done to us, a purely individual and personal matter, rather than as sharing in a communal celebration in which we "meet the Lord." For example, many people, when they celebrate Eucharist, think of it solely as a matter of personal devotion, an occasion for saying their own private prayers and for receiving the body of the Lord for personal sanctification. Our language betrays our misunderstanding. We "receive" holy communion, we have water poured on us and "are baptized," we are "confirmed by the bishop" and "married by a priest." The impression created by this manner of speaking is that we are passive entities instead of active participants with the church. We need to change our language and our way of sharing the sacramental celebration.

2. Sacraments Arise out of Life

Sacraments come from the basic and shared experience of human living. The things that we celebrate in the sacraments are ordinary human things, such as eating, washing, anointing, laying on of hands, embracing, exchanging promises. It is difficult, if not impossible, to enter into celebration where there is no shared experience to celebrate. Think of how bored you were when you were invited to your spouse's class reunion! Sacraments flow from the common experience of life; they are symbols which "make present" that which they signify; through them we "meet the Lord." Thus Our Lord Jesus Christ took some important aspects of ordinary human life and specially sanctified them so that they would symbolize and confer the special grace of his love; the sacraments were instituted by Christ (CCC 1114).

3. We Must Experience before We Celebrate

We do not celebrate for celebration's sake. This has important repercussions for the sacraments. We do not celebrate the body and blood of the Lord in the Eucharist if we have not felt a hunger for his presence in our lives. We do not celebrate the Lord's forgiveness in the sacrament of Reconciliation unless we truly experience that we are forgiven. We do not celebrate marriage unless we have begun to experience the mutual love and self-giving that it involves, a love which begins with sincere human friendship.

4. *Each Sacramental Symbol Is Brought into Concrete, Sense-Perceptible, Living Reality by Appropriate Words and Actions*

We experience the cleansing waters of baptism and hear the words pronounced by the church: "I baptize you . . . ." We eat the bread of the Eucharist and hear the church pronounce that this is the body of the Lord. We feel the oil of anointing and hear the church pronounce that this will bring us the healing of Christ. But, as we pointed out above, ritual that loses its roots in symbol and meaning becomes mere magic. The practice is there, but real religion is dead. We must be extremely careful not to make the sacraments a form of magic. In magic, the magician waves his wand, says the magic words, and presto! pulls a rabbit out of a hat. The sacraments are sometimes treated in the same way: perform the action (washing with water), say the words ("I baptize you . . .") and presto! God's grace is automatically given. It is of course true that, as the Catechism points out, "From the moment that a sacrament is celebrated in accordance with the intention of the Church, the power of Christ and his Spirit acts in and through it, independently of the personal holiness of the minister." In other words, the sacraments confer grace by the very power of the Holy Spirit acting in the performed ritual itself. However, the sacraments are not inert instruments of grace. In order to meet the living God, active and "faithing" participation is required. And so the Catechism continues, "Nevertheless, the fruits of the sacraments also depend on the disposition of the one who receives them" (CCC 1128).

The Sacraments – Meeting God at the High Points of Human Life

God is present to us in every aspect of our lives, but we recognize and celebrate God's presence more fully and with more solemnity at certain high points, or marker points. We recognize also that with each of these marker points God's gift of grace is, as it were, specially adapted to the event we celebrate. Sacraments confer the grace they signify. For example, the washing of baptism signifies a death to sin and a rising to new life. The grace of baptism helps us to live up to the promises we made, to live the new life of a Christian.

The sacraments are classic examples of the principle of sacramentality at work. They are concrete sense-perceptible actions built around ritual. These concrete human actions are signs that point beyond themselves to the transcendent God. But, more than that, they are symbols that participate in the power of that to which they point and therefore "make present" to us the unseen God and bring us into contact with him. The sacraments are expressions of the life of the church. It is in the church, working through the events of our very human lives, that we meet God, that we build up a loving relationship with God, that we honour and worship the God of mystery who is present to us. The Roman Catholic church recognizes seven such special symbols associated with the high points of human life. Each sign, or symbol, is made effective as a bearer of God's grace, by words and by actions that are outward signs of inner meaning. The seven sacraments are as follows.

1. High Point of Human Life: Being Born into the Human Family

Religious Celebration: Baptism

Through baptism we are born into the Christian community. We celebrate being born into a new life in the Spirit, freed from sin (CCC 977-978, 1265). Being freed from sin, however, does not deliver us "from all the weakness of nature. On the contrary, we must still combat the movements of concupiscence that never cease leading us into evil" (CCC 978). At this point let us say a word about infant baptism. People often ask: Why do we baptize infants who cannot experience the celebration and need to have their commitment to live the Christian life made for them, without any free decision on their part? Without going into detail on a somewhat sticky theological problem, for the moment we will say that the tradition of infant baptism is a very ancient one in the church (CCC 1282). The practice was in place long before any theological justification for it was attempted. Adults who came forward for baptism just wanted their children baptized as well so that, in growing up, they would share in all the benefits and the influences that the Christian community could provide. This latter point is still the main reason for continuing the practice. Infant baptism may also have its hazards, as illustrated by the story of the young boy attending his infant sister's baptism. "Be careful," he warned the priest, "she bites!"

Religious sign: Flowing water and the prayer of the church "I baptize you . . ."

Religious symbol: The symbolism of water has a long and continuous presence in the Bible, from the account of creation, to the flood, to the crossing of the Sea of Reeds in the salvation of Israel, and in many other places. Just as God saved the Israelites from almost certain death and brought them by the passage through water to a new life as a people, so also does Jesus Christ save us by passing through death to a new and resurrected life. The religious symbolism of baptism is precisely this passing through death by water to a new life in the Spirit mediated through the Christian community. We experience this salvation and new life and celebrate it by the appropriate ritual of baptism. The death-to-new-life theme is a constant one in Christian tradition, and it comes directly out of everyone's own life-experience. It is the eternal cycle of all nature.

2. High Point of Human Life: Reaching Maturity, Growing Up, Rite-of-Passage Ceremony

Religious Celebration: Confirmation

We grow up to our Christian responsibility, just as we have to grow to maturity in the normal course of human life. We take charge of our own Christian commitment, so to speak.

Religious sign: The laying on of hands, the signing with oil and the saying of appropriate words by the minister (usually a bishop) in the name of the church.

Religious symbol: Confirmation is not an easy sacrament to pin down. There are many symbolic themes vying for our attention. One of the principal ones is that of oil. In the early days, olive oil was extensively used to cure ailments. Athletes used it to tone up the system before a contest, to give strength and vitality and to ease sore muscles afterwards (CCC 1293). The symbolism for the sacrament is that our faith is strengthened, toned up, confirmed; it comes to maturity by the special gift of the Spirit. We "share more completely in the mission of Jesus Christ" (CCC 1294). The gift of the strengthening and empowering Spirit is one of the major themes of the celebration. It is also symbolized by the bishop laying hands on the candidates, the "passing of the baton" of faith, as it were. The "laying on of hands" symbolizing the gift of the Spirit is, in fact, one of the earliest Christian symbols (Acts 8:17). The whole Christian community should have a part in this celebration. This community participation is symbolized in the ritual by each candidate choosing sponsors who "lay hands" on the candidate during the ceremony. In fact, the candidates call all to celebrate the presence of the Spirit active in their community.

3. High Point of Human Life: The Human Necessity of Eating and Drinking as the Central Point, or Focus, of Celebration and Togetherness in Community

Religious Celebration: Eucharist

Religious sign: The offering, and eating, of bread and wine. The bread and wine become the body and blood of Jesus by the power of God's Spirit acting through the words of the ordained priest, who voices the faith of the community.

Religious symbol: Bringing the community together round the table of the Lord. The religious celebration also encompasses the need to offer oneself to God as an act of worship, to offer sacrifice in union with the sacrifice of Christ that is re-enacted in the Eucharist. (This sacrament is so central to the church, and to our life in it, that it will be dealt with in far more detail in the following chapter.)

The Sacraments of Initiation

The three sacraments of baptism, confirmation, and Eucharist are called the sacraments of initiation (CCC 1275, 1533). In the ancient church, when most of the new Christians were adults, these three sacraments were celebrated in a single ceremony, with the final one, Eucharist, being the community's celebration and welcome to the new Christians. The ceremony was usually presided over by the bishop. Eastern Rite Catholics have maintained this same order to this day, with the three sacraments being administered even for infant baptism. In the Western church, however, when the numbers of Christians grew too great for the bishop to be involved in every such ceremony, confirmation became separated from baptism. At this time, too, many infants were presented for baptism, and so only the first stage of the initiation process was undertaken, thus becoming separated from the other two. The latter two stages were deferred until the children were more mature and able to appreciate what they were doing. In recent times, the church has reintroduced the Rite of Christian Initiation of Adults (R.C.I.A.). This new rite is an attempt to recapture, for new adult Christians, the ancient sequence of events in Christian initiation. The rite, with the three sacraments in order, is celebrated at the Easter Vigil.

4.   High Point of Human Life: Choosing a Career, Making a Life Commitment

By virtue of their baptism everyone is called to minister to others, to serve others, to take care of their needs as Jesus taught us. But for the continuation of the church as founded by Jesus Christ, the presence of specially ordained ministers, who give a special service, is essential. "They are consecrated in order to preach the Gospel and shepherd [i.e., lead and serve] the faithful as well as to celebrate divine worship as true priests of the New Testament" (CCC 1564).

Religious Celebration: Holy Orders, Ordination

The whole community should participate in this ceremony of providing special ministers in the vineyard of the Lord. It is not only the work of the bishop.

Religious sign: The laying on of hands by the bishop, representing the Christian community, and the saying of appropriate prayers. As part of the ordination ritual, it is customary for all the priests in attendance also to lay hands on the candidates as a sign of solidarity and unity in their special ministry.

Religious symbol: The laying on of hands is a typical human ceremony of commission and empowerment. Parents lay hands on and embrace their children when they leave home, passing on the family heritage and tradition, as it were. The sword was laid on the shoulders of the new knight; the hood is laid on the shoulders of the new graduate. The religious symbol signifies the empowering grace of the Holy Spirit that comes from God through the community and the ordaining minister. The newly ordained priest is "sent" to minister to the community, just as the Lord sent forth the disciples (Mt 10:5 ff.; Mk 16:15).

5. High Point of Human Life: Getting Married

The majority of people will choose this form of human commitment.

Religious Celebration: Marriage

God is very much part of this celebration. The love of the partners for each other will call forth God's creative power to produce new life; the marriage partners are co-creators (CCC 1652). They are empowered by God's grace in their task of co-creating and parenting. Too few marriage partners seem to understand this grace and to call on it for help during married life.

Religious sign: The exchange of consent by the partners. Thus, the two partners administer the sacrament to one another. They are not "married" by the priest; the priest or deacon is only there as the church's official witness (CCC 1662).

Religious symbol: The exchange of consent as a symbol of the love of the two partners expresses the love of God for us. St. Paul calls it a symbol of the union of Christ and the church (Eph 5:25-32). Therefore, God is always the third party in a marriage, intrinsically uniting the partners to each other and to the whole community. Some authors have called Christian marriage the "basic sacrament"; "If we realize the fundamental sacramentality of all human experience and the way Jesus transformed this sacramentality, there is good reason for seeing human friendship as the most basic sacrament of God's saving presence to human life. . . . Within human friendship there is a paradigm role played by the love between a Christian wife and husband."[142]

6. High Point of Human Life: The Need to Forgive and Be Forgiven

Evil is the number one problem for human beings. Everyone is conscious of his or her own personal evil. Not to admit this, St. John says, is to make liars of ourselves (1 Jn 1:8). The need to seek forgiveness, to experience forgiveness and to be reconciled with those we have hurt or who have hurt us is a human psychological need that is essential for our psychological health and well-being.

Religious Celebration: The Sacrament of Reconciliation

God raises this natural human need to the level of a religious celebration for, as we have seen, in perpetrating evil on our neighbour we also damage our relationship with God. And celebration it should be – a happy and consoling experience, not a fearful, worrying one.

---

[142] *Sacraments and Sacramentality*, p. 93.

Religious sign: The purely human sign of asking for and receiving forgiveness before the church becomes the religious sign of asking God for forgiveness. Thus we tell (i.e., openly speak) our transgressions and ask for forgiveness. From the minister (priest), we openly receive the forgiveness of God and the church. Both acts must be externalized in some way: by signs or gestures or words.

Religious symbol: Human forgiveness is a symbol of the compassionate love and forgiveness of God, who will never be outdone in mercy and generosity.

7. High point of human life: Sickness and Death

Paradoxically, death is the most important part of life. In effect, we live so as to die well, for death is inevitable. It is only through death that we can pass to new life.

Religious Celebration: Anointing of the Sick

"Are any among you sick? They should call for the elders of the church and have them pray over them, anointing them with oil in the name of the Lord" (Jas 5:14), (CCC 1523). The Lord is especially present to us in sickness and at death because this is the most crucial of all human experiences (CCC 1500-1501). We celebrate that presence with the church. "Death needs to be celebrated, and that is why there are funeral rites. Mourning is a form of festivity which enables us to absorb the experience of death so that we can go on with life. Sickness is a profound experience that needs to be owned, and that is why there is a sacrament of the sick."[143] As far as possible, this sacrament should be celebrated in the presence of family members and any others able to be there with the sick person. The sacrament should involve as many of the community as are able to come, for it is the prayer of the church that will cure the sick person.

Formerly Anointing of the Sick was known as Extreme Unction: that is, anointing in danger of death. But if we wait till death is imminent, we are really asking God to work a miracle to heal the sick person. Also, the sick person is less able to participate consciously and fully in the sacrament. Somehow families got the impression that, once the priest was called in for the Sacrament of the Sick, the sick person would immediately think that he or she was dying and become fearful and disturbed. No, the anointing of the sick is principally for the sick, not the dying. For the dying there is Viaticum (literally, food for the journey). The dying person receives the sacrament of the Eucharist to help prepare and to be strengthened for the experience of death and the journey to a new life (CCC 1524).

---

[143] *The Book of Sacramental Basics*, p. 21.

Religious sign: The anointing with oil and the saying of appropriate prayers by the minister and the whole church.

Religious symbol: Again, the symbolism is that of the curative properties of oil.

Reflection Questions

1. What is your understanding of the principle of sacramentality? Give some examples from your own life of how you experienced this principle in action.

2. Why is symbolism such an integral part of human life? Describe some symbols that have particular meaning for you. Why are they meaningful?

3. What do you understand by ritual? What rituals do you experience in your religious life and in worship? What is your reaction to these rituals?

4. Describe some ways in which you would attempt to put the principle of sacramentality into practice in your teaching career.

5. Discuss the problems of a proper integration of celebration and worship.

6. Explain carefully what is meant by saying that "the church is a sacrament to the world." Do we have any part to play in this?

7. "The seven sacraments are not individual events. They are not actions of personal devotion." Do you agree with this statement? If the sacraments are not actions of personal devotion, what are they?

Further Reading

Bausch, William J. *A New Look at the Sacraments* (Mystic, CT: Twenty-Third Publications, 1983). A useful book by a well-known author. Individual sacraments are treated in detail, but the section on sacramentality is somewhat sketchy.

Browning, Robert L., and Roy A. Reed. *The Sacraments in Religious Education and Liturgy* (Birmingham, AL: Religious Education Press, 1985). A standard reference work. Should be in every school and departmental library.

Cooke, Bernard. *Sacraments and Sacramentality* (Mystic, CT: Twenty-Third Publications, 1983). An expanded and updated edition is expected in the near future. A short book by an outstanding theologian that deals with all the important points covered in this chapter.

Guzie, Tad. *The Book of Sacramental Basics* (New York: Paulist Press, 1981). Introduces some fresh, new ideas and has a good section on the sacramental process.

16

EUCHARIST

Introduction

One of my most vivid memories from my days as a student in Rome came from my attending some of the public sessions of the Second Vatican Council. . . . The Pope, Pope Paul VI, would concelebrate mass with a dozen or more bishops. The other bishops were in attendance and the rest of the basilica was crowded with humanity of many sorts and shapes and sizes. And as the Pope began the Mass and this vast congregation thundered their responses, it always seemed to me that here in a quite exceptional way the church was at prayer. It brought home to me the saying: the church is never more truly itself than when Mass is being celebrated. In St. Peter's during an ecumenical council that truth is evoked most powerfully but it is equally true at every celebration of the Mass.[144]

Anyone who has had the privilege of participating in a eucharistic celebration in St. Peter's in Rome will most assuredly concur with the above account. The vastness and the surpassing architectural beauty of the basilica itself, in a sense the epicentre of the church, already stirs the emotion of togetherness with Christians everywhere, the feeling of belonging, a sense of the ineffable presence of God. But all these emotions and feelings are made even more real when the Eucharist is being celebrated. The church is never more the church than when it is celebrating together the Lord's Supper. The Eucharist is the central act of worship of the People of God. It is the Eucharist that cements, that binds together this very People of God into one body, one caring, sharing community. Down through the centuries, through all the historical vicissitudes to which the church has been subjected, through all the heresies that have beset it, through all the internal strife that often seemed to threaten the very existence of the church, it was always devotion to and faith in the Eucharist that kept the body together. Pope Pius XII, in his encyclical letter *Mediator Dei*, says that "all the faithful should be aware that to participate in the eucharistic sacrifice is their chief duty and supreme dignity" (No. 80). "The Eucharist is 'the source and summit of the

---

[144]   Roderick Strange, *The Catholic Church* (Oxford, UK: Oxford University Press, 1986), p. 100.

Christian life' . . . For in the blessed Eucharist is contained the whole spiritual good of the Church, namely Christ himself, our Pasch" (CCC 1324). Very simply, the church without Eucharist is impossible.

This intrinsic connection between Eucharist and church was very clearly expressed in the Constitution on the Sacred Liturgy of Vatican Council II. The Pope and bishops realized very clearly that if the Council was to be a significant instrument for the renewal of the church, then the Eucharist, and the reanimation of participation in it by the faithful people of God, must be the very focus of that renewal. Therefore, before attending to any other important matters, the Council addressed itself to the forming of a document on the Sacred Liturgy. From this document have come many changes in the form of celebration of the Eucharist, an important one being the use of the vernacular instead of Latin in the Latin Rite church.

Passover

We cannot understand the Christian Eucharist unless we go back in Jewish history to the Passover event.

As far as we can tell, Passover was an ancient rite of the people of the land of Egypt. It pre-dated the advent of the family of Jacob in Egypt, but this people adopted it from their Egyptian hosts as a religious service. Because of subsequent events this religious service became associated with the Israelite belief that God had saved them from the Egyptians.

From reading the Book of Exodus (Chapters 5 to 12), we learn that just before the actual exodus, the going out from Egypt, the country had been subject to the so-called plagues, which were probably a series of natural disasters (we cannot know for certain). The Jews read these disasters as punishments sent by God on the Egyptians because Pharaoh would not free them from slavery and let them leave. The last and most powerful of these tragedies was the death of many children and animals, the cause of which the Bible does not make clear. In the history of Israel's faith, however, it was God who preserved the Israelites from this last catastrophe. The "Angel of Death" *passed over* the houses of the Jews that had been marked with the blood of the lamb that was sacrificed.

READ: Exodus 12:1-28.

The Passover event is associated with the eating of a meal of roasted lamb, bitter herbs and unleavened bread. The ritual eating of this meal became the memorial of the Exodus – the central experience of Jewish faith – to be repeated through all generations.

> *You shall observe this rite as a perpetual ordinance for you and your children. . . . And when your children ask you, 'What do you mean by this observance?' you shall say, 'It is the passover sacrifice to the Lord, for he*

passed over the houses of the Israelites in Egypt, when he struck down the Egyptians but spared our houses.' (Ex 12:24-27)

When the Jewish people celebrate Passover and eat the Seder* meal, what are they doing?

1. They are remembering God's saving act on their behalf

It is more than mere remembrance, however – more than simply recalling a past event. The ritual requires that in their minds and hearts they re-live the great event. They must enter into it spiritually, emotionally. They must imagine that they are actually there experiencing it themselves. They must experience again the bitterness of slavery, rejection and being held in contempt. They must experience the joy and relief of being saved by God and must ask themselves what they must do now to bring about the reign of God in the world.

2. They are giving thanks for God's saving act

They thank God for the experience of freedom from slavery and oppression, an experience that now becomes the paradigm for freedom from all kinds of slavery, whether personal or societal.

3. The whole ritual constitutes an act of worship of God

After Moses' injunction to the people to eat the Passover meal as a constant remembrance of their salvation, the Book of Exodus remarks: "And the people bowed down and worshipped" (Ex 12:27). It is a worship that will be enjoined on them by the covenant (First Commandment).

4. They are renewing their sense of being a people, a community formed by covenant with God

They are bound together forever and share this special gift of God.

All this is important for us, for as Christians we are the direct inheritors of that same tradition. What we do at the celebration of the Eucharist is basically what the Jewish people do in celebrating Passover (CCC 1164).

The Last Supper

READ: Luke 22:7-8, 14-20.

Scripture scholars are somewhat divided as to whether the last meal celebrated by Jesus with his disciples was in fact the ritual Passover supper. That uncertainty is not really of great consequence, for all agree that the meal that was eaten had strong Passover connotations and overtones and partook of the very ceremonial of the Paschal meal (see Mk 14:12, 1 Cor 5:7).

At this last Passover supper with his apostles, Jesus introduced a new dimension to the Jewish ritual meal. The saving act of God at the Exodus is now to be re-enacted in a most dramatic way. Following the Passover ritual, after giving thanks Jesus distributes the unleavened bread to his disciples, saying that this bread is his body which is given for them. Similarly, the cup of wine "that is poured out for you is the new covenant in my blood" (Lk 22:20; "for the forgiveness of sins" – Mt 26:28).

Thus, through the passion, death and resurrection of Jesus, God was once again to seal a new covenant with his people – the new covenant in the blood of Jesus. The Passover lamb, the victim of the Jewish sacrifice, is now Jesus himself, who becomes the victim of the sacrifice of the new covenant. And so in our present celebration of the Eucharist, Jesus is spoken of as the "Lamb of God who takes away the sin of the world." Jesus requested that his followers repeat this ritual meal "in commemoration of me." And his request is honoured every time we celebrate the Eucharist. Eucharist comes from the Greek *eucharistia*, meaning "thanksgiving." Following the Jewish ritual of the Passover meal Jesus "gave thanks" to God before he distributed the bread and wine. The name Eucharist has come down to us from what Jesus did at the Last Supper with his disciples.

And so, just as the Jews re-enacted the original Passover and commemorated their freedom from oppression in the ritual Passover supper, we Christians re-enact the sacrifice of Jesus, the installation of the New Covenant, in the celebration of our Eucharist. This mystery "stands at the centre of the Good News that the apostles, and the Church following them, are to proclaim to the world" (CCC 571).

Eucharist as Mystery

In its essence, Eucharist is a deep mystery. It belongs irrevocably to Christian faith. Here we are in the realm of sacrament, an earthly reality that reveals God to us. We are in the realm of signs and symbols that point beyond themselves to an unseen reality and which make that reality "present" to us. The deep mystery that is the Eucharist is not something that we can discover for ourselves; it is a gift of God's revelation. Certainly, it is beyond full human explanation. It is an aspect of God's presence to us in the midst of life. However, as we have said before, mystery is not mystification and we must attempt to read as much as we can into this mystery. To that end we shall deal with Eucharist under three major headings:

1. Eucharist as presence;
2. Eucharist as communion;
3. Eucharist as sacrifice.

1. Eucharist as Presence

There is an anecdote from the life of St. John Mary Vianney (1786–1859) that goes something like this. St. John, parish priest of the small town of Ars in France in the 1800s, observed a man who used to come to his church and sit for hours just staring at the tabernacle,* not seeming to say any prayers. When St. John asked the man about it, the man replied that there was no need for formal prayers because, as he said simply, "I know that he is there, and he knows that I am here."

This story focuses on the very Catholic understanding that the person of Jesus is specially present in the eucharistic bread reserved in the tabernacle (CCC 1374, 1377). It is a sacramental presence that belongs to the realm of symbol, a symbol that "makes present" the reality to which it points. The matter is well stated by the Final Report of the Anglican–Roman Catholic International Commission.*

> What is here affirmed is a sacramental presence in which God uses the realities of this world to convey the realities of a new creation: bread for this life becomes bread for eternal life. Before the eucharistic prayer, to the question: 'What is that?' the believer answers 'It is bread.' After the eucharistic prayer, to the same question he answers: 'It is truly the Body of Christ, the Bread of Life.'[145]

After the recital of the eucharistic prayer the bread and wine are now said to be consecrated. If any is left over after communion it is not just ordinary bread. It is bread that is "truly the body of Christ, the Bread of life," the Eucharist of the Lord. This Eucharist, under the form of bread and wine, this Eucharist that "contains" the whole person of Christ, is kept in the churches in a special receptacle, the tabernacle, which in Roman Catholic churches is the focus and centre of prayer (CCC 1378, 1380).

In their understanding of Eucharist most other Christian denominations will not go as far as this. There are no tabernacles in their churches, for there is no consecrated bread to reserve. They believe that the bread and wine only signify (point to) the presence of Jesus. Union with the Lord is achieved in the act of eating the bread and wine in the course of a eucharistic celebration. The bread left over, though blessed, is of no special significance.

In the words of the Catechism (1375) the bread and wine are "converted" into the body and blood of Christ. Precisely how this conversion takes place is a deep mystery. The traditional teaching of the church, stated in the decrees of the Council of Trent (1545–1563), is that a process of "transubstantiation" takes

[145] Anglican-Roman Catholic International Commission I, *The Final Report* (Cincinnati: Forward Movement Publications, 1982), p. 21.

place whereby the substance of bread and wine become the substance of Christ's body and blood. The accidents of bread and wine, however (that is, those things that enable us to see, feel, taste, smell, etc.), remain unchanged. Thus, it looks, feels, tastes and is broken like bread but it is really the glorified body of Christ. And so, Jesus identifies bread and wine with himself changing them into himself in order to remain with us. The bread and wine we receive, therefore, is no mere symbol, or pointer; rather it is the risen Lord's real body, it is Jesus himself.

In addition to this special sacramental presence in the eucharistic bread, we believe that Jesus is present in the church in many other ways. For example, Jesus is present in the word of Scripture, particularly when this word is spoken and explained to the community and associated with some liturgical action such as the Eucharist. Again, when Christians gather to pray together they have faith in Jesus' presence in the community, as he said "For where two or three are gathered in my name, I am there among them" (Mt 18:20). All these elements are brought together in the eucharistic celebration. The Christian community is gathered in his name to do in his memory what he did at the Last Supper and thus enter into the mystery of his passion, death and resurrection. It is the "entering into" the passion, death and resurrection of Jesus (just as the Jews "enter into" the experience of being saved by God at the Reed Sea), through the gathering together for prayer, through the proclamation of the Scriptures, through the consecration of bread and wine and the eating of the body and blood of Christ, that Jesus becomes present in the eucharistic community. The priest does not celebrate Eucharist by himself; rather, the whole community celebrates. The priest is their representative who calls the community to celebrate and leads them in the celebration. Without community, without a caring, sharing, forgiving, loving family there is no true Eucharist, for the Eucharist is both the sign of unity among Christians and the power of God's Spirit that brings about this unity.

2. Eucharist as Communion

The story is told of a Christian missionary in India who was distributing copies of the Christian Scriptures to anyone who would accept them. One day while travelling on a train he offered a copy to a man sitting next to him. The man took the book, angrily tore it into pieces and threw the pieces out the window. As it happened, there was a man walking beside the railroad track that day, and he picked up a piece of paper on which was written "the Bread of Life." He did not know what it meant, but one of his friends told him that it came from a Christian book that he should not read. But the man said, "I want to read the book from which this beautiful phrase came," and he bought a copy of the New Testament. In it he read the passage from which the original scrap of paper had come, in which Jesus says, "I am the Bread of Life." This was the beginning of his conversion to Christianity. Through the power of God's grace, that little scrap of paper had indeed been for him the Bread of Life.[146]

Jesus is the Bread of Life given to us in the Eucharist. For us to understand this phrase better we must take a look at the symbolism of bread and wine.

Symbolism of Bread and Wine

Bread and wine are basic elements of food. In our culture, wine is an expensive and little-used commodity. Not so in many other cultures, and particularly the culture to which Jesus belonged. But food itself is full of deep symbolism: it points to something beyond itself that is not easy to explain.

1. Food is nourishment

Just as food is nourishment for our bodies, the Eucharist is nourishment for our spiritual life. As Jesus said,

> Those who eat my flesh and drink my blood have eternal life, and I will raise them up on the last day; for my flesh is true food and my blood is true drink. Those who eat my flesh and drink my blood abide in me, and I in them. (Jn 6:54-56)

Eating the eucharistic bread will bring us into close union with him who is our Lord and saviour (CCC 1331, 1416).

2. Food speaks the language of love

A little baby best understands that it is loved and cared for when it is fed, particularly when it is fed at its mother's breast with much caressing and tenderness. Such feeding and loving produce a sense of security that, child psychologists assure us, is very necessary for a healthy, balanced and emotionally stable development. There is no mystery in the fact that if we love someone we will feed them; it is something that is cut deep in our human experience. Jesus himself makes the point very clearly in his parable about the end of time: "I was hungry and you gave me food, I was thirsty and you gave me something to drink" (Mt 25:35). God loves us by feeding us with himself in the Eucharist.

3. Eating together is central to celebration and unity

Often when people gather together to celebrate, or just to be with one another, they eat. If you study the gospels, you will find that stories about eating have a prominent place. Jesus seems to spend a lot of time eating! Jesus ate with his disciples, with his friends, with publicans and other "unsavoury" character; in fact, one of the big accusations against him was that he ate with sinners!

---

[146] Adapted from Monika Hellwig, *Understanding Catholicism* (New York: Paulist Press, 1981), p. 143.

A meal together cements friendship, expresses care and consideration, and produces *koinonia* (caring, sharing, togetherness). Correspondingly, we do not like eating with people with whom we do not get along, and we rarely plan to eat with our enemies. One of the most powerful and emotional episodes of the *All in the Family* series on television had to do with Archie Bunker's son-in-law inviting a friend to Christmas dinner. Archie discovered that this friend had been a Vietnam War draft-dodger. The tension that developed when Archie refused to eat with him was a powerful reminder that eating together means expressing love and acceptance of those with whom we eat. It has been said that the family that prays together stays together. Can it not also be said that the family that eats together stays together? One of the greatest tragedies of modern fast-paced living is precisely that families do not seem to be able to find the time to eat together. A meal together is, in fact, a *com-union*, or union with.

The act of eating together at the table of the Lord, at the eucharistic celebration, is not only a "com-union" with the Lord, it is also cements our "com-union" in the church. Sharing Christ together in the Eucharist also means that we share ourselves with one another; we are brought together in the experience of close unity in the church (CCC 1325, 1407).

One of the astronauts on the very first voyage to the moon in July 1969 was Edwin "Buzz" Aldrin. Before leaving Earth, Aldrin had prepared a special kit containing a cup, some wine and some bread that had been given to him by the minister of his church, bread that would be used in the communion service at that very church. He had also prepared some Scripture readings from the gospel of John appropriate to his communion. While sitting in the lunar module before walking on the moon surface, Aldrin read from the Scripture and performed his personal communion service. In his account of this experience, Aldrin remarked that he had felt a strong sense of unity with the people of his own church back home and with the church everywhere in the world.

Please note that above we said: "eating together." While it proved a very significant religious experience for him and was a courageous act of faith, "Buzz" Aldrin's solo communion service is not the norm. We Catholics have an unfortunate tendency to look upon Holy Communion as a purely personal matter between ourselves and God. Most of the time we are not even conscious of the other people with whom we are sharing the meal. Clearly, in a large church it is difficult to get the sense of a communal meal. Nevertheless, that is what it is; it is not purely a personal contact between myself and God. The depth and intimacy of God's presence to us in communion is as much a function of the depth of our communal union as it is a function of Jesus' presence in the eucharistic bread.

Because of the difficulty of sensing communal union in a large gathering for Sunday Mass, for example, we should try as much as possible to foster such community outside of the eucharistic celebration. Bernard Cooke expresses it well:

> In simpler times, there probably was much more sharing of life's experiences among people as they met and conversed before going into the church building; and the meaning they had for one another passed unnoticed but importantly into what they then did during the liturgy. If, for example, someone learned before Mass that a friend's young daughter was dangerously ill, that was certain to be part of that person's Prayer of the Faithful. Perhaps we should try to regain some of this interchange among the assembled group, even capitalize on it to make the entire eucharistic celebration more personally meaningful.[147]

In other words, we should not just walk in and out of Mass immersed in our own thoughts. We should meet and greet people, share with them our experiences and concerns, try to strengthen our community ties in whatever way possible. All the effects that flow from a happily shared meal should flow from sharing the Eucharist together – increased understanding of others, more caring, sharing, helping and forgiving. Everything, in other words, that helps to build true community, and the kingdom of God. The *koinonia* established around the table of the Lord should be the *koinonia* of our lives as Christians.

3. Eucharist as Sacrifice

The English word "sacrifice" comes from the Latin *sacrum facere*, meaning to make sacred. When something is set aside from its ordinary use and made over to God, it is made sacred. The key element in sacrifice, therefore, is that of making a gift to God. God receives our gift and thereby makes it sacred, or holy.

The more popular understanding of sacrifice tends to focus on the killing of a victim, with all the attendant implications of destruction and the shedding of blood. Another popular understanding of sacrifice is that it implies giving something up, doing something unpleasant, like giving up candy for Lent. It is probable that this notion of sacrifice came to us from an imperfect understanding of Jewish sacrifice which, for the most part, seemed to involve the messy killing of animals. But, for Jewish religious worship, the essence of sacrifice was not the killing of an animal. The essence of the sacrifice revolved around blood. In their pre-scientific understanding of things blood was life, and only God was the author of life. In their ritual the blood was poured out over the altar. The symbolism of this act is that, since only God is the author of life, the pouring out of blood (life) points to the fact that only God has supreme power over life, that

---

[147]   Adapted from *More Quotes and Anecdotes*, p. 217.

God is the sovereign God, the Lord of the universe. Thus, it is a formal act of worship, an offering to God, a sign and a symbol that the people also give themselves to God – a sacrifice.

Perhaps even more pertinent for our understanding of Jewish ritual is the importance for them of the peace offering. Essentially, this is a meal shared by God and the people, a meal that cemented the covenant relationship, or restored it if it had been broken. The Passover celebration, in which God's saving act was "remembered," re-lived, was such a meal. By sharing in this meal the Jews participated in the peace offering and in sacrifice.

Jesus' Sacrifice

Traditionally, Roman Catholics have held that Jesus' passion and death on the cross are a "sacrifice." But how are we to understand this? Does it mean that we concentrate on the painful shedding of blood on the cross? Or does it rather mean that we concentrate on Jesus' giving of his life, his most precious human possession, for his friends? If we understand the essence of sacrifice to be in the gift-giving, then this latter meaning makes most sense. That gift began at the Passover supper ("This is my body which is given for you"). It is continued on the cross as one continuous act of giving (CCC 1367).

Where does all this leave us?

1. We must participate in Jesus' sacrifice, his offering of himself to his Father, by offering ourselves in union with him: that is, by making a gift of ourselves and all aspects of our life to God. The gift of ourselves is symbolized by the gifts of bread and wine; they are our small gifts to God. Jesus takes these gifts, wonderfully identifies himself with them in the course of the eucharistic celebration and then returns them to us as nourishment for our spiritual life of union with him and work for the kingdom of God.

    What this means is that we must recommit ourselves to the Christian life, accepting the guidance of the church. We recommit ourselves to efforts to establish the kingdom of God on earth, we recommit ourselves to personal union with Jesus. If we are to participate fully in the eucharistic celebration we must make this recommitment in our minds and hearts at some stage during the celebration.

2. To seal this offering we must partake of the eucharistic meal: we must "eat the flesh of the Son of Man and drink his blood" so that we may have life (Jn 6:52 ff.). Partaking of the eucharistic meal is an essential complement to the offering. Unless we are conscious of complete separation from God by mortal sin we should eat the bread of the Eucharist when we participate in

the Mass.[148] This act of eating brings us right back to the symbolism of the meal as mentioned above.

Thus, the symbolism of sacrifice and the symbolism of the meal are inextricably woven together in the Eucharist. We cannot have one without the other.

The Rite of Eucharistic Celebration

The Mass

Why is the eucharistic celebration called the Mass? The term "Mass" comes from the Latin *missa*, meaning sent, or dismissed. In the early days of the church, any ecclesiastical celebration was concluded with a blessing and a sending forth of the people, a dismissal. In the course of time this term *missa*, which evolved into Mass, came to be used only for the eucharistic celebration.

In order to promote the dialogue between priest and people, which is essential if we are to participate properly in the Eucharist, it is useful to have a book in which the parts of the celebration are clearly laid out. Such a book we call a missal, of which there are several available. We should note that the missal is not an end in itself. It is not meant to be a distraction or a barrier to our participation in the ceremony. It is simply a help in focusing our attention, in making us aware of what is going on and in promoting our thorough involvement in what is very much our Eucharist.

Finally, we should be aware of the fact that the rite of the Eucharist (that is, the order and form of the eucharistic celebration) varies in different parts of the church. What we shall describe here is the rite used in the so-called Latin churches and does not apply, for example, to the Ukrainian Catholic churches. However, no matter what rite is used, the essential parts of the Eucharist are the same.

The Mass of the Latin Rite

The Mass consists essentially of a repetition of what Jesus did at the Last Supper. Go back to the Gospel according to Matthew (26:26).

While they were eating, Jesus took a loaf of bread, and after blessing it he broke it, gave it to the disciples, and said "Take, eat; this is my body."

There are three actions here: 1) Jesus took the bread; 2) he blessed it; 3) he gave it to his disciples to eat. These three actions constitute the central part of the

---

[148] CCC 1393 points out that "Holy Communion separates us from sin." Receiving the eucharist with good dispositions is a way of having our venial sins forgiven. Many people still think that it is necessary to have one's sins forgiven in the sacrament of reconciliation before one can receive Christ in the Eucharist. No. Venial sin can be forgiven by the Eucharist; one is not obliged to confess unless conscious of mortal sin.

Mass. To these the church, in the course of time, added others: a) the opening, or penitential rite, in which we confess our sinfulness and ask for forgiveness; b) the rite of the word of God; c) the rite of dismissal at the end.

And so we may say that the Latin rite Mass consists of six parts.

1. *The opening penitential rite*

We join with the priest in confessing our faults before the whole church community and asking for God's forgiveness, that we may enter into the celebration with the proper dispositions, forgiving one another as God forgives us. This part also includes the *Gloria in Excelsis*, a hymn of praise to God. This is followed by the special prayer of the day (always a prayer of petition that we make to God through Jesus Christ Our Lord).

2. *The liturgy of the Word*

This consists of readings from Sacred Scripture appropriate to the day. We believe that God is present to us in the word of Scripture, and this serves as an important prelude to the presence of Christ in the Eucharist itself. Most often, this word of God is explained in the homily, or sermon, which is designed to help us understand the Scripture better and to meditate on how we can apply it to our own lives. On important days of celebration, such as Sunday, the Creed is recited, our common act of faith as a Christian community. The Creed summarizes the principal articles of our faith contained in the readings and the whole celebration.

3. *The preparation of the gifts of bread and wine*

As we mentioned above, these ordinary gifts of bread and wine are our gifts to God; they represent us, they represent our self-giving to God just as Jesus gave himself for us. This self-giving is symbolized by the procession in which representatives of the celebrating community bring up the gifts to be presented to the presiding minister. The priest prays in the name of all the people:

> Blessed are you Lord, God of all creation. Through your goodness we have this bread to offer, which earth has given and human hands have made. It will become for us the bread of life.

Then the priest invites us to join in this prayer of giving and we ask the Lord to accept our gifts (ourselves):

> May the Lord accept the sacrifice at your hands, for the praise and glory of his name, for our good, and the good of all the church.

4. *The liturgy of the Eucharist itself*

This, undoubtedly, is the central part of the Mass. The priest recites (again in the name of all the people) the special eucharistic prayer with its repetition of the actual words of Jesus at the Last Supper with his disciples. In the course of time, other parts were added to this prayer to recall more fully the passion, death and resurrection of the Lord. As a result, now we have more than the words of Jesus recorded in the gospel. The eucharistic prayer concludes with a great exclamation of praise and adoration to God:

> Through him, with him, in him, in the unity of the Holy Spirit all glory and honour is yours, almighty Father, for ever and ever.

And all the people answer Amen – yes we believe it, yes we want it so, yes we unite ourselves with this expression of praise and worship.

5.   *The communion rite*

Now Jesus gives us back our gifts, made holy in the eucharistic action. We begin by reciting the prayer of all Christians, the Our Father, the prayer that unites us as a community, the prayer that expresses our deepest desires, the prayer that Jesus asked us to pray. To cement that unity, to further bring us together as a community, we express peace to one another in any way we see fit (handshake, embracing, a word or two of greeting). And then we eat the body of the Lord and drink his blood. As we have already mentioned, this Holy Communion should be an intrinsic part of any eucharistic celebration. For various reasons (not always cogent reasons, one has to admit), drinking from the cup is not always available. But it is enough to partake of the bread, for in the Eucharist the whole person of Christ – body, blood, soul and divinity – is contained under the species of bread and wine.

6.   *The conclusion and dismissal*

The priest in the name of the people says a concluding prayer of petition. It is a prayer that makes specific reference to the Eucharist in which we have just participated. Then the priest gives us God's blessing and invites us to go forth and live out what we have just experienced.

> "Go, the mass is ended" (*Ite, missa est*) – we are sent forth to love and serve the Lord.

The Directory for Masses with Children

In its Constitution on the Liturgy, Vatican Council II had spoken of the need to adapt the liturgy to suit the needs of various groups, especially children. Children must be helped to participate as fully as possible in the eucharistic celebrations of the church. For this reason the *Directory for Masses with Children* was produced, for, as the Directory points out, "Children cannot always understand everything that they experience with adults, and they easily become weary. It cannot be expected, moreover, that everything in the liturgy will always be intelligible to them."[149] The Directory does not create a special rite for the Eucharist different from the one used for adults. All the parts of the Mass described above are retained. However, some elements are shortened or simplified and texts more suitable for children's understanding are built into the rite. "All who have a part in the formation of children," says the Directory, "should consult and work together. In this way even if children already have some feeling for God and the things of God, they may also experience the human values which are found in the eucharistic celebration, depending upon their age and personal progress. These values are the activity of the community, exchange of greetings, capacity to listen and to seek and grant pardon, expression of gratitude, experience of symbolic actions, a meal of friendship, and festive celebration."[150]

It goes without saying that the Directory is an important document for all teachers involved with the religious formation of young (pre-adolescent) children. They should be familiar with its contents and be able to use it in planning eucharistic celebrations for children.

Conclusion – "Do This in Memory of Me"

We should now be able to see that at the Last Supper Jesus was doing essentially what his Jewish ancestors had done for centuries (CCC 1403, 1409). All the Passover symbolism enters deeply into the symbolism of the Eucharist. This act, so central to Christian worship, is to be continued in the church forever – "Do this in memory of me."

As we mentioned at the beginning of this discussion, what we do in celebrating the Eucharist is basically what the Jewish people do in celebrating Passover.

1. *We remember*, in the active sense of that word. We make present again the saving act of God in the gift of Jesus for us. As do the Jewish people in celebrating Passover, we should remember as we try to feel ourselves being present with Jesus on those fateful days, try to experience in ourselves the saving love that was poured out for us, try to be part – in our mind and heart – of the passion, death and resurrection.

2. *We give thanks* for God's goodness and generosity. We give thanks for God's fidelity to his promises; we give thanks for the new covenant offered us in Jesus. We give thanks for the grace of God in Jesus by which we are offered freedom from the slavery of sin. We give thanks for this anticipation of heaven (CCC 1402).

---

[149] *The Roman Missal, Directory for Masses With Children*, No. 2 (Ottawa: Canadian Conference of Catholic Bishops, © 1973, ICEL).
[150] *Ibid.*, No. 9.

3. *We worship* God by participating in the eucharistic celebration. In our worship of God, Jesus is our personal representative and mediator. Because the act of worship is performed by Jesus himself there is no greater act of worship on earth than the Eucharist.

4. *We renew our sense of being a people called together by God – a church.* We are the people of the new covenant, the church of Jesus Christ through which he continues to live and work on earth. We are his body, his hands, his feet, his voice; through us he continues his work of establishing the kingdom of God on earth. The Eucharist is the very centre of unity in the church (CCC 1325).

A final word. It should not be difficult to see why the church places such supreme importance on celebrating the Eucharist together, regularly and often. As we have said often enough, but never too often, the Eucharist is the very centre of unity in the church. Through celebrating the Eucharist we are brought together as a caring, sharing, helping community which carries on Jesus' work in the world. The Eucharist is also the source of our growth in personal union with God; it sustains and nourishes our spiritual life. The Eucharist is the focus of the new covenant. We have no option. If we are to be true followers of Jesus we must celebrate Eucharist together.

Reflection Questions

1. How do you personally experience the Eucharist? How do you see it as meaningful in your life?

2. What is the intrinsic link between Jewish Passover and Christian Eucharist?

3. How would you attempt to answer those who say that they do not go to Eucharist on Sunday because they find the whole procedure dull and boring, the sermon out of date and not related to their daily life, and because they find that they can pray better at home?

4. When we say that Jesus is "present" in the Eucharist, what do we mean?

5. "It is as a meal shared that the Eucharist has its particular significance, not simply in the sharing of food, but in the sharing of food as representative of the loving service which the members of the assembly offer one another" (Ralph A. Keifer). Comment on this quote. How do you relate to it personally?

6. What do you understand by the notion of sacrifice? In what way is the Eucharist a sacrifice? How would you attempt to teach this aspect of Eucharist to fairly young children?

7. What do we mean when we call Jesus the "Lamb of God?"

Further Reading

Cooke, Bernard. *Sacraments and Sacramentality* (Mystic, CT: Twenty-Third
    Publications, 1983). Already recommended for the chapter on
    Sacramentality. Excellent section on the Eucharist.

Coyle, Tom. *This Is Our Mass* (Mystic, CT: Twenty-Third Publications, 1989).
    Simply written, but with many deep insights which will help us to deepen
    our faith and love for the Mass and to live out our eucharistic participation in
    our everyday life.

Guzie, Tad W. *Jesus and the Eucharist* (New York: Paulist Press, 1974). This
    book addresses "the kinds of questions asked today by college students,
    religious educators and interested adults" concerning the Eucharist. It does
    so in clear and straightforward prose and with singular success. As one
    reviewer put it, "Simply the best thing I have ever read on the subject."

Henderson, J. Frank, Kathleen Quinn, and Stephen Larson. *Liturgy, Justice, and
    the Reign of God* (New York: Paulist Press, 1989). Highlights the intrinsic
    connection between worship and social justice, between eucharistic
    participation and working to establish God's kingdom in the world.
    Particularly useful for teachers.

Part IV

MORALITY, SIN AND RECONCILIATION

17

PRINCIPLES OF MORALITY: THE TEN COMMANDMENTS

Fundamental Principle of Morality

The most basic principle of morality is deceptively simple: do good and avoid evil. But this simplicity hides a wealth of complexity. We shall spend this chapter trying to disentangle some of that complexity. We find Jesus stating the Christian version of this adage in the gospels. Jesus does not propose it as his own particular and distinctive advice, but rather as a principle that is instinctively ingrained in our human consciousness: do unto others as you would have them do unto you.[151] This maxim subsequently came to be called the "Golden Rule of life." Jesus also puts his own special seal, as it were, on this advice by stating the two greatest commandments: love God, and love one another. To love someone is to seek to do good to them, and certainly, at the very least, to avoid doing them evil.

What Does "Moral" Mean?

For a better understanding of this basic principle of morality we need to explain what we mean by good and evil. But first, let us say something about the very word "moral." The word is derived from the Latin *mores*, meaning customs, habitual ways of doing things. Customary ways of doing things can, of course, be either right or wrong, good or evil. When we say that something is "moral" we generally mean that it is "good." In the historical past, in times when the social milieu was more uniform, doing the right thing meant that you did what the generally good people in society did because this ultimately benefited the whole community. To show responsibility for the community is clearly one of the ways in which we "do unto others as we would have them do unto us." *In morality the fundamental value is always the human person and the person in relationship with society.* We belong to society and the human community by the

---

[151] The Catechism deals with this under the heading of The Natural Moral Law which "expresses the original moral sense which enables man to discern by reason the good and the evil" (CCC 1954-1960).

very nature of our birth; thus, personal morality can never be divorced from our responsibilities as members of that society.

Since customs, practices, habitual ways of doing things vary from culture to culture, it can be expected that there will be varying approaches to morality. That there should be varying approaches to morality even among Christian groups, and particularly Catholic groups, is a fact that sometimes gives rise to misunderstanding and even scandal. In the East, for example, "saving face" is a moral value little comprehended in the West. In many parts of Africa, the good of the tribe is the principal determining factor in moral situations, while in the West, many of our moral decisions are focused on the good of the individual. In the past, Christian missionaries (mainly from Europe) in foreign lands sometimes attempted to "Christianize" (which too often meant "Westernize") moral codes that they little understood, perceiving them only to be "pagan," or non-Christian. The results were often disastrous.

As we can see, the major issue in these varying approaches to morality is that people have different views of what is good or evil. It is time for us now to attempt to shed some light on what we mean by good and by evil. Is it possible for us to find meanings that can be applied trans-culturally, to all peoples?

Good and Evil

Every human person has an innate tendency to seek his or her fulfillment and perfection. The mere fact of being alive and being human means that one has purpose, one has goals, one seeks meaning in life. Also it means that one has needs and desires pursuant to keeping oneself alive and seeking one's own fulfillment. This fulfillment, or perfection, we call "the good." Hence, we can state another fundamental moral truth: *Anything contributing to the full actualization of human potential and the proper development of the human person is good, or moral.* Those who believe in God see and understand God as the final end and purpose of human life, the supreme good. For the believer, human development and human perfection are undertaken in accordance with God's will, the guiding principle of which is love. God is love. But more about this presently.

Just as anything that contributes to the proper growth and development of the human person is good, so anything that frustrates or acts against this proper growth and development is considered to be evil. What are some of the things that frustrate human life and development, and which everyone would therefore consider evil? Here is a partial list: death, suffering and pain, disability, deprivation of freedom, discrimination that deprives one of opportunity to improve oneself, deprivation of worth and self-esteem. We call these "pre-moral" evils (that is, evils in the objective sense before any moral slant has been added).

Human beings may be deprived of what they need for their growth and development as persons in different ways. One way that pre-moral evil may be caused is by natural disasters such as earthquakes, floods, epidemics, accidents and, in general, things which are outside of human control. We call such evils "physical evils." But, as we know quite well, most of the evil in the world does not occur in this way. Most of the evil in the world is brought on by the free, deliberate and unjustified actions of human beings. We call such evils "moral evils." *And so, moral evil occurs when we voluntarily and deliberately become involved in the spread of pre-moral evil.* A convenient division may be made as follows:

Physical Evil (pre-moral evil): evil brought on by forces normally outside human control, e.g., natural disasters, sickness, accident.

Moral Evil: evil brought on by the free, unjustified action of other humans.

While the above may be a helpful distinction, it is not always as clear-cut as it looks. Sometimes what may at first appear to be purely physical evils are in fact the result of culpable human carelessness or negligence – the motorist who does not check his car's brakes, the meteorologist who through negligence does not accurately predict a hurricane, the careless smoker who causes a fire. What all this reaffirms is that, for the most part, it is the free, unjustified action of human beings that frustrates the legitimate personal needs of other humans or, in other words, causes evil. Most evil is moral evil.[152]

At this point you may be wondering where all this talk about evil is leading. Your patience is about to be rewarded, for some important considerations follow from the above.

1. *Morality has to do with who and what we are as human beings and with our legitimate development as persons.* It applies to all human persons, whether or not they have made a religious commitment. One does not have to be a religious person, or express belief in God, to be bound by morality. "Society expects those who have no allegiance to any religion to be responsible for their conduct as are those who do. This would be a preposterous expectation unless it were possible to understand right and wrong, good and bad, apart from a religious commitment."[153] No society can function properly for the good of its members unless there is some form of agreed upon moral code that binds everyone. Right is right, and wrong is wrong, apart altogether from religion.

---

[152] The Catechism deals with the distinction between physical and moral evil in 309-311.
[153] Richard Gula, S.S., *Reason Informed by Faith* (New York: Paulist Press, 1989), p. 46.

2. *Authority does not create morality.* The church, the government, or anyone else in authority cannot arbitrarily declare something to be immoral. Whatever it is must be immoral (i.e., inflict unjustified pre-moral evil) *in and of itself* before it can (or should) be so declared. Therefore, when someone in authority declares something to be immoral, the declaration is nothing more than a reminder to us that we are in fact dealing with immorality. An example may help us to understand this. The major argument against abortion is not that the church forbids it. Rather, it is the other way around – the church forbids it because it is wrong, because it inflicts unjustified pre-moral evil. And so, I am against abortion, not primarily because I am a Catholic but primarily because I am a member of the human race.

   The same may be said about the authority of God. Nothing is immoral simply and only because God says so. To hold that would mean that God could arbitrarily create evil, which is a silly and impossible assertion. God has made us, and the world we live in, after his own creative plan or design. By that very fact God has already determined the things that could cause pre-moral or physical evil; we suffer if we come into conflict with the law God has established in creation – we don't break the law of gravity, it breaks us! Whether such pre-moral evil becomes moral evil is always dependent on human free will. And that is a circumstance over which, in truth, God has no control. The commandments of God, therefore, are not arbitrary prohibitions forbidding us to do this, that or the other. We should look upon the commandments as God's very good advice to us as to how we can best develop our personality and live at peace in society. Therefore, even for the non-religious person, following God's advice makes eminent good sense. Let us repeat the important principle: *things are not wrong because they are forbidden; rather, things are forbidden because they are wrong.*

3. *Immoral and illegal are not the same thing.* Sometimes authorities (whether civil or religious) make laws about things that are not in themselves pre-moral evils. Laws like these are made only to help regulate society for everyone's benefit. Things forbidden by such laws are illegal, but not necessarily immoral. Driving through a red light may be illegal, but unless there is a danger of pre-moral evil to the public, or to oneself, it is not immoral. It would be nice if authorities would make laws and regulations about things that have moral significance, but that hope is not always realized! We note, for example, and with sadness, that in most countries abortion is legal, but it is certainly immoral. Similarly, doing bodily harm to oneself may not be illegal, but it is almost certainly immoral.

By and large, contemporary North American society is very law-oriented. We use such expressions as "There ought to be a law!" when we feel strongly about some issue. We tend to want things well-regulated, legislated, everything wrapped in a neat package so that we will know where we are and how far we can go. This legalistic mentality has had the unfortunate (some would say pernicious) result of making people think that whatever is legislated in law is by that very fact moral. The law becomes the yardstick of morality. In other words, we feel morally justified in doing something as long as it is not forbidden by law – "There's no law against it!" Upright and moral persons cannot allow themselves to take this easy way of easing their consciences. Pre-moral evil – damage to persons, physical or psychological – is the yardstick of morality. If there happens to be a law against such evil then so much the better, but we must not allow only the law to sensitize us and do our thinking for us.

Morality and the Human Condition

It is probably true to say that evil is the number one problem for human beings. Pain, suffering and human deprivation, particularly of the innocent, strike us as being "unfair," not in keeping with our innate sense of what is right. Believers find it hard to reconcile evil with a good and loving God. Unbelievers find it a tremendous stumbling block to faith. Down through the centuries philosophers, thinkers and theologians have attempted many explanations of evil but none is perfectly satisfactory. All explanations leave us with unanswered questions. Evil is indeed a deep mystery (CCC 309).

We who believe in Jesus Christ should note that Jesus did not attempt to explain evil; he simply accepted it as part of the burden of being human, a normal part of the human condition. What he did do was to spend a good part of his life trying to alleviate the effects of evil, of human suffering in all its forms. He also gave us a way of coping with evil so that our personal sufferings can become meaningful and even helpful to our development as persons.

It is a basic fact of experience that all of us try to avoid evil. In one way or another we all seek the "good life"; we all seek happiness. It is also a basic fact of experience that in seeking the "good life" for ourselves we may bring evil on other people. We trample on others, both to attain our own selfish ends and to escape the evil that others bring on us. And, what is even more troubling is that we often try to rationalize our actions with such thoughts as "I need this," or "I'm only getting what is mine." Our selfishness makes us insensitive to the harm we do to others.

We are all caught up in the vicious cycle of the spread of evil. That surely is the basic insight of the story of Adam and Eve in the Bible, as it is the insight of the story of the Tower of Babel (Gen 11:1-9). God's creation is good in itself; it is we human beings who have sullied and spoilt it. Since we all have to live together and to share this world, it seems obvious that we should avoid bringing evil on others if only to save ourselves from having evil done to us – the Golden Rule again. A society that does not have a moral code of care and concern for everyone cannot endure for long. One cannot help but remark that the disintegration of the moral code of Western societies is cause for grave concern.

Reasons for Being Moral

To be a moral person will require that we sometimes have to make sacrifices of our own needs and desires, and give up what we most want to do for the good of others. What will motivate us to do this?

In the first place, perhaps we might act morally just to avoid punishment. If avoiding punishment is our only motivation, then, if there is no chance of being caught, we just go ahead and act as we please. Clearly, this is a selfish and unsatisfactory answer. Such a way of acting does nothing for one's own self-esteem and one's own fulfillment as a human person.

Second, we might be persuaded to be moral simply out of enlightened self-interest. The argument would go like this: if we inflict evil on others, then individuals, or the society in which we live, might do the same to us. So in order to avoid evil we act morally. Again, this is a rather selfish and unsatisfactory motive.

Third, we might act morally because of the inner conviction that human persons are unique, precious and worthwhile, that there is great intrinsic value in the human person, and that human persons are worthy of our love. There is no way that we can absolutely prove this intrinsic value of the human person. We just know it and feel it deep inside us, a gut instinct, if you will, an innate sense of what is right. And, as the philosopher William James has said, "The nobler thing tastes better to us, and that's all that can be said about it." It "tastes" better: we feel better about it, and we are more at peace with ourselves.

Application to Teaching

This basic insight into the intrinsic nobility and value of the human person has deep and important ramifications for parents, teachers and anyone concerned with teaching morality, particularly to youngsters. Generally speaking, we can get children (and older people too) to do what is right by training: by sanctions, by rewarding good acts and punishing evil ones. Psychologists might call it a process of conditioning. Such a process of conditioning may well be necessary at certain stages of moral development. However, the challenge of good parenting and good teaching is to get people to do what is right because of the inherent value and nobility of the human person. This inherent nobility and value demand that human persons should not suffer unjust pre-moral evil. Teachers and parents can tell young people about this inherent nobility, and the telling is manifestly necessary, but the key to good teaching is to bring students to experience that preciousness and value for themselves. The real challenge for parents and teachers is to create the environment in which young people can experience for themselves this most important moral truth so that not only will they do right but they will want to do what is right.

One very effective way in which we can reshape our desires so that we want to do what is right is to select the proper role models, people who find (or found) meaning and fulfillment in activities we know are right and good. If one spends most of one's time with a crowd who think that videogame arcades are the place to be, then after a while one gets "sucked in." The role model is wrong. If, on the other hand, one spends one's time with people who find work for social justice and for the poor and disabled fulfilling, very probably one shall come to feel that way, too.

Finally, a word on heroism. A call to the heroic, a call to do something special, something significant, something out of the ordinary, can be terribly important in building human character. North America, and most of Western society, is struggling with a culture that is badly entrapped by rampant self-interest, individualism, narcissism. The evidence of this is ample and compelling. As a result, ours is a culture that discredits heroism because heroism generally means some form of personal sacrifice. Ernest Becker writes as follows:

> The crisis of modern society is precisely that youth no longer feel heroic in the plan of action that their culture has set up. We are living a crisis of heroism that reaches into every aspect of our social life. . . . of course, [this is] the crisis of organized religion too: religion is no longer valid as a hero system, and so the youth scorn it. If traditional culture is discredited as heroics, then the church that supports that culture automatically discredits itself.[154]

One reason why the fundamentalist cults are making such progress may well be that they demand a certain heroism from their adherents. The adherents feel "special," different from others, affirmed by the group. If the church is to be effective in attracting youth (and, we may add, grown-ups too), it must insist in whatever way it can on some form of heroic action, such as has often been demonstrated in Christian history. Precisely the same advice can be given to parents and teachers engaged in helping young people to adopt a proper moral stance. They should find what they are looking for in the demands that Catholicism makes on its adherents. They should find it also in the example of the many holy and heroic people who have responded wholeheartedly to these demands.

---

[154] Ernest Becker, *The Denial of Death* (New York: Free Press, 1973), pp. 6-7.

Are There Objective Standards of Morality?

We noted earlier in this chapter that different cultures often have different approaches to morality. This fact, and other considerations also, have led some to hold that there are no objective standards in morality; everything is relative and situational. In other words, our moral stance will vary with the situation in which we find ourselves. We call this "moral relativism."

We may distinguish two types of moral relativists: the social relativists and the personal relativists. The former hold that whatever a particular society accepts and approves is the only standard of morality. For example, if a particular society accepts and approves of child sacrifice or of slavery, as did some early cultures, then child sacrifice and slavery are moral. Also, what we might call customs, or conventions, assume strict moral force. "When in Rome, do as the Romans do" might become a moral dictum instead of just good advice about getting along in a foreign country.

For the personal relativists the principal criterion of morality is their own personal satisfaction. Their slogans are well known in today's moral climate: "Whatever suits me is right," "My way is as good as your way," "Don't force your morality on me," "Do your own thing." Then there are those relativists whose principal moral criterion is "whatever makes me feel good." If I feel good about it, then it is right.

Some form of relativism will always exist in human society because relativism is a product of the basic selfishness that infects us all. One of the factors that contributes to the persistence of relativism in society is our inability to distinguish clearly between morality and custom or convention. Here is how one psychologist puts it: "For example, we are sure that infanticide is immoral but what about polygamy (one husband with two or more wives) . . .? Maybe in our culture where marrying for love is the accepted norm, we simply cannot understand cultures where marriage plays another role." While it may sometimes be difficult to distinguish between the moral and the merely conventional, we cannot "generalize from the ambiguity of a few cases, a very few, to the ambiguity of all cases," which is what the relativists do.[155]

Most nation members of the United Nations are signatories to the Declaration on Human Rights. It is painfully evident that not all of them live up to the obligation they have undertaken in signing the declaration. Nevertheless, their having signed is testimony of the recognition and acceptance in diverse cultures that there are human values that apply to all. These human values are the basis of an objective morality. Without such an agreed-upon basis for morality we cannot

---

[155] Joanmarie Smith, *Morality Made Simple (But Not Easy)* (Allen, TX: Argus Communications, 1982), pp. 31-32.

have any international discussion of what is good for the human person, what contributes to development of peoples and what evils are to be avoided – in other words, what is morally right. We conclude, therefore, the following:

Ethical values are objective, not relative or purely subjective. Everyone who considers himself or herself human is bound by morality.

Covenant Morality – The Ten Commandments

Covenant Morality

As we have already seen in an earlier chapter, a covenant is an agreement between two or more parties. It is like a contract, as we understand that term today. It establishes certain rights, with the corresponding responsibilities, among the participants. But a covenant goes further than a mere legal contract. It establishes a deeper personal relationship that cannot easily be spelled out in purely legal terms. It establishes a relationship of friendship, or love, or even a quasi-familial relationship of brotherhood or sisterhood. In the covenant that God made with the Jewish people through Moses (Ex 19–24, Deut 1–30) he offers to the Israelite people a special relationship in words that ring with familial concern, care and tenderness: "I shall be your God and you shall be my people." God promises them that if they are faithful to their side of the bargain they will become his "treasured possession out of all the peoples," "a holy nation" (Ex 19:5-6).

As well as the Decalogue (from the Greek meaning, literally, "ten words"), God gave the Israelites many other prescriptions and regulations concerning even minute details of their daily life. These also they are required to observe as part of the agreement with God. True Israelites understand these regulations as the will of God, as what God wants of them. These laws constitute the basis of Israelite morality. Israelite morality, then, is religious; it arises from their faith, from their sensitivity to the presence of God in their lives. As one writer puts it, "True Israelite religion does not consist only in acts of worship. It involves the whole of life."[156] Israelites live and behave in a certain way because that is what God wants. They entered into an agreement with God to obey his command-ments – "All the words that the Lord has spoken we will do" (Ex 24:3) – and they sealed this agreement with a religious ceremony (Ex 24:1-18) (CCC 2060).

Covenant morality, then, is a morality of faith. People who have entered into a covenant with God act morally because they believe that is what God wants of them. They believe that the morality of their actions, the way they deal with one another, affects their relationship with God. They now have an added reason for

---

[156] John Gallagher, C.S.B., *The Basis for Christian Ethics* (New York: Paulist Press, 1985), p. 71.

being moral, namely, their faith and their love of God. We Christian believers have accepted the new covenant brought us in Jesus Christ. This new covenant is firmly based on the covenant entered into by God and the Israelite people. Jesus made it abundantly clear that he wanted to fulfill not abrogate the original covenant (Mt 5:17).

The other laws and regulations notwithstanding, the centrepiece of the covenant entered into on Mount Sinai is the Decalogue which Moses had chiselled on tablets of stone. It is to this Decalogue that Jesus most frequently refers in his teaching. He was once asked, "Teacher, what good deed must I do to have eternal life?" Jesus replied, "Keep the commandments." "Which ones?" persisted the questioner. In reply, Jesus gives a quick summary of the Decalogue. "You shall not murder; You shall not commit adultery; You shall not steal; You shall not bear false witness; Honour your father and your mother" (Mt 19:16-19). He then adds one that is not in the Decalogue given on Mount Sinai but is found in the book of Leviticus, "You shall love your neighbour as yourself" (Lev 19:18). This latter commandment Jesus uses to sum up the whole meaning of human relations, how people should behave towards one another. Together with the commandment to love God, he says, these two commandments sum up all the teaching of the law and the prophets (Mt 22:32-40).

The Ten Commandments

Vatican Council II has urged that moral theology should be "drawing more fully on the teaching of holy scripture."[157] One of the ways we can fulfill this urging of the Council is to focus on the commandments, a focus which is certainly in keeping with traditional Christian catechesis (CCC 2064-2065). To be an effective instrument of moral teaching, however, the commandments must be viewed in the light of Jesus' insistence that love is the true basis for morality. If we love God we shall keep his commandments.

We are perhaps most familiar with the commandments in the way they are stated in the Bible: in *negative* form ("Thou shalt not . . ."). This is a Semitic legal device coming out of the period in which the Bible was written. There are advantages to stating the commandments in this negative form. 1) It makes the commandments easy to remember. That is an important consideration when we realize that all teaching in those days was oral; there were no books. 2) Clear prohibitions ("don't do it") generally bring people up short; they have a psychological impact, and stick in our minds. Both these considerations are probably still true today. Nevertheless, even granted these advantages, too many of us see the commandments only as negative strictures. We tend to perceive them as limiting our freedom, as forcing us not to do things we might want to do. The

---

157   *Vatican Council II, Decree on the Training of Priests (Optatam totius)*, No. 16.

result is that we miss the aspect of invitation; we do not see the commandments as loving proposals from a loving God. We do not see them as God's gift to us for our own good (CCC 2059). It is far more helpful to present the commandments as positive statements (invitations, guides) rather than as negative commands. This, we hope, will be particularly helpful for those who are teaching the commandments today. At the same time, it is also important for us to preserve the more familiar negative biblical form. Thus, the two forms, the biblical form as well as its more positive aspect, will be presented in our enumeration of the commandments. We shall also indicate some ways we might reflect on each commandment and questions we might ask ourselves so that we can better apply God's invitation to our life.

The second thing we should note about the commandments is that the ones that refer to our neighbour (numbers 4-10) simply represent basic human morality (CCC 2070). It is morality that applies to everyone, religious believers and non-believers alike. These commandments not only recognize but emphasize the intrinsic value, the preciousness of the human person. They indicate the way human persons should live in order to get along with one another in society and make a success of their life. Once again, therefore, it should be clear that God proposes the commandments to us *as his loving advice for our own good*. They are proposed to us for the peaceful ordering and harmony of human society and thus for our own better development as human persons. "Since they express man's fundamental duties towards God and towards his neighbour, the Ten Commandments reveal, in their primordial content, *grave* obligations. They are fundamentally immutable, and they oblige always and everywhere. No one can dispense from them. The Ten Commandments are engraved by God in the human heart" (CCC 2072).

Jesus said that the twin commandments of loving God and loving one another sum up and contain the whole law and the teaching of the prophets (Mt 22:37-40). The first three commandments of the Decalogue may be brought together under the one heading of "love God."

First Commandment

Negative Form: *"You shall have no other gods before me. You shall not make for yourself an idol, whether in the form of anything that is in heaven above, or that is on the earth beneath, or that is in the water under the earth. You shall not bow down to them or worship them" (Ex 20:3-5).*

Positive Form: Recognize, accept and worship only the One, True God.[158]

---

[158] For further development the reader is referred to the extensive treatment in the Catechism, 2084-2141.

Explanation: This commandment is more than an affirmation that there is but one God. It asserts that this one God is unique, transcendent. Though revealed in and through human history, this God is in fact the Lord of history, the Lord of life. The commandment requires us to recognize that this one God has offered us a special and unique relationship, a continuing presence in every aspect of life. Not only must we accept and recognize this but we must "pay attention" to God and do nothing to sully the relationship.

Reflection

Where is God in our hierarchy of values? Does God come a poor second to popularity with others? to friends? to money? to career? to self? to power and influence? to sex? to winning at sports?

The need to worship God is clear. Do we pray in private, and with others, particularly with the Christian community at the Eucharist? Does our prayer rise out of our profound sense of God's love for us?

Do we accept and recognize that God is present in the most intimate way in every aspect, in every circumstance of life? How often do we turn to that loving God who is the very core of our being?

Are there any false gods that we worship, that have power over us, to whom we have sold our souls? A line from the Paul Simon song "Sounds of Silence" should give us pause: "And the people bowed and prayed to the neon god they'd made." Has TV become our god so that we spend hours "worshipping" before it?

Are our lives ruled by superstition? Do we attribute magical or divine power to ordinary created things (hats on the bed, spilling salt, the number 13, fortune tellers, horoscopes, palm readers)?

Second Commandment

Negative Form: *"You shall not make wrongful use of the name of the Lord your God" (Ex 20:7).*

Positive Form: Respect and reverence God.[159]

Explanation: To understand this commandment we must fully appreciate the meaning of "name" in the Hebrew culture. For the Semitic peoples the name was the person. To give someone a name was to say something about the person. Thus, for example, "Jesus" means "God saves"; the name tells us what the person is about. Therefore the bottom line in the second commandment is that we must reverence God himself, the Transcendent, the Holy One, not subject to anyone, least of all those he has created out of nothing. To show disrespect or insult God's name is to insult and show disrespect to the person of God. When

---

[159]   See Catechism, 2142-2167.

we use the name of God we should do it with honour and respect and with great consciousness of what God means to us.

Reflection

Do we dishonour God by using his name flippantly? "But I really didn't mean anything bad," we say. "It's just a way of speaking, maybe a bad habit." Would that be a good thing to say after we had insulted a police officer for giving us a ticket?

Do we dishonour God's name by perjury (lying although we have called on God to witness that we are telling the truth) or by cursing (calling on God to harm someone) or by swearing (taking an oath without just cause)? Jesus taught that we should always tell the truth and therefore there would be no need to swear – "Do not swear at all," he said (Mt 5:34).

Third Commandment

Negative Form: *None*

Positive Form: "Remember the sabbath day, and keep it holy" (Ex 20:8).[160]

Explanation: The Jewish Sabbath probably originated in response to the social need for a day of rest from work and for family reasons. Israel, being such a religious nation, "came to ascribe a religious value to each of its ethical precepts. . . . Eventually this day of rest . . . saw the religious motivation so predominant that the day of rest became a day of cult."[161] The Jewish Sabbath has become the Christian Sunday because the resurrection and the day of Pentecost both occurred on the first day of the week, a change dating back to the earliest days of Christianity. The holiness of Sunday revolves around the positive worship of God, but as a family day it should also be seen as helping to preserve an important social value. It is entirely fitting that we should set aside some sacred time for worship both as private persons and as a community, which has received everything from God (First Commandment). The Christian Eucharist is the centre of our community worship, which is why Sunday Eucharist is not an option but a duty and a responsibility. The commandment should not be seen exclusively in terms of Sunday worship. We need to let God speak to us, and therefore we need to slow down from time to time and listen to God.

Reflection

Do we perceive Sunday as a valuable family day and day of worship?

---

[160] See Catechism, 2168-2195.

[161] Raymond F. Collins, *Christian Morality: Biblical Foundations* (Notre Dame, IN: University of Notre Dame Press, 1986), p. 55.

Do we easily find excuses for not worshipping with the community? "So, could you not stay awake with me one hour?" Jesus complained to his sleepy disciples (Mt 26:40). Does he make the same complaint to us?

What are we looking for in Sunday worship – entertainment? Or do we really want to make a gift of ourselves to God?

Do we perceive Sunday worship as an essential aspect of being "church"?

Do we take time to create a Sunday for God in our heart?

Commandments 4 to 10 have to do with how we should relate to one another in a well-ordered society. They are God's commandments to us for how we should love one another.

Fourth Commandment

Negative form: *None*

Positive Form: "Honour your father and your mother" (Ex. 20:12).[162]

Explanation: The focus of this commandment is that we are born into a society of persons. We cannot develop as full human persons outside of human society, both the smaller society of our own family and the larger society of the country or nation to which our family belongs. It is in our own best interest to do everything in our power to maintain the family as a strong and stable unit that, in its turn, will contribute to a strong, stable and moral nation.

We tend to think of this precept as one which tells children to obey their parents. That is a mistake. When God gave the Decalogue it was given to the whole people, adults and children alike. Also, families in those days were more like clans, or what we would call today extended families. Honour was due not only in a specific way to parents but to the "elders" of the clan in general. The concept can be easily extended to include respect and honour for anyone who holds legitimate authority in the community. We should also reflect on the fact that the commandment does not say "obey your father and mother" but "honour your father and mother," a far wider and all-embracing concept that would include all forms of respect.

The honour due to parents, as required by the fourth commandment, extends to the support we owe to them in their old age. This component of the precept is clearly echoed in the book of Proverbs (Prov 19:20), and Jesus re-emphasizes it in the gospel (Mk 7:9-13; Mt 15:3-9), so there can be little room for misunderstanding.

---

[162]   See Catechism, 2197-2257.

We have already emphasized the intrinsic value and preciousness of the human person. This important truth is part of the fourth commandment. It is extremely well put by Raymond Collins:

> The fourth commandment . . . indicates that human value lies in something other than human function. The temptation was strong in ancient Israel as in other primitive societies to banish or destroy those humans who were not functional, the aged, the weak, the sick, the orphans, etc. With the fourth commandment Israel radically banished the concept of function-based worth. Might one not say that *the fourth commandment is based on a view which sees man's worth in his innate and God-related dignity rather than in his societal or functional value?*[163]

Reflection

Pope John Paul II says: "There is no law that lays it down that you must smile! But you can make a gift of your smile; you can be a leaven of kindness in your family." What have we done lately to preserve family unity and happiness? How often have we told our parents that we appreciate them? (Refer to the story of Tommy in Chapter 2.)

Pope John Paul II also says: "Every effort to make society sensitive to the importance of the family is a great service to humanity." Have we made any efforts in this regard with our politicians?

Does the difference between honouring our parents and merely obeying them mean much to us?

"Human value lies in something other than human function." Do we merely pay lip service to this dictum? How far do we really see God as the basis of human dignity and act accordingly?

St. Paul wrote: "Let every person be subject to the governing authorities; for there is no authority except from God" (Rom 13:1). We have been nurtured by a civil community and culture; do we feel any sense of loyalty and thankfulness? Are we, in fact, willingly "subject to the governing authorities"?

Have our aged parents just become an intolerable burden? What is intolerable?

Fifth Commandment

Negative Form: *"You shall not murder" (Ex. 20:13).*

Positive Form: Respect life, and the bodily integrity of every person, including your own.[164]

---

[163] *Christian Morality: Biblical Foundations*, p. 57; emphasis added.
[164] See Catechism, 2258-2330.

Explanation: We are made in the image and likeness of God and loved by God. Our bodies participate in our intrinsic dignity as persons. Our bodies must not be defiled or mutilated, nor must life be unjustly terminated. Our bodies must not be subjected to moral evil. "You shall not murder" is the translation provided in the New Revised Standard Version (NRSV) of the Bible. It is better than the more familiar "You shall not kill." With the NRSV translation we don't need to explain that the precept does not forbid killing as an act of war or as self-defence. Everyone has a right to life and to bodily integrity, but society also has a right to protect itself and the general good of its citizens, whether this general good comes under attack from individuals or from other societies.

Often enough we hear people say, "It's my body; I can do what I like with it." They think that this kind of reason justifies them performing some form of self-mutilation, or in ruining their health. Think hard about what this means when it comes to the decision to use drugs or alcohol, or to smoke (now more than ever proven to be seriously dangerous to health), or to engage in extremely dangerous sport (e.g., professional boxing). The fifth commandment clearly indicates that God, and God alone, is the Lord of life. We are but the stewards of God's creation; we are its proprietors, not its owners, and that includes our own life. Our life is our own, yes, but we don't own it.

There is something else we should think about. The bishops at Vatican Council II have shown us how this precept should be given wide application. Regarding the desperate poverty and want of so much of the world's population, the Council had this to say:

> Faced with a world today where so many people are suffering from want, the council asks individuals and governments to remember the saying of the Fathers: 'Feed the people dying of hunger, because if you do not feed them you are killing them,' and it urges them according to their ability to share and dispose of their goods to help others.[165]

A stark reminder indeed of our responsibility for human life.

Reflection

Have we ever reflected on the morality of war, or do we leave this to the politicians? Do we feel any responsibility in this regard?

Can we sincerely call ourselves peacemakers?

Have we ever seriously considered suicide?

Where do we stand on abortion? euthanasia? capital punishment?

---

[165] *Pastoral Constitution on the Church in the Modern World*, No. 69.

Does the damage we inflict on our own bodies by abuse of alcohol or drugs (medical and/or recreational) or by smoking strike us as a moral matter?

Vatican Council II stated, "There is growing awareness of the sublime dignity of the human person . . . [who] ought to have ready access to all that is necessary for living a genuinely human life . . . food, clothing, housing . . . rightful freedom even in matters of religion." How have we sought to meet the needs of the poor?

Do I share God's concern for the oppressed and unprotected peoples of the world?

Sixth Commandment

Negative Form: *"You shall not commit adultery" (Ex. 20:14).*

Positive Form: Respect the integrity of married life.[166]

Explanation: Ancient Israel considered adultery to be a sin against someone else's marriage rather than one's own. For example, a Hebrew male was not considered to have offended against his own marriage by sexual liaison with a prostitute. For the ancient Israelites, therefore, personal sexual misconduct was not the major issue in adultery. Rather, adultery was the shattering of someone else's marriage relationship. The sin of adultery was a sin against justice. It was an offence against human society, the stability of which depends on stable marriages and families.

In the past, Christian moral theology tended to refer all kinds of sexual sin to the sixth and ninth commandments. However convenient this may be, it certainly stretches the biblical text beyond allowable scriptural limits. For the Christian, immoral sexual conduct is more adequately dealt with in other parts of Scripture, particularly the New Testament. However, it does us no harm to be reminded that the foundation of the marriage relationship is love, and love expressed in a sexual way. Roman Catholic teaching has always held that sex is a gift of God reserved exclusively for celebrating married love. Furthermore, the celebration of married love must always respect both the unitive (loving mutual self-gift of the spouses) and procreative (conceiving of children) functions of sex. The Playboy philosophy (to view sex as some form of recreation) still infects much of Western society. It is virtually taken for granted by the arts and entertainment industry, which seems to portray it as a perfectly ordinary and integral part of our culture. With this philosophy, adultery becomes a form of sport, or at least nothing more sinister than personal pleasure. It is a philosophy that goes hand in hand with today's divorce-infected social climate, a climate in which there is little respect for the permanence of the marriage commitment. It is

---

[166] See Catechism, 2331-2400.

a deeply immoral philosophy because it deals in evil and injustice, and it damages relational growth of persons and the stability of human society.

Reflection

St. Paul (Eph 5:25-33) compares love in marriage to the love of Christ for the church (for us, the People of God). Have we ever meditated on this beautiful passage?

Writers of fiction have often portrayed adultery as fulfilling some deep need for personal expression and growth. For example, "It was less than a tenth part of me, but I had to have it." Or, "In that moment the past and the present came thundering together and he was master of it all." How do we feel about this kind of thinking? Where is God in the marriage relationship?

Preserving one's sexual expression for one's marriage partner requires self-discipline. Can we see such self-discipline as good for our development as persons? Or do we, like Oscar Wilde, say, "I can resist anything except temptation"?

Most agree that sex must be responsible. Is this purely a social statement, or does it have deep religious connotations as well?

Seventh Commandment

Negative Form: *"You shall not steal" (Ex. 20:15).*

Positive Form: Respect the personal freedom of others.[167]

Explanation: This commandment is reiterated in the Book of Deuteronomy (5:19). Because of the peculiar grammatical construction in Hebrew, many Scripture scholars are of the opinion that this commandment does not refer so much to stealing property as it does to kidnapping people. The question of property is more clearly dealt with by the ninth commandment. In early biblical times, kidnapping was a crime as real as it is for us today. Note, for example, the kidnapping of Joseph (Gen 37), as well as the stricture in Ex 21:16, "Whoever kidnaps a person, whether that person has been sold or is still held in possession, shall be put to death." Human freedom is the value that is protected by the commandment.

Reflection

The moral evil of unjustly depriving someone of freedom is clear enough. We should reflect, however, that we don't have to put people in prison to deprive them of their freedom. A domineering personality can deprive others of their freedom of expression; unjust laws can make people prisoners of their conscience; dire poverty can deprive people of their freedom to develop as human

---

[167] See Catechism, 2401-2463.

persons; lack of education, or blatant discrimination, can deprive people of their freedom of opportunity. Kidnapping? There are many ways we can "kidnap" others, deprive them of their freedom, and therefore be guilty of moral evil.

How do we measure up in light of the above?

Eighth Commandment

Negative Form: *"You shall not bear false witness against your neighbour" (Ex 20:16).*

Positive form: Respect the truth.[168]

Explanation: Under Israelite law a guilty sentence could be passed upon the testimony of only two witnesses; there was no possibility of appeal. Now, to us that is rather harsh jurisprudence, but we can easily see why the giving of false evidence under such circumstances is indeed grave, and therefore why this commandment is necessary to protect the innocent.

While it is true that the commandment is immediately concerned with lying in a legal case, the basic immorality is the subversion of the truth, which brings real evil on someone. Hence, it is perfectly acceptable to extend the prohibition to all lying that perpetrates evil and hurts people.

In our day truth is in deep crisis. It is not an exaggeration to say that the eighth may well be the most sinned-against commandment of all. The scandalous disregard for truth in diplomatic relations and in politics is an odious disgrace. The "slanting" of news by the news media (particularly television) is so blatant that now people are openly discussing whether the role of the news media is to give us entertainment rather than news. At the personal level, the operative question too often seems to be "Can I get away with it?" One wonders whatever happened to the old adage "Honesty is the best policy."

Truth is the basis of all human communication because it is the basis of trust. Human society – all relations between individuals and nations – is founded on mutual trust. If we cannot normally expect people to tell the truth, if we constantly suspect that they may be lying, then we cannot trust them, and cannot really communicate with them. Since, in order to develop as human persons, communication with others is essential, and communication is so badly undermined by lying, it should be easy to see how totally destructive habitual lying is.

The human virtue that most marked the life of Jesus was that of personal integrity, candidness, honesty. The sin that angered him the most was lying hypocrisy, an iniquity that moved him to vigorous indignation and even invective (see Mt 23). He suffered, and ultimately paid the supreme price, for his

---

[168]   See Catechism, 2464-2513.

honesty and integrity, his refusal to turn from his appointed mission. There is a deep lesson here for us.

Reflection

Many research studies have pointed to the pervasiveness of cheating in schools and universities. Have you ever reflected on why cheating is immoral?

"Truth is not only violated by falsehood; it may be equally outraged by silence" (Henri Frederic Amiel). Have we ever thought about this? Is it true of us?

"Indeed it is not in human nature to deceive others for any long time, without in a measure deceiving ourselves too" (John Henry Newman). Have we reflected on the self-destructiveness of lying, which exposes our deep-seated selfishness?

Detraction means to ruin a person's good name by telling the truth, for example, revealing a person's private sins through gossip. Is gossip a big factor in our lives?[169]

Ninth Commandment

Negative Form: *"You shall not covet your neighbour's wife" (Ex 20:17).*

Positive Form: Respect the integrity of marriage even in intention and desire.[170]

Explanation: To covet means to desire eagerly, to long for, to yearn for. It might seem easy enough to connect this commandment with Jesus' statement "But I say to you that everyone who looks at a woman with lust has already committed adultery with her in his heart" (Mt 5:28). And again, "For out of the heart come evil intentions, murder, adultery, fornication, theft, false witness, slander. These are what defile a person . . ." (Mt 15:19-20). Both the commandment and Jesus' statements remind us that sin is ultimately in the intention. We must remember,

---

[169] Reflect on the following:
   I maim without killing. I break hearts and ruin lives.
   The more I am quoted the more I am believed. . . .
   My victims are helpless. . . .
   To try to track me down is impossible.
   The harder you try, the more elusive I become. . . .
   I topple governments and wreck marriages. . . .
   I make innocent people cry in their pillows. . . .
   I am called Gossip.
   Office gossip. Shop gossip. Party gossip. . . .
   Before you repeat a story, ask yourself:
   Is it true? Is it fair? Is it necessary?
   If not - SHUT UP.
   (Anonymous)
   Quoted by Mark Link, S.J., *Path Through Catholicism*, p. 197.
[170] See Catechism, 2514-2533.

however, that according to Hebrew understanding, mere mental things such as thoughts, desires and intentions were not of great consequence. The Hebrew mind did not separate the spiritual from the material; it had no grasp of "soul." That kind of dualistic thinking, which we Westerners take for granted, is the result of the influence of Greek philosophy. The Hebrew mind dealt in concrete realities. Reality meant that, to be significant, desires and thoughts had to be externalized, concretized in physical action. The Hebrew mind would never separate the thought from the acting person. To covet one's neighbour's wife, therefore, already includes in some way the physical act of adultery.

Reflection

Jealousy is an insidious form of desire. Are we jealous over someone else's marriage?

What positive steps have we taken to guard against the possibility of covetousness?

Do I regard my spouse as my "possession"?

Tenth Commandment

Negative form: *"You shall not covet your neighbour's house . . . or anything that belongs to your neighbour" (Ex 20:17).*

Positive form: Respect the right of your neighbour to own property.[171]

Explanation: We noted above that the seventh commandment seems more aimed at curbing the evil of kidnapping than at forestalling theft of goods. The theft of goods is dealt with by the tenth commandment. Here again we have to take account of the Hebrew mind-set, which is focused mainly on the concrete. We can hardly improve on what Raymond F. Collins has to say:

> The language of the Hebrew text [of the commandment] encompasses within the scope of the precept not only the theft itself but all the intrigue which preceded the act of theft and which is part of the act in its fullest human reality. Thus the precept is concerned with the world of thought, but only in so far as this world of thought becomes externalized in the world of act.[172]

Covetousness is concerned with and ultimately leads to unjust acquisition of that which is coveted.

The commandment indicates that the Bible recognizes that people have a right to private property and that right must be respected by others. Some private property is necessary for the full and proper development of the human person.

---

[171] See Catechism, 2534-2557.
[172] *Christian Morality: Biblical Foundations*, pp. 61-62.

Even in societies that have freely renounced the right to private property, such as religious orders, it is recognized that some things have to be regarded as "personal," as reserved for the individual's personal use. Former Communist societies, which abrogated the right to private property without the free consent of the citizens, have begun to realize the disastrous results for human development that inevitably follow. It is a denial of a deep and basic human instinct. On the other hand, the right certainly can be abused. The greedy acquisition and accumulation of property and money by the rich, usually at the expense of the poor, is an iniquity as scandalous as stealing a poor person's livelihood.

Reflection

Are we content with what God has given us in the way of human talent, or do we wish we were someone else?

Do we often feel that someone else "got all the breaks"?

Is the accumulation of wealth and prestige the engine that drives and motivates us?

What is our personal understanding and measurement of "success"? Acquisition of material goods? power? influence? Or is it our improvement as loving, caring human persons?

Conclusion

It is worth repeating that the commandments are concerned with basic human morality, basic human values. These values have to do with human life and freedom, marriage and family, justice and property, truth. In other words, *the commandments deal with values that are necessary if we are to live successful human lives.* These values spring from who we are as human beings; they must therefore be observed as basic morality by everyone, believers and non-believers alike. It should not take us long to realize the importance of these values if we simply reflect on what the world would be like if everyone lived according to the Ten Commandments. Does that sound like heaven on earth? Well, it is. It is these values that are at the heart of the Declaration of Human Rights. The Bible, however, makes it clear that these are God's values; they are built into who we are as humans by God's creating hand; they form the foundation of our relationship with God. God not only created us but is intimately concerned with our human life and the way we live together as a human society, wanting always the best for us. Our God is a loving God who is revealed in the very heart of human history.

Note: The Numbering of the Commandments

We have followed the traditional Roman Catholic way of numbering the commandments. Another way, more favoured by other Christian groups, is to make two commandments of the Roman Catholic first commandment: 1) "You shall have no other gods before me;" and 2) "You shall not make to yourself an idol." Numbers nine and ten are then telescoped into one commandment against coveting. In either case the number ten is preserved.

Reflection Questions

1. Distinguish between illegal and immoral. Give some examples of things that are illegal but not immoral and things that are immoral but not illegal. Why do you think that many people regard the civil law as the norm of morality?

2. "I don't believe in the Catholic church because it is always telling me that things that everyone else is doing are wrong, such as pre-marital sex, divorce and abortion. The church is interfering with my liberty." Deal with this objection.

3. How would you go about explaining the basic principle of morality to students?

4. "All morality is relative; it depends on the situation you find yourself in and what is best for you in that situation." How would you answer such an objection?

5. Explain how the Ten Commandments represent a development and practical application of the basic commandment "Love God, and love one another."

6. What do you think is the most sinned-against commandment in Western culture? Why?

Further Reading

Collins, Raymond F. *Christian Morality: Biblical Foundations* (Notre Dame, IN: University of Notre Dame Press, 1986). A standard work on the subject that is highly respected for its scholarship and readability.

Gula, Richard M. *Reason Informed by Faith* (New York: Paulist Press, 1989). One reviewer calls it "the best one-volume presentation of fundamental moral theology now available." Requires careful reading but will reward study. An excellent reference book.

18

SIN AND CONSCIENCE

Section 1 – Sin

What Is Sin?

The story is told about a certain king who once visited a prison in his domain. One by one he asked the prisoners what crimes they had committed. They all claimed that they had been wrongly accused and were victims of a miscarriage of justice. All except one, that is, who owned up to what he had done and declared that he deserved his prison sentence. The king ordered his immediate release, "For," he said, "this man has no business here among all these innocent people."

Refusal to accept responsibility for one's misdeeds is but one of the factors that has contributed to the present-day demise of the notion of sin. It does not take a genius to see that the notion of sin has fallen on hard times. People even avoid using the word; euphemisms are the order of the day. For example, stealing is now referred to as "lifting something"; people don't lie, they simply "misrepresent the facts"; no one kills an unwanted baby, they just "terminate a pregnancy." Many people complain that even the clergy have reneged on their moral leadership; they no longer preach powerfully and clearly about sin (the "fire and brimstone" sermon). As the parishioner said to the priest who was being transferred to a different parish, "I'm sorry you're leaving, Father. We never knew what sin was until you came!"

The decline in the appreciation and understanding of sin is certainly linked to the steady decline in moral responsibility in our present-day culture. The great tendency today is to blame one's transgressions on a variety of factors, rather than to accept personal responsibility. The decline in moral responsibility and the factors to which it is attributed have been extensively treated in theological and psychological literature; we shall not go into the details here.[173] Let us just say that if we have lost a sense of sin then we have lost a sense of the presence of God in our life; we no longer feel that God is an essential element in our life.

---

[173] For a good summary of the reasons for this decline see Sean Fagan, *Has Sin Changed?* (Wilmington, DE: Michael Glazier, 1977), pp. 2-6. See also Dr. Karl Menninger, *Whatever Became of Sin?* (New York: Hawthorn Books, Inc., 1973); M. Scott Peck, *People of the Lie* (New York: Simon & Schuster, 1983).

More than that, we have also lost a sense of God's goodness and compassion, of how much God loves us. We have simply become lethargic about evil.

The question we must now ask is, how is moral responsibility linked to sin? In the last chapter, we saw that the responsibility to be moral is a human responsibility that falls on everyone. Not only must we promote human good but we must avoid bringing real evil on ourselves and on others. But for us believers who have accepted the covenant with God initiated by Jesus Christ, there is an added dimension to our moral responsibility. We believe that the way we behave towards others affects our relationship with God. "Love God" and "Love your neighbour as yourself" are the two great commandments. They go together; we cannot have one without the other. We love God by loving one another. The core of Jesus' message to us is that we must be thoroughly human, thoroughly moral. We must respect, love and work for the nobility, the preciousness, of every human being; when we do, we are in fact loving God and cementing our relationship with him.

Sin must be seen from the point of view of our covenant relationship with God in Jesus Christ. Since the covenant relationship is a relationship of love, sin is lovelessness. Sin may be defined as *the damaging or total rupturing of our love relationship with God in Jesus.* We are made in the image and likeness of God and sin robs us of this relationship, of this likeness (CCC 705).

It should be evident that the word "sin" is, in fact, theological language. It is a word for believers; it belongs in a world where God is recognized and accepted as a personal influence in one's life. For an unbeliever to speak of sin makes little or no sense, even though the word "sin" has now become part of common speech. It should also be evident that sin is personal and subjective – it has to do with a personal relationship (CCC 1868). Morality, on the other hand, is objective in that it has to do with the human person and with proper human development that applies to all, believers and unbelievers alike.

Understanding Sin

Sin in the Bible

To better understand sin, we should start with the Bible. For biblical writers, sin is an ever-present and pressing reality. It is the Bible that tells the story of our covenant with God, and it is there that we have the clearest expression of what sin is. The Bible story is the story of God's incredible goodness and his love for us. It is also the story of our transgressions and God's compassionate willingness always to forgive. The fact that we do renege on God's love, that we do turn away from our covenant promises and therefore need forgiveness, is central to the Bible story. In fact, many spiritual writers and scripture scholars would go so far as to say that the forgiveness of sin is probably the key theme of the Bible, certainly of the New Testament. The whole meaning of Jesus' mission on earth, his very name even (Jesus means "God saves") centres on the forgiveness of sin, "for he will save his people from their sins" (Mt 1:21). Jesus himself sums up his whole mission on earth at the Last Supper with his apostles. In giving them the cup he said, "Drink from it, all of you; for this is my blood of the covenant, which is poured out for many for the forgiveness of sins" (Mt 26:27-28).

In the Bible, sin is always understood as a refusal to do God's will. What God wants is that we should love God and love one another, that we should be thoroughly moral people (CCC 1850). Nowhere is this theme, together with God's mercy and forgiveness, better expressed and explained than in Jesus' parable of the Prodigal Son (Lk 15:11-32; it will be fully explained in Chapter 20). The Prodigal Son, having spent his time and money on "riotous living," returns home and says, "Father, I have sinned against heaven and before you" (Lk 15:18; 15:21). In sinning against his father, the Prodigal had also sinned against heaven. When we fail to love one another, by that very fact we fail to love God, we damage our relationship with God, we sin.

Sin as a State

When the Bible speaks of sin, it doesn't only mean "sins," that is, individual personal acts against the will of God. The Bible also refers to a state or condition of sinfulness in which we find ourselves in the world. There is a power of evil in the world to which we are all subject and which influences us toward sinfulness. We experience that evil from the moment of birth; indeed, many would say we experience it even in the womb. As the child grows, no matter how sheltered his existence, he becomes conscious of people who lie and who cheat, people who are cruel and uncaring, people who are selfish and greedy, people who are involved in the whole catalogue of moral evil. Every child finds himself in a world where the formative social and cultural influences are riddled with evil. Unable to escape these influences, every child is eventually drawn into sin.

From the mere fact of being born we are all influenced by this state of sin even before we can make a conscious decision of our own, even before we can morally discern right from wrong. We come into the world with a strong "inclination to evil," a tendency to self-centredness. As our human personality develops, we eventually make a conscious decision to accept and be part of this evil, to commit our own personal sins. We are influenced by the evil in the world in such a way that, in the course of our human development, personal sin becomes inevitable – we cannot *not* sin. And so, the Bible recognizes that all of us are sinners: "If we say that we have no sin, we deceive ourselves, and the truth is not in us" (1 Jn 1:8). We cannot recover from this state of sinfulness by our own effort and volition; we need to be healed. That healing comes to us through the redeeming grace of Jesus Christ which is freely offered to us through the merits of his life, death and resurrection (CCC 421, 615).

The early biblical writers, and the whole Jewish tradition, were acutely conscious of this state of evil in the world. That posed a serious problem. How could their experience of evil be squared with their faith in the goodness of God and the essential goodness of God's creation? They offered their explanation in the form of stories. The story of Adam and Eve and their fall from grace (Gen 2:15-3:24) is one such story, perhaps the principal one. The Adam and Eve story need not be taken as historical; in fact, to take it as historical creates more problems than it solves. It is a story, but a story with a purpose and a message. The purpose of the story is to explain that God is not the author of evil – human beings are. God's creation is essentially good; it is we human beings who have sullied it. We must take responsibility for the state we find ourselves in. What the Bible is saying is that evil came into the world as the result of sin, as the result of our refusal to accept and respond to God's invitation to love. For invitation it is; God will not do violence to our free will.

If we should not take the Bible story of Adam and Eve as literal and historical then we do not know how sin came into the world. It is as simple as that. The Bible story has it that the first sin was one of disobedience and, indeed, this is truly a deep insight into the human psyche. Adam and Eve were forbidden to eat of a certain fruit but they ate anyway. But, it was more than mere disobedience. The story depicts them as wanting to have "knowledge of good and evil." "But the serpent said to the woman, 'You will not die; for God knows that when you eat of it your eyes will be opened, and you will be like God, knowing good and evil'" (Gen 3:4-5). Now, "good and evil" is just a Semitic way of saying "everything" (much as we might describe all our movements as "comings and goings"). They wanted to have all knowledge and thus be equal to God, not subject to him. And so the sin is depicted as the ultimate rebellion of the creature against its creator, the selfishness that chooses its own way rather than God's way (CCC 398). And isn't that our own personal parable, too, and our personal tragedy? Can we not all easily relate to it? We, too, are faced with moral choices in life. Because of our selfishness we make the wrong choices – we choose to satisfy ourselves rather than God; we commit sin. We are Adam, we are Eve. The Adam and Eve story is a wonderful story, full of deep insight into the human condition ruined by sin, the miserable experience of self-alienation, the falling out of harmony with our world, the pathetic effort to blame someone else for our mistakes. It is a story that will repay careful study, for it is our story.

Conditions for Sin – Degrees of Sinfulness

Since sin involves a personal human decision, the psychological conditions for such a decision must prevail before anyone can be said to have sinned. The

Catholic tradition has always held that there are three conditions for sin, conditions that have to do with making human decisions:

a)   sufficient knowledge, or reflection;

b)   full consent of the will, or personal freedom;

c)   real evil to oneself or to others.

Should either sufficient knowledge or full consent be absent, for whatever reason, the act is not considered to be a human act. Thus, for example, someone cannot commit sin while sleepwalking; there is neither knowledge nor consent. If either sufficient knowledge or personal freedom is impeded in some way, then one's personal responsibility is correspondingly diminished. We cannot sin if we don't want to, or are not aware of it. In effect, therefore, *sin is in the intention*. And so, for example, someone who in genuine error judges something to be good, when in fact it is evil, does not commit sin. Conversely, an evil intention can make an objectively good act sinful.

Finally, we say the act must involve real (pre-moral) evil, either to oneself or to others. Often the gravity of the evil caused determines the gravity of the sin.[174]

Taking these three conditions into consideration, Catholic theology has traditionally distinguished degrees of sinfulness: mortal sins and venial sins. Now, measuring out degrees of sinfulness is generally not a very helpful practice, and we should not let ourselves get too caught up in it. Too often it is associated with assigning blame and determining punishment. We must not let ourselves think of God as some kind of heavenly taskmaster who has the recording angel keep our accounts, so to speak, and who "punishes" our sins. God does not punish us – God is a God of love and compassion. Nevertheless, while we must guard against becoming too legalistic in our judgment of sin, this distinction between mortal and venial is helpful.

Mortal sin is sin that causes a complete break in our relation with God. The word comes from the Latin *mors*, meaning death. Mortal sin causes spiritual death. We make a conscious decision to turn completely away from God's offer of love. We turn away from the recognition of God in our life, and we go our own way (CCC 1855-1856).[175]

Venial sin is sin that does not completely separate us from God but represents a cooling in our relationship, a strain, a temporary falling out. The word comes from the Latin *venia*, meaning grace, or favour. Thus, we remain in God's

[174] It would be well, at this point, to review what was said about pre-moral (real) evil in the previous chapter.
[175] CCC 1472 deals with the consequences of unrepented grave sin (loss of communion with God and eternal life).

favour and grace but we have been less than consistent in our commitment to our covenant promise (CCC 1862-1863). Clearly, this inconsistency, this strain in our relationship with God, can be more or less serious depending on (a) the evil we have caused – grave evil means grave sin; (b) the circumstances of the act – e.g., stealing a small amount from a wealthy person versus stealing a person's whole livelihood.

In his commentary on paragraph 1858 of the Catechism, Gerald J. Hughes, S.J., makes some helpful points:

> In distinguishing between mortal sin and venial sin, the Catechism repeats [St. Thomas] Aquinas's doctrine that the Ten Commandments deal with matter which is itself serious. This [too] is to be taken in the context of his immediately following remarks. The Catechism is not saying that all sins against the Ten Commandments involve grave matter, but merely that they involve the kind of areas which are potentially grave matter. Thus, killing, adultery, lying are by their nature serious issues. But every failure to observe the commandments is not equally serious.[176]

The Psychological Dimension

To better understand degrees of sinfulness we must turn to psychology. We ask this question: How do we make moral decisions? What is the psychological basis for these decisions?

We can envisage the human person as a complex, multi-level being. Different levels of the psyche may be thought of as layers radiating out from a central core.[177] The different levels of the psyche represent the different levels of personal involvement in moral decision making.

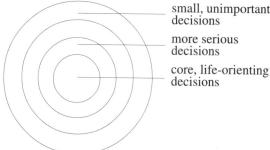

small, unimportant decisions

more serious decisions

core, life-orienting decisions

The Human Psyche

---

[176] Gerard J. Hughes, S.J., "Our Human Vocation," in Michael Walsh, ed., *Commentary on the Catechism of the Catholic Church* (Collegeville, MN: The Liturgical Press, 1994), p. 351.

[177] Richard Gula, S.S., prefers to envisage it as a spiral moving outwards from a centre of identity. This is a somewhat more complex image but some people may find it more enlightening. See *Reason Informed by Faith*, p. 78.

When we make small, unimportant decisions connected with everyday life (such as brushing our teeth or eating) we engage only the outer portions of the psyche. Ordinary, everyday actions do not require us to delve deep into the psyche. They are not important decisions. They do not require deep convictions; they do not engage us profoundly as persons.

Other decisions engage us far more profoundly and may touch our deep convictions. These may be called serious decisions (choice of a career, choice of a particular lifestyle). Still others go to the very core of our being and determine the whole direction and orientation of our life. They determine how we express our personality; they make us who and what we are.

Our commitment to God in the covenant engages us at the core of our being. It is a life orientation that ultimately determines everything for us. What we understand by mortal sin is precisely something that engages us at the core of our being. We consciously reject our relationship of love with God. We choose self instead of God. It is as though we have built a shell of selfishness around ourselves and refuse God entry to our person. God does not cease to love us; no, we have ceased loving God. We choose to make ourselves the centre of our lives instead of God. Our relationship with God is dead. This is what we call mortal sin.

Sin and the Single Act

How many times have you asked, or thought of asking, "Is that a sin?" "Is it a sin to . . .?" Questions like that may indeed come from a genuine and sincere conscience, a genuine desire to please God. More often, they come from people who want to give in to themselves as much as possible and still stay on the right side of God. This is particularly true when the action is understood as serious sin or as mortal sin.

In the past, we tended to make a link in our mind that mortal sin, in fact any sin, was connected with an individual act. In moral theology the individual act became the paradigm by which we judged sin. Faithful Catholics who confessed their sins in the sacrament of Reconciliation were advised to tell their sins "according to kind and number." Each separate act was considered to be a separate sin. Each penitent approached the confessional with a "grocery list" of sins. But following our present-day understanding of the human decision-making process outlined above, we now prefer to look more at a person's whole life-orientation, rather than at individual acts. A life-orientation involves the very centre of one's being, the entire outlook that motivates our life, the core of one's freedom.

Let us take an example. If someone were to give up praying completely over a long period, that might indicate a total orientation away from God, a nonrecognition of God in their life. But we know from experience that things usually don't happen that way. Generally, we don't give up praying in one single, carefully thought-out and deliberate act. More probably we simply get careless. At first we make decisions about prayer with the outer portions of the psyche. After a time we realize that we have been lax, but we do nothing about it. That is a decision made deeper in the psyche. Finally, we end up making a decision that we can get along quite well without prayer, thus cutting off our relationship with God.

Is it possible, then, for someone to commit mortal sin in one single act? Yes, it is possible, but probably happens infrequently. Yes, it is possible for us to think of someone who with very deep malice aforethought would commit a heinous crime, a crime so evil, in fact, that our *human* judgment would have to say that such a person had separated himself or herself totally from God. All we are saying is that such an occurrence, while possible (we do have free will, after all!), may well be rare; that is not the way most human beings normally behave. Mortal sin involves a whole life-orientation, and life-orientations do not generally occur as a result of single acts. The Catechism does not specifically deal with this issue of completely tying mortal sin to a single act; it does point out, however, that "mortal sin is a radical possibility of human freedom, as is love itself" (CCC 1861). This wording, which makes "a comparison between mortal sin and love perhaps suggests that mortal sin is unlikely to be an isolated action."[178]

Is it possible for us then to know with certainty if, and when, we have completely separated ourselves from God? No objective and all-encompassing answer can be given to that question; only our own inner conscience can be the final arbiter. Ultimately, no one other than we ourselves can make that judgment. It is well to remember, however, as Timothy O'Connell reminds us, that we are not speaking about "some legal definition of particular acts, but about the intrinsic effects of behaviour, and of their underlying human decisions, upon relationships with God and neighbour."[179]

Sins and Sinfulness

In a small town in Ireland, two men stood watching as a funeral passed up the street. Said one man to the other, "Now, who's that?" "Paddy Riley," said the second man. "Ah, is Paddy dead, then?" "That he is," said the other man soberly. "What did he die of?" "Well now," came the reply, "I don't rightly know. But whatever it was, I don't think it was anything serious."

---

[178] Hughes, S.J., "Our Human Vocation," p. 351.
[179] Timothy E. O'Connell, "A Theology of Sin," in Lawrence Cunningham, ed., *The Catholic Faith: A Reader* (New York: Paulist Press, 1988), p. 212.

On the side of a mountain in the Rockies lies what is left of a huge tree. Botanists say that it was several hundred years old. By examining the tree, scientists were also able to tell that in the course of those years it had weathered several natural disasters, such as storms, ice damage, avalanches and being struck by lightning, all of which had failed to kill it. But a horde of beetles attacked the tree. The beetles ate into the bark and cut off the tree's ability to distribute to the root system the food it had manufactured in the leaves; its inner life was destroyed. And so, this forest giant that had withstood all that nature could throw at it for hundreds of years was felled by beetles so small that they could easily be crushed in one's fingers.

Nothing we have said in the previous section should be taken to mean that single individual acts, particularly ones of small moral significance, are of no importance in the world of sin. No, all sin is reprehensible. All sin damages our relationship with God, weakens our love and sets us up for a definitive break, the destruction of our inner life. All sin requires forgiveness. We are human, and sin simply follows us in our human behaviour patterns. Thus, giving in to ourselves in small things will eventually develop into a bad habit, a drift into selfishness that will, in the long run, lead us away from God. If, for example, I easily let myself drift into the habit of lying or cheating, I could end up with a very poor regard for the truth. Then the big criterion of truthfulness becomes what suits me. It is that sort of selfishness that could eventually exclude God from my life.

The point we really want to make is that we should be talking less about individual sins and more about sinfulness. The question we should ask ourselves is not so much "what wrong things have I done, and how often?" Rather we should be asking ourselves, "How do these wrong things I have done indicate my general orientation to God, my love for God, my love for my neighbour?" "What are the desires, the tendencies, the habits, the values that govern my life?" "Where is my life heading?" "Have I said 'yes' to life and accepted God's gift with gratitude and humility, even though I experience hard times?" There are many people whose life may appear to be extremely good. They don't seem to do many wrong things. But if the truth were known, perhaps one would find that their lives were ruined by suppressed anger or envy or recrimination. They may be full of resentment towards God or rebellion against their lot in life. They may be alienated people.

Conclusion

As we conclude this section, let us emphasize again that sin is a reality. We cannot escape it, we must not ignore it; we must name it, we must confront it. It is the personal tragedy of every believer's life; it is a personal experience of alienation. It is alienation from oneself, and from God, well described by St. Paul:

For I do not do the good I want, but the evil I do not want is what I do. Now if I do what I do not want, it is no longer I that do it, but sin that dwells within me. (Rom 7:19-20)

As one author has it, sin is "much less something we do than it is something in which we find ourselves." It is much less a single act than it is sinfulness: a direction of life, an orientation, a disposition, a habit of introverted selfishness. It is this alienation that needs forgiveness and healing so that we may be restored to wholeness. Catholics find healing in the sacrament of Reconciliation.

Section 2 – Conscience

Deeply aware of the decline of a sense of moral responsibility in our society today, psychologists and moral theologians are calling for a rehabilitation of the notion of sin. Eminent psychoanalyst Dr. Karl Menninger, in his book *Whatever Became of Sin?* insists that we would all be healthier, even in a purely psychological sense, if we could better grasp and respond to the need for repentance and conversion. For this to happen we have to have a keen sense of when we have done wrong. That is the work of conscience.

What Is Conscience?

Somewhere, somehow, we may have heard that "conscience is the voice of God telling us what is right and what is wrong and making us feel guilty if we have done something wrong" (CCC 1777, 1795). But the matter is not so simple. We need to say more; we need to take a closer look at what conscience really is and to say something about guilt.

1. Judgment

At the practical level, the first thing that conscience is concerned with is an immediate decision as to what should be done about a certain course of action. We may define conscience as a judgment about the rightness or wrongness of some action (CCC 1778). In any such judgment two things are always involved: knowledge and obligation. First, we know that certain things are right and that others are wrong. Second, we also experience that we are obliged to do the right thing. Doing the right thing produces a feeling of peace and contentment – we are "at one" with ourselves, our dignity is upheld (CCC 1780). Doing what we know to be wrong produces a feeling of guilt and remorse – we are "at odds" with ourselves.

Right away we notice something extremely important that has telling consequences: *feelings are not conscience*. Feelings of contentment and peace, or feelings of guilt, may (and in fact generally do) *accompany* the judgment our conscience makes, but these feelings do not determine the morality of the action. Some people do the most horrible things and feel no guilt or remorse (e.g., the

Nazi plan for the holocaust), while others feel guilt over matters that have no moral significance (e.g., being neat and tidy in one's person).

In practice, therefore, we should be extremely cautious about judging morality by feelings and emotion. Many times we hear people say, "It must be right because I feel good about it." Jane Fonda had a slightly different version of this. Years ago, on a national TV show, talking about her protest activity she defended herself by saying, "How can I be wrong when I am so sincere"(!). It does not seem to have occurred to Jane that someone can be sincerely wrong or sincerely mistaken. What we have to be sincere about is making a sincere effort to clear up doubts and thus develop a clear and correct conscience. Someone may feel very good but still may have made the wrong moral judgment.

2. Knowledge

In order to make a correct practical judgment, we must know what is right and what is wrong. But how do we know?

(a) The law within us

In the first place, our knowledge comes from the general sense of who we are as human beings. God speaks to us through the prophet Jeremiah when he says,

> But this is the covenant that I will make with the house of Israel after those days, says the Lord: I will put my law within them, and I will write it on their hearts; and I will be their God, and they shall be my people. (Jer 31:33)

This "law" Jeremiah speaks of is a metaphor for that instinctive knowledge we all possess of what we must do to be true to ourselves and not act against our very nature. The "law" is also a metaphor for the basic urge we all feel to achieve inner peace, harmony, psychological balance, "at-one-ness" within the self, and to uphold our dignity. This is something that is built right into our human nature by God who created us and who "writes it in our hearts." It is something that makes for psychological health and that, experts increasingly believe, has a great effect on our physical well-being also. This inner sense of our own personhood includes the knowledge of such basic moral principles as " do good and avoid evil" and "treat others the way you would like them to treat you." No one has to teach us these principles. We all have a general sense of human value, of responsibility, and of the rules we need to follow if we are to preserve our integrity and successfully live together in human society. When we act against these basic instincts and principles, we experience a sense of discordance, an uneasiness, nagging worry, a restlessness; we are "out of sorts." We call this guilt.

Vatican Council II has much to say about conscience. Some people have even gone so far as to call it the Council of conscience. One of the clearest of the texts (slightly amended) is as follows:

> Deep within their consciences men and women discover a law which they have not laid upon themselves and which they must obey. Its voice, ever calling them to love and to do what is good and to avoid evil, tells them inwardly at the right moment: do this, shun that. For they have in their hearts a law inscribed by God. Their dignity rests in observing this law, and by it they will be judged. Their conscience is people's most secret core, and their sanctuary. There they are alone with God whose voice echoes in their depths.[180]

It is God who has made us who we are, it is God who has put these basic instincts in us, it is God who wants us to act according to our human nature and be true to ourselves. Therefore, there is certainly a sense in which we can say that conscience is "the voice of God." Nevertheless, we should remember that the "voice of God" is only a metaphor. We do not take it literally. God does not whisper into our ear the same way that Jiminy Cricket whispered into Pinocchio's ear. God's call comes to us in the heart of the very human process of making moral judgments; it is not an extra voice that dictates new moral information to us. Thus, God calls to us through our conscience, and we can only be true to ourselves when we act in accordance with what our conscience tells us is right. In the telling words of Thomas Babington Macauley, "The measure of a man's character is what he would do if he knew he would never be found out." No one else knows, but God knows.

Since with conscience "we are alone with God whose voice echoes in our depths," conscience is, ultimately, the sole arbiter for us of what is right and what is wrong. If God is calling to us in the depths of our conscience then there is no escaping it, we must follow that call (CCC 1800). Conscience is inviolable. Consequently, no one should be forced to act against his or her conscience. St. Thomas Aquinas, one of the greatest theologians of the Catholic church, dramatizes the obligation of conscience in the following fashion:

> Anyone on whom ecclesiastical authority, in ignorance of the true facts, imposes a demand that offends against a clear conscience should perish in excommunication, rather than violate his conscience.

To act against our conscience would be to do violence to our true selves, to the person God wants us to be; we damage our relationship with God, we sin.

---

[180] *Pastoral Constitution on the Church in the Modern World*, No. 16. This description is repeated in CCC 1776.

For us Christian believers, what God wants us to do and how God wants us to act is made explicit by Jesus. We are called by Sacred scripture to think like Jesus Christ: "Let the same mind be in you that was in Christ Jesus" (Phil 2:5); to espouse the same values and principles that governed his life; to take his life as the example of how we should act.

(b) Forming conscience

It is one thing to say that the "law" of how God wants us to act is written in our hearts, but frequently this "law" is not clear to us. We may need to improve our knowledge, to clarify the principles for action, to make quite sure that we know how we should act. We must follow our conscience, it is true, but we also have an obligation to make sure that our conscience is correct and not mistaken. We call this process "forming one's conscience."

Richard Gula correctly points out that forming one's conscience is not simply a matter of answering the question "What ought I to do?" Forming one's conscience should take into account not only the question "What sort of person am I?" but also "What sort of person ought I to become?" What is the sort of person that God wants me to be? In other words, our whole moral outlook and character is also important. Our moral character, our way of seeing and approaching moral matters is, in fact, the background against which we make moral judgments. If our moral character is bent, or "skewed" in a certain direction, that is how we shall make our moral judgments. For example, am I easygoing, liberal, non-judgmental, anti-authoritarian, not very reflective? Or am I law-oriented, judgmental, conservative, careful? Clearly, properly forming one's conscience requires a certain degree of self-knowledge – we must know what kind of person we are and how we would normally act in certain circumstances. Gula indicates four sources of what he calls "moral wisdom" that can help us in forming our conscience.

1. On the purely human level we look to our own experience, our own personal character. We look for help from family, friends, experts, people who know more than we do but who are honest and will not simply tell us what we want to hear.

2. On the Christian level we have the help of sacred Scripture, our faith, the example of virtuous Christians: people who have really lived the gospel values. We also have the work of theologians and scripture scholars, who will help us to interpret God's word.

3. We belong to a Christian community that has traditions, stories, rituals, devotional practices that help to form our spiritual outlook and character. "The mature conscience," says Gula, "is formed and exercised in community in dialogue with other sources of moral wisdom." Particularly

should we note the importance of prayer, for prayer is essential if we are to form our consciences properly.

4. As Catholics we also have a rich tradition of moral discernment. More specifically, we believe that the official teaching church is there to help and guide us in matters which may not have clear-cut moral answers. For us, the teaching magisterium headed by Christ's vicar, the Pope, is a special and authoritative source of moral wisdom. We must give it our full and loyal attention[181] (CCC 1788, 1789).

Looking at the above four points, one might be inclined to feel that forming one's conscience is an impossibly complicated exercise, far too difficult for the likes of you and me. But take heart. The four points are only meant to be indications of where we might get help; they are not prescriptive. What we have to be convinced of is that *there is a real obligation to do our best to develop a correct conscience*. We can't slough off this obligation just because we are too lazy, which is precisely where so many of us fail.

Conscience and Super-Ego

Sigmund Freud was the first to describe what he called the "super-ego." The super-ego is a part of our psyche, which is like a storehouse. In the course of our development from childhood, we accumulate in this storehouse all the obligations, all the do's and don'ts together with the threats of punishment and promises of reward foisted on us by various authority figures – parents, teachers, priests, the teaching church, police and the like. If we go against these taboos, the super-ego plies us with guilt: we feel bad, which puts us out of sorts with ourselves. It is precisely this weapon of guilt and fear that authority figures have used to "keep us in line." An example we can all relate to is how we react when we are driving and we notice a police car behind us. We have done nothing wrong, but immediately our pulse quickens and we begin checking our speed, our seatbelt, our driving position, etc. Our super-ego is at work, spreading the fear that the cop may catch us breaking the law. That police officers are authority figures with the power to arrest us has been well and truly planted in our psyche in the course of our growing up.

There is little doubt that the quality of many people's lives is still governed by the dictates of the super-ego. They have never matured enough to be able to make their own moral decisions. They are still harking back to what was decreed for them by the authority figures of their youth. This is rather tragic. But it still leaves us with the problem of how to distinguish between the guilt (that is, the

---

[181] *Reason Informed by Faith*. For a full treatment of the formation of conscience see Chapter 10.

unease, the out-of-stepness) that comes from an overactive super-ego and guilt that comes from genuine conscience. In truth, it's no easy problem to solve.[182]

Distinguishing between a true conscience and the super-ego requires a great degree of self-knowledge. We have to know our past, the influences that shaped us, our own character, our worldview, our manner of reacting. As Richard Gula points out, "The difference between the working of the super-ego in the child and the adult is one of degree and not of kind."[183] The super-ego is always there. As we mature, we should develop more and more skill at distinguishing the dictates of a genuine conscience from those merely of the super-ego. "The super-ego may also be felt by the morally mature person," says Sean Fagan, "but he is not dominated by it. He recognizes its presence but he has it under control. Such a person can respect law and authority, but his life is governed more by freely chosen values."[184] As mature persons we recognize and accept our limitations and weaknesses, but we are always open to new avenues of moral growth. Above all, we believe that, no matter what, God loves us and only asks of us that we be sincere and true to ourselves in trying to come to correct moral decisions.

While we should be aware of the working of the super-ego, it would be wrong to think that every feeling of guilt is the product of an overactive super-ego. Let us close with one final and helpful word of warning on this matter from Sean Fagan:

> It would be a pity if, whatever the flaws in our early training and the psychic and social influences at work in our subconscious, we overlooked the definite and obvious possibility that we feel guilty because we are guilty. If our guilt feeling is the result of a personality disorder we may get help from a counsellor or psychiatrist. There is no need for repentance. But if our guilt is sin, no amount of counselling or psychiatry will help. What is needed in this case is repentance, conversion, atonement. The remedy is simple and easily available. God has given us the means to cope with sin. His forgiveness is there for the asking.[185]

This quotation gives a good lead-in to the next chapter of this book, where we shall consider the whole matter of the forgiveness of sin.

---

[182] See particularly John W. Glazer, "Conscience and Superego: A Key Distinction," in C. Ellis Nelson, ed., *Conscience: Theological and Psychological Perspectives* (Newman Press, 1973). Richard Gula carefully summarizes Glazer's distinctions in *Reason Informed by Faith*, p. 127.

[183] *Reason Informed by Faith*, p. 129.

[184] *Has Sin Changed?*, p. 137.

[185] *Ibid.*, pp. 143-144.

Conclusion

In conclusion, let us remind ourselves that the human virtue that most marked the life of Jesus was integrity. He was true to himself as a human being. He led his life according to the way he understood his conscience to be calling him, to do the will of God his Father. In this respect, as in all other respects, Jesus is our model. As we have seen, conscience is the "voice of God," calling us to act in accordance with our true selves as human persons and as believers in God, who is love. Consequently, conscience is the final arbiter of how we stand in our relationship with God. We must not act against a clear conscience, for this is what we mean by sin, and our conscience can be blunted by sin. By allowing ourselves to become immersed in the selfishness of sin we damage the psyche's ability to make sound moral judgments. Almost always we have a hidden agenda of selfishness influencing our decisions. "The worst thing in the world," said the well-known writer and broadcaster Bishop Fulton Sheen, "is not sin; it is the denial of sin by a false conscience – for that attitude makes forgiveness impossible." When we deliberately bury our conscience under a mound of self-serving rationalizations, we cut off communication with the God who is so intimately part of our life; in other words, we don't want to be forgiven. The only sin that God cannot forgive is the sin for which we don't want to be forgiven, and that, as Bishop Sheen says, is the worst thing we can allow to happen to us.

Reflection Questions

1. Distinguish between mortal sin and venial sin. How would you explain the difference between the two?

2. What do we mean by sinfulness, as distinct from individual sins?

3. "No one ever became evil all at once" (the Roman writer Juvenal). Comment on this statement.

4. In what way can it be said that conscience is the "voice of God" in our heart, telling us what is right and what is wrong?

5. Why should we be extremely cautious about judging morality by feelings and emotion? Is the way we feel always an infallible guide to a clear conscience?

6. Explain carefully what you understand by guilt. Does God make us feel guilty?

7. What is meant by "forming one's conscience?"

Further Reading

Fagan, Sean. *Has Sin Changed?* (Wilmington, DE: Michael Glazier, 1977). As clear and thorough a treatment of the subject of sin as is available at the present time. Easy reading in large print. Should be a standard reference book.

Glazer, John W. "Conscience and Super-ego: A Key Distinction," in C. Ellis Nelson, ed., *Conscience: Theological and Psychological Perspectives* (Newman Press, 1973). A useful article if somewhat esoteric in its treatment of the subject.

Menninger, Karl. *Whatever Became of Sin?* (New York: Hawthorn Books, Inc., 1973). One of the first books to detail the modern tendency to play down the notion of sin. Rather bulky and detailed but can be used as a reference. Should be in the school library.

O'Connell, Timothy. "A Theology of Sin," in Lawrence Cunningham, ed., *The Catholic Faith: A Reader* (New York: Paulist Press, 1988). A short, easy-to-read article on the subject of sin.

Peck, M. Scott. *People of the Lie* (New York: Simon & Schuster, 1983). Takes up the same topic as Menninger but perhaps in a simpler, more readable form.

19

TEACHING MORALITY

The purpose of this short chapter is to provide some sort of conclusion and summary to the section on morality. The following points are not meant to be a complete "how-to" on the teaching of morality – far from it. They simply represent some reflections based on the experience of many teachers, which we hope will be useful for helping to shape a person's moral outlook and response to concrete moral situations. And so, let us note the following:

1. We teach *the message of Jesus*. That message makes certain demands on our moral behaviour. The core of Jesus' message is love for one another, love that is truly self-sacrificing, as was his love for us.

   This self-sacrificing love, therefore, *is the principal moral norm that we must teach*. Not only must we teach it but, most importantly, we must be an example of it. It is this love that expresses itself in all the values proposed by Jesus' gospel preaching and example. And so we affirm love and respect for all persons; we affirm the need for justice in all its forms; we affirm the positive value of and need for peace; we teach respect for property and for the earth given us by God, respect for truth, respect for the sanctity of marriage, respect for personal integrity, respect for the sanctity of human life from conception to the grave.

2. We must teach *the clear reality of personal sin* which damages our relationship with God and which contributes to the spread of evil in the world. We have to accept responsibility for our part in this evil. We must not hide behind a battery of excuses (blaming circumstances or the "system" or other people) for our moral laxity. We teach that sin needs repentance and conversion.

3. We teach *how one's conscience is to be formed* according to the Christian moral code as interpreted by the teaching church. We help people distinguish between conscience and super-ego, but we also teach them that conscience does not depend on personal whim or on an emotional response that gives rise to a spur-of-the moment decision. We teach that while feelings may accompany a moral decision, feelings are not a sure guide to morality. We are required to reflect, to think and to pray. We help people to gather the tools for making their own good moral decisions; we do not make

moral decisions for them. Pope John Paul II, at Czestochowa during his 1983 visit to his homeland of Poland, gave this advice:

"I must make an effort to be a person with a conscience. I do not stifle this conscience, and I do not deform it; I call good and evil by name, and I do not blur the difference; I develop in myself what is good, and I seek to correct what is evil, by overcoming it in myself."

4. We teach that *there are objective standards of morality*. Everyone cannot adopt one's own personal standards of morality; this would be a recipe for anarchy. A society that does not have an agreed-upon moral code is destined for disintegration. Therefore, morality is not determined by what suits us at the moment. There are objective values that must be respected by all if we are to properly live and develop as human persons. "My way is as good as your way" is definitely not a moral norm.

5. Following from No. 4 above, we teach that *polls and surveys do not determine morality*. There is no "morality by Gallup"! The pollster's method is as follows: take a survey to discover what people think and do; the more people there are who think it is right, or who are doing it, the more right it becomes! A classic example is that of divorce. If, as the surveys tell us, more than one-third of all marriages end in divorce, then people begin to think, "so many others are doing it, it can't be that wrong. It's just the way society is today." That kind of thinking weakens the marriage bond; a divorce mentality develops. Instead of trying to work out their difficulties, spouses think that divorce is the best and easiest way out. Polls are not moral norms; as the old saying goes, two wrongs cannot make a right.

6. We teach that *the fundamental value in morality is always the human person with his or her capacity for love and the relation between the person and society*. Anything that causes real evil to persons is immoral in itself. Civil law does not determine morality; we cannot use the civil law as our yardstick for judging morality. The fact that there is no civil law against something does not make it moral or "all right." Actions are wrong in and of themselves, not because someone has declared them to be so. Things are not wrong because they are forbidden, they are forbidden because they are wrong.

7. We teach what are the *false values* that are so strong in our present-day Western culture and that pull us away from the values proposed by Jesus in the gospel.

    Individualism: My personal needs and desires take precedence over everything; always claiming my "rights" instead of looking to my duties and responsibilities to the community and to society.

Privatism: We all have a right to privacy, but not to the extent of going against established moral norms (for example, the decision of the United States Supreme Court that abortion may be justified on the grounds of a woman's right to privacy); excessive privacy is another manifestation of the pervading selfishness of the modern age.

Narcissism: The ego, vanity, as the measure of everything (such as this slogan from the l'Oréal hair-colour commercial: "It costs more, but I'm worth it!" "It makes me feel good about myself"). Narcissism produces relational paralysis. One is so enamoured with oneself that nothing has value except in relation to self. In such a climate it is extraordinarily difficult to form lasting relationships.

Success in life: Measured by one's material possessions and position in society, not by what one has become as a person (having a Mercedes makes one better than someone who drives an old Chevrolet).

Consumerism: Buying what we don't need just for the sake of buying to satisfy our greed; shopping as a sport – "shop till you drop"; wasteful rape and pollution of the environment so that we may have a more luxurious lifestyle.

Violence: Thinking that violence is the right reaction when you cannot get what you want, or when you think you are right; the rapid increase of violence in our society is indeed frightening.

False love: Confusing love with sexual infatuation.

8. We teach people *how their moral outlook is being subtly manipulated* by advertisers and by the media in general, and we help them to discern and work against this manipulation. In particular, we alert them to the great violence done to truth by the media which, among other things, often manipulate news to enhance its "entertainment" value. This loss of human integrity (that great human virtue exhibited by Jesus) is perhaps the most subtle – but very real – contribution of modern society to the evil in the world.

Pedagogy

There are many ways we may go about teaching morality. The following steps are suggestions only. They are taken from the generally accepted procedure of basic catechesis. They are presented here as principles only; the pedagogical details will have to be worked out for each particular teaching situation.

1. *Put people in touch with their present experience.* Thus, help them to come to an awareness, a conscientization of their present moral vision and moral standards. Many people, because they have been so conditioned by the moral climate in which we live, seem totally unaware of proper moral

norms. All good pedagogy uses present experience as a jumping-off point for new learning. So for the average person (depending on age, social class, or present circumstances), what are the present moral decisions they have to make, and do make: cheating at school or in business? pre-marital sex and adultery? shoplifting? lack of respect for parents and for the property of others? injustice to one's employees? Have people try to discover it and to name it, to become completely and specifically conscious of it. The teacher should only be a guide; he or she should not do the naming for those being taught unless it becomes necessary.

2. *Bring their ideas, their perceptions, their experiences into dialogue with the Christian vision of life* as presented by a) the teaching of Jesus, b) the teaching of the church, c) the experience and traditions of our Christian community, and d) the example of countless faithful and heroic Christians.

3. *Formulate some concrete plan of action* to bring about a synthesis of the two preceding points. Question: What are we going to do about it?

20

RECONCILIATION

The Effects of Sin

In order to understand reconciliation, we must first take a look at what sin does to us. The word that probably expresses it best is "alienation." We are alienated from self, from the community (church), and from God.

1. Alienation from Self

As we noted in a previous chapter, it is more important for us to focus on our state of sinfulness rather than on individual sins. The important thing is our "fundamental attitude towards oneself, and the world, and God."[186] What sin does to us on the personal level is alienate us from our true goals in life, the goals that we know will make us better persons. We opt for selfishness rather than openness; we opt for comfort, safety and security rather than accepting our responsibilities towards others in society. But we cannot escape the fact that we are social beings. We develop as persons in a social context. We can only be truly human, true to ourselves, in the context of relationship with other humans. One of our most basic needs as human persons is the need to love and be loved, but how can we reach out in love towards others if we are only focused inward, only intent on loving ourselves?

As sinners we need forgiveness, we need healing, we need to be reoriented, revitalized, at peace with ourselves. But forgiveness and healing can only come when we want it and when we are prepared to take the necessary steps to change, to be converted. To be converted means to be turned around, to change direction, to focus on our true goal, which is God, rather than on our own selfish desires. To be healed of our alienation we must first forgive ourselves. Now, forgiving ourselves does not mean that we condone our wrongdoing or our sinful state, but rather that we do not wallow in self-pity or become overly miserable about our mistakes. It is largely something we have to do for ourselves, but others can help us. In fact, ministering to sinners, assisting them in the process of conversion, is one of the chief ministries of the church because it was one of the chief ministries of Jesus.

---

[186] Bernard Cooke, *Sacraments and Sacramentality*, p. 191.

An important part of the healing process is the experience of being forgiven. At the purely human level, the experience of forgiving and being forgiven is an essential aspect of proper human development. We really cannot experience the forgiveness of God unless we have experienced human forgiveness, since all our experiences of God are based on the analogy of human experience. And here, surely, is one way in which we can truly minister to the sick – those sick in sin. The love and the forgiveness of God are mediated to us through the love and forgiveness of other persons. Part of our following of Jesus, part of our imitating his ministry, is to help bring healing and forgiveness to those in need, just as he did.

Now, if we want to be forgiven, it stands to reason that we ourselves must be forgiving people. How can we really experience God's forgiveness if we harbour grudges, if we seek revenge, if we refuse to accept a sincere apology, if we do not do our best to patch up quarrels? That Jesus recognized the importance of this crucial aspect of human relationships is clear from the way he taught us to pray: "Forgive us our sins as we forgive those who sin against us." God's forgiveness is only offered to us on the condition of our own willingness to forgive others. But that may not always mean public reconciliation. For example, suppose someone were to slander your reputation, using private information you had provided; you would forgive that person, but it might not be wise to be reconciled in the sense of taking that person back into your confidence at the same level of trust. Surely this is something we need to reflect on and pray about constantly.

2. Alienation from Community

As we noted in the previous section, we are social beings: we only develop as persons in a social context. The important consequence of this is that we cannot deal with God on a purely individual basis. Our relationship with God necessarily involves our relationship with others. Contemporary (Western) culture is a culture that is highly individualized and privatized. As a consequence it is a culture that has difficulty recognizing community. It is a culture excessively concerned with "self," often to the point of narcissism. The self has become the measure of everything. Translated into moral terms, what this means is that what suits us is right, what doesn't is wrong. The operative word in our society is *right* – everyone is out to claim their own individual rights. The words "obligation," "responsibility," "duty," which are words of the community, as it were, are largely forgotten.

In such a cultural climate it is extremely difficult for us to thoroughly grasp the notion that our relationship with God is closely determined by our relationship with people. Our first instinct is to regard our relationship with God as a purely personal and private matter, no business of anyone else's but our own.

And so my sins, my transgressions, are matters which concern only God and myself, no one else. *This kind of mentality is totally foreign to the Bible and totally foreign to our understanding of church.* We are a covenanted people; the reality of our interdependence is as important as the reality of our independence.

What follows from the above is vitally important if we are to properly understand reconciliation.

1. All sin is simultaneously an offence against God and against the community.

2. All sin has a social dimension.

3. There is no such thing as a purely private sin.

Even our so-called private sins make us more selfish, they make us more introverted, they affect our human growth and therefore have an effect on how we relate to others in community.

If all sin is simultaneously an offence against God and against the community, then it follows that *forgiveness of sin must involve the community in some way.* It is true that only God can forgive sin but, because of the covenant, because of the way God has chosen to deal with us, God's forgiveness comes to us in and through the community of believers, the church, who must welcome us back to God's family.

3. Alienation from God

God's love is unchanging and constant. God's fidelity is never in question, no matter what we have done. As we have seen in an earlier chapter, a Hebrew word used in the Bible to describe God's love is *hésed. Hésed* designates the faithfulness and loyalty that bind two parties together in a true relationship of love and self-giving. Thus, God is described as "abounding in steadfast love and faithfulness" (Ex 34:6). God has *hésed* for us. God is revealed as freely giving this total love and fidelity, not because of any legal obligation, but out of complete goodness, graciousness and generosity. What God wants is our steadfast love, a love that shows itself in a desire to do God's will. Thus the prophet Hosea says, "I desire steadfast love and not sacrifice, the knowledge of God rather than burnt offering" (Hos 6:6). It is not that God stops loving us; no, it is we who stop loving God, who alienate ourselves from God's everlasting love. We need to repent and be converted.

The message of repentance and conversion is one that appears in the very earliest stages of Jesus' ministry. In fact, it was the central theme of the preaching of Jesus' precursor, John the Baptizer.

*John the baptizer appeared in the wilderness, proclaiming a baptism of
repentance for the forgiveness of sins. And people from the whole
Judean countryside and all the people of Jerusalem were going out to
him, and were baptized by him in the river Jordan, confessing their sins.
(Mk 1:4-5)*

After Jesus' resurrection, on the day of Pentecost, when Peter, full of the
Holy Spirit, had finished his first enthusiastic speech to the people proclaiming
the Lord Jesus, they anxiously asked him and the other apostles, "'Brothers,
what should we do?' Peter said to them, 'Repent, and be baptized every one of
you in the name of Jesus Christ so that your sins may be forgiven'" (Acts 2:37-
38).

The Greek word used in the Bible for conversion, repentance, is *metanoia*,
which means "change of heart," "changing direction," "retracing one's steps." If
we are in a state of sin, then we must "change direction" to return to God. Being
alienated from God means that we have chosen other goals in life than the ones
we know God wants. We have decided that we can find meaning in life apart
from God – in fact, that we ourselves can be our own meaning.[187] The decision
that we do not really need God in our life is the basic sinful decision. Our
alienation from God is self-imposed and personally chosen; we need to change
our goals, to change direction, to re-orient ourselves: we need to repent.

Jesus and the Forgiveness of Sin

We noted in a previous chapter that our sinfulness and God's forgiveness
are a key theme of the Bible. An integral part of the message preached by Jesus
is that God is always willing to welcome back in reconciliation anyone who
sincerely asks for forgiveness. This, indeed, is great Good News. Consider
sayings like these:

I was sent only to the lost sheep of the house of Israel. (Mt 15:24)
*Those who are well have no need of a physician, but those who are sick;
I have come to call not the righteous but sinners. (Mk 2:17)*

*Drink from it, all of you; for this is my blood of the covenant, which is
poured out for many for the forgiveness of sins. (Mt 26:27-28)*

There is no sin that God will not forgive unless it be the sin for which we do
not want forgiveness. Not only did Jesus preach the message of God's forgiveness, he also built a good deal of his active ministry around this theme.

Even a quick reading of the gospels indicates how central the forgiveness of
sin was to Jesus' whole ministry. Repeatedly he tells those who showed great

---

[187] A look back to Chapter 18 will remind us that this is precisely the sin of Adam and Eve as
depicted in the Bible.

faith in him, "Your sins are forgiven." He did this often for people who had not specifically asked for forgiveness, but rather for some other favour, such as healing from illness (see Lk 5:22-26; Lk 7:36-50). But perhaps nowhere better is Jesus' healing ministry and the forgiveness of sin explained than in the parable of the Prodigal Son. The famous English novelist Charles Dickens was once asked what, in his opinion, was the best short story he had ever read. He replied: "The story of the Prodigal Son." Let us now try to see what Jesus was teaching in this "best short story."

The Parable of the Prodigal Son

The gospel itself does not give this parable any specific title; in fact, it might just as well be called The Parable of the Generous Father, for God is the central figure in the story, which is indeed about his lavish love and generosity. The parable really tells the story of two sons: one who left home, the so-called prodigal, and one who didn't. Both sons are important for the teaching that Jesus gives, but for the specific teaching on forgiveness and conversion it is the prodigal that we must focus upon.

This parable has been worked over extensively in scriptural and spiritual literature. We can only give a short summary here, but the parable is indeed a gem worth mining fully.

READ Lk 15:11-32.

We may note that the parable graphically depicts the plight and desperation of the younger son, who had hit rock bottom. He is starving and has no money. He is hired to feed pigs, unclean animals according to Jewish law. The pigs were fed the bitter-tasting pods from the carob tree that he would gladly have eaten but, says the story with great pathos, no one even offered him some of the swine's food. There is an old piece of rabbinical wisdom that avers, "When the Israelites are reduced to eating carob pods, they repent!" And so the stage is set for the real heart of the parable, the story of reconciliation.

The process of reconciliation has two sides to it: the willingness of the sinner to be reconciled and the willingness of the Father to receive the sinner. Both of these are beautifully illustrated in the parable.

But before we examine the process in more detail we should keep reminding ourselves of something that we have already mentioned several times in different contexts: our understanding of how God deals with us is patterned on our understanding of human relationships. Thus, our understanding of the reconciliation of the sinner with God is patterned, by analogy, on our understanding of the reconciliation of human persons who have become estranged as the result of wrongdoing on the part of one or both of them. We can easily see this process at work in Jesus' story of the prodigal son.

a) *From the point of view of the sinner*

1. The first stage in the healing of alienation is a two-step process:

    i)   recognition of brokenness, the recognition that all is not as it should be
         (recognition by the Prodigal that he had hit rock bottom);

    ii) recognition of one's own personal role in the brokenness ("but when he
         came to himself").

    We have to "come to ourselves," and that is really the heart of the matter for
    so many of us. The denial of guilt seems to be endemic in contemporary
    times, and that is very distressing. We tend to be lethargic about evil. Even
    if we recognize evil in the world, we are reluctant to see it in ourselves or to
    see how we have personally contributed to the evil in the world. We find it
    extremely difficult to admit that there is anything wrong with our lives. If
    we do admit it, we tend to blame everything but ourselves: other people,
    circumstances, health, social conditions, the economy, whatever. But we are
    not just victims of our circumstances. If we do not recognize and accept our
    guilt, accept responsibility for the state of alienation we now feel, how can
    we honestly and sincerely arrive at a decision to say we are sorry? We have
    to be sorry for something. One of the most important tasks for pastoral
    workers is to help people to come to this recognition of personal
    responsibility. They must be helped to recognize their own contribution to
    the evil that they feel exists in their own lives.

2. Recognizing and accepting our guilt implies a self-examination. When the
    young man in the parable "came to himself," he examined the situation
    brought on by his dissolute living ("Here I am dying of hunger"). He
    examined his state of sinfulness, brought himself to a full realization of what
    he had done. This, too, is a necessary and basic step in the process of
    reconciliation.

3. Accepting one's guilt and realizing what one has lost (the security and
    comfort of home, with all that that word implies) opens one's heart for
    repentance, for conversion. It opens one's heart to say "I'm sorry" ("I will
    get up and go to my father"). "Father, I have sinned against heaven and
    before you" is a clear recognition that a sin against the father is
    simultaneously a sin against God. To be forgiven by God we must ask
    forgiveness of those we have hurt.

4. The fourth stage in the process of reconciliation is the willingness to make
    up for our wrongdoing, and that requires an act of humility. It is always
    humiliating to admit that we are wrong, to admit that we are less than
    perfect. Making up for our wrongdoing most often takes the form of an
    apology, but often an apology is not enough. If we have caused material

damage, we have to make restitution. If we have damaged someone's good name, we have the obligation of doing our best to restore that good name in the eyes of those who have heard our lies or slander. Another way of looking at it is that we must try to restore some human dignity to the person we have hurt. When both parties to the process of reconciliation can come away from the event with their human dignity restored and enhanced, then the process has been a success. In the story of the prodigal son, the son plans to return to his father and say to him, "I am no longer worthy to be called your son; treat me like one of your hired hands" (Lk 15:19).It was a deep act of humility, a personal acceptance of the fact that he had wronged his father and himself; he was prepared to make up for it by working as one of his father's hired hands, thus forgoing the privileges and comfort of the household.

b) *From the point of view of the Father (God)*

In the parable, the response of the father to his returning son is particularly poignant and beautiful. It is exactly the pattern of how God treats us sinners as we seek reconciliation.

1. In the story, the father is presented as the epitome of everything we expect from one who loves. He does not wait for the son to ask forgiveness or to deliver his little prepared speech; in his joy and eagerness to greet the young man he runs to meet him, throws his arms around him and kisses him. It is a poignant and heartfelt "welcome home." When the son finally does get to say, "I have sinned . . .," the father brushes him off as though not interested in any explanations, any expressions of sorrow, so impatient is he to get on with the welcome. He does not want his son to humiliate himself or to grovel for forgiveness. This, indeed, is the ideal of how we should treat others when they ask forgiveness for having wronged us. The father's forgiveness was there long before the son had time to say, "I'm sorry"; God's forgiveness of us is not triggered by our saying we are sorry. His love is a permanent, forgiving love that is eternal; it is pure grace, pure goodness, for that is God's nature. Saying we are sorry is an admission to ourselves that we are in need of that grace. The dynamic is beautifully expressed by Robert Farrar Capon: "Confession," he says, "is not a transaction, not a negotiation in order to secure forgiveness; . . . Forgiveness surrounds us, beats upon us all our lives; we confess only to wake ourselves up to what we already have."[188]

---

[188]   Robert Farrar Capon, *The Parables of Grace* (Grand Rapids, MI: Eerdmans, 1988), p. 140.

2. The father's forgiveness, as we have said, is already there; it did not have to be triggered by the son's admission of guilt. But the parable has the father do something that is deeply symbolic, something that signals his welcome and forgiveness in an expressive and tangible way: he calls for sandals to be put on his son's feet. The young man who had done slave's work feeding swine is no longer to be considered a slave and go barefoot, as slaves did. His status as son is restored – sons wear shoes.

3. But the putting on of shoes was not enough. The young man must further be welcomed back into the family and take his rightful place in the family circle. He must be made to feel at home once again; there must be no further embarrassment among the members of the household. And so the father calls for a ring and a robe to be put on him so that everyone in the little entourage would easily be able to see and accept the return of the prodigal. Some commentators on this parable have pointed out that the father was, in fact, taking a risk. He must have known that there would be some criticism, and even anger, at his fulsome forgiveness. We all know from our own experience that there are always some people who do not forgive easily. There are always some who want miscreants to pay as much as possible for their transgressions. As it turned out, the elder son was quite angry; there may well have been others of the household who felt the same way. The father was also taking a risk that his generosity would make the younger son even more profligate when he realized how easy it was to be forgiven. Does God take the same risk with us when we are granted the same openhearted forgiveness and are welcomed back? Does the ease with which we are forgiven make it more likely that we shall sin again? It is indeed something for us to ponder, but it is also a deep revelation about the kind of person God is, and the kind of love that is poured out on us.

4. And then there is the celebration: the killing of the fattened calf, the feasting, the music, the dancing. The whole community must share this happy moment. In another parable Jesus says that this kind of joyful celebration is but a reflection of the joy that takes place in the community of heaven. "Just so, I tell you, there will be more joy in heaven over one sinner who repents than over ninety-nine righteous persons who need no repentance" (Lk 15:7).

Summary

The story encapsulates beautifully what happens when the church celebrates Reconciliation with us. A short summary is in order. In celebrating the sacrament of Reconciliation, *we sinners:*

- examine ourselves and reflect on our sinfulness;
- recognize and accept our guilt ("I know it is my fault");
- confess our sinfulness (i.e., openly say we are sorry);
- make up for our wrongdoing.

God our Father:

- embraces us and welcomes us home;
- forgives us fully;
- makes us members of the family once again;
- initiates a community celebration.

We should be able to see how the process outlined in the parable initiates the healing of the three forms of alienation that are the result of sin: alienation from oneself, alienation from the community and alienation from God. It is but another indication of how acutely conscious Jesus was of the devastating effects of sin and how much he directed his ministry toward the healing of these wounds.

The Sacrament of Reconciliation

Since Jesus' ministry to sinners and his forgiveness of sin were such an important and integral part of his whole mission on earth, it is only natural for him to arrange the continuation of this ministry in the church. In fact, it is quite clear from the New Testament that Jesus did indeed grant to his church the continuing power to reconcile sinners and forgive sin in his name (CCC 1446). It is reported in the Gospel according to Matthew, for example, that Jesus gave his apostles the power to "loose" and to "bind" in the name of God (Mt 16:19). The Gospel according to John records that shortly after the resurrection, when Jesus had appeared to the apostles, he said to them,

> *"As the Father has sent me, so I send you." When he had said this, he breathed on them and said to them, "Receive the Holy Spirit. If you forgive the sins of any, they are forgiven them; if you retain the sins of any, they are retained." (Jn 20:21-22)*

The church has faithfully carried out that commission to this very day.

A Short History of the Sacrament

Perhaps we should mention first of all that the early church, almost from the beginning, understood that participation in the Eucharist was an effective way of having one's sins forgiven (CCC 1393-1394). Participation in the Eucharist with the Christian community is in fact a participation in Christ's sacrifice on the cross offered for the forgiveness of our sins. As William Bausch puts it, the addition of the words "for the remission of sins" in the gospel accounts of the Last Supper "were meant precisely to underscore the primitive insight that the Eucharist is a real, expiatory sacrifice of atonement which causes the forgiveness of sins."[189]

In spite of this primitive insight about the expiatory nature of the Eucharist, the church first understood the forgiveness of sin as coming through the sacrament of Baptism. In his very first speech after the experience of receiving the Holy Spirit at Pentecost Peter urged the crowd, "Repent, and be baptized every one of you in the name of Jesus Christ so that your sins may be forgiven" (Acts 2:38). And so, the church has always regarded Baptism as the prime sacrament for the forgiveness of sin (CCC 985). To become a Christian in the early centuries meant a complete change of lifestyle, a complete break with the accepted culture. It was indeed a heroic act. People did not undertake such heroism lightly. It is not difficult to see why the early church expected that, once one had confessed to the Lord Jesus and had been converted and baptized, this conversion would last a lifetime.

It did not take them long, however, to realize that this was an unrealistic expectation. Some converts fell away; some betrayed the community that had accepted them and thus caused great scandal. People, therefore, still continued to sin seriously after Baptism; in particular, murder, adultery and apostasy* were considered to be very grave sins. The community's response was to exclude such public sinners from their gatherings, and particularly from participation in the Eucharist. They were excommunicated.* One could always have one's less serious sins and transgressions forgiven in the Eucharist, but the denial of one's baptismal promises, and the great scandal caused the community by public apostasy, was far too serious. The question then became this: How would the church deal with the problem? Could such persons be re-admitted to the community? Could Baptism be re-administered? And, in view of the likelihood of someone falling away again and again, how often could this be done?

The resolution of these problems, which resulted in the development of the sacrament of Penance (now called Reconciliation), took many centuries. The church's understanding of how Jesus' ministry of forgiving sins was to be applied in practice underwent a slow evolution. The sacrament was first conceived as a means of reconversion after a falling away from one's baptismal promises. It was received only once in a lifetime. Sinners confessed to a minister representing the community, usually the bishop. They had to go through a

---

[189] William J. Bausch, *A New Look at the Sacraments* (Mystic, CT: Twenty-Third Publications, 1983), p. 156.

protracted period of public penance, such as, for example, standing at church doors and asking for forgiveness and for prayers from the people entering. Today we would consider such conditions for forgiveness to be impossibly harsh. Nevertheless, they do impress on us one very important aspect of the sacrament of Reconciliation that tends to be forgotten: namely, that the church has always understood this sacrament as belonging to the *whole community*. It is the whole church that mediates God's forgiveness, and this communitarian aspect of the sacrament must be adequately signed and signified. The sinner is reconciled with God, but only by being reconciled with the whole community (CCC 1469). Reconciliation, therefore, is emphatically not a purely private matter between the sinner and God; it must be the church community that welcomes home the sinner, thus making repentance and conversion possible. It surely doesn't surprise us that many people did not use this difficult form of Reconciliation. Often enough they put off their conversion till their deathbed.

There were some local variations in the form that the sacrament of Reconciliation took but, in general, matters stumbled along for centuries until the invasion of the barbarians changed the face of Europe. Monks from Ireland were instrumental in spreading the Christian faith among the new Europeans. In time, many barbarians and their descendants accepted Christianity, thus bringing new peoples and new cultures into the church. These newcomers, it seems, did not take kindly to the accepted form of celebrating Reconciliation in the church. The Irish monks, skilled in spiritual direction, offered assurance of God's love and forgiveness for sinners. They, it seems, had grasped the theological truth that God's forgiveness is ever present and should not be limited in any arbitrary way.

As people came to the monasteries seeking forgiveness, a new rite of Reconciliation gradually developed, which we now know as private confession. The evolution was slow and difficult, with many changes and variations. Eventually, by the seventh century, what emerged was a rite that took the form of a) private confession to a priest (representing the church community), b) the imposition of an adequate penance to make up for one's sins, c) immediate reconciliation with the church without having to wait or do public penance. This form of Reconciliation was challenged and discredited by the Protestant Reformation. The reformers insisted on the adequacy of personally and privately asking God for forgiveness in the silence of one's heart and believing that one is forgiven. In response to this Protestant challenge, the Council of Trent (1545–1563) formally gave approval to the established method of celebrating Reconciliation through private confession.

The Name of the Sacrament

Until quite recently, the sacrament was most often called the sacrament of Penance (CCC 1423). The word "penance" derives from the Latin *poena*, meaning pain, or suffering. It indicates that the church has always understood that one has to make some reparation for one's sins – one has to undertake some form of self-denial to make up for the selfish indulgence of sin. Such self-denial is hurtful, painful, unpleasant, something we might rather not do, hence the word "penance." In the rite of the sacrament, the priest usually assigns some penance, that is, some prayer, some form of self-denial, as a reminder to the penitent of the need to make reparation for sin (CCC 1460, 1494). During such periods as Lent and Advent, the church has always advocated that we keep before ourselves this constant need to make reparation for sin and that the traditional means of doing this are by self-denial, prayer and almsgiving. Self-denial has always been understood as an important plank in the spiritual development of the Christian. Think of these words of Jesus: "If any want to become my followers, let them deny themselves and take up their cross and follow me" (Mk 8:34).

The sacrament also used to be known as Confession (CCC 1424), but that terminology was always a misnomer. Confession is the act by which we tell our sinfulness to another – in this case the priest. There is more to the sacrament than the mere telling of sins, as we shall see.

The preferred name today is Reconciliation. This word more accurately indicates what is really going on and what the whole purpose of the exercise is. To be reconciled means to re-establish a relationship, and that is exactly what happens. We become reconciled to God and to the whole church community; we re-establish the relationship of love that we had lost by mortal sin. God welcomes us home as the father did the prodigal in the gospel parable.

Celebrating the Sacrament

While private confession remains the norm for celebrating Reconciliation in the church today, many pastoral problems remain, such as the following:

1) The community, though represented by the priest, really has no effective part to play. Privacy, while having certain advantages, tends to preclude the joyful experience of being welcomed back by God and by the community, as was the prodigal son.

2) Another problem with private confession is that to a large degree the element of celebration is missing. Private confession can sometimes be sombre and joyless.

3) The fact that it is so easily available may tend to make it routine and mechanical. Presently the church is experimenting with different forms of reconciliation, such as communal Reconciliation services, which aim at overcoming these difficulties.

Since Reconciliation is a sacrament, four things are required for its celebration.

1. *The specially designated (i.e., ordained) minister* (CCC 1456, 1461, 1495). The minister represents God and the church, the two parties that are essential for reconciliation. Only God can forgive sin; therefore, the minister is only God's instrument. When we confess, we confess to God, not merely to the priest. Likewise, the church community must take part in the act of forgiveness. All sin, as we have said in an earlier chapter, affects the whole community because we are a covenanted people. There is no such thing as a purely private sin. In private confession the minister acts on behalf of the community; the minister is the church's representative who offers forgiveness in the name of God and of the community.

2. *The external sign.* All sacraments, in accordance with the principle of sacramentality, are celebrated in an external, sense-perceptible way. Sacraments are external signs. In the sacrament of Reconciliation, the sign is twofold:

    a) the active confession, or telling of sins and sinfulness, and the asking for forgiveness;

    b) the signing of forgiveness by the minister in the name of God and of the whole community.

    All of this must be done in a sense-perceptible way: for example, by words, gestures or writing. The signing of forgiveness and the communitarian nature of the sacrament are beautifully expressed in the words of absolution pronounced by the priest over the penitent:

    God, the Father of mercies, through the death and resurrection of his son Our Lord Jesus Christ, has sent the Holy Spirit into the world for the forgiveness of sin. Through the ministry of his church may God grant you pardon and peace. And I absolve you from your sins in the name of the Father, and of the Son, and of the Holy Spirit.

3. *The penance.* The priest usually assigns a penance, as has already been noted. The penance should come out of the sin itself and be appropriate to it (CCC 1460). Very often it is difficult to do this and so the priest just assigns some prayers, or perhaps some penitential exercise such as making the stations of the cross. Now it should be obvious that saying some small prayers is not going to make up for our sins. So what is the purpose of the small penance? First, it is a reminder that we should do penance. Self-denial and penance are lifelong duties for we are all sinners, but, lazy and selfish as we are, we need to be constantly reminded of this duty, and reminded in a tangible way. Secondly, the penance is a sign to God, and to ourselves, that we are indeed sincere in our expression of sorrow and determined to change our life.

4. *Amendment.* It is taken for granted that we will do our best to change or
   amend our life – to turn from our sinful ways – to be truly converted. If I
   apologize to someone for some wrongdoing, the apology must include the
   implicit promise to cease and desist from similar occurrences in the future;
   otherwise, my apology is hardly sincere. If this is the ordinary way we
   behave towards other human persons, then we should do no less with God.
   Of course, we may know very well from past experience that bad habits die
   hard, that despite our promise of amendment we may well do the same thing
   again. Indeed, it is one of the strengths of private confession that it takes
   account of this propensity to recidivism and allows us to seek God's mercy
   and pardon again and again. Nevertheless, on each occasion that we ask
   forgiveness we must be sincere in trying to reform.

Why Confess to a Priest?

For many, this is a burning question. Most people find confession a humili-
ating experience. Opening the less pleasant side of one's character to another
person is difficult. Most of us would rather not have to do it. Why can't we just
ask God for forgiveness in the privacy of our mind and heart? After all, it is not
the priest who forgives but God, and God knows each one's conscience intimately. Many Christian denominations, after all, do not have any formal ritual
for the forgiveness of sin; why can't Catholics be like them?

First, let us note that we should always ask God for forgiveness in our mind
and heart and promise to mend our ways. We do this as an essential aspect of our
preparation for the sacrament of Reconciliation. When we do this we are indeed
forgiven, immediately, unreservedly. God's forgiveness, as we have pointed out,
is never lacking. Why, then, do we need to confess to a priest?

We offer four reasons:

1. When we sin, we sin against the whole community. There is no such thing as
   a purely private sin. Every sin has social consequences. We are not purely
   private individuals; we are a covenanted community, and that is how God
   deals with us. The community, therefore, must take part in the forgiveness;
   it does this through its representative, the ordained minister. Reconciliation
   belongs to the church.

2. Reconciliation is a sacrament. Sacraments are sense-perceptible, outward
   signs of God's grace. Roman Catholics are a sacramental people who
   believe that God comes to them in and through the created sense-perceptible
   universe. We are body-persons, not disembodied spirits. Reconciliation is
   offered to the *whole* person, and therefore it must be signed in a sense-
   perceptible way, which necessarily includes the body. We have already
   pointed out above how this takes place in the rite of the sacrament.

3. When our forgiveness is outwardly signed (spoken by the priest), we know with certainty that we are forgiven. God speaks forgiveness through the priest. We experience it more intensely because it comes to us in sense-perceptible form and not merely in our mind or our imagination, as it would if we spoke to God only in the privacy of our own prayer.

4. From a purely human psychological point of view, unburdening oneself to someone is a tried and true therapeutic formula. Organizations such as Alcoholics Anonymous have recognized the therapeutic value of opening up one's personal weakness to another human being. Commenting on Step 5 in the AA process, the manual says, "Somehow, being alone with God doesn't seem as embarrassing as facing another person. . . . When we are honest with another person, it confirms that we have been honest with ourselves and with God."

Lee Iacocca, the brilliant automobile executive who rescued the Chrysler Corporation from bankruptcy in the late 1970s, mentions in his autobiography how misunderstood this sacrament is. Though it took him a while, he came to realize that the regular examination of conscience, the distinguishing of right from wrong preparatory to celebrating the sacrament of Reconciliation, was the best therapy he ever had.[190] Being honest with oneself about one's transgressions and speaking to another about them brings with it a true sense of freedom and peace. The priest is trained to listen, to give advice and help.

Sins and Sinfulness

In celebrating the sacrament of Reconciliation, many people use what might be called the "shopping list" approach. They make up a list of all the sinful acts they can remember and the number of times they have done them. Apart from everything else, that approach may well put an unnecessary burden on the memory. Instead of being a pleasant, even joyful experience, celebrating the sacrament can thus become a sweaty worry.

As we pointed out in the chapter on sin, there is a difference between "sins" and "sinfulness." What we should tackle is our sinfulness. Instead of burdening ourselves trying to remember each and every sinful act, what we should be looking for are trends in our life – trends such as growing selfishness, more and more frequent lying, a tendency to bitterness and criticism, using others for our own purposes, and so on. Sinful acts point us in the direction of the life-trends that alienate us from God. For example, the question is not so much whether I break the sixth commandment by going to bed with someone to whom I am not married. Rather, some of the questions to ask are these: What does this say about

---

[190]   Lee Iacocca, *Iacocca: An Autobiography* (New York: Bantam Books, 1984), p. 8.

my attitude toward God and toward others? Am I simply using someone, or are we using one another, to satisfy a selfish pleasure with little or no love or commitment and little regard for the consequences? Does such an act make me a more caring or a more selfish person? What does it say about my attitude towards God's love for me?

In the process of seeking reconciliation with God there is much room for selfish deception. Rather than just saying "I broke the sixth commandment," the above questions will help us to probe far more deeply into the real causes of our infidelity and get to the bottom of assessing our sinfulness and our relationship with God. Ultimately, sin is a state of mind that prevents me from arranging my life in response to God's love for me. Sin has more to do with how I arrange my life than with keeping score of the number of times I do this or that.

How Often?

How often should we celebrate the sacrament of Reconciliation? The short answer is, as often as we feel the need for a re-orientation in our life. In a sense, we can compare the human psyche to a machine. To keep machines in good working order they need regular checkups. If we wait for a major breakdown to occur, the cost of repairs is higher and more traumatic. If we do not make a regular practice of examining our conscience, of periodically reviewing our life, we might easily slip into not doing it at all.

There is no obligation to seek reconciliation in the sacrament unless we are conscious of mortal sin – sin that completely separates us from God. As we have already mentioned, there are other ways of having our sinfulness forgiven, such as participation in the Eucharist. But, since we have this unerring capacity for deceiving ourselves, we should seek reconciliation at regular intervals. The grace of the sacrament is precisely the grace that will help us to be more sensitive to our failings and help us avoid the occasions of sin.

Conclusion

In the popular movie *Love Story*, one of the characters offered this piece of advice: "Love means never having to say you're sorry." Now surely this statement cannot be ranked as one of the shining examples of moral philosophy! In fact, it is nothing more than a slogan that stirs the emotions but is very far from the truth and is removed from real life. The truth is that love frequently requires us to say we are sorry. In fact, saying we are sorry is a strong indication that we love someone enough to be genuinely disturbed over our hurtful behaviour. The sacrament of Reconciliation gives us an opportunity to do just that. Properly celebrated, the sacrament of Reconciliation can make an important contribution to our development as persons and to the enhancement of our love relationship with God. Let us make use of it.

Reflection Questions

1. What is the meaning of penance? The church teaches that doing penance must be an integral part of every Christian life. Why?

2. As we examine our conscience in preparation for the sacrament of Reconciliation, what are the principal things we should pay attention to?

3. Distinguish between sins and sinfulness. Why was the older brother in the parable of the Prodigal Son probably more at fault than the one who left home?

4. How would you attempt to convince a Protestant friend of the advantages of confessing one's sins to a priest?

5. Why must the church community be part of the reconciliation process?

6. What does it mean to say that sin alienates us from ourselves?

Further Reading

Bausch, William. *A New Look at the Sacraments* (Mystic, CT: Twenty-Third Publications, 1983). A standard reference work on the sacraments that is non-technical and written for the educated lay person. Full of fresh insights, it provides practical applications to the Christian life.

Cooke, Bernard. *Reconciled Sinners* (Mystic, CT: Twenty-Third Publications, 1986). A concise and simple treatment of the whole process of reconciliation in which the author centres the discussion of sin and reconciliation in the context of human behaviour and attitudes. Cooke's other book, *Sacraments and Sacramentality*, has already been recommended.

Perkins, Pheme. *Hearing the Parables of Jesus* (New York: Paulist Press, 1981). A particularly brilliant treatment of the parables. More than useful as background reading for the parable of the Prodigal Son.

21

SOCIAL JUSTICE

Action on behalf of justice and participation in the transformation of the world fully appear to us as a constitutive dimension of the preaching of the gospel or, in other words, the church's mission of the redemption of the human race and its liberation from every oppressive situation.[191]

These words of the church's bishops gathered in synod in Rome, 1971, sharply remind us that if we are sincerely to call ourselves Christian and followers of Jesus Christ, we have a serious obligation to work for justice in the world. Work for justice, therefore, is not an option; it is an integral part of the practice of our faith. As we pointed out in Chapter 2, there are three major aspects to the active expression of our faith: believing, trusting and doing. The "doing" of our faith means carrying on Jesus' work in the world, in the effort to establish the kingdom of God. The kingdom of God is a kingdom of peace and justice, which means that we must become peacemakers and promoters of justice in the world. "Blessed are those who hunger and thirst for righteousness, for they will be filled," said Jesus; "Blessed are the peacemakers, for they will be called children of God" (Mt 5:2-11). But first, what is justice?

Justice

Justice is the virtue by which we respect the inherent rights of others and render to them and to God what is their due in fairness and uprightness (CCC 1807). Sacred scripture makes a strong connection between God's justice and the steadfast love and faithfulness that we expect from God. God's justice is an expression of God's love for us (see Micah 7:8-20). In the same way our justice towards others should be an expression of our love for them. Faith is never a purely private matter between an individual and God; it has clear social implications. In being just and promoting justice, we are carrying out Jesus' commission to us: "Love one another as I have loved you." We are "doing" our faith.

Justice and Charity

Because justice has so much to do with love, many people confuse it with charity. The word "charity" is derived from the Latin *caritas*, which is the word

---

[191] Introduction to *Justice in the World*, a document produced by the 1971 Synod of Bishops in Rome.

used in scripture to designate the love that Christians give one another. Charity is the virtue by which we put into practice the command of Jesus that we should love one another. Part of this commandment involves our acting justly towards others; consequently, charity and justice are closely bound together. However, the word charity has assumed a related meaning in our present society. According to the dictionary it can mean "a kindly liberality and helpfulness, especially toward the needy and suffering" and "aid given to those in need" – alms to the poor. Appeals for the poor are often made in the name of "charity." This makes some people think that when they give alms to the poor, or when they act with a kindly liberality and helpfulness, they are satisfying their obligation in justice. Far from it. Justice means respecting someone's rights: the right to life, liberty, and all the other human rights. Charity, in the sense outlined above, means giving of our surplus; it means doing for others over and above what is a person's strict right, which may or may not help to promote justice.

Justice is concerned with human rights, but human rights are never absolute; they are always relative to the rights of others. I cannot express my right to free speech if it means that I will cause injustice to another person. I cannot practise my right to commerce and trade if it means that I exploit my workers. Looking out for others is the most radical demand of the gospel; we must truly love one another. True love may demand that I sometimes give up my strict rights in favour of another. True love always demands personal sacrifice. Only when this imperative of love for one another is recognized and practised can the whole human community progress and prosper.

Justice and Equality

It is sometimes said that justice demands that everyone should be absolutely equal, particularly in the economic sense, but this is a misunderstanding of the meaning of justice. Justice does not mean absolute equality; what it means is equality of opportunity. Everyone should have the opportunity to develop their human talents, which means the rich should not have greater opportunity than the poor. We must make every effort to redress this kind of inequality in society. (What we are putting forward here is an ideal. In practice, giving everyone equality of opportunity may well depend on the general health of the economy of a country.) Nevertheless, no matter how much we try to give everyone the same opportunity to develop their talents, some people may waste their opportunity and that will give rise to a de facto inequality in society. Furthermore, it is clear from experience that we are not all created equal in talent or ability. Society tends to reward those with more talent, whether these rewards are in the material sphere (such as higher salaries) or in the spiritual and moral sphere (such as high esteem of one's peers). This type of "inequality" tends to be accepted as appropriate. We may grumble at the enormous sums of money paid to athletes or entertainers, but still we seem prepared to pay the price to see them perform! We rejoice at the adulation and prestige given to Nobel Prize winners even though we know that such achievement is beyond our abilities.

Social Justice

Justice extends beyond the rights of the individual. It also must be social in its application. We do not live as individuals only – we are social beings. The reality of our interdependence is every bit as important as the reality of our independence. We agree to regulate our social life by systems, structures and institutions. These systems and structures (for example, the capitalist or communist system, or the structures set in place by governments) are sometimes unjust in their application and practice; rather than promoting the good of people they may well be instruments of oppression. Justice must be social also; it must apply to the systems, structures and institutions by which society is regulated. This kind of justice we call "social" justice.

Let us now take a look at the church's stand on social justice.

The Church and Social Justice

Particularly in the present century, it is probably safe to say that the Catholic church's manifest concern with social justice issues is unmatched. From the time of Pope Leo XIII (1878–1903) to the present Pope, there has been a steady stream of teaching on the topic of social justice, the documents of which would now fill a very large volume. The church has addressed itself with vigour to matters of the political and social order that impinge on the rights of peoples. The church has a vision of the divine destiny of all people in accordance with gospel teaching and hence has no option but to promote all aspects of justice. Michael Ryan expresses it well:

> The church now sees that the social order is a dimension of the human person and, therefore, that the environment itself falls under the gospel judgment. Its mission of redemption, therefore, extends both to individuals and social structures. The Church has a vision of the human person, and of what the human person is called to be. Since the person is a social being, that vision necessarily has social consequences.[192]

Many people have criticized the church for "meddling in matters that do not concern it." Many people believe that the Pope and bishops have no business making pronouncements on political and social matters and that they should stick to promoting the spiritual good of people. But our God is a God of life and human history. The kingdom of God on earth has to do with improving the

---

[192] Michael T. Ryan, *Solidarity: Christian Social Teaching and Canadian Society* (London, ON: Guided Study Programs in the Catholic Faith, 1990), p. 17.

quality of human life and the alleviation of human suffering, as Jesus did during his public ministry. Issues concerning the improvement of human life and the alleviation of suffering are moral issues, not merely economic issues. Morality has to do with the principles and values that regulate our dealings with each other in society. The church has a right and duty to speak out on such issues. "To the Church belongs the right always and everywhere to announce moral principles, including those pertaining to the social order, and to make judgments on any human affairs to the extent that they are required by the fundamental rights of the human person or the salvation of souls" (CCC 2032). To say that the church should stick to spiritual matters is to interpret spirituality in a narrow or disconnected way. We can only develop spiritually within the context of our social life and our interaction with others. One of the classic errors of modern thinking is to assert that spiritual development is purely a private matter between the individual and God. On the contrary, everything that impinges on the social development of peoples (psychological, cultural and economic) impinges on their relationship with God. This is simply an admission of who we are as a people redeemed by Christ, and into whose life God has entered in a most intimate fashion through the incarnation of Jesus. It is also an acceptance of our destiny to be with God for all eternity; this is the point and purpose of all human life. God must be integral to every aspect of our life; "The moral life is spiritual worship" (CCC 2031).

We should note, however, that the church does not attempt to offer practical and concrete solutions to all problems related to social justice. The church does not have a specific political, economic and social program that will apply across the board to all peoples for all times. To quote the document *Justice in the World* again, "Of itself it does not belong to the Church . . . to offer concrete solutions in the social, economic, and political spheres for justice in the world." The church recognizes that different peoples will have to develop their own social and political systems to suit their own needs, provided that such programs conform to the general principles of social justice.

Church Teaching on Social Justice

We shall now develop the major principles of the church's social teaching under five headings:[193]

1.   The nature of the human person

2.   The social character of sin

---

[193]   In the schema that follows the author is deeply indebted to Professor Lee Cormie of the University of St. Michael's College, Toronto, for sharing some of his unpublished material on the subject.

3. Liberation from oppression

4. Preferential option for the poor

5. Priority of labour over capital

1. The Nature of the Human Person

Church teaching takes an unashamedly theological view of what it means to be human. The view that comes out of Christian faith is that we are destined to an eternity with God, and that Jesus Christ has infinitely ennobled and dignified human nature by becoming one of us. In a real sense, therefore, we are all taken up into Christ, we all share in the Incarnation (CCC 460). Adopting this incarnational perspective means that we must view persons not merely as economic entities but as having spiritual, psychological, cultural and social needs, if they are to develop as true human beings. Human nature is social – we are created into a society by which we are nourished materially, spiritually, culturally. Our human personalities are shaped by our interrelatedness in community. Community relationships are integral to our proper development as human persons (CCC 1879-1880). The Vatican II document on the Church in the Modern World puts forward a theological rationale for this:

> God . . . desired that all men and women should form one family and deal with each other as brothers and sisters. All, in fact, are destined to the very same end, namely God himself, since they have been created in the likeness of God.[194]

But then the document further spells out this human interrelatedness in more sociological terms:

> The fact that human beings are social by nature indicates that the betterment of the person and the improvement of society depend on each other. Insofar as humanity by its very nature stands completely in need of life in society, it is and it ought to be the beginning, the subject and the object of every social organization.[195]

What follows from all this is that true human development must take account of the whole person: spiritual, moral, economic. It is the duty of all, particularly of the institutions that regulate our life (such as the government), to promote such integral development. "Development," says Pope Paul VI, "cannot be limited to mere economic growth. In order to be authentic, it must be complete – integral; that is, it has to promote the good of every person and of the whole person."[196] Therefore, the success of the social systems that we institute to

---

[194] *Pastoral Constitution on the Church in the Modern World*, No. 24.

[195] *Ibid.*, No. 25.

[196] Encyclical letter *Populorum progressio*, No. 14.

help human development must be judged not only by whether they promote material and economic development but by whether they are of benefit to persons, whether or not they promote human dignity and true spiritual and moral growth.

Clearly, if we take this broad view of the factors that contribute to human development, as we must, we can broaden the scope of our definition of injustice. For example, it is not only unjust to crush people economically, to keep people poor, to curtail their opportunities for personal development; it is also unjust to deprive them of the right to practise their religion, and it is unjust to support a moral climate that acts against true human development (such as the promotion of abortion). If we are to promote true social justice, then we must react against any injustice of this kind.

2. The Social Character of Sin

A second important element in the teaching of the church on social justice is the recognition of the social character of sin. As was pointed out above, we are social beings and we regulate our lives in society by various structures and institutions. It is these very institutions and structures that are sinful, for they often perpetrate injustice by inhibiting integral human development. It is true that sin is always personal – sin always begins in the hearts and minds of individuals as egotistical selfishness and greedy ambition that lead to evil by disregard for the good of others. But this personal sinfulness creeps into the very systems that we set up in society. These systems become impregnated with the evil values of materialism and greed. It is this that we call social sin. Thus, the structures that regulate trade and commerce (such as the system by which food is produced and distributed, or gambling on the commodities market) often have the effect of promoting poverty among peoples, thus hindering their integral human growth. These structures are sinful. Pope Paul VI dramatically brought this to the attention of the world in his 1967 encyclical letter *Populorum progressio* (The Progress of Peoples):

> Today, no one can be ignorant any longer of the fact that in whole continents countless men and women are ravished by hunger, countless numbers of children are undernourished, so that many of them die in infancy, while the physical growth and mental development of many others are retarded and as a result whole regions are condemned to the most depressing despondency.[197]

The people who promote such structures, which make the rich richer and poor poorer, and who operate within them, are not only cooperating in sin, but also promoting sin even at a personal level. This fact was already recognized in

---

[197] *Populorum progressio*, No. 45.

Vatican II. The Pastoral Constitution on the Church in the Modern World says this: "Whenever they [men and women] are confronted with an environment where the effects of sin are to be found, they are exposed to further inducements to sin." (No. 25). Lee Cormie comments: "Sinful structures reflect the past sins of those who established them and promote further sins in the present by undermining the dignity and well-being of whole classes of people."[198]

In order to redress the evil and correct the injustices, we must reform the system; we must get at the causes of injustice. Such action may well mean attacking systems that are presently considered basic to human freedom: for example, the free enterprise system. But the very systems that have made the countries of the Northern Hemisphere prosperous are the ones that have made others dependent and poor. Social justice will always be a struggle because those who are rich will fight vigorously to keep what they have.

3. Liberation from Injustice

The result of social sin is that people are oppressed and their full human development is curtailed. Church teaching clearly indicates that it is the duty of all to work for the elimination of such oppression. This is what we mean by liberation. The teaching on liberation is certainly in keeping with the message of the Bible given particularly through the prophets (see Chapter 9). Economic and other forms of oppression were already well established in biblical times. The need to react against such oppression and redress the evil it causes is explicitly stated in God's revelation to us through the prophets.

But we have to understand the meaning of this word "oppression." In modern times its meaning has been much broadened and yet weakened. To claim that one is "oppressed" is often an easy way out of dealing with life's problems. Adopting the martyr complex, frequently claiming that one is a "victim," is disingenuous, to say the least, and may well mask a certain laziness or a certain defect of character – an unwillingness to take control of one's life. The word "oppression" should be applied only to those who have no power to react. There are many factors that may give rise to the inability to react to oppressive situations: (a) fear (as in the case of many innocent people caught up in the throes of war, or fear of the authorities – secret police and death squads); (b) grinding poverty, when all one's energies are channelled into the struggle to survive (characteristic of much of the world's population); (c) lack of education, whereby one is not even able to recognize one's state of oppression (as is the case for ordinary people in many South American countries); (d) sheer despondency at the perceived uselessness of "fighting City Hall."

---

[198] Lee Cormie, *Elements in Contemporary Catholic Social Teaching.* Unpublished manuscript.

True liberation in the social justice sense means empowering people to manage their own affairs, to take control of their lives. Such empowerment may come through the elimination of abject poverty; through promoting proper education; through reforming oppressive bureaucratic structures in society (for example, giving workers representation on boards of management); or through all of these things. As has been said, the church does not attempt to give a detailed plan that will suit every case. Rather, the church points out the general principles on which liberation should be based and urges the implementation of these principles.

4. Preferential Option for the Poor

Whenever this aspect of the church's social teaching is discussed, this question inevitably arises: "What do you mean by 'poor?'" Who, or what, are the poor? In the purely material sense poverty, of course, is relative. People who are declared poor in North America are, by the standards of other nations, extraordinarily wealthy. While lack of material wealth is certainly an aspect of poverty, it is by no means the whole story. If we search the Old Testament, we find that the term "the poor" refers not only to those who are economically deprived but also to those whose social status is low and who therefore are often treated unjustly. They have no "clout," they are not listened to and are often exploited by the unscrupulous.

The Scriptures also make it very clear that God has a special care for such people. The God of the Hebrews, our God, was first revealed among the oppressed slaves of Egypt. In Jesus Christ this God became incarnated as one of us. Jesus grew up in the despised and forgotten village of Nazareth ("Can anything good come out of Nazareth?" – Jn 1:46). He refused to use the weapons of glory and power to impress the people with his message (Mt 4:5-10). And from the very outset he identified himself with the sinners, the outcasts of society, with the children and with the "little" people who had no voice in society.

What do we mean, then, by a "preferential option" for the poor? Donal Dorr, in his excellent book *Option for the Poor*, seems to hit the nail on the head. "I would want to insist," he says, "that the choice in question is not essentially an act of private asceticism or even face-to-face compassion for a poor person. It is specifically a response at the level of the wider society as a whole, a response to the unjust ordering of society."[199] He then goes on to point out that the established structures of the society in which we live tend to perpetuate injustice in the

---

[199] Donal Dorr, *Option for the Poor: A Hundred Years of Vatican Social Teaching* (Maryknoll, NY: Orbis Books, 1983), p. 3.

form of the continued dominance of the rich over the poor. These structures are most often administered and applied by middle-class bureaucrats who, probably without any ill will, find it difficult to think in terms of the poor. This can also be said of some of the services administered by the church itself. If we are to take seriously this option for the poor, then we must disassociate ourselves from being more identified with those at the "top" of society. Identification with the poor means looking at things from their point of view. "The preferential option for the poor means that the first task in confronting issues of development is to listen to the poor and unemployed, to get their perspective on the issues and options, and to include them in the decision-making process."[200] In any decisions made by governments or other agencies that affect the structure of society, the needs and concerns of the poor must take precedence over the needs of the rich and powerful. It is abundantly clear that in our society it is the rich who influence political and social decisions for their own benefit by their large financial contributions to political parties.

Identifying ourselves with the poor does not mean that we have to adopt a lifestyle of material poverty, though, for some people, it may (as is the case with the members of many religious orders). What it should mean is that we try to simplify our lifestyle, and get rid of the excess and clutter of material goods that constantly seem to pile up and are often unnecessary for a good and generous life. It also means that we can never be condescending towards the poor but should try to understand things from their point of view.

5. Priority of Labour over Capital

A key document of church teaching on this matter is the encyclical letter On Human Work (*Laborem exercens*), by Pope John Paul II. The Pope repeats aspects of Catholic social teaching mentioned above: namely, that our personalities and our human growth are influenced and shaped by the material and social environment in which we live. In fact, he says, even our spiritual development is so affected.

Whatever factors (such as social systems and structures) dominate that social environment profoundly affect our personal development. One of the major factors contributing to our spiritual and personal development is work, and therefore the conditions in which we work. "Human work," says the Pope, "is a key, probably the essential key, to the whole social question." Often it is by the type of work in which people are engaged that they define themselves socially and personally and by which, as the Pope says, they become human. The Pope also stresses the importance of work as a means of subsistence, and

---

[200]   Lee Cormie, op. cit.

therefore the basis on which people can start families and contribute to the continuance and growth of human society.

From these general principles follow some important practical considerations:

1. The rights and human dignity of the worker take precedence over the work itself. Put another way, this means that labour takes precedence over capital. The well-being of the workers and their families must take precedence over the consideration to maximize profits. There is a delicate balance to be observed here. Without profits there is no capital investment; without capital investment there is little or no work. Labour and capital must work together for the benefit of both. But the human dignity of the workers must not be sacrificed to greedy investors bent on squeezing every ounce of profit they can out of the business.

2. Since work is so important for human development, it follows that everyone should have the right to a job. In the words of Lee Cormie, "Strategies which promote full employment have a priority." In addition, this means that "workers and local community people should participate in the decision-making process concerning economic development strategies," and that therefore "strategies which promote co-operation and democratic decision-making have a priority."[201]

Monitum

Many people have pointed out that the church's documents on social justice seem to concentrate on condemning the evils of the free enterprise capitalist system of economics. To a large extent this is true, because that system presently dominates world economics and has given rise to several abuses. But the fact that the church condemns such abuses does not mean that the church endorses socialism or communism, which are the opposite of capitalism. These systems are fraught with their own kinds of evil: limits on human freedom, totalitarianism, poor economic performance leading to reduced human development. The church speaks out against these evils also. The main concern of all the church's teaching is the preservation of the integrity of the human person and the fostering of a climate of work in which the human person can live and develop in dignity.

A final word. Armchair quarterbacks should beware of proposing simplistic solutions to immensely complicated social and economic problems. Our society is too full of modern-day Robin Hoods who suggest that we take from the rich to give to the poor – a nice, neat, easy-to-understand way of redressing the evils in society. Over-simplified solutions, particularly when given to our young people,

---

[201] Lee Cormie, op. cit.

who do not have the experience or the knowledge to make the necessary distinctions and evaluations, can cause serious harm.

Some Particular Cases

Since it is impossible to list and discuss all the particular cases of injustice in the world, we have chosen a few that seem to have particular relevance in society today.

Justice for the Races

> All men and women are endowed with a rational soul and are created in God's image; they have the same nature and origin and, being redeemed by Christ, they enjoy the same divine calling and destiny; there is here a basic equality between all and it must be accorded ever greater recognition.

Thus does Vatican Council II (Pastoral Constitution on the Church in the Modern World, No. 29) call attention to the basic equality before God of all peoples (see also CCC 1934-1935). Racism sins against this desire of the Creator, for it establishes distinctions and inequalities among the various races of the earth. In many societies today, racism is an undeniable and odious fact of life. No matter how much we may protest our openness, most of us, if we dig deep enough into our consciousness, will find there some racist attitudes. We find it difficult to adjust to people who are different from us, particularly if that difference is one of race. Racism has led to injustices of all kinds, even to such horrible crimes as genocide and ethnic cleansing.

Hard as it may be, we must convince ourselves that the fact that we are different does not mean that we are better. God created us all human, all destined for the same eternal glory, and that is the only basis on which to deal with one another. Therefore, before accusing others of racism let us honestly examine our own attitudes and pray for healing.

Justice for the Sexes

> For in Christ Jesus you are all children of God through faith. As many of you as were baptized into Christ have clothed yourselves with Christ. There is no longer Jew or Greek, there is no longer slave or free, there is no longer male and female; for all of you are one in Christ Jesus. (Gal 3:26-28)

God created the human race male and female but, as St. Paul points out, we are all "one in Christ Jesus."[202] While sexual differences remain, therefore, there should be no inequality. Statistics show us how far we have drifted from this ideal in modern society. In most parts of the world, including our own, cases in which men are discriminated against in favour of women are comparatively rare;

---

[202] The Catechism deals with this issue extensively; see CCC 355, 369-373, 1605, 2333.

women have borne the brunt of sexual discrimination. Economically, women are far more likely to be living below the poverty line than men. While we are making progress in this area, in many cases women's salaries for equally demanding work are still not commensurate with those of men. Women hold fewer positions of authority than men, particularly in the business world. Commercial enterprises use women as sex objects to sell products rather than treating them as persons. Because they are physically weaker than men, women are far more likely to suffer abuses of various kinds of power; their human dignity is belittled; they are mistreated, beaten, raped. In our male-dominated society, everything seems to point to the fact that women are inferior. It is a sad fact that even the Catholic church cannot escape criticism on this question.

It is our duty as Christians to deplore the sin and redress the evil.

War between the sexes will do nothing to advance our society and contribute to human development. First, we must examine openly and honestly our own attitude towards equality among the sexes and tackle our own faults in this area with courage. Second, if we want to know how to act to establish justice among the sexes, we should read the gospels. Particularly regarding discrimination against women, an excellent practical exercise for us to undertake would be to collect from the gospels all those passages in which Jesus has dealings with women. We shall find there attention to women's needs, an upholding of women's dignity and their place in society, compassion, understanding, and forgiveness.[203]

> *So God created humankind in his image, in the image of God he created them; male and female he created them. . . . God saw everything that he had made, and indeed, it was very good. (Gen 1:27, 31)*

Justice for the Unborn

Of all human rights, the right to life is surely the most basic, for it is the condition for all the others. Yet it is this very right that seems to reveal a dreadful split in our society. On the one hand, we are prepared even to go to war to protect the right to life; many countries have banned the death penalty for criminals; our medical services become more and more sophisticated with every passing year to protect our health and prolong our life. Yet, on the other hand, we seem to be moving more and more towards a "pro-death" stance. Our laws allow the killing of the unborn; assisted suicide is a new and burgeoning issue; caring for our aging population is eating away at our medical dollars – can euthanasia be far away? At one end of the corridor our doctors are assisting mothers to give birth, while at the other end of the corridor they are destroying the unborn.

---

[203] An important document on the role of women in the church is the apostolic letter *Mulieris dignitatem* by Pope John Paul II, 1995.

The basic question is this: what value do we put on the human fetus? If we see it as merely a pile of cells, then we need have no qualms about removing it as an inconvenience and a hazard, much as we might remove a wart. If, however, we understand the fetus to be human – in the subtle words of Pope Paul VI, "a person in the act of becoming" – then we must protect it and give it the right to be born no matter what inconvenience it causes. The fetus' right to life does not cede to the right to health, or life, of the mother or of anyone else. The church's stand is quite clearly expressed in the 1974 Declaration on Procured Abortion.

> Any discrimination based on the various stages of life is no more justified than any other discrimination. The right to life remains complete in an old person, even one greatly weakened. In reality, respect for human life is called for from the time the process begins. From the time the ovum is fertilized, a new life is begun which is neither that of the father nor of the mother; it is rather the life of a new human being with its own growth. It would never be made human if it were not human already.

The measure of the moral fibre of a society is always how it treats its weak and helpless members, of whom the unborn form a more than significant part. They are helpless; they cannot act for themselves, but they still have a right to justice, the justice that the Bible demands for the poor and oppressed, to whom Jesus devoted so much of his ministry.

While we cannot condone abortion, there is little use deploring it with great wringing of hands if we do nothing about it. We must work against the causes of the killing of the unborn. One such cause is lack of education as to the true value of the human fetus and as to its life independent of the mother, and a lack of education about the true purpose and proper use of human sexuality.

> Our society has tried to ignore the connection between love-making and life-making, and has come to treat fertility as a disease. Instead, we need to see this connection as necessary, natural and beautiful. The responsible expression of sexuality respects this fact and appreciates that all our actions have consequences.[204]

Also, removing the fetus is a violent solution to what for some is a profound human problem. We must try to convince people that non-violent solutions are always to be preferred. Mahatma Ghandi and Martin Luther King are great modern examples of a non-violent approach to pressing social problems. They realized fully that violence rarely solves anything. Another cause is poverty and, in some countries, the profound devaluation of female children. We must make every effort to ensure that our society will provide alternatives to abortion, such

---

[204]   Catholic Office of Religious Education, Archdiocese of Toronto, *Social Justice: 1981-1991*, (Toronto, 1990), p. 44.

as support services for unwed mothers (for example, Birthright, started in Toronto in 1968 by Louise Summerhill), grants for children, shelters for the abused and unwanted.

Conclusion

Work for social justice is an integral part of establishing the kingdom of God on earth. It is an integral part of preaching the gospel; it is to follow in the footsteps of Jesus. The kingdom of God is a kingdom of justice and peace. Our challenge as Christians is to look to the needs of those who "hunger and thirst for justice" and to be peacemakers. For some, this call of the gospel may well mean a whole life devoted to social justice causes. But while we are not all called to such dedicated service, social justice means that at a personal level we all should be just in our dealings with one another. It means respecting life and the dignity of everyone from conception to the grave; it means forgiving and asking for forgiveness; it means espousing the cause of non-violence and never condoning violence as a way of solving human problems; it means working for the elimination of oppression; it means combatting discrimination and the belittling of people because of their race or sex; it means taking to heart and working to solve the problems of the poor; it means being a peacemaker in one's own little circle; it means praying for world peace.

It seems fitting to close this chapter by quoting the prayer attributed to St. Francis of Assisi that so beautifully expresses so many of the things we have been dealing with.

Lord, make me an instrument of your peace:
>   where there is hatred, let me sow love;
>   where there is injury, pardon;
>   where there is doubt, faith;
>   where there is despair, hope;
>   where there is darkness, light;
>   where there is sadness, joy.

O, Divine Master, that I may not so much seek
>   to be consoled as to console,
>   to be understood as to understand,
>   to be loved as to love.

For it is in giving that we receive,
>   it is in pardoning that we are pardoned,
>   it is in dying that we are born to eternal life.

Reflection Questions

1. What is justice? How would you distinguish it from charity?
2. What is meant by social justice?
3. From the five major aspects of church teaching on social justice, select the one most relevant to you at the present time and explain how you would act on it.
4. What is meant by "preferential option for the poor"?
5. Who, or what, are the "oppressed" of the world? Do you consider yourself oppressed in any way? Explain.
6. Someone says to you that the obvious way to solve social problems is to take from the rich and give to the poor. How do you reply?

Further Reading

Catholic Office of Religious Education, Archdiocese of Toronto. *Social Justice: 1881-1991* (Toronto, 1990). An easy-to-read, well-presented treatment of a century of Catholic social teaching. Highly recommended for beginners.

Dorr, Donal. *Option for the Poor: A Hundred Years of Social Teaching*, rev ed., (Dublin: Gill and Macmillan, 1992). An excellent single-volume survey and discussion of church teaching on social justice. Dorr traces the historical development of the teaching and shows the evolution of church thinking on this matter over the years.

Selected Church Documents on Social Justice

Pope Pius XI, *Quadragesimo anno*, 1931. Encyclical letter to commemorate the fortieth anniversary of *Rerum novarum*, the ground-breaking work of Pope Leo XIII.

Vatican Council II, *Pastoral Constitution on the Church in the Modern World* (Gaudium et spes), 1965.

Pope Paul VI, Encyclical Letter *Populorum progressio*, 1967.

Synod of Bishops at Rome, *Justice in the World*, 1971.

Pope John Paul II, Encyclical Letter *Laborem exercens*, 1981.

Proclaiming Justice and Peace: Papal Documents from Rerum novarum through Centesimus annus, rev. ed., edited by Michael Walsh and Brian Davies (Mystic, CT: Twenty-Third Publications, 1991).

Do Justice! The Social Teaching of the Canadian Catholic Bishops (1945-1986), edited by E.F. Sheridan, S.J., (Sherbrooke, QC: Édition Paulines, 1987).

Part V

THE LAST THINGS

22

DEATH AND BEYOND

Introduction

Many times in this book we have asserted that human life has meaning and dignity – human life is worthwhile. Furthermore, we have emphasized that the earth we live in, the environment that nurtures this human life, is sacred and valuable and demands that we treat it that way. In face of these assertions, is it then fair to say that human life is worthwhile only because it leads to something better, to something more worthwhile? We have often heard it said, perhaps in sermons or in our early education, that the real life is yet to come, that we are tending towards something better than we have now: eternal life, heaven, being with God, the "beatific vision" (CCC 1028). Thus, the disappointments, the difficulties, the sorrows and tragedies of everyday living must be endured as we look forward to a life without all these miseries.

While all this is true, if we see life only as meaningful in terms of the future, then we have effectively devalued this life. If the real and true life is yet to come, then why bother about this one? Why struggle with the daily reality we face? Why try to improve this life, particularly for those who suffer so much want and injustice? Is all the gospel teaching about trying to establish the reign of God on earth just so much wishful thinking?

We are faced here with another of those Christian paradoxes – in fact, an extension of the paradox of the reign of God, which is both a present and a future reality. If we look at the present as having relevance only in view of the future, we shall have missed the significance of the life of Jesus Christ. A religion that sees this world merely as a place of passage, something to be endured for the sake of the future, is not a Christian religion. Sigmund Freud and Karl Marx called attention to the falsity of this kind of religion, the latter describing it as the "opiate of the people," a drug that assuages the pain of living a full human life. Those who take this drug will have no incentive to change the world for the better, to improve the quality of human life for all.

If the focus of our attention should be on this life, then how do we deal with what we have called the "end things": death, judgment, hell, heaven? Can we even speak about them in any meaningful way? The New Testament gives us some help. In an oft-quoted passage, Paul says, "But, as it is written, 'What no eye has seen, nor ear heard, nor the human heart conceived, what God has prepared for those who love him'" (1 Cor 2:9). This verse is often taken as some sort of prediction of heaven, but that is a less than accurate interpretation. The verse is actually from the prophet Isaiah, and Paul uses it to point out that in fact we *do* know something about what God has prepared. We know it, Paul says, because we "know the mind of the Lord," because we have the "mind of Christ" (1 Cor 2:16). The Spirit of Jesus Christ has been given to us at the heart of our real Christian life. It is this Spirit that enables us to look into our lives and to discern from our own present earthly experience "the mind of the Lord." Undoubtedly, the "mind of the Lord" is that we should work to establish the kingdom of God on earth, as Jesus did. As we carry out this commission from God, our daily experience will give us some glimpse of the future, even though, as Paul says again, "For now we see in a mirror, dimly . . ." (1 Cor 13:12). We see dimly, partially, with a certain fuzziness, for we do not have any direct revelation about heaven, or hell, or judgment in such fashion that we can know *exactly* what they will be like. In fact, the "end things" are the subject of much scriptural and theological speculation. There has been some private revelation on these matters but, as we have already pointed out in a previous chapter, we are not bound to have faith in private revelation; we already have all the revelation we need for salvation.

Before we begin our discussion proper, let us reiterate a crucially important principle already mentioned several times in this book: we can only speak about God in analogical or metaphorical language because all human language is based on human experience, and none of us has *directly* experienced God. All experience of God is mediated through the created universe. Similarly, since none of us has directly experienced what goes on beyond the grave, we can only speak about it in symbolic or metaphorical language. Two things follow from this.

First, metaphors should not, and cannot, be taken literally. In our insatiable curiosity to know about the future, the mysterious, the not yet, we tend to take the metaphors about the last things as being literally true. If we do, we are bound to end up with misunderstanding and false ideas.

Second, we can only say what things are "like" (analogy) if we already know some aspect of the reality, however vague and incomplete. Therefore, if we are able to speak of the "last things" at all we must have experienced these things (death, heaven, hell, etc.) in some analogous fashion, however nebulous, in our everyday living.

As we can see, the last things are simultaneously present and future realities; we only can get some idea of the future, however vague, by reference to the present. There are no easy, pat answers to death and its beyond; our enquiries will leave us with as many questions as we think we have answers. For, in reality, all these things point to the mystery of life itself, a mystery with which we shall struggle till our death.

Death and Resurrection

"It is a poor thing for anyone to fear that which is inevitable," said the early Christian theologian Tertullian (155-245 C.E.). That death is inevitable no one will deny; we have no evidence of anyone who has escaped it. We have to die and most of us don't want to. As the poet Dylan Thomas has written, "Do not go gentle into that good night. . . . Rage, rage against the dying of the light." We avoid talking about death as much as possible, and when we do we tend to use euphemisms. We talk of someone "passing away," or as being "in God's hands," and so on. But is it really a "poor thing" for anyone to fear death? After all, Jesus was afraid to die. The scriptural evidence seems quite compelling.

> *In the days of his flesh, Jesus offered up prayers and supplications, with loud cries and tears, to the one who was able to save him from death, and he was heard because of his reverent submission. (Heb 5:7)*

From the cross came the anguished cry, "My God, my God, why have you forsaken me?" (Mk 15:34). There is no need for any of us to be ashamed of being afraid to die; it is quite natural that, as we frequently do in life, we should recoil from the uncertainty of the unknown. While we cannot deny the reality and finality of death, Christian belief softens the blow by helping us to look beyond death to the promise of total fulfillment in God. We seek to overcome our fear of the unknown, our fear of "that good night," by our hope in the promises of Christ for our resurrection and transformation in God. This is a hope that Dylan Thomas (and, along with him, many unbelievers) does not seem to have had.

Can we have any experience of what death will be like even in the midst of a healthy life? Yes. Every time we lose something precious and valuable, something or someone that we love and are attached to, something we have worked hard to achieve, we die a little – we lose a part of ourselves. The wrenching and gnawing we experience at such a loss can give us some idea of what death may be like. Paradoxical as it may sound, therefore, death and dying are an integral part of living. The final moment of death is the supreme moment of life. Death is what the psychologists call a "peak experience." It should not merely be endured with passivity and acceptance, rather it should be a free and conscious act of life, the final gift of ourselves to God, as Jesus did on the cross: "Then Jesus, crying with a loud voice, said, 'Father, into your hands I commend my spirit'" (Lk 23:46) (CCC 1009, 1011).

Christians believe that through death we shall emerge into resurrection exactly as Jesus did through his death (CCC 990-991). When discussing the resurrection of Jesus in an earlier chapter, we said that resurrection means that after death we shall continue our existence as persons in a new way. We know very little about the precise nature of this new life except that we shall no longer be subject to the contingencies and limitations of this present life. We shall not be different persons; our resurrected life will be continuous with this one but different from it; we shall exist in a new mode of being. Jesus' death seemed to take him from his great work of establishing the kingdom of God on earth; it seemed to separate him from his great desire and dedication. But yet, this was the supreme moment of the endorsement by God of his whole life, a life given to doing his Father's will. In the same way death may seem to take us from what we love and desire, but it is the supreme moment of our endorsement by God, an endorsement that is sealed by resurrection.

How can we speak in any meaningful way about resurrection? We can do so because we already have some experience of it, however feeble. Michael Simpson, S.J., puts it well:

> Are moments of true achievement, of creative inspiration, of love, of prayer, destined to final destruction and annihilation? Is death simply the end of all that has been achieved in life, or has this some lasting value? We cannot really bring ourselves to believe that all that we have loved and valued and created will simply be destroyed and lost. That would seem to imply a contradiction within the very roots of our being: that all that seems most significant, most valuable, is in fact an illusion, that it is the mocking taunt of ultimate absurdity and destruction. It would seem to make the whole of life a lie.[205]

We experience in the depth of our being the very roots of eternity; the experience of "the beyond" is intrinsic and immanent to us in every human action. Thus, resurrection is both a now and a future event – the future will make permanent what for now is an ephemeral experience. And since it is the whole person that experiences, body and spirit together, so will the whole person be taken up by God in resurrection.

Eternal Life

Death leads to eternal life (CCC 1020). As we have just said, there is an aspect of permanence to every human action, a permanence that cannot be explained by reference to this life alone. Every truly human act reaches into eternity, belongs to eternal life. Eternal life is something that is often referred to in scripture. For example, in the Gospel according to John alone there are 17

---

[205] Michael Simpson, S.J., *Death and Eternal Life* (Notre Dame, IN: Fides Publishers, 1971), p. 52.

references to eternal life. Jesus speaks about it frequently: "And this is eternal life, that they may know you, the only true God, and Jesus Christ whom you have sent" (Jn 17:3). To know God[206] is something of lasting value, something that cannot face the absurdity of ultimate destruction. The church, too, persistently makes reference to eternal life in liturgical prayers and invocations. In fact, one might be tempted to say that eternal life is one of the dominant themes of all liturgical prayer. But what is eternal life?

Let us first say that eternity does not mean unending time. We cannot understand eternity in terms of time and space. Time is a measure of succession and change, of moment succeeding moment. In eternity there is no time as we experience it now. We cannot, therefore, think of eternity as though it were time; but that is precisely what we tend to do. Stories of this type of thinking abound. For example, some of us were told as children that the way to think about eternity was to think of a bird coming along every thousand years and removing one grain of sand from the world's deserts and beaches. When all the sand was removed, eternity would not yet have begun! The Bible deals with eternity by using images and metaphors. Thus, heaven is depicted as a banquet; the vision of God as piercing, all-enveloping light; hell in the language of burning and fire. None of this can be demonstrated by empirical evidence. Of course, that does not mean that heaven and hell do not exist, nor does it mean, on the other hand, that we must take any of these images literally. As we have already said, if we are to derive any meaning from the notion of eternal life then, in some way, that meaning must relate to the experience we have now. We are often urged to hope for eternal life, but how can we hope for something of which we have had no experience? It follows that, though eternity is not fully within our grasp, we must be able to relate to it, and we can hope for it because we already experience it partially. The truth is that we have already begun to live our eternal life in the midst of our present life. Eternity is now – all our present actions have eternal significance. We must not think of eternity as beginning only after death – as some kind of reward (or punishment) for our life on earth.

Can we give any examples of this partial experience of timeless eternity? Yes, we can. There are many moments in life when we truly transcend ourselves, when we rise above the constricting circumstances of any given moment or experience and reach out totally towards another. There are moments when we lose ourselves, as it were. Such moments may come in prayer; they frequently come in the self-gift and experience of true love. To lose oneself in the gift to another, when we rid ourselves completely of selfish interests, is a moment of transcendence which, while being in time, is also outside of time; time, as we

---

[206] Please refer to Chapter 1 for an explanation of what it means to know God.

say, stands still. The moment of transcendence also may come in the depths of an exceptionally moving aesthetic experience.

A friend once said she had been "taken out of herself" at her first experience of live ballet. To be "taken out of oneself" – to experience ecstasy (from the Greek "to stand outside [oneself]") – is a peak experience in which we lose consciousness of time and often of space.

In dealing with the concept of eternal life we have thus far concentrated on the meaning of eternity, but what about life? What does life mean in these circumstances? Here we are on even less sure ground than in trying to understand eternity. Again, let us turn to Michael Simpson for assistance.

> One can give no picture of how we can experience a participation in the eternal life of God in a mode no longer subject to the spatio-temporal conditions of this world. All one can say is that all the positive creations and achievements of one's life – all one's true personal relationships, all in fact that helps to constitute the person one has become – are not destroyed but are experienced in a way that transcends the conditions of our present world.[207]

Therefore, although the essence of eternal life will be the "vision of God" (CCC 1023) it will not be merely a passive and static absorption in the wonder of God revealed. Eternal life in heaven will be active, closely related to our present life. Similarly, all one can say about the eternal life of those who have totally alienated themselves from God is that it will be a continuation of that ruinous and unproductive self-absorption that characterized their earthly life.

Reincarnation

Many religious groups hold that the human soul may have pre-existed in some other human or non-human form before becoming united with the present body. Upon death of the present body the soul may then pass into another body, thus giving rise to the possibility that we may have lived a different life at a different time, perhaps even several different lives. This is the doctrine of reincarnation. Such a doctrine is at odds with the Christian belief that each person is created in the image and likeness of God and is unique. The soul and the body are specially fitted together in the one person. The body is an integral part of the person. We cannot be a person other than we are. If the soul could migrate to another body then there would be a different person who would no longer be me. It is the me that has come from God and that will go to him. "When the single course of our earthly life is completed, we shall not return to other earthly lives: 'It is appointed for mortals to die once' (Heb 9:27). There is no reincarnation after death" (CCC 1013).

---

[207] *Death and Eternal Life*, p. 73.

Judgment

"I am ready to meet my Maker," said Sir Winston Churchill. "Whether my Maker is prepared for the ordeal of meeting me is another matter." Tongue-in-cheek as this may sound, Sir Winston, it seems, was well and truly imbued with the Christian belief that upon our death we shall meet God and be asked to give an account of our actions, upon which God will pass judgment. There are many references to God as judge, and to the day of judgment, in the Bible; for example, "But I tell you that on the day of judgment it will be more tolerable for the land of Sodom than for you" (Mt 11:24). St. Paul does not mince words with the Romans: "But by your hard and impenitent heart you are storing up wrath for yourself on the day of wrath, when God's righteous judgment will be revealed" (Rom 2:5). God, we have frequently said, is a God of love, but that does not mean that God is like a benign grandparent, dispensing gifts and totally overlooking our transgressions. God's love must be tempered by justice; otherwise, his love is trivialized. God's love is trivialized when we ignore the very real evil that we experience in the world. According to Sacred Scripture, God's just dealings with us will be revealed on the "Day of the Lord," that moment when we can no longer hide from God as we have so often done during life. But, as is made abundantly clear in the New Testament, this "Day of the Lord" has already come. It has come in Jesus Christ, in whom God is fully revealed. In the Apostles' Creed we profess our faith that Jesus "will come to judge the living and the dead." We understand this expression of faith as meaning that, in Jesus, we are already judged; his life and message are the judgment passed on the world. The Gospel according to John reminds us of this:

> And this is the judgment, that the light has come into the world, and people loved darkness rather than light because their deeds were evil. . . . Those who believe in him are not condemned; but those who do not believe are condemned already, because they have not believed in the name of the only Son of God. (Jn 3:19, 18)

Thus, the very fact of unbelief is condemnation in itself; God does not have to inflict condemnation. God does not judge us, we judge ourselves. Our every action contains in itself a judgment according to how it conforms or does not conform to the message of the gospel.

The church teaches that upon our death we experience judgment and immediately we become fully aware of the outcome of our life (CCC 1051). This judgment we have carried with us through life, but its final result may not always have been apparent. Clearly, judgment is a metaphor, a symbol, and should not be taken literally. Many people, taking the symbol literally, imagine themselves before God, who weighs their good deeds against their bad deeds and pronounces judgment. We cannot take God's judgment to mean the same thing as our human understanding of the scales of justice.

How, then, might we think of it? When we die we shall immediately become fully conscious of our real self, that is, the self we have fashioned throughout our life in relation to the God who created us and called us. We shall recognize immediately how we have responded to God's commandment to love him and to love one another; the value of our response, or the shame of it; the goodness, or the selfishness of our life. Thus, we are judged by being opened to the truth, which we have either hidden from or recognized and responded to in life. As we have said, this is a self-judgment, not a sentence pronounced by God.

The church also teaches that, in addition to our own personal judgment, there will be a "Last Judgment," a final accounting for the whole human race to take place at the end of time and the second coming of Jesus Christ (CCC 1059). This is not an easy symbol to interpret. Perhaps we might think of it as follows. We are social beings, not mere individuals. Our response to God is always in the context of our relationship to others. We have responsibilities towards the community and towards the environment that support us. Just as at our personal judgment we come to a full awareness of how we have responded to God, so also at the Last Judgment we shall become fully aware of how we, as a people, stand in relation to God's plan for the human race. The symbol of the Last Judgment strongly reminds us of our obligations to the whole human race and to the environment of which we are part.

Hell

Many of us grew up with the idea, and the fear, that hell is a place of fire with Satan, the prince of darkness, presiding over his minions (the disobedient angels and the lost souls). Influenced perhaps by St. Augustine, who held that more people were damned than saved, we tended to adopt a rather pessimistic attitude towards the final end of humanity. But how, we may argue, can a good and caring God allow anyone to go to hell? The modern tendency is to dismiss the notion of hell as a medieval fantasy.

We must remember what was said above about God's love being tempered by justice; not to appreciate this is to trivialize that love. God owes it to himself to be true to his own nature, to his own perfection and holiness. If we want to enjoy the vision and presence of God, we too must come to the perfection of which we are capable.

There can be little doubt that much of the discussion of the existence or non-existence of hell has to do with a literal interpretation of the symbol. As we have said, we cannot interpret symbols literally. What then can we say?

Let us begin by unflinchingly grasping the nettle. *It is firm, undoubted Christian teaching that human beings can really damn themselves and that hell is a real possibility* (CCC 1035). The teaching on hell has been derived from many sources in both scripture and tradition, but it is also perfectly logical. If we hold that human beings are free, then we must hold that we are free to totally reject the love of God. Our understanding of love is that, if it is not freely given, it is not love. God will not force us to love him, God will not miraculously change our hearts if they are set on evil. God will not save us unless we want to be saved. As St. Augustine has said, "He who made us without ourselves, will not save us without ourselves." If we withhold our love, if we surround ourselves with a cocoon of selfishness, if we freely choose not to respond to God's call and die in that state, then the state that we have already created in our life will become permanent. *It is that state of permanent estrangement from God that we call hell.*

And so, the major "pain" of hell is the irrevocable loss of God. Can we get any idea from our own experience what that might be like? Yes, in a very limited sense, we can. Hell is loneliness, the loneliness of a thoroughly selfish person. To get some idea of what hell might be like, we can expand as far as we wish any experience of loneliness we have ever had. The notion that we shall have the company of others who are in a similar state, who will share our misery and thus provide some consolation, is a fantasy for which we have absolutely no evidence, scriptural or otherwise. Hell is *total frustration*, the frustration of being called by God, of having experienced God's love and generosity, and of never being able to reach the fulfillment of that call. Again, we can expand as far as we like any experience of frustration we have ever had. Hell is *horrible remorse*. We realize that we have rejected God's offer of love and now there is no going back on our own free choice. As we say, we have blown it. Remorse is depicted very vividly in Scripture as a worm that constantly gnaws and eats away inside us. "And if your eye causes you to stumble, tear it out; it is better for you to enter the kingdom of God with one eye than to have two eyes and to be thrown into hell, where their worm never dies, and the fire is never quenched" (Mk 9:47-48, quoting the prophet Isaiah 66:24).

Let us conclude by making two important points. The first is that God does not predestine anyone to hell, or arrange things in a person's life so that they cannot escape hell no matter what they do. This pessimistic doctrine is held by some Christian sects. But this would be a total denial of human freedom, which we cannot accept (CCC 1037).

Second, as the Catechism puts it, "The affirmations of Sacred Scripture and the teachings of the Church on the subject of hell are a *call to the responsibility* incumbent upon man to make use of his freedom in view of his eternal destiny. They are at the same time an urgent call to conversion" (CCC 1036).

Does God Punish?

We read in the Bible in many places that God rewards the good and punishes the wicked. For example, the theme of punishment is strongly developed in the gospels according to Matthew (13:40-42) and Mark (9:43). Not only that, but Matthew depicts Jesus as himself administering the punishment (Mt 13:41; 25:41). In the Book of Revelation there are lurid descriptions of the tortures of the damned. Based on this kind of scriptural evidence, a common way of talking about hell is that "God punishes us for our sins" or "God sends us to hell for our sins." How literally can we take these statements? Not literally at all.

God does not punish us, we punish ourselves. As we saw in the chapter on sin, all sin inflicts some evil on others. As a result of sin there is a web, a network of evil in the world, and all of us are caught in it. Hell is the culmination and the sum of that evil. By our sins we freely choose to be part of the evil in the world, and we suffer the consequences of that choice. Therefore, hell is not something inflicted by God; it is something that we create for ourselves, something that we begin to experience long before our death. Hell is the symbol for all the despair, the frustration, the physical and mental pain, the remorse over lost opportunities, the deep dissatisfaction of pervasive selfishness that we impose on ourselves during life. Above all, hell is the failure to love, the failure to love God and to love one another.

The "Fire" of Hell

There is perhaps nothing more calculated to inspire fear than the thought of an eternity spent in everlasting fire, the fire mentioned in the Scriptures (see Mt 25:41, Mk 9:48). This fire, as we have sometimes been led to understand, causes all the misery of burning but does not consume. For example, consider the following:

> To impress upon us what the loss of the soul through mortal sin meant, my father would light a match, grab your hands, and hold them briefly over the flame, saying: "See how this feels; now imagine that for all eternity."[208]

This notion of real fire in hell has arisen from a literal interpretation of certain passages in Scripture, such as the ones mentioned above. Catholic teaching does not require us to take these passages literally. The fire of hell can, and should, be understood symbolically. We know what happens when fire burns – it consumes what it burns and effects a chemical and physical change. How, we may ask, does the fire of hell burn according to our understanding of fire? What is consumed? What change takes place? If the fire of hell is in some way different from our scientific fire so that it can cause the misery of burning

---

[208]   Patrick Buchanan, "Tales from 'Blessed Sacrament'," *Crisis*, April 1988.

without consuming what it burns, then we have absolutely no experience of it and therefore cannot speak about it.

Fire is a common and much-used symbol in human speech. We speak of being "consumed by the fire of love." The Holy Spirit appeared at Pentecost as what seemed to be "tongues of fire." We speak of being "burned up with anger." Thus, fire can be a symbol of the good (love), or the bad (anger); it can also be a symbol of the presence of the Spirit. We burn incense in the worship of God; we also burn garbage to get rid of something injurious to our health. Because we are deeply aware of the horrible effects of burning, we associate it with all that is dreadful. In this way it is a fitting symbol for hell.

In conclusion, then, hell is a reality; we cannot explain it away or give in to some emotional aversion to its presence. That God is all-good and all-loving has tended to make some say that hell is just an unpleasant myth. Not so! We create our own hell by our selfish withdrawal from God; therefore, the finality of hell remains a distinct possibility. Having said this, we have no evidence that hell is actually a "place" and that anyone is in fact "in" hell. The church has many times declared that the saints enjoy the perfect vision and enjoyment of God's presence; the church has never declared that there is anyone in hell, not even Judas.

Fear of God

An important consequence of what has been said above is that we should never fear God as someone who will inflict dire punishment if we do not measure up. God is always our friend, our saviour, our loving father. But the Bible does talk of the fear of the Lord in many, many places. For example, "The fear of the Lord is the beginning of wisdom, and the knowledge of the Holy One is insight" (Prov 9:10). How are we to understand this fear?

Fear is a perfectly natural human response to certain experiences and to certain sets of circumstances. Psychologically and physiologically we know how we respond to fear: the "fight or flight" reaction, butterflies in the stomach, a tensing of the muscles, a racing of the heart, and so on. We may distinguish between two types of fear: the fear of fearfulness, that is, the fear that we experience in face of terrifying circumstances; and the fear of love, that is, the fear that we experience when we have hurt someone we love. The human person reacts identically to both types of fear; the physiological and emotional reactions are the same, the experience is the same, but for very different reasons. When we truly love someone, we are afraid to hurt them, and we experience that fear as gnawing away at us, worrying us. By analogy we can apply that same type of fear to our relationship with God, and that is what we mean by fear of God. We damage our relationship with God by sin. We fail to respond to God's invitation, to God's call; we fail to become the persons God wishes us to be as a result of our own negligence and evil purpose. What we can genuinely be afraid of is the evil our own free actions bring upon us and others.

Satan: The Devil

Once, after giving a talk, the great English Dominican preacher Fr. Vincent McNabb was sarcastically questioned by an unbeliever in the audience. "Padre," he said, "when I get to heaven how will I get my shirt on over my wings?" "You won't have to worry about that," replied Fr. McNabb. "What you'll have to worry about is how to get your trousers on over your tail!"

Stories about the devil, humorous or otherwise, abound. In these stories, and often in art, the devil is pictured as a horrible creature with pointed ears, horns, fiery eyes and a sharp tail – the epitome of evil. Add to this the fact that down through the ages and into our present time a cult of Satanism, or devil worship, has flourished, and we are left with evidence of a strong belief in the existence of the devil. But the devil is nothing if not controversial, and many people pour scorn on the idea of the existence of Satan, claiming that in this enlightened scientific age we should be rid of such nonsense. Nevertheless, even the hardiest of skeptics tend to hedge their bets when it comes to the devil. As one woman is reported to have said when asked why she bowed her head in reverence at the mention of Satan, "It costs nothing to be polite!"[209]

In the teaching of the Catholic church, we are not at liberty to do away with the reality of Satan, but we certainly should try to understand what we mean by that symbol, for symbol it is.

First, what do the words mean? The name "Satan" comes from the Hebrew word *satan*, meaning the adversary, the foe, the enemy; the word "devil" comes from the Greek *diabolos*, meaning "one who confuses." We tend to give the devil a personality and speak of "him." This usage is well supported by the New Testament, which has several references to the phenomenon both under the name "devil" and under the name "Satan." There is no doubt that giving the symbol a personality makes it far more compelling, and it would be wrong for us to completely do away with this idea for, as we shall see, it points to something real enough in our experience.

What is the experience to which the symbol of Satan points? It is the experience of evil in the world.[210] There is a tendency to think of evil only in personal terms: there are evil people but not evil as such. Many scholars point out that we cannot think of the evil in the world merely as the sum total of all the

---

[209]   Adapted from Hubert Richards, *Death and After: What Will Really Happen?* (Mystic, CT: Twenty-Third Publications, 1987), p. 57.
[210]   Please refer to the Chapter 17 for an explanation of the meaning of evil.

evil committed by individual persons. The unjust decisions taken in a corporate boardroom, or by governments, for example, often turn out to have disastrous consequences beyond the intentions of the people who took those decisions and who, when the evil becomes evident, would probably want to disassociate themselves from it. Thus, the evil seems to take on a life of its own – what we might call corporate evil. It is for this reason that we say there seems to be *intelligent opposition* to the establishment of the kingdom of God; it is almost as if the forces of evil are guided by an evil intelligence.

It is this experience of corporate evil that makes us think of the devil as a person, with an intelligence and an evil will. It is why we call it the devil "the one who confuses," the one who pulls the wool over our eyes so that evil is disguised as good. We also call him/her/it Satan, the one who is the adversary of God, the enemy of God, the deceiver. Everyone is aware of the evils of the former Soviet communism, as we were aware of the evils of the Nazi system of so-called National Socialism and the evils of regimes presided over by tyrannical dictators. But to identify Satan as an individual person would be like saying that the evils of Soviet Communism in Russia, National Socialism in Nazi Germany, and the regime of Saddam Hussein in Iraq were due to the fact that Josef Stalin, Adolf Hitler and Saddam Hussein were possessed by the devil. Also, to personalize Satan as the head of the fallen angels driven out of heaven by Michael is to literalize a biblical symbol and stretch it beyond allowable limits (see Rev 12:7-9). When we talk, therefore, of being "tempted by Satan," what we mean is that we are being lured into the evil of the world by our own weakness and selfish tendencies. When we pray in the Our Father not to be led into temptation, we pray for God's help to resist the attractiveness of evil in the world.

Therefore, to completely do away with all talk of the devil would leave us without a tremendously compelling symbol. The symbol of the devil is a very useful one for reminding us of the genuine existence of corporate evil, the forces of evil that seem to take on a life of their own. The personal conversion and repentance of individuals will not completely cure this problem. We need to turn to Our Lord Jesus Christ, who promised a "new earth," a "new life" through the power of his salvation. By his death and resurrection Jesus has conquered the forces of evil. Because we possess the power of his Spirit, we have nothing to fear from Satan. We have but to prepare ourselves as best we can for the "day of the Lord," when his victory over evil will be manifest.

One or two final points. First, probably because we tend to think of the devil as an individual person, some people seem to develop an unnecessary paranoia about the presence of Satan. We need not look for the devil in every dark corner of our lives. Our experience shows us that we ourselves are responsible for a lot of the evil in our lives because of our bad habits and selfish desires. (In some cases, psychiatric disorders may be the cause.)

Second, can we say anything about possession by the devil so dramatically portrayed in such movies as *The Exorcist*? There is no way we can make a perfectly clear distinction between diabolical possession and what may be a psychiatric disorder. With advances in medical science today, the tendency is to treat such manifestations as medical rather than spiritual phenomena. It may sound strange to some people, but it seems that often enough his Satanic Majesty can be treated medically! The church still does retain the ritual of exorcism for diabolical possession, but it is used much less often today.

Purgatory

The word comes from the Latin *purgare*, meaning to purge, to get rid of, to remove something that is having a bad effect. The church teaches that purgatory is a process whereby we are purged of residual selfishness so that we can enter into perfect union with God, who himself is totally self-giving (CCC 1030, 1031).

First, let us note that this teaching is perfectly logical given our understanding of the nature of God and the nature of sin. As we have mentioned in a previous chapter, not all sin is mortal, not all sin is deadly, not all sin totally separates us from God. When we die, most of us will have some unresolved problems in our life. Probably we will have failed to achieve the goal of perfect self-development: there will be selfish attachments that have not been broken, forgiveness that has not been asked, evils that have not been repaired. If we understand God to be perfectly just, then he owes it to himself that nothing that is imperfect should be allowed to enter into complete union with him. There must therefore be some process of purification, some process of being rid of this residual evil. If this purification does not take place during life, then it must take place after death. For this reason we say that the process of purgation will be painful. We say it because we know from our experience that to give up our selfish desires and actions is a painful process. To give up something to which we are attached is always painful, and probably more so when this attachment is sinful.

Having said all this, when we come to try to discover how precisely this purgation can take place after death, and what the pain will be, we find that there is far more darkness than light. In fact, we simply do not understand it, nor can we offer any clear explanation of the process because we have no direct experience of it. The mistake that is most often made is to take the metaphor literally. This, as we have pointed out, is the basis of most of the mistakes about the last things. To try to explain the literal existence of purgatory as a "place" where souls spend some "time" having themselves cleansed of imperfection through a painful process leaves us with innumerable problems. Not the least of these problems is how we can apply the concepts of time and space to a non-spatio-temporal world. Because these and other problems have no obvious solution, many people find it convenient just to discard the whole teaching. But the teaching on purgatory does correspond and point to the experience of deep realities in our life; therefore, in no way should we abandon it. As Hubert Richards says, "Like talk of hell it is not to be taken literally, but it should be taken seriously. It too is a projected picture of a present experience – that of the painful contrast between God's unswerving love and the meanness of our response."[211]

How, then, may we interpret the symbol? First, the teaching on purgatory is an expression of our faith in the justice and mercy of God, which is a reality that we experience in and through our own understanding of human justice and mercy. To show mercy and condescension is an integral part of the love that Jesus enjoins on us if we are to develop as true human persons. Similarly, we act justly and expect justice from others as an integral part of our adherence to the teaching of Jesus. It is the experience of the justice that we ourselves show and expect in all our human dealings.

Second, the symbol of purgatory is a stark reminder of the obligation to pursue wholeness in our own human development – that is, the development in ourselves of the values that marked the life of Jesus. It reminds us of our experience of the true and the false in our lives and of the need we feel to eradicate the false. In the early church, it was precisely the belief in purgatory that encouraged people to pray for the dead. They believed that our prayers here on earth could help the dead get through their period of purification, though how this process can take place was never satisfactorily explained. Roman Catholic doctrine still firmly holds that *we can and should pray for the dead*. Praying for the dead enhances our image of God as a forgiving God and also strengthens our faith and hope that even beyond death, healing and change can take place. Praying for the dead shows that we are in some way in communion with those who have died; the oneness of the human family is not destroyed by death, for we believe that beyond death, life is changed but not destroyed. The most effective prayer is the special prayer of the Eucharist: hence the custom of having Masses said for the dead.[212]

---

[211] *Death and After: What Will Really Happen?*, p. 82.

[212] On the difficulty of explaining how our prayers help the dead and what, in effect, praying for the dead means, see *Death and After: What Will Really Happen?*, pp. 81-82.

Heaven

We have all heard the old joke that for those who lead a good Christian life "the pay is not great, but the retirement benefits are out of this world!" The belief that heaven exists "out of this world" is one that is so firmly fixed in our culture that it has become the stuff of songs ("Heaven can wait, this is paradise"), common expressions ("Heavens above!"), names of foods ("Heavenly Hash"), even the hymns we sing in church ("Now thou art high in thy mansions above"). A common way of speaking is to refer to heaven as "up there," "beyond the clouds." Even the Christian Scriptures seem to underscore this conception of heaven. At the Ascension of Jesus we are told that "he was taken up to heaven" (Acts 1:2). And again, referring to the apostles gathered to bid goodbye to Jesus, "When he had said this, as they were watching, he was lifted up, and a cloud took him out of their sight" (Acts 1:9). All this leaves us with the image that Jesus has gone "up" to his rightful place in heaven, seated in glory "at the right hand of the Father."

To maintain this kind of vision is to make the capital error of mistaking the image for the reality. The word "above" simply means greater than, superior to; God is superior to the world, totally transcendent, and in that sense "above" the world. Christians do not believe that God dwells "above" in the spatial sense; Christians believe that God is in the world sustaining it by his power and presence. If God is in the world, then heaven is already in the world and should, in some way, be part of our experience.

Further evidence can be offered from the Christian Scriptures, particularly in the writings of St. Paul. He reminds us that we are "in" Christ; by faith in Our Lord Jesus Christ we are already taken "up" into him.

So if anyone is in Christ, there is a new creation: everything old has passed away; see, everything has become new! (2 Cor 5:17)

Thus, our resurrection to a new life already is a reality while we still live this one. Again, Paul says,

Blessed be the God and Father of our Lord Jesus Christ, who has blessed us in Christ with every spiritual blessing in the heavenly places. (Eph 1:3)

We already experience the spiritual blessings that belong to heaven: union with God and personal fulfillment. And again,

If with Christ you died to the elemental spirits of the universe, why do you live as if you still belonged to the world? (Col 2:20)

We are in the world, but not of it. By our Baptism we have died to sin and risen to a new life in which we share the divine life of God. This new life is a present experience; we must not go back to the old one. Thus, the Christian Scriptures strongly suggest that the heaven we hope for is a present experience, not a purely future one; it is part of the eternal life we have already begun to live. Now we experience it "darkly," "as in a mirror," but this life shall be transformed into a full and perfect experience of God.

What might we point to as experiences of heaven in this life? One of the most poignant, surely, is the death of a loved one. If we do not despair, it is because of our hope and inner conviction that the person is not lost and gone forever. Our hope is a clear experience that "in" heaven we shall be reunited with our loved ones. In a sense, we already experience that reunion, for the dead person lives on in our memory.[213] The satisfaction we experience for a job well done, the fulfillment of our legitimate desires, the achievement of goals we set ourselves, are all images of the happiness of heaven.

There are several symbols and metaphors for what heaven might be like. One that is most frequently used is by St. Paul, who said that heaven means the "face-to-face" vision of God, what is called "the beatific vision." Clearly God does not have a face (though Jesus does), but this image is a very useful one. "Face to face" means a deep and enduring *understanding* of God, an understanding that is more than an intellectual exercise but is a full personal experience. It is helpful to use the analogy of a face-to-face encounter with someone we love, for one can understand so much by looking into someone's face. The face is the part of the human body that best conveys human emotion and all the little nuances we associate with the self-givingness of love. This face-to-face vision will bring immense joy and satisfaction, as is experienced by true lovers.

One danger of pushing this analogy of the face-to-face vision too far is that it tends to make us think of heaven as a very personal, isolated, almost selfish experience of God. God did not send his Son purely for our own individual salvation but for the salvation of the whole world. Our experience of heaven will depend to a large extent on how we have carried out the commission given us by Jesus to change and transform the world, to establish the reign of God with all that that means. Our enjoyment and vision of God are inextricably bound up with our relationships and our responsibilities towards others. Because of all this, another helpful image of heaven is that of the great banquet with all the saints. It is around the meal table that we share *koinonia*, union, friendship, togetherness, care for one another. Again, the image is one of great joy, satisfaction, belonging, security, a taste of which we already have in similar situations on earth.

Therefore, let us say it again. Heaven already exists on earth; it is not something that will arise like a phoenix out of the ashes of what we have now.

---

[213] The Catechism refers to heaven as "blessed communion with God and all who are in Christ" (CCC 1027). Included in this communion, of course, will be Christ and Mary the Mother of God (1024).

Heaven exists in the transformation of our human life that has been brought about by the advent of Jesus.

> . . . the creation itself will be set free from its bondage to decay and will obtain the freedom of the glory of the children of God. We know that the whole creation has been groaning in labour pains until now; and not only the creation, but we ourselves, who have the first fruits of the Spirit, groan inwardly while we wait for adoption, the redemption of our bodies. (Rom 8:21-23)

Human life – the whole of creation – will be transformed, not destroyed; the seeds of that transformation have already been sown, and now "we wait for adoption, the redemption of our bodies." That is the vision of St. Paul so arrestingly developed in the writings of the Jesuit priest Pierre Teilhard de Chardin.[214]

Thus we may say that the images of heaven reaffirm our images of hope. We hope and trust that this life is worthwhile and not absurd; heaven assures us that it is. Heaven assures that we are not puppets on the stage of history; we have infinite value. God cares for each one of us and for the whole universe. Life is moving towards fulfillment, and we contribute to that fulfillment if we care for and love one another. "You have made us for yourself, O Lord, and our hearts are restless until they rest in you."

Conclusion

Reading the Scriptures we are left in no doubt that Jesus's preaching and message were couched in terms of the present. He said that "the kingdom of God is among you." It is here; we do not have to wait for it in the future. The presence of the kingdom demands life-shaping decisions and commitment now. We are in the "last times." Eternal life is not a future phenomenon, not something that only comes on us after death, but a present reality intrinsic to every aspect of life.

Therefore, and most importantly, *all questions about eternal life are, in fact, questions about this life*. We do not ask questions about eternity out of curiosity but rather that we may learn to live better now. All the realities of eternity are dealt with in Scripture in the form of image, symbol and metaphor. We must not take this language literally. This does not mean that the realities do not exist; what it means is that, since we do not have any direct experience of them, we must form symbols of them out of the ordinary experience that we do have. The symbol points to the reality and makes the reality present, but it is not the reality.

---

[214] See, for example, Pierre Teilhard de Chardin, S.J., *The Divine Milieu* (Harper & Row, 1965).

Heaven, hell and purgatory are symbols for the eternal significance of human existence; they are not to be thought of as "places" to which we "go" or are "sent" after death. Insofar as we open ourselves to God and our neighbour *now*, then our life shares in the life of God. Insofar as we shut ourselves off from others by our unbridled egotism, we have already excluded God from our life. In truth and in fact, therefore, heaven and hell enter into every human decision we make. We experience heaven when we experience wholeness, integrity and a genuine good conscience that are born of honest self-giving. We experience hell in the frustration and emptiness and loneliness of unbridled selfishness.

Reflection Questions

1. Since we have no direct experience of death, heaven and hell, we can only speak of these things after the analogy of something we have experienced. In what way can we experience death while still living this life?

2. What do you understand by eternal life? Will this be a reward for having lived a good life on earth?

3. "God does not judge us, we judge ourselves." Explain this statement.

4. We are told in sacred scripture that "The fear of the Lord is the beginning of wisdom." Explain what we mean when we talk of the fear of God.

5. What does it mean to say that "the image of heaven reaffirms our images of hope?"

6. Is it strictly correct to say that anyone is "in" heaven or "in" hell? Give reasons for your answer.

Further Reading

Richards, Hubert. *Death and After: What Will Really Happen?* (Mystic, CT: Twenty-Third Publications, 1987). Deals with the issues in this chapter in a way that college students, church educators, counsellors of the bereaved and preachers will find inspiring and extremely helpful.

Simpson, Michael, S.J. *Death and Eternal Life* (Notre Dame, IN: Fides Publishers, 1971). This slim volume provides a more theological and philosophical treatment of the topic. Requires more careful reading but will reward study.

Appendix

THE CATHOLIC SCHOOL AND
THE CATHOLIC TEACHER

In this section, as we speak about curriculum we do not only mean courses of study. Curriculum will be taken to include all aspects of the total program of the school, as well as what we might call the overall "faith-tone" and Catholic environment of the school. We shall deal with it under three headings: 1) the Catholic school; 2) the Catholic teacher; 3) the aim of religious education.[215]

1. The Catholic School

The Catholic church has always had a strong commitment to education. Indeed, Catholic education has an illustrious history. Unfortunately, a full treatment of that history is outside the scope of this book. But any commitment to Catholic education has its origin in the command of Our Lord Jesus Christ that the good news should be preached to everyone: "And he said to them, 'Go into all the world and proclaim the good news to the whole creation'" (Mk 16:15). The Catholic church has always regarded education as one of the main ways in which the good news is proclaimed and spread. But this last statement has to be understood properly.

Evangelization and Human Development

The aim of evangelization is 1) to bring people into contact with the person of Jesus Christ; 2) to spread the gospel message; and 3) to promote an active faith. The message of the gospel is a message for the good of the whole person. It is a message that helps us to develop properly as good human beings; it is a message that enables us to live in society with other people in an atmosphere that

---

[215] The text in this section is based mainly on five sources: The Sacred Congregation for Catholic Education, *The Catholic School* (Rome, 1977); Ontario Conference of Catholic Bishops, *This Moment of Promise* (Toronto, 1989); The Catholic Private Secondary School Principals of Toronto, *A New Covenant: Catholic Secondary Schools and Public Funding*; Canadian Catholic Trustees Association, *Catholic Education: From Principle to Practice in Catholic Schools* (Toronto, 1975); Sacred Congregation for Catholic Education, *The Religious Dimension of Education in a Catholic School* (Rome, 1988).

will promote our whole human good. Here is what Pope Paul VI says in his encyclical letter on the evangelization of peoples, *Evangelii nuntiandi*:

> The church evangelizes when she seeks to convert, solely through the power of the divine message she proclaims, both the personal and collective consciences of people, the activities in which they engage, and the lives and concrete milieu which are theirs. (No. 18)

The Pope speaks of conversion, but this must not be taken only in the narrow sense of trying to convert someone to Catholicism. If this was indeed the case, then Catholic schools would be open to the frequently laid charge of proselytism. Therefore, a conversion, yes, but a conversion that involves the whole of our very human life, what we might call conversion in the broad sense. Applying this to the Catholic school, the Sacred Congregation for Catholic Education in Rome says,

> The Catholic school is committed thus to the development of the whole person, since in Christ, the perfect human being, all human values find their fulfillment and unity. Herein lies the specifically Catholic character of the school. Its duty to cultivate human values in their own legitimate right in accordance with its particular mission to serve all people has its origin in the figure of Christ.[216]

An intrinsic part of the mandate of the Catholic school is to "cultivate human values in their own legitimate right." And so, we may well ask, how specifically does the message of the gospel contribute to full human development?

1. The gospel message keeps reminding us of the "transcendent goal which alone gives life its full meaning."[217]

The real meaning of human life is that we are destined for a closer union with God than we have now. To help people to understand this and to regulate their lives accordingly is a great contribution to human development. One of the incredibly sad features of the secularized life that so characterizes the contemporary world is the inability to find meaning and purpose. According to the well-known French author François Mauriac, "If there is no God, and everything, therefore, is permitted, the first thing that is permitted is despair."[218] The inability to find meaning in life, which often brings with it hopelessness and despair, is, without doubt, one of the important factors militating against full human development. Gospel

---

[216] *The Catholic School*, No. 35.
[217] Pope Paul VI, *Allocation to Cardinal Gabriel-Marie Garrone*, November 27, 1972.
[218] Tony Castle, *More Quotes and Anecdotes*, p. 122.

teaching provides us with such meaning, as well as hope for the future and a vision of life's fulfillment.

2. The gospel message provides us with values that enhance our human development.

    The great message of the gospel is that we should love one another as God loves us. A life based on self-sacrificing love, and not on selfishness, should be the goal of every human being, not only those who are professedly religious. A concomitant benefit is that this self-sacrificing love surely will bring the peace that is so necessary for proper human development.

3. Gospel teaching provides an antidote to the false values that pervade our society today and which, ultimately, act against proper human development.

    Such false values are dealt with elsewhere in this book (see Chapter 19) and it might be well to review this section now. Christianity is, by its nature, counter-cultural in the best sense of that word. To be true to its mandate, Christianity must keep pointing out the false values that exist in any culture, false values that impede proper human development.

We could add many more examples of how teaching the gospel contributes to balanced and integral human development. For the moment, the above will have to suffice. Catholic education, therefore, aims to develop the whole person and to produce better human beings. It is certainly not only a matter of teaching institutionalized religion as such. Those who think otherwise are simply not in touch with reality; they misunderstand the nature and methods of Catholic education.

The Role of the State

For the most part, governments, which officially declare themselves to be non-religious, or a-religious, have control of education. The state schools are not only non-religious but in most cases do not even attempt to inculcate a moral code. We affirm strongly that parents have the prior right in the education of their children. Nevertheless, one cannot deny that the state also has the right and duty to supervise and promote the education of its citizens. But it is a truism that a nation cannot live on material values alone. History has shown that the denial of the higher values, the spiritual and moral values, is disastrous, not only for nations but also for whole civilizations. To paraphrase the gospel, we do not live on bread alone.

In North America, and indeed in Western civilization in general, Christianity and Christian values have been integral to the laws and general ethical stance that regulate these societies. In North America, and in many other countries, Christianity has been an integral part of the founding of these nations. In general, Western civilization still lives by the Christian code of ethics. In many cases, the

Catholic faith and Catholic education have been integral parts of the cultural mosaic, even though today Catholicism may not be the dominant Christian religion.

Characteristics of a Catholic School

It is not our intention here to go into all the details of what makes a Catholic school. There is a considerable body of literature dealing with the subject. Nevertheless, it seems appropriate to point out two or three of the most important features.

1. The school, a community of faith

A Catholic school is not a school in which Catholic students are segregated; not a school that is staffed by Catholic teachers; not a school in which religion is taught for two hours a week. Basically, a Catholic school is one in which God, his truth, his life are integrated into the entire syllabus, curriculum and life of the school.[219]

The Catholic school should aim to be a community of faith, and that includes everyone: teachers, students, support staff. They have the same faith, the same commitment to gospel values. When we say community we mean just that. Those who belong to the community will be a caring, sharing, helping, forgiving, peace-promoting, loving, self-sacrificing group of people. As in any community, the older, more adult members of the community (principal and teachers) have an obligation to help the younger members (the students) grow in their faith. This means that all classroom teachers, no matter what their area of competence or expertise, together with other members of the staff, must be examples to the younger members of the school community of a committed Christian and Catholic lifestyle. To many, this may seem impossibly idealistic. Some of the adult members of the community may be struggling with their own faith and feel unable to lead others in the right direction. While the ideal may never be achieved perfectly, no one is absolved from trying to achieve it.

2. The school, a promoter of service to others

Not only must the school community itself live by the values of the gospel, but also living these values will mean promoting the ideal of service to others, notably the poor and disadvantaged (as Jesus did), both in the developing world and at home. Jesus' statement about himself and his life is quite clear: he defined himself by service to others. "For the Son of Man," he says, "came not to be served but to serve, and to give his life a ransom for many" (Mk 10:45).

---

[219]   *This Moment of Promise*, p. 7.

3. *The school, a sacramental community*

A sacramental community means two things. First, celebration of the Eucharist, and indeed the other sacraments, should be the centre point of unity and community in the school. The whole school community should pray together and especially gather around the table of the Lord in the Eucharist. Second, the school must be seen to promote the very principle of sacramentality. As has already been pointed out in Chapter 15, the principle of sacramentality states that all created things can and should mediate the presence of God to us. Therefore, in a Catholic school one should ask, Are the staff and students sacraments to one another by mediating the presence of the unseen God? Are there permanent and tangible reminders of the presence of God in the school – a chapel (the location of which will encourage students to visit it), statues, art work, bulletin boards with special presentations on feast days or the liturgical seasons, religious plays, crucifixes, a Bible in every classroom, and so forth? For these external reminders to be truly sacramental they must reveal the deeper realities of faith and community in the school.

2. The Catholic Teacher

It is a truism to say that the school is only as good as the teachers in it. To an even greater extent does that apply to the principal. All the research of recent years testifies unequivocally that the leadership of the principal is vital in determining the nature of the school and its commitment to the ideals of Christianity.

For the Catholic teacher, teaching is far more than a job; it is more than a means of putting food on the table. It is a ministry, a calling from God. If permanent employment is the only motivation for becoming a Catholic teacher, we have no hesitation in saying that such a person is in the wrong business, or at least the wrong place. If the business of the Catholic school is to share in the spreading of the gospel message and the human improvement of the young people committed to its care, then the teacher is a minister of the gospel *par excellence.*

The word "minister" is important. It comes from the Latin *minister*, which means servant, one who serves, one who spends oneself in the service of others. As we have seen above, Jesus describes himself as such. To be a minister of the gospel is more than a job: it is a call to serve, a vocation. It demands a specific commitment. Those who do not feel themselves imbued with this ideal of service to others and to the church should seriously query whether their motivation for wanting to be a Catholic teacher is appropriate.

The Purpose of Catholic Teaching

In order to better understand the role of the Catholic teacher, it may be helpful to take a look at the aim and purpose of our Catholic schools in a slightly different way from that already put forward above.

Our schools exist as distinct from public schools only because of their religious goals. If these religious goals are not actively upheld and promoted by teachers, we shall have failed in our duty as servants of the Roman Catholic public, and also as ministers of God's word. As we have already pointed out, it is a serious mistake to think that "religious" goals are substantively different from "humanitarian" goals: that is, human development in all its aspects. We are far too adept at separating the religious from the human, almost as though the former had little or nothing to do with the latter. For someone who believes in Jesus Christ, to be a religious person is to be an excellent and well-developed human person. To repeat the oft-quoted aphorism of St. Irenaeus, "The glory of God is man fully alive."

We may distinguish four things that Catholic schools should offer students:

1. A broad and total education of excellent quality

We take this for granted. Our schools should be as good as and better than public schools. If they are not, then we have no business running schools. Every teacher must bring to the teaching of a discipline a Catholic viewpoint, an orientation personal and professional, that will communicate itself to students no matter what the subject may be. Obviously, some subjects (for example, literature) lend themselves more readily to this orientation than others. Once we understand that human improvement and human development are an important goal of evangelization, then we shall have fewer problems with those who ask, How does one teach Catholic mathematics?

2. The opportunity to enter into a personal relationship with God and to strengthen their membership in the church

Teachers will have great difficulty in accomplishing this goal if they themselves are not living the gospel authentically and have only a tenuous attachment to the church. Not every teacher will have achieved a fully mature faith; some may be struggling with doubt and uncertainty.[220] Therefore, everyone should understand that the church is a structured community that is open to dynamic growth. At certain stages of their own faith journey, some people may not be able to subscribe fully to all aspects of church teaching and practice. Also, some may not feel able to live up to all the ideals of behaviour demanded of a committed Catholic.

---

[220] At this point it may be helpful to review what was said about doubt in Chapter 5.

Despite all this, loyalty to the Catholic tradition requires that teachers have 1) a great respect for the church, a church which is not the Pope and bishops only, but ourselves (see Chapter 12); 2) a positive attitude towards participation in the church's continuing life and development; and 3) a determination to work on their own faith life and conversion. Loyalty to the church further demands that teachers should not present their own personal problems of faith, or attachment to the church, or of acceptance of church teaching in a negative or pejorative manner before the students. This does not exclude reasonable expression, suitable to the age of the students, of the fact that a variety of opinion does exist on certain questions within the Catholic tradition. However, teachers should beware of presenting their own opinion or "feeling" as equal to or better than the current official teaching of the church. That is a particularly objectionable form of arrogance.

Sadly, it is often the case that those who feel that they cannot subscribe to certain aspects of church teaching really have not properly understood the teaching and argue only from a "gut reaction" or a media-influenced perception. It is no secret that the media have a poor reputation regarding truth and completeness in presenting matters concerning religion. Often people who are having difficulties with their faith have not taken the trouble to inform themselves properly of the reasons for and the background to church teaching. It should go without saying that all Catholic teachers need to become better informed about current Catholic theology and teaching by reading, consultation, discussion and further study. No professional person can ignore the need for constant updating, and teachers are professional people.

In attempting to achieve the above goal, teachers should also be fully aware of the prevalent cultural milieu in which they work. This is a milieu in which there is increasing fragility in families and family life. Too often the home is only minimally Christian. Parents, while wanting their children to have the benefits of a religious education, do not themselves give good example of active practice of the faith. Fragmented and broken homes are a particularly serious problem. Added to this is the fact that parish resources are becoming overextended and the numbers of clergy are seriously diminished. This situation means that the school may well be the place where many young people experience their first real contact with the church, a church that teaches them to try to live more by faith, hope, and love than by the values of a consumer society.

Teachers should aim to make this primary experience of the church a pleasant and fruitful one for the students.

3. *The opportunity to learn more about Catholic teaching*

This aspect is dealt with in detail below in section 3, "The Aim of Religious Education." It is worth noting, however, that this is not solely the responsibility of the religious education teacher; it is the duty of every teacher in a Catholic school.

4. *The opportunity to build a religiously based set of values*

As has already been said, one of the great duties of the Catholic school is to expose the false values that exist in our society, values that are not consonant with the gospel. The false values that exist in society must be exposed by putting them up against the values exhibited in the life and teaching of Jesus. Once again we must make the point that gospel values are human values, not merely religious values. Living out the gospel values in our life will make us better human beings. It is terribly important that the students experience these gospel values in the life of the school community, for example speaks louder than words. As has already been said, the teachers have a grave responsibility to help create that experience.

It seems appropriate to end this section with a quote from the document *The Religious Dimension of Education in a Catholic School* (No. 26), which sums up much of what we have been saying:

> Prime responsibility for creating [a] unique Christian school climate rests with the teachers, as individuals and as a community. The religious dimension of the school climate is expressed through the celebration of Christian values in Word and Sacrament, in individual behaviour, in friendly and harmonious interpersonal relationships, in a ready availability. Through this daily witness, the students will come to appreciate the uniqueness of the environment to which their youth has been entrusted. If it is not present, then there is little left which can make the school Catholic.

3. The Aim of Religious Education

As we have seen, two of the major purposes of a Catholic school are 1) to help students develop a close personal relationship with Jesus Christ and 2) to provide them with the opportunity to learn about Catholic teaching. We have also seen that all teachers, no matter what their subject area, must be involved in this enterprise. This being the case, it should be very useful for everyone to know the whole aim and purpose of religious education and also something about how that goal is achieved. Religious education should not be confined to the course of study laid out for religion, taught, perhaps, as a separate subject. As was pointed out at the beginning of this chapter, curriculum is to be taken in the broad sense as including everything in the school that promotes faith and a religious outlook.

The Gospel of John presents Jesus summing up the whole purpose of his life and teaching in these words: "And this is eternal life, that they may know you, the only true God, and Jesus Christ whom you have sent" (Jn 17:3). We have already talked about what it is to know Jesus (see Chapter 1). It is not mere cerebral knowledge but a knowledge that is active, influencing the whole of one's life. We have already quoted Pope John Paul II on this subject, but his words are worth repeating:

> In the first place, it is intended to stress that at the heart of catechesis we find, in essence, a Person, the Person of Jesus of Nazareth. . . . Accordingly, the definitive aim of catechesis is to put people not only in touch, but in communion, in intimacy, with Jesus Christ.[221]

This, indeed, is the heart of the matter.

While knowledge of and union with Jesus is the definitive aim of religious education, there is a process by which this aim is achieved, or rather by which one attempts to achieve this aim. As we have already seen above, intimate knowledge of and faith in Jesus Christ is a gift of God not within the teacher's province to give. Nevertheless, the teacher must prepare the ground for God's gift. And so we can look at religious education as taking place at three levels:

1. *Information* (the objective level)

2. *Formation* (the subjective level)

3. *Transformation* (the intersubjective and conversion level)

Level 1: Information

Roman Catholics should know their faith. Educated Catholics should know what they believe and why they believe it. We would, for example, consider the education system to have failed if some went through a country's school system and emerged with little or no knowledge about the country, its history, its geography, its government, its life in general. Similarly, one of the roles of the Catholic school is to produce educated Catholics. For this purpose, basic information about the Catholic religion is essential.

The basic information we refer to would consist of such things as statements and explanations of doctrine and official teaching, creeds of belief (e.g., the Apostles' Creed), moral values (e.g., the Ten Commandments), historical information (e.g., Bible history, the history and structure of the church), the structure of scripture and something about its meaning and interpretation, sacraments and symbols, liturgical celebration: in short, everything you ever wanted to know about the Catholic faith but were afraid to ask!

---

[221] Pope John Paul II, *Catechesi tradendae*, No. 5.

It is vitally important to insist that our faith be a reasonable, informed faith; it is not a blind adherence to teaching that we do not and cannot understand. "'Faith seeks understanding': it is intrinsic to faith that a believer desires to know better the One in whom he has put his faith and to understand better what He has revealed; a more penetrating knowledge will in turn call forth greater faith, . . . In the words of St. Augustine, 'I believe, in order to understand; and I understand, the better to believe'" (CCC 158). One of the clear distinguishing features of Catholicism down through the centuries has been the commitment to a faith informed by clear theological reasoning. It has hardly been better stated than by a Protestant theologian of the University of Chicago: "Throughout Catholic history [there has been] a drive toward rationality, the insistence that the divine mystery manifest in tradition and sacramental presence be insofar as possible penetrated, defended, and explicated by the most acute rational reflection."[222] Catholic schools have often been accused of failing to provide basic theological information in religious education classes, thus producing a crop of Catholics who "know nothing" about their faith. While it would be wrong to put all the blame for these "know-nothing" Catholics on the school (the home, too, has a large influence here), if the teaching is bad the school must accept some responsibility for this.

Thus, the information aspect of religious education corresponds to the believing aspect of faith. Our belief system must be built on a solid foundation of knowledge that will help us in the active practice of faith.

Level 2: Formation

Faith cannot survive only on information. Religion is as much a matter of the heart as it is of the head. The religious response stems from the whole person. The level of formation goes beyond the level of information and, in a sense, is built on it, but not necessarily in sequence.

The level of formation is the level of affect, or emotion, or value. Students must be helped to feel deeply that what they are being taught has personal value for them – that it is relevant to their present or future situation and to their experience. Unless teachers can succeed in doing this, they will not make progress in reaching the ultimate goal of religious education. Religion must be taught in such a way that students come to grasp it as a value, as something worthwhile, as something they hold dear, as something speaking to their life, as something that adds meaning to their life. We cannot, for example, ask someone to be committed to Jesus Christ, or to the church, if Jesus Christ, or the church,

---

[222] Langdon Gilkey, *Catholicism Confronts Modernity: A Protestant View* (New York: Seabury Press, 1975), p. 22.

has no gut-level meaning for them, does not speak to their life or experience, or in other words, is not relevant. So it is for any aspect of faith or religious practice.

Right away we should be able to see that the role of the teacher at level two is somewhat different from that at level one. At level one the teacher can be quite objective – stand back from the material, so to speak, and let it speak for itself, much as one would do in a science or mathematics class. In fact, some teachers of theology are guilty of just that: trying to teach theology in a sterile, objective, non-involved atmosphere devoid of faith. But religious education is not the same as teaching theology. The teacher cannot stand back and be objective. The teacher has necessarily to become a model for the students. The students are far more likely to reach level two if they can see the teacher as a deeply committed person. The teacher teaches as much by example as by words.

Teaching at this level involves a lot of faith sharing. Sadly, it has to be said, so imbued are we with the cultural bias that faith is a private, personal matter that some teachers seem to be afraid of sharing their faith with others. Good religious education is bound to suffer when this is the case.

And so, if the teacher comes across to the students as enthusiastic about religion, as deeply committed, as caring and reverent, the students are far more likely to be led to value and commitment themselves. What we are saying is that the teacher should be a *proclaimer* (from the Latin *pro-clamare*, to cry out) of the good news. Cardinal Newman expresses it very beautifully:

> The heart is commonly reached not through the reason, but through the imagination, by means of direct impressions (i.e., experience) . . . . Persons influence us, looks subdue us, voices melt us, deeds inflame us. Many a man will die upon a dogma; no man will be a martyr for a conclusion.

As we can see, the formation aspect of religious education corresponds to the trusting and doing aspects of faith. As Newman says, we must approach the heart and the emotions that are so important in any act of trust. The personal trust developed between teacher and student is very important in preparing the ground for faith. And, Newman says, deeds inflame us. Yes, deeds form a crucially important aspect of proclamation; we *do* our faith. The type of religion that Jesus proposed is "doing the will of the Father," thus, an active, lifestyle-oriented religion. And so proclamation must include active work to establish the kingdom of God on earth. In this regard, the teacher must be a leader by example. Newman says again, "The heart is commonly reached through direct impressions." We must aim to get students to experience what it means to be a religious person by active work for the spread of the kingdom (e.g., work for justice, work for the poor, work for the sick).

Level 3: Transformation

The Gospel of John tells the story of how Jesus met a Samaritan woman at Jacob's well (Jn 4:7-42). They had a long discussion (though he should not have spoken to her, since she was a woman he did not know, and, worse yet, a Samaritan). At its conclusion she was convinced that he was the promised Messiah. She went back into the village to tell everyone. The villagers themselves came out to meet Jesus. When they had met him and spoken with him, they said to the woman:

It is no longer because of what you said that we believe, for we have heard for ourselves, and we know that this is truly the Saviour of the world. (Jn 4:42)

There, in a nutshell, is expressed very well what should be our role as teachers, as parents, as administrators, as leaders in Catholic education. We must attract the villagers to come out and meet Jesus so that, after speaking with him face to face, they will be convinced that he is the Saviour of the world.

This story of the Samaritan woman serves as a good introduction to the third level of religious education: transformation. This is the level of personal contact with Jesus, the level of conversion. As did the Samaritan woman, the teacher can initiate this contact; the teacher should set the environment for the encounter with Jesus, but ultimately the outcome will depend on the grace of God and the free choice of the person. We can bring a horse to the water, but we cannot make it drink. We cannot force faith on anyone, and even God will not force faith on anyone. The free human will is supreme; God will not act against it. Teachers, therefore, should not become dispirited if, despite their best efforts, there are still some unbelievers among their students.

So, when it comes to transformation, the role of the teacher is limited. What teachers can and must do, however, is to present to the students the challenge of Jesus, the challenge of faith, the challenge of vocation and commitment. "Are you with me, or against me?" Ultimately, whichever way one looks at it, that is the basic choice everyone has to make. We choose to be faithful to Christ. But, as we are all very much aware, it is not a choice that we make once and for all. To be faithful to God and the teaching of Jesus is a choice we have to keep on making throughout our life. From time to time we shall fall away and we shall need conversion, a return to intimacy with God. Therefore, faith is not a once-in-a-lifetime thing – we must constantly review it, adapt it to changing circumstances, renew it. But always the question of the gospel remains as a test to our faith: Are you with me, or against me?

And so, what we are aiming at in the level of transformation is to help the students to develop and renew their faith, to make a personal commitment to Jesus, a commitment that involves knowledge and gut-level emotion, a commitment that makes Jesus Christ become real and present to every aspect of life and fills that life with meaning. Here we are at the heart and soul of religious education, the conversion experience.

At the level of transformation, therefore, three things seem important for the teacher:

1) Present the direct challenge of the gospel message; be a proclaimer;

2) Give a good example of living out the gospel message, with enthusiasm and commitment;

3) Help the students to pray, and pray with them, so that they can come to "meet the Lord Jesus."

Integration of Levels

Religious education must be pursued at all three levels, and the levels must be properly integrated. In order to have a comprehensive program or unit or even sometimes a lesson, we should have a balance of all three levels. Sometimes in the delivery of such a comprehensive approach we may need to emphasize one or another of the levels, but none should be left out.

It is possible that these levels may occur in sequence – level 1 to level 2 to level 3 – but this is not necessarily so. Thus, for example, we can integrate a value approach to Jesus with a factual and informational investigation. In the very same context we can present Jesus as a personal challenge, as calling us to commitment. How the three levels are integrated will be up to the individual teacher in each particular situation. The important thing to remember is that all three levels are essential. It can safely be said that most of the major mistakes made in the teaching of religion come from a misplaced emphasis, or lack of emphasis, on one or another of the levels. Teachers who feel more comfortable with one level or another will tend to emphasize that level at the expense of the others. That is a mistake.

Finally, we should note that these three aspects or levels of religious education provide a good self-evaluation model for teachers. We must look back on our teaching and seriously consider how well and how integrally we are proclaiming these three aspects: in other words, how professional we are in this most important part of our teaching ministry.

Reflection Questions

1. What are the principal characteristics of a Catholic school?
2. What must Catholic teachers aim to achieve in their teaching?
3. Articulate carefully why you want to teach in a Catholic school and not any other type of school.
4. Review your own particular discipline (e.g., science, English) and devise ways in which to bring the gospel teaching into your own teaching. (For example, detect Catholic and Christian themes in literature.)
5. How would you aim to promote community in the school?
6. Put together some ideas on how you would promote the aim of transformation in your teaching situation.

Further Reading

Lee, James Michael, ed. *The Spirituality of the Religious Educator* (Birmingham, AL: Religious Education Press, 1985). An important work for the religious development of all who are committed to religious education. Part I shows how religious education activity can itself deepen the religious educator's own spiritual life. Lee's own personal contribution, "Lifework Spirituality and the Religious Educator," is particularly recommended.

Mulligan, James. *Evangelization and the Catholic High School* (Ottawa: Novalis, 1990).

Mulligan, James. *Catholic Education: The Future is Now* (Ottawa: Novalis, 1999).

Archbishop Philip Pocock. "What Is a Catholic School?", an address to F.C.E.A.O., (Toronto, March, 1971).

The Sacred Congregation for Catholic Education. *The Catholic School* (Rome, 1977).

The Sacred Congregation for Catholic Education. *The Religious Dimension of Education in a Catholic School* (Rome, 1988).

The Sacred Congregation for Catholic Education. *The Catholic School*, No. 35.

GLOSSARY OF TERMS

Adonai: Instead of reading the name Yahweh (the name of God was so sacred it should not be uttered), the Jews substituted *Adonai,* which means "Lord." Term still kept in many editions of the Bible.

Agnostic: One who claims that we cannot know anything with certainty about God, or an after-life. A religious skeptic.

Analogy: (From the Greek, meaning "proportion.") A way of indicating realities that are both similar and dissimilar. To say God is "love" means that God's love is both similar to ("like") human love and essentially dissimilar to it.

Anglican–Roman Catholic International Commission (ARCIC): A Commission consisting of pre-eminent Roman Catholic and Anglican theologians set up to try to find common ground in the Roman Catholic and Anglican approaches to Eucharist and other matters. The first stage of this work is complete and the commission has issued its Final Report (1982), which has not been fully accepted by the authorities on either side. A second commission (ARCIC II) has now been established to carry on the work of the first.

Anthropomorphism: Making God into the image of a human being whether physical (having a human body) or emotional (having human emotions such as anger or joy).

Apocalypse (Apocalyptic): Name given to the last book of the Bible (the book of Revelation) which relates extraordinary, cataclysmic, mystical revelation. Refers to the signs that will signal the end of the world and to the style of writing that portrays such visions and signs (e.g., the books Daniel, Revelation and the Gospel According to Mark, Chapter 13).

Apocrypha: (Greek for "hidden," or "not genuine," "of doubtful authenticity.") Those books of the Bible not recognized by Protestants and Jews as inspired by God and are often put at the end of Protestant editions.

Apologetics: The formal and rational arguments mounted in defence of the truths of faith. Based on the principle that our faith is reasonable and not simply a blind adherence to things we are told to believe.

Apostasy: The sinful act by which one abandons externally (by outward act) and internally (in intention) the Catholic faith in which one is baptized and which one formally professed.

Atheist: One who denies the existence of God. Atheism exists in many forms and may range from militant rejection of God to a tolerant indifference to God's existence.

Authoritative interpretation of Scripture: Interpretation provided by the teaching authority of the Pope and bishops. The Catholic church holds that such authoritative interpretation is necessary if we are to be able to properly adjudicate between competing interpretations and thus preserve the one faith for the whole church.

Bible: (From the Greek *ta biblia,* "the books.") A compilation of selected Israelite and early Christian traditions ranging over the whole life of the people. Accepted as inspired by God and normative for faith. Divided into two main parts: the Hebrew Scriptures or Old Testament, and the Christian Scriptures or New Testament.

Biblical fundamentalism: The position which states that, since the Bible is believed to be God's word, everything in it must be accepted at face value: that is, the words mean exactly what they say. Biblical Fundamentalists do not accept that the Bible has to be interpreted. There are many grades and shades of Biblical Fundamentalism.

Biblical fundamentalists: Those who believe that the Bible is to be understood as literally true: that is, the words must be taken to mean exactly what they say.

Canaan, Canaanite: The name of the land lying between Egypt and Syria in which the Israelites settled. In several places the Bible notes the strong influence the Canaanites and Canaanite religion and culture had on the Israelites.

Canonical: (From the Greek *canon* – "measuring stick," "list," or "rule.") Books of the Bible accepted by the church as genuine and authoritative revelation from God and forming the rule of faith. Thus canonical books are distinct from apocryphal or non-canonical ones.

Christian Scriptures: A collection of selected traditions of the early Christian church written within about 100 years of the death of Christ. Believed to be inspired by God and therefore constituting authentic revelation.

Conversion: (Meaning, literally, "to turn away from.") We turn away from our old and sinful ways to greater intimacy once more with God. A greater recognition of the presence and purpose of God in our life.

Cosmology: A comprehensive study of the universe from the point of view of its origin, nature and destiny.

Covenant: A mutual agreement, a contract made between God and the people, initiated by God and freely entered into by the people, whereby God promises certain benefits if the people observe God's requirements.

Creed: A list of the principal beliefs of Christian faith stated in concise form and developed in response to early heresies and from the need for some statement of faith in connection with baptism.

Excommunication: The formal expulsion of someone from the community of the church and especially from participation in the Eucharist.

Exegesis: The process by which we try to get into the mind of the scriptural author in order to "lead out" what was intended when the words were written.

Exodus: 1) The going out from Egypt and the escape at the Reed Sea. 2) The name of the second book of the Pentateuch, which relates the story of the Exodus.

Fundamentalism (*See* Biblical Fundamentalism)

Gentile: General term used for those who are not of the Jewish faith.

Gospel: (From the Old English *God-spell.*) The Good News of salvation and the ushering in of the reign of God brought by Jesus Christ. Also refers to the books that recount the story of Jesus' life and teaching.

Hebrew Scriptures: Written traditions of the Jewish people, largely written in Hebrew, which began to be collected and written about 1000 B.C.E.

Heresy: (From the Greek meaning "choice.") Knowing and willful rejection of the orthodox doctrines of faith by a baptized person.

Hierarchy (Hierarchical): (From the Greek meaning "order," "rule by priests.") In general means a "top to bottom" ordering of things. Applied to the church, it generally refers to the ordering of ordained ministers – Pope, bishops, priests, deacons. This ordering of ministers is also the hierarchy of authority in the church. Proponents of the institutional model of church hold that this hierarchy belongs to the essence of the church as established by Jesus Christ.

Immanence: (From the Latin *immanere,* "to remain in.") God "remains in" creation. God is present everywhere by his ongoing act of creation. The complementary term to "transcendence"; both terms are needed to adequately describe God's relationship to creation.

Incarnation: (From the Latin *in-caro*, literally "in the flesh," "to enflesh.") Applied especially to the acceptance by Jesus (as God) of a true and complete human nature.

Inerrancy: The Bible is free from error in those religious affirmations which are made for the sake of our salvation. The Bible contains error but teaches no error.

Inspiration: (From the Latin *in-spirare,* "to breathe into.") The Holy Spirit "breathed into" the minds of the Scripture writers so that, as true authors, they consigned to writing everything and only those things he wanted.

Israel: 1) Name given to Jacob by the angel who contended with him. 2) The Northern Kingdom after the breakup of the country in 922 B.C.E.

Israelite: 1) Descendant of Jacob; more properly used after the Exodus and the covenant united the people into a single group. 2) Citizen of the Northern Kingdom after the breakup.

Jew: Name derived from Judah, son of Jacob. Used collectively to designate the whole people, particularly those associated with the Southern Kingdom in and around Jerusalem.

Kerygma: (From the Greek, meaning "the proclaiming of a message," or "the message proclaimed.") The heart of the message of good news brought by Jesus Christ and so proclaimed in the earliest preaching of the church.

Koinonia: A Greek word meaning "togetherness," "fellowship," "loving union." A quality that should be characteristic of the community that is the church as it was characteristic of the early church communities.

The Law: Another name for the Torah. Gives a rule of life derived from God's requirements in the covenant, the divine guidance for living.

Left-brain language: The left side of the brain is more concerned with scientific data, mathematics, particularities, reasoning.

Literal meaning of Scripture: What the scriptural author(s) intended the words to mean.

Miracle: An event which bears the marks of a special intervention by God; an act of God's power which seems not to follow the normal laws of nature and carries a religious message for those who believe.

Monotheism: Belief in only one God.

Mystery: (From the Greek, meaning "secret.") Not something we cannot know but something we cannot *wholly* know, since it "goes beyond" our human understanding. The mystery of God is now revealed to us in Jesus Christ in a language that we can understand.

Myth: (From the Greek, meaning a fable or a story.) A story which, by symbolic, metaphorical and imaginative language, attempts to put us in touch with the deep but mysterious truths of human existence incapable of being expressed by rational concepts. Myth does not mean "untrue"; it corresponds to a deep reality that we experience within ourselves as true but incapable of expression in "left-brain" language.

New Covenant (Testament): The new agreement between ourselves and God, introduced by Jesus Christ, which enhances and replaces the old agreement made by the Israelite people through Moses.

New Testament: 1) The covenant made between God and ourselves in and through Jesus Christ. 2) Collective name for the written traditions (Christian Scriptures) of the early Christian communities (up to about 100 C.E.) about Jesus and their response to his teaching.

Normative: Providing the rule, the exemplar, the standard, the reference point, by which we judge things. The Bible is the norm by which we judge all revelation.

Old Testament: 1) The covenant made between God and the Israelite people. 2) The collective name for the written traditions (Hebrew Scriptures) of the Israelite people. First part of the Bible.

Pantheism: From the Greek *pan* (everything, or all), and *theos* (God). A theory that identifies God with the world and the world with God. Characteristic, in varying degrees, of some religions. Christianity affirms the total transcendence of God but at the same time recognizes that creatures receive their being from him.

Parable: A story taken from nature, or from human life, to illustrate some religious or moral truth. Challenges the listener to refer the story to his or her own life and to act in accordance with the religious or moral truth.

Para-liturgical: Prayer/worship ceremonies based on the sacramental principle that help participants to come into closer contact with God in the form of some external rite. They are close to full liturgical ceremonies but not necessarily presided over by an ordained church minister.

Pentateuch: The first five books of the Bible providing the earliest traditions of the Israelite people and revered by them as representing God's special teaching and guidance.

Polytheism: Belief in more than one god.

Prophet: (From the Latin *pro-fari,* "to speak on behalf of someone.") Someone inspired by the Spirit of God to give God's message, to interpret events in relation to God's will, to re-emphasize certain aspects of the message that may have been forgotten or not sufficiently acted on.

Right-brain language: The right side of the brain is more concerned with the poetic, the symbolic, the metaphorical, the aesthetic, reaching into realms not easily described in basic scientific terms.

Seder: Seder means "order," the order of service for the night of the Passover. The Jewish family gathers together for a family meal and worship service; the meal commemorates the eating of the Paschal Lamb before the Jews left Egypt.

Septuagint: The Greek translation of the original Hebrew of the Hebrew Scriptures made by seventy Jewish scholars around 200 B.C.E. Includes certain books or parts thereof not originally written in Hebrew and now accepted by the Catholic church as inspired by God. Protestants reject these books as apocryphal.

Synod: (From the Greek, meaning "council.") A gathering of bishops and others who meet to discuss and determine matters of church teaching and practice. Synods can be local and diocesan (the local bishop meeting with priests and lay people from his diocese) or they can be representative (the Pope meeting with the synod of bishops, with delegates from every episcopal conference, every three years in Rome), or they can be ecumenical (a full meeting of the Pope and all the world's bishops).

Synoptic: (From the Greek, meaning "seen together," "with one eye.") Refers to the gospels according to Matthew, Mark and Luke which, drawing on similar sources, are very close in their presentation of the story and message of Jesus.

Tabernacle: (From the Latin *tabernaculum*, meaning "tent, canopy.") The small hut or receptacle in the church in which the Blessed Eucharist, in the form of consecrated bread, is reserved after Mass and serves as a centre of prayer. Frequently covered with a canopy, or tabernacle veil.

Testament: From the Latin *testamentum*, meaning "mutual agreement," "contract."

Torah: Literally means "teaching." The special teaching given by God to the Israelite people concerning their part in the covenant which is translated into a rule of life (the Law) and found in the Pentateuch.

Transcendence: (From the Latin, meaning "to surpass.") Refers to the "otherness" of God, who is "above" and "beyond" the world and human understanding. Sometimes used of human beings to explain a state in which they rise "above" the constricting earthly circumstance of any given moment and "go out" of themselves.

Vatican Council I: An ecumenical council that ran from 1869–70. It was interrupted by the Italian revolution and never resumed. The major decree to come out of this council is the decree on papal infallibility.

Vatican Council II: An ecumenical council of the church held at the Vatican from 1962–1965, in which Pope and bishops met to discuss, rework and reformulate church teaching. The decrees of the Council have had a great effect on modern theology and church practice. Called Vatican Council II because it is the second ecumenical council held at the Vatican.

Yahweh: Sacred name of God used in certain parts of the Bible. The third person singular of the verb "to be" in Hebrew, meaning he/she is, or he/she who is. God's name is "he who is."

Index